TIFFANY CHUNG

INDELIBLE TRACES

TIFFANY CHUNG
INDELIBLE TRACES

Orianna Cacchione and Tiffany Chung

with Heidi Amin-Hong, Mark Bradley, Erik Harms, and Sarah Newman

Art, Design & Architecture Museum, UC Santa Barbara | Hirmer Publishers

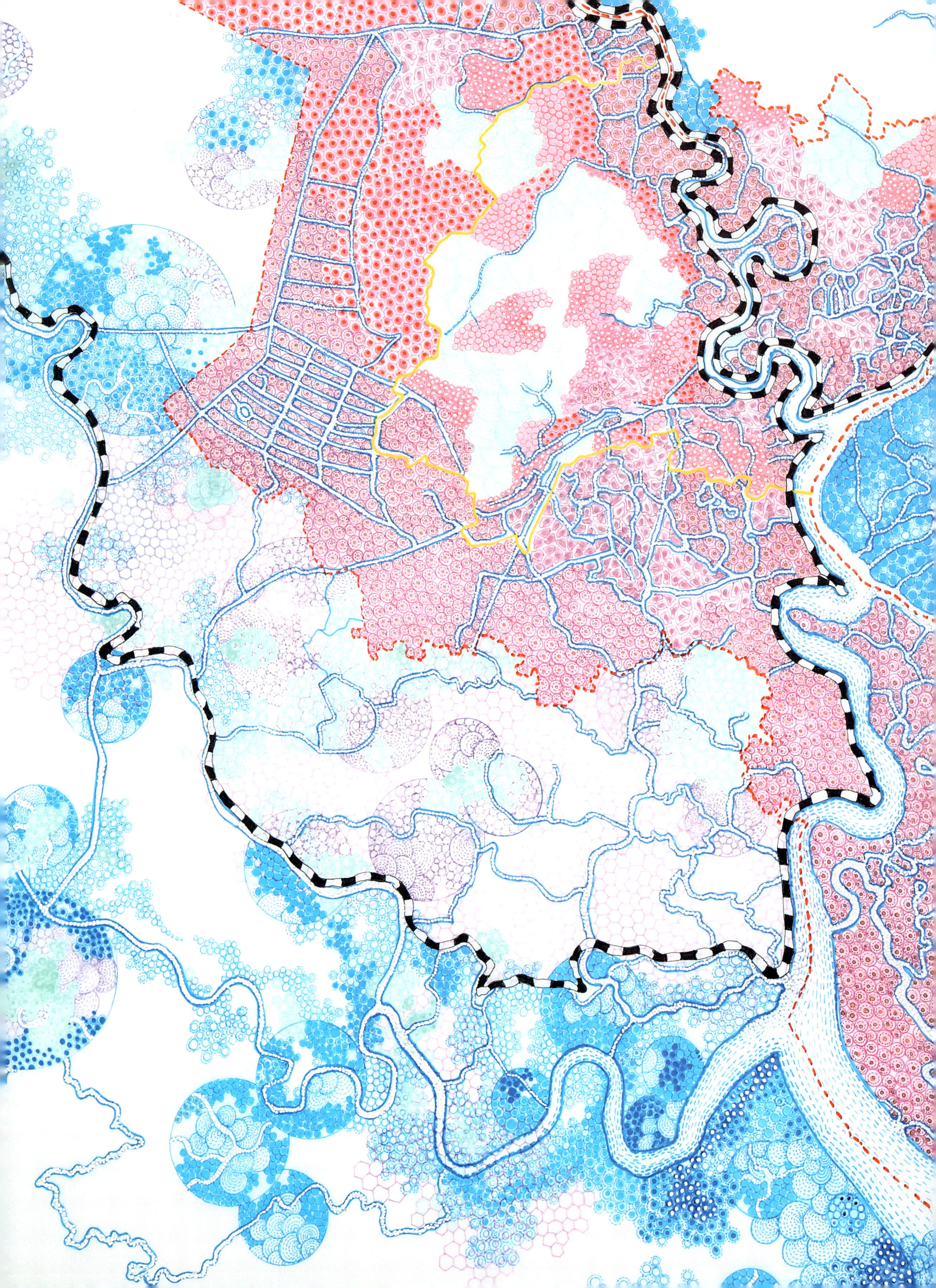

TABLE OF CONTENTS

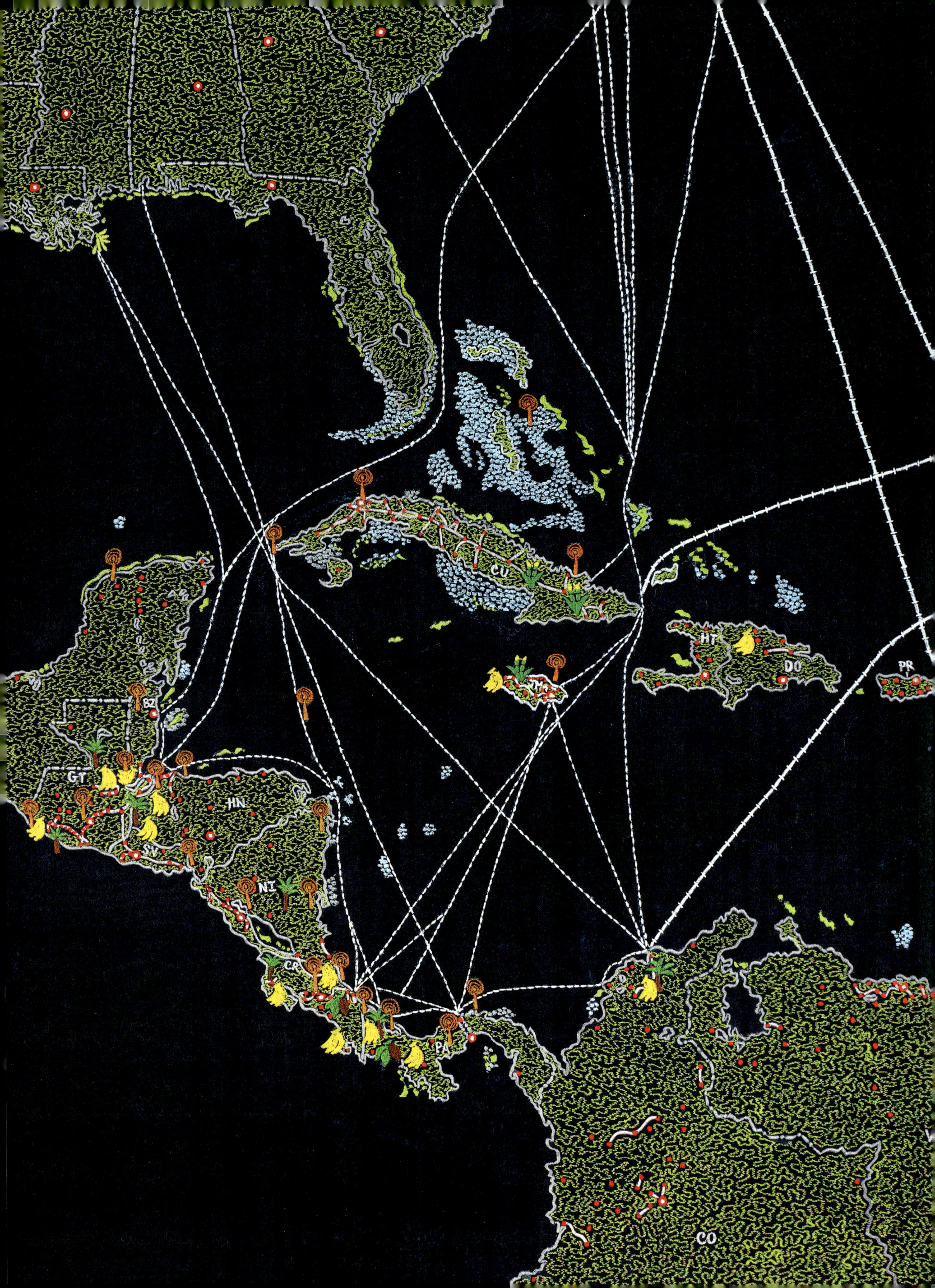

CU
HT
DO
PR
BZ
GT
HN
SV
NI
CR
PA
CO

DIRECTOR'S FOREWORD

I first encountered the art of Tiffany Chung in 2015 at the 56th Venice Biennale, curated by the venerable Okwui Enwezor. There, in the large expanse of the Arsenale, Chung presented colorful cartographic works from her series *The Syria Project* (2012–ongoing). Meticulously executed in oil on vellum, these precise maps utilize a complex system of coded shapes and colors to articulate pressing issues of global crisis, uncertainty, and instability. Each map is informed by intense research and data collection, giving a compelling visual form to the mass displacement of peoples due to war and/or climate change.

However, what is most arresting about Chung's art is her ability to document and give voice to the memories etched into these landscapes. In much of her work, the artist takes on the role of ethnographer and historian to chronicle what the cartographic records and statistics cannot: the lived experiences and personal accounts these topographies have witnessed. Ultimately, Chung is able to translate vast datasets and world histories into aesthetic objects that speak from the heart in deeply moving and personal ways.

Realizing the exhibition *Tiffany Chung: indelible traces* at the University of California, Santa Barbara, the artist's alma mater, marks the fulfillment of a promise I made when I first took on the role of director. Tiffany Chung received her MFA at UCSB in 2000, and a little over twenty-five years later, it only feels fitting for the Art, Design & Architecture Museum to host her first mid-career survey. Just as Tiffany's practice is steeped in abstracted notions of site specificity, it was important to realize this exhibition here in Santa Barbara, marking a return for the artist to one of her many homes away from home.

indelible traces is painstakingly curated by Orianna Cacchione, the former Assistant Director and Curator of Exhibitions at the AD&A Museum. Orianna has worked tirelessly to organize this exhibition, ensuring that the artist's voice is present at every turn, making both the exhibition and its accompanying catalog a true collaboration in every sense. This spirit of collaboration extends beyond the AD&A Museum's galleries to include the presentation of Chung's first digitally native artwork in partnership with the AlloSphere Research Facility here at UCSB.

This ambitious exhibition and accompanying catalog are made possible thanks to generous grants from the Terra Foundation for American Art and the Henry Luce Foundation, as well as support from UCSB's Art Equity Commons, the Billy Rose Foundation, and the AD&A Museum Council. Additionally, my heartfelt thanks goes out to the numerous lenders to the exhibition—both public institutions and private collectors—for entrusting our museum to share Tiffany's powerful work with a national audience. I am also deeply gratified by the participation of the Weisman Art Museum and the Blaffer Art Museum in the exhibition tour.

Today, as our national borders are further reified and immigrants unjustly vilified, the work of Tiffany Chung is more vital than ever. It not only reminds us of our shared histories and humanity, but also asks us to reimagine these ongoing global crises on a uniquely personal scale.

Gabriel Ritter
Director
Art, Design & Architecture Museum, University of California, Santa Barbara

From the initial conception of this exhibition, Tiffany and I were committed to engaging UC Santa Barbara's campus community as much as possible. I am grateful for the tireless support of Professor Emeritus Kim Yasuda. She is a champion not only for Tiffany but also for countless art students, constantly innovating new collaborations for artists across campus. My deepest thanks is owed to the extraordinary team at the AlloSphere, led by Professor JoAnn Kuchera-Morin with Dr. Tim Wood and Dr. Gustavo Alfonso Rincon. JoAnn and her team were exceptional partners and collaborators, allowing us to realize the newly commissioned artwork, *Spheres of Time*. I must also thank Tiffany's collaborators Isaac Hernández Campos, Adam Kaleta, and Mario Norton, who worked closely with Tiffany to imaginatively compose the melodic soundtrack and design the immersive environment. UCSB Assistant Professor of English Heidi Amin-Hong has been an enthusiastic interlocutor, having long researched Tiffany's artwork in her scholarship, and is committed to teaching with this exhibition.

I am deeply appreciative for all of this support.

Orianna Cacchione

ARTIST'S NOTE

I am forever grateful to my parents, whose struggles and fortitude set a profound example for overcoming hardship with dignity and faith. Their love and presence were felt even at times when we were apart, and have shaped the relationship between my siblings and me. They've taught us what family means and how actions speak louder than words.

As I work on my first ever survey exhibition, I cannot thank enough those who taught, mentored, and opened the door for me with boundless generosity and consistent support: Neil Chapman, Kim Yasuda, Colin Gardner, Dinh Q. Lê, Steven Pettifor, and Tyler Rollins. I want to acknowledge and sincerely thank the curators and writers who have worked closely with me and championed my art in their exhibitions and texts throughout the course of my career, including Zoe Butt, Okwui Enwezor, Sarah Newman, Russell Storer, Hiromi Kurosawa, Vivian Li, Paul Farber, Việt Lê, Pamela Nguyen-Corey, Erik Harms, C. A. Xuan Mai Ardia, Mark Bradley, and Heidi Amin-Hong, among many others.

My career has been enabled and sustained through the irreplaceable support of Tyler Rollins of the former Tyler Rollins Fine Art (New York), Quynh Pham and Rob Cianci of Galerie Quynh (Sài Gòn), Lorraine Kiang and Edouard Malingue of Kiang Malingue (Hong Kong/New York), Jeff Lee of RYAN LEE Gallery (New York), Alberto de Juan of Galería Max Estrella (Madrid), Post Vidai (Geneva/Sài Gòn), and others. I would not have been able to create my work were it not for the ongoing support and invaluable expertise of a dedicated group of collaborators who have played a crucial role in my practice: Tiêu Lộc, Nguyễn Thị Thúy Nga, Bùi Kim Thông, Đoàn Mỹ, Hồ Hưng, Dương Anh Tôn, Brian Barr, Isaac Hernández Campos, Mario Norton, Matthew Seamus Callinan with UAP and RZ-1 Fine Art Solutions, Alex Beaumier, Adam Kaleta, and the visionary AlloSphere team led by JoAnn Kuchera-Morin.

Finally, this mid-career survey exhibition was made possible by the vision and championing of the AD&A Museum Director Gabriel Ritter, as well as the hard work of the whole museum team and dedicated interns, and our partner institutions, the Weisman Art Museum and Blaffer Art Museum. I also want to thank all the funding foundations that have believed in my practice. Most of all, I want to express my gratitude to curator Orianna Cacchione, who has worked tirelessly to organize and see this exhibition through to the end with an unwavering determination and sharp focus. I have been so blessed to work with her over the past several years. She has been involved on all fronts, including her brilliant edits and close work with book designer Jena Sher, copyeditor Natalie Haddad, and the team at Hirmer Publishers, to produce the first comprehensive academic publication spanning twenty-five years of my work. I hope that long after my exhibition and its US tour end, this book will continue to be an important resource for those who are interested in my interdisciplinary practice.

Tiffany Chung

THE INDELIBLE TRACES IN TIFFANY CHUNG'S CRITICAL CARTOGRAPHY

Orianna Cacchione

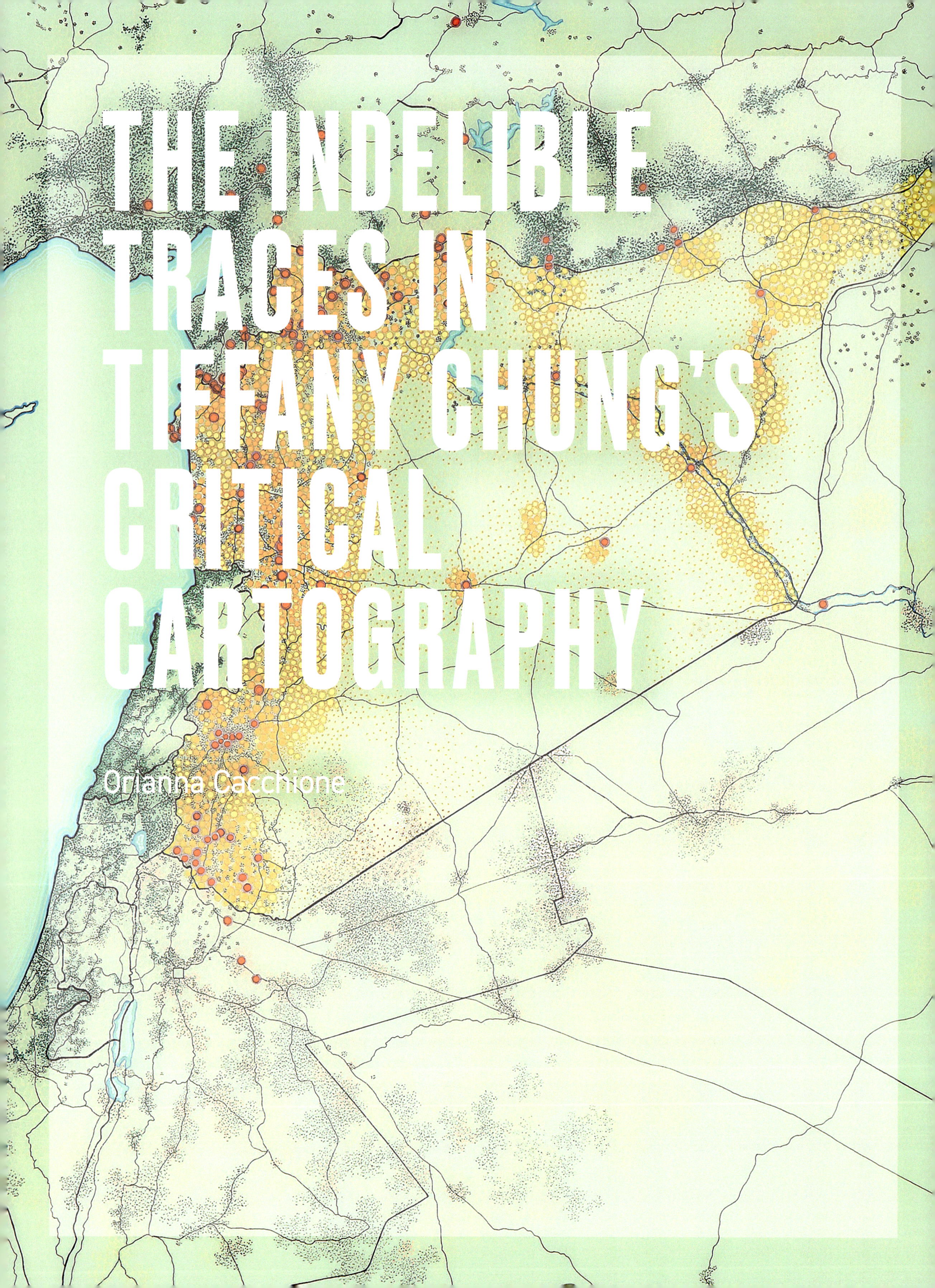

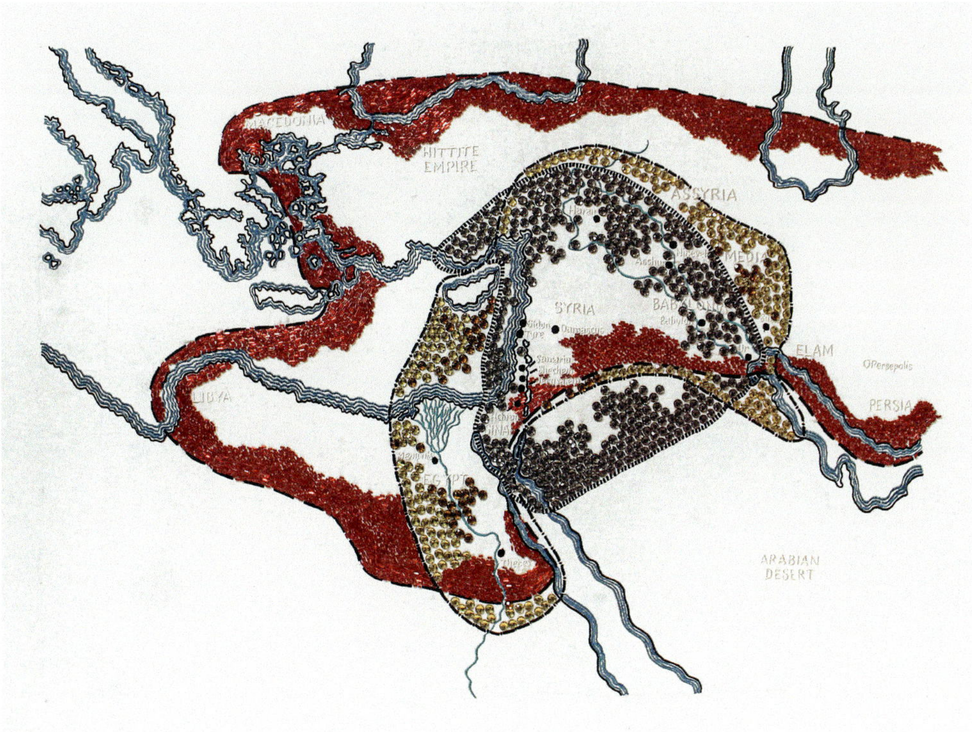

FIGURE 1 Tiffany Chung. *Life, which you look for, you will never find–the ancient Near East,* 2015. Embroidery, beads, plastic gems, 85 × 115 cm (33 ½ × 45 ¼ in.).

Shining rhinestones and red glass beads cluster in the center of Tiffany Chung's *Life, which you look for, you will never find—the ancient Near East* (2015, fig. 1, see pp. 110–111). The finely embroidered lines of blue thread that snake between them suggest rivers. Stitched in a cream color, the words Syria, Babylonia, Assyria, Hittite Empire, Macedonia, Libya, Egypt, Elam, Arabian Desert, and Sinai recede from the background and slowly come into focus. Supplanting a key, the title of the tapestry-*cum*-map is taken from the Epic of Gilgamesh, first recorded in Akkadian during the second millennium BCE. Mourning the death of his friend Enkidu, the warrior king Gilgamesh seeks the secret to immortality. The eponymous line that Chung selected is a response to Gilgamesh's fear-driven pursuit and reinforces the inevitability of death. Gilgamesh's compulsive quest evokes the insatiable search for knowledge itself that is threaded through Chung's practice, a search that is never straightforward. Here, the glittering map acts as a mirage or enticement to dig deeper into the history its surface only faintly reveals. Created four years after the Syrian revolution in 2011, the tapestry investigates the historical origins of the conflict. It is part of Chung's long-term *Syria Project* (see pp. 110–125), a series of maps that trace the civil war, the resulting humanitarian crisis, and the forced displacement of civilians. The elegantly detailed works also document the number of refugees, locations of camps, border crossings, areas of conflict, military positions, and changing geographies—for instance, *13 Oct 2013 NYT/UNHCR: Syria 4,250,000; Jordan 543,000; Turkey 504,000; Lebanon 790,000; Iraq 197,000; Egypt 126,000* (2014, fig. 2).

The Syria Project emerged in tandem with Chung's research into the exodus of more than two million refugees following the end of the war in Việt Nam in 1975, a crisis she personally experienced. Despite its immense scale, the exodus is still not recognized by official histories in Việt Nam. Resisting what she has identified as this "politically driven historical amnesia,"[1] Chung is "concerned with how my work can document and discuss the micro, hidden histories to counterbalance the 'grand' narratives produced through statecraft."[2] Seeking to fill in the gaps left out of official reports, Chung draws on the Japanese concept of *ma*, which refers

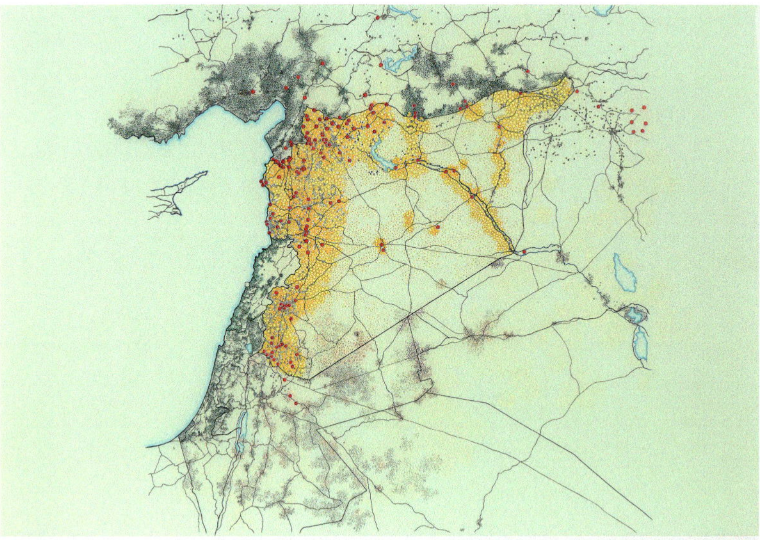

FIGURE 2 Tiffany Chung, *13 Oct 2013 NYT/ UNHCR: Syria 4,250,000; Jordan 543,000; Turkey 504,000; Lebanon 790,000; Iraq 197,000; Egypt 126,000*, 2014. Ink and oil on vellum and paper, 79 × 100 cm (31 × 39 ⅜ in.).

to the emptiness or space between things, looking for what is missing in order to challenge historical narratives that are written by those who hold power or influence. She works with statistical data, archival records and documents, even written policies, but acknowledges that "you also need the refugees' experiences to make the story complete."[3] In the *Vietnam Exodus Project*, she has undertaken extensive research, including combing through records at the United Nations High Commissioner for Refugees (UNHCR), talking with refugees, and studying flight and boat manifests to create maps (fig. 3, see also pp. 98–101) that recuperate and make visible individual refugee migrations. The resulting maps provide some of the most comprehensive documentation of the Vietnamese refugee crisis, yet they remain tacitly incomplete: national borders go undrawn and blank expanses compete with the details shown, leaving space for what is still unknown. She has stated, "Together with *The Syria Project,* [the *Vietnam Exodus Project*] will form a comparative study of forced migration as committed in different national contexts."[4] This has led art historian Benjamin H. D. Buchloh to argue that her projects press "the epistemes of cartography and the diagram into service of the most productive project drawing could currently attempt."[5] As such, her artworks join those of many contemporary artists who have developed new forms of artistic representation for the politically unrepresented by creating an "empowering system of imagery to analyze and challenge the potential existential reduction that states of exception entails," as art historian T. J. Demos describes.[6]

Cartography emerges as both a method and medium in Chung's practice. Maps, in fact, allow Chung to synthesize large amounts of data and complex relationships—from refugee movements to pirate attacks, master planning to urban development, climate change to global trade. Her artworks might be seen through the lens of experimental geography, defined by curator Nato Thompson as emerging from moments of rupture, "born when the extant frame is not wide enough and we must begin to understand the mechanism of power, finance, and geopolitical structures that produce the culture around us."[7] Her reworking of cartography thus positions her within a long genealogy of projects by artist-geographers, including the study of the physical and social implications of urban space in the rambling psychogeography of the Situationist International; the location pieces of Douglas Huebler; the daily geographic documentations of On Kawara; the deconstructions of colonial cartographic systems of Anna Bella Geiger; the abstracted landscapes of Julie Mehretu; the mapped migrant journeys of Bouchra Khalili; and the investigative practices of Trevor Paglen. Yet, Chung's works are always threaded with emotion, or what geographer Nigel Thrift calls the "spatial politics of affect," to provide the texture of experience alongside its graphic representation.[8]

Like *Life, which you look for, you will never find—the ancient Near East*, many of her maps are adorned with beads and embroidery sewn by hand, providing a visual manifestation of the time put into their own making but also nodding to traditions of narrative tapestries that hold family and cultural histories—Vietnamese hand embroidery, Hmong story cloths known as *paj ntaub* (flower cloth), African American quilting in the Southern United States, or narrative Afghan war rugs woven during the Russian occupation. Situating Chung's practice within a genealogy of feminist craft, art historian Pamela Corey argues for the work's "conceptual and linguistic intervention in 'statecraft'" as much as "handicraft."[9] Importantly, Chung acknowledges that her use of embroidery as a medium was inspired by stories of Vietnamese women patching soldiers' uniforms and stitching US Army parachutes into blankets during the war as well as her own practicing of embroidery in the post-1975 period. The map's colorful and curving lines form ornate patterns that are at once alluring and intimate, but their titles disclose geographic coordinates, historical events, and specific sources, asserting a critical tension between the abstracted lines and dots drawn or sewn on their surface and the decidedly political subject matter they reference. Seductively rendered as jewel-toned drawings and elaborately stitched embroideries, Chung's maps complicate the ostensible neutrality of mapmaking.

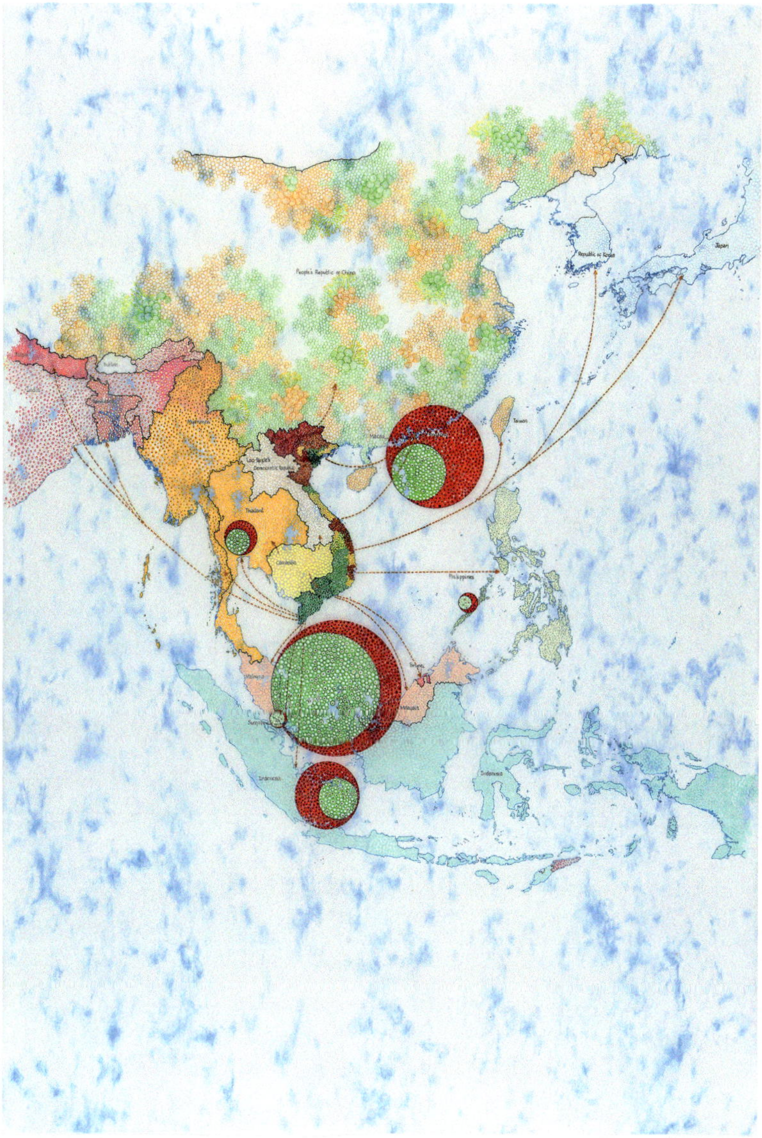

FIGURE 3 Tiffany Chung, *UNHCR records and figures: remapping regional movements, arrivals and resettlements of V-refugees in 1979*, 2016. Ink and oil on vellum and paper, 110 × 70 cm (43 ¼ × 27 ½ in.). Sifang Art Museum, Nanjing, China.

The meticulously rendered infographics shuttle between legibility and illegibility, recognition and erasure, the poetic and the empirical, setting up a dialectical tension that is threaded throughout Chung's work. *Destination Songkhla: pirate attacks in the Gulf of Thailand, Oct–Dec 1985* (1999/2019, see p. 106) and *Destination Pulau Bidong, Dec 1985–June 1986* (1999/2019, see pp. 104–105) were painted and hand-stitched on handkerchiefs. As their titles suggest, these maps depict pirate attacks on Vietnamese refugee boats in the Gulf of Thailand, but the works themselves only obliquely reference the attacks through a series of dots and curving lines that are veiled by geometric patterns. They manifest art historian and author Việt Lê's description of cartography as a process that negotiates "discrepant mappings that are at once legible and illegible to dominant forces."[10] In this way, cartography emerges as an active process of world-making and becoming. Despite the solemn subject matter that much of Chung's work addresses, each project leaves open space for speculation and filling in the gaps between lines and dots, territories drawn and those left to be imagined. In this way, cartography provides a means to not only reckon with history, but also project into the future. Ultimately, in Chung's artworks, the map emerges as a subversive palimpsest of histories erased, overlooked, ignored, intentionally disremembered, and yet to be written.

However, this focus on cartography alone oversimplifies her work. Chung developed her iconic maps alongside and in tandem with photography, sculpture, video, installation, and performance. These projects investigate landscapes and migratory networks marked by climate change and natural disasters, colonialism and nation building, post-industrialization and urbanization, and war by tracing the relationships between living beings, the built environment, nature, and forces of power. Seen through this broader lens, her practice should be considered within the emergent framework of investigative aesthetics, coined by theorists and artists Matthew Fuller and Eyal Weizman. Investigation, here, functions to contest official accounts by producing a "counter-reading, a counter-narrative that gathers all of these different kinds of trace, and is attuned to their erasure,"[11] while aesthetics acts as the "careful attunement and noticing extending to the elaboration of precise means of sensing and sense making."[12] In making investigation an aesthetic practice, Chung is able to synthesize the traces of histories erased and make them both sensed and sensible. In her artworks, Chung unravels the complex and often hidden entanglements of history, politics, economics, and ecology that accrue in landscapes and shape conflicts and migrations in order to reveal systems of power and cycles of transformation—natural or human-made, resilient or destructive—across stretches of geological time.

In much of her work, Chung excavates the histories of specific locations to unearth the chronology of a site that has been hidden or forgotten to time. For the *Fukagawa Shokudo* (*Fukagawa Dining Room*) project from 2010 and 2011, she created a series of site-specific artworks that investigate the urban heritage of the only surviving public dining room in Tokyo. A plaque outlines the chronology of the site (fig. 4 and 5), starting with the building's official opening in 1932, and including its partial bombing during the United States air raids on Tokyo in 1945, its renovation and reopening as a public employment center and later

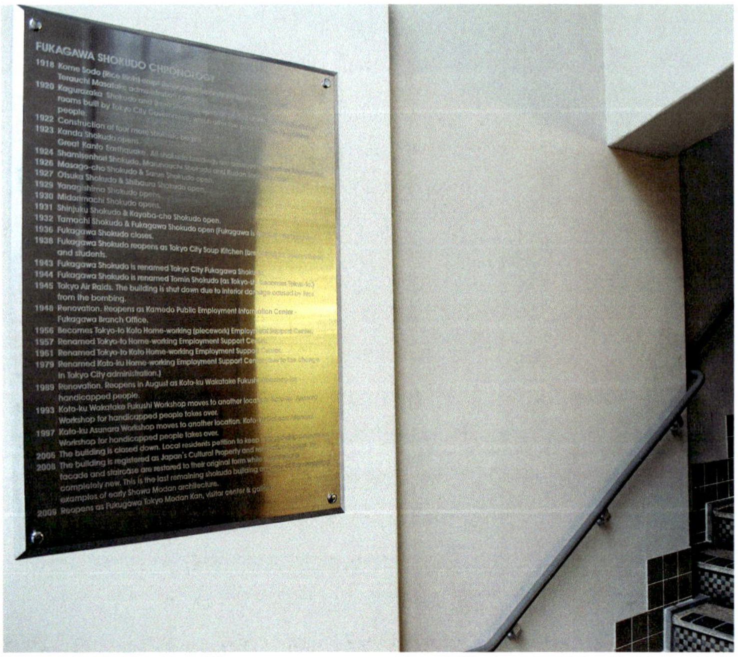

FIGURE 4 Tiffany Chung, *Fukagawa Shokudo Chronology,* 2011. Etching on steel plate, 120 × 84.5 × 2 cm (47 ¼ × 33 ¼ × ¾ in.). Installation view, *Fukagawa Shokudo,* Tokyo Modan Kan, Tokyo, 2011.

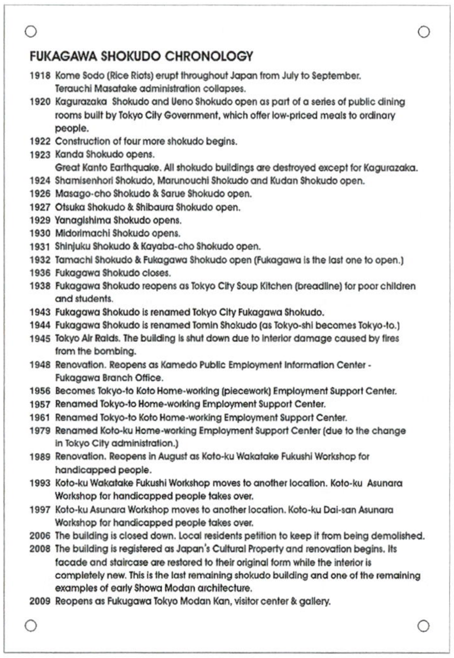

FUKAGAWA SHOKUDO CHRONOLOGY

1918 Kome Sodo (Rice Riots) erupt throughout Japan from July to September. Terauchi Masatake administration collapses.
1920 Kagurazaka Shokudo and Ueno Shokudo open as part of a series of public dining rooms built by Tokyo City Government, which offer low-priced meals to ordinary people.
1922 Construction of four more shokudo begins.
1923 Kanda Shokudo opens.
Great Kanto Earthquake. All shokudo buildings are destroyed except for Kagurazaka.
1924 Shamisenhori Shokudo, Marunouchi Shokudo and Kudan Shokudo open.
1926 Masago-cho Shokudo & Sarue Shokudo open.
1927 Otsuka Shokudo & Shibaura Shokudo open.
1929 Yanagishima Shokudo opens.
1930 Midorimachi Shokudo opens.
1931 Shinjuku Shokudo & Kayaba-cho Shokudo open.
1932 Tamachi Shokudo & Fukagawa Shokudo open (Fukagawa is the last one to open.)
1936 Fukagawa Shokudo closes.
1938 Fukagawa Shokudo reopens as Tokyo City Soup Kitchen (breadline) for poor children and students.
1943 Fukagawa Shokudo is renamed Tokyo City Fukagawa Shokudo.
1944 Fukagawa Shokudo is renamed Tomin Shokudo (as Tokyo-shi becomes Tokyo-to.)
1945 Tokyo Air Raids. The building is shut down due to interior damage caused by fires from the bombing.
1948 Renovation. Reopens as Kamedo Public Employment Information Center - Fukagawa Branch Office.
1956 Becomes Tokyo-to Koto Home-working (piecework) Employment Support Center.
1957 Renamed Tokyo-to Home-working Employment Support Center.
1961 Renamed Tokyo-to Koto Home-working Employment Support Center.
1979 Renamed Koto-ku Home-working Employment Support Center (due to the change in Tokyo City administration.)
1989 Renovation. Reopens in August as Koto-ku Wakatake Fukushi Workshop for handicapped people.
1993 Koto-ku Wakatake Fukushi Workshop moves to another location. Koto-ku Asunara Workshop for handicapped people takes over.
1997 Koto-ku Asunara Workshop moves to another location. Koto-ku Dai-san Asunara Workshop for handicapped people takes over.
2006 The building is closed down. Local residents petition to keep it from being demolished.
2008 The building is registered as Japan's Cultural Property and renovation begins. Its facade and staircase are restored to their original form while the interior is completely new. This is the last remaining shokudo building and one of the remaining examples of early Showa Modan architecture.
2009 Reopens as Fukugawa Tokyo Modan Kan, visitor center & gallery.

FIGURE 5 Text from *Fukagawa Shokudo Chronology.*

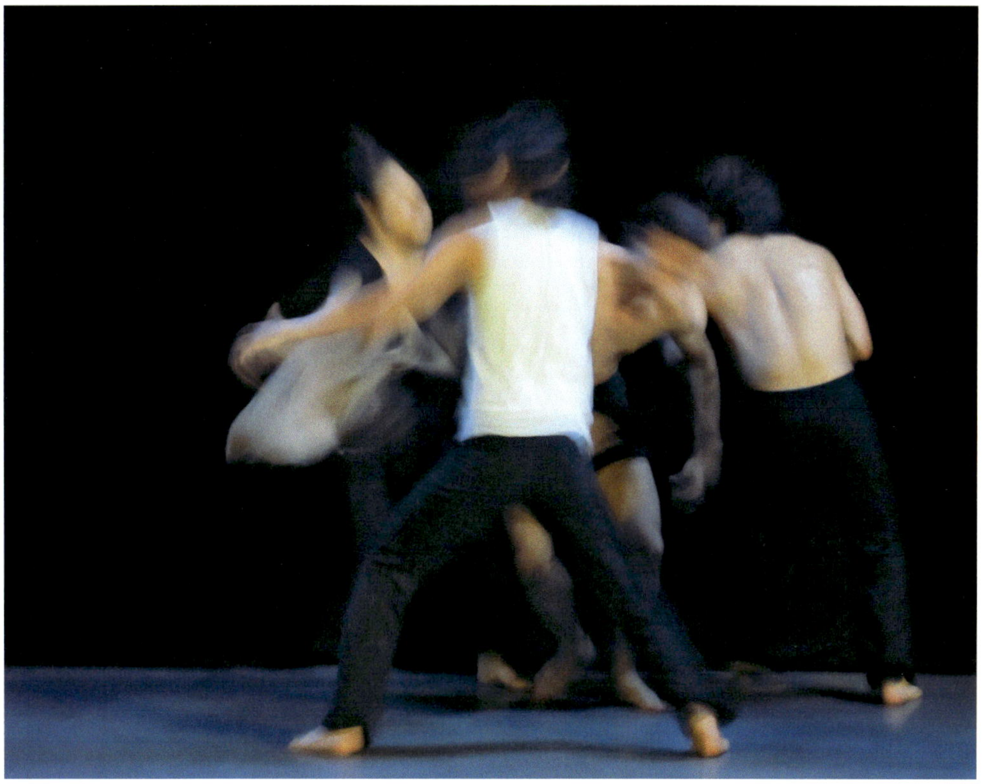

FIGURE 6 Tiffany Chung, *well-side gatherings: rice stories, the rioters, the speakers, and the voyeurs*, 2011. Video still. HD, audio, 8:24 mins.

a workshop for people with disabilities, and its conversion into Fukugawa Tokyo Modan Kan, a visitor center and art gallery in 2000. A series of maps contextualize the building within a changing city, documenting Tokyo at different historical junctures: during the Edo period, at a time of increased urban planning following the 1923 Kanto earthquake, and during World War II when the US created strategic bombing surveys of the city. Text-based works provide recollections of the rice riots that led to the construction of the public dining rooms sourced from historical and narrative accounts. The video *well-side gatherings: rice stories, the rioters, the speakers, and the voyeurs* (2011, fig. 6) delves into the origins of the rice riots, a protest initiated by the women living in a fishing village in Toyama Prefecture in July 1918 that spread throughout the country. Chung translates the roles these women played and the communal discussions they held during the food shortages into bodily actions and choreography for performers in the Arabesque Dance Company, based in Sài Gòn (present-day Ho Chi Minh City). Moving against the black backdrop of a darkened stage, the dancers reimagine the experience of food shortages more broadly. Taken together, these artworks intertwine historical narratives, cartography, community activism, and urban change within the building itself, evoking the Latin word *chorographia*, which describes mapping as a "portrait of a place."[13]

Importantly, the rice riots in Japan resonated with Chung's experience of the 1975–86 subsidy period (*thời bao cấp*) in Việt Nam—so closely, in fact, that segments from *well-side gatherings* are integrated into another video work, *Recipes of Necessity* (2014, see pp. 94–95) focused on the subsidy period, to draw out the parallel experiences of people in different times and places. In *Recipes of Necessity*, Chung creates an unexpected portrayal of the subsidy period through the recipes people remember their families cooking during that time. These stories are juxtaposed with a collective meal in which these dishes are served and clips of the dancers in *well-side gatherings* are shown to bridge the experiences in Việt Nam and Japan. This produces a collapsing of time and space that is central to Chung's work, where different temporal and spatial relations coexist through the superimposition of layers and clips, or the juxtaposition of several maps in one space.[14]

Three maps created as part of the long-term project *Archaeology for Future Remembrance* (2013–16, see pp. 56–63) manifest a speculative form of Chung's temporal layering. The maps trace different urban plans for Sài Gòn: Charles Le Brun's 1795 plan for the colonial capital, the 1972 USAID wartime development plan for the Thủ Thiêm district, and a 1996 plan to create the Thủ Thiêm New Urban Area. Approved by the city government, the massive redevelopment project evicted approximately 15,000 multigenerational households. Inspired by archaeological discoveries of Óc Ec cultural settlements in the Mekong Delta, Chung resisted the erasures of this community by "excavating in advance," to use art historian Colin Gardner's term, the remains of the neighborhood after it was razed. She collected found objects from the demolished houses—windows (see fig. 7) and tiles (see p. 54)—and shoes left behind by those who were displaced. She exhibits these objects in pristine museum vitrines to combat the state's rhetoric of "reclaiming wastelands" (*khai hoang*), which was frequently deployed by the government to justify national land development projects throughout different periods in the country's history.[15] For Gardner, Chung rejects "the conventional *ex post facto* placement of peoples within already historicized places in favour of situating them as a 'people yet to come' (in [Gilles] Deleuze's terminology) for future remembrance, as an act of becoming that presupposes a projected collective agency."[16] In this way, Chung's investigations into the impacts of master planning work against the dispossession of the residents of Thủ Thiêm and what Việt Lê calls the "traumas of development."[17]

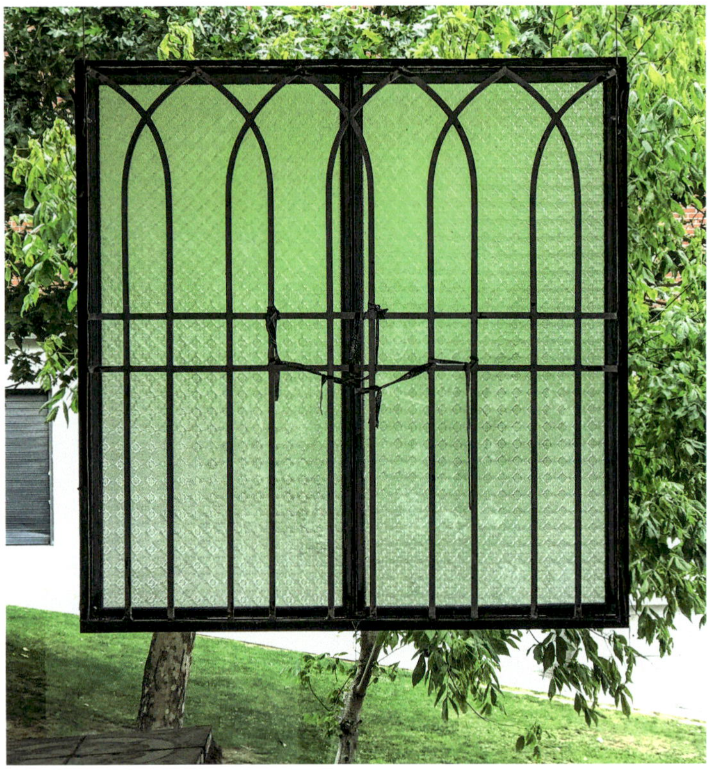

FIGURE 7 Tiffany Chung, *erasure begins from the will to knowledge*, 2013. Recovered windows from demolished homes, 126 × 126 × 20 cm (49 ⅝ × 49 ⅝ × 7 ⅞ in.). Installation view, *Archaeology for Future Remembrance*, Maumaus/Lumiar Cité, Lisbon, Portugal, 2019.

Chung's appropriation of the map as the tool of urban planning gives rise to her signature iconography of colorful, proliferating dots and concentric circles. This system developed first in maps such as *10.9677°N 106.4667°E* (2007, see pp. 52–53) and *34°15'5"N 131°17'58"E* (2007/2011, fig. 8). Their titles reference GPS coordinates in Việt Nam and Japan, respectively, that their abstracted surfaces withhold. In each, obsessively drawn dots and lines grow like mold or fungi overtaking roads and dashed line boundaries as if superficially imposed on cryptic topographies. They reveal cartography as a subjective and subversive practice—reimagining the locations, stakes, and determinations that the maps portray. The later maps, *25°15'8"N 55°16'48"E Dubai 1973* (2010, fig. 9) and *25°15'8"N 55°16'48"E Dubai 2020* (2010, fig. 10), explicitly address the transformation of Dubai from 1973 to the government-sponsored 2020 master plan, threading this visual system concretely to urban planning. Anthropologist Erik Harms describes, "The landscape collapses beneath the weighty vision of the plan, the 'growth' it feeds seems also to eat away at the very landscape it ornaments."[18] For Pamela Corey, "Chung's vibrant proliferation of dots, circles, and

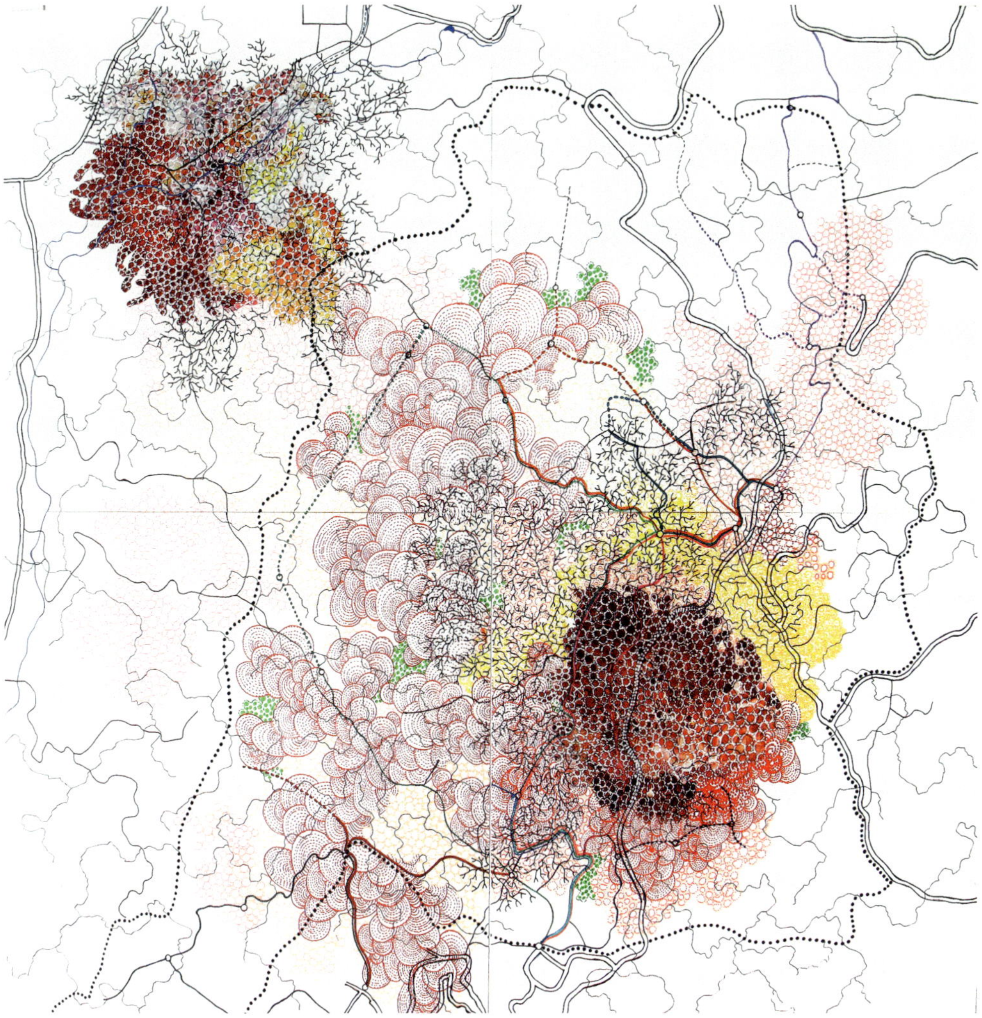

FIGURE 8 Tiffany Chung, *34°15′5″N 131°17′58″E*, 2007/2011. Ink, oil, and collage on paper, 4 panels, 116 × 116 cm (45 ⅝ × 45 ⅝ in.).

amoebic forms deliberately crowds the surface, literally reproducing explosive growth, density, and uncontained spread."[19] This graphic system replicates the growth, swell, and later migrations that she investigates, creating a shorthand for these shifting geographies.

Informed by the historic 1978 flood of the Mekong River Delta, *The River Project* investigates the evolving geographies caused by the intensification of climate change and hydropower development alongside the resulting displacement of people. After the war, Chung's family was forcibly relocated to a New Economic Zone, established in the Mekong River Delta, where they witnessed the flood. The boldly embroidered map *up and down the river-migration of the fish* (2010) recreates Chung's memories of "leaping silver-colored fish" during the flood.[20] Every year during the monsoon season, the Mekong River expands beyond its banks, sending water upstream into Tonlé Sap Lake, flooding the surrounding forest and populating the fishery; this gives the river its poetic name: the river that runs backward. Other cartographic drawings trace both flood predictions for Sài Gòn and the greater Mekong River Delta based on models developed by the International Centre for Environmental Management (ICEM) (see p. 43). As a countermeasure to the extreme flooding effects that are intensified by sea level rise, Chung created *stored in a jar: monsoon, drowning fish, color of water, and the floating world* (2010–11, see pp. 48–51), a model city of houseboats floating above the gallery floor. The models are inspired by indigenous building techniques adapted over generations by communities living on floodplains throughout Asia. The schematic complexity of the houseboats in *stored*

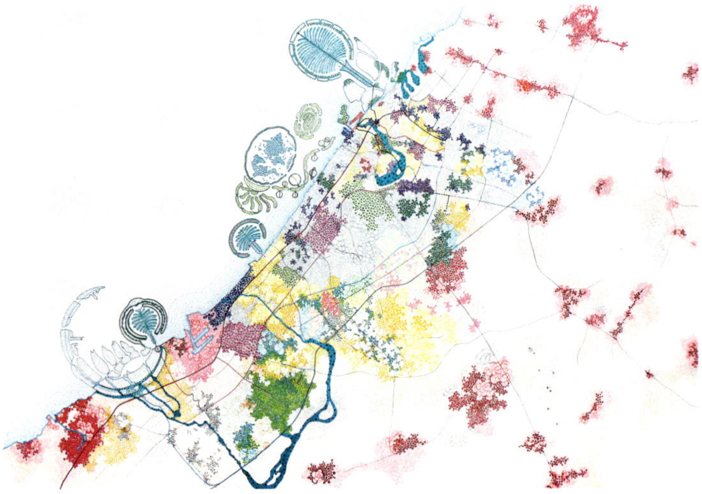

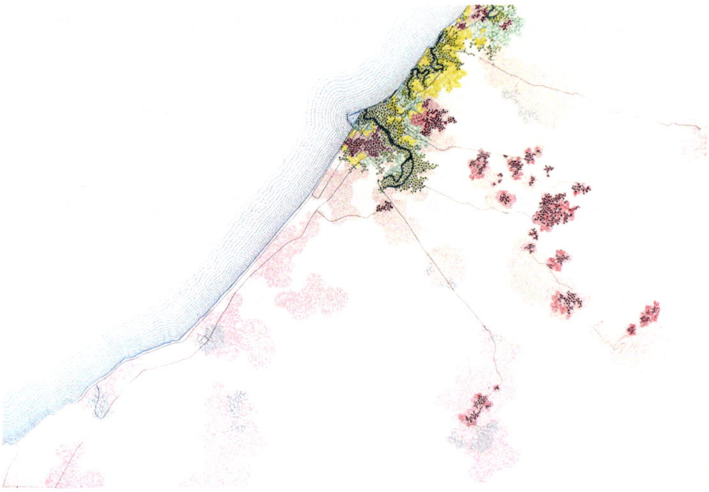

FIGURE 9 Tiffany Chung, *25°15′8″N 55°16′48″E Dubai 1973*, 2010. Ink, oil, and Copic marker on Arches paper, 110 × 165.5 cm (43 ⅜ × 65 ⅛ in.).

FIGURE 10 Tiffany Chung, *25°15′8″N 55°16′48″E Dubai 2020*, 2010. Ink, oil, and Copic marker on Arches paper, 110 × 165.5 cm (43 ⅜ × 65 ⅛ in.).

in a jar contrasts with the earlier installation *From Sidewalk Cafes to the Stars* (2006, see p. 166), a model city constructed with Styrofoam and adorned with saccharine-colored decorative tape. Its slipshod construction comments on the hollowness of rapid urban development in both Japan and Việt Nam. Here, the sturdy houseboats stand in stark contrast to the high-rises reaching to the skies, and local ingenuity acts as a persuasive antidote to the frenzied international investment and state-led master planning programs that Chung experienced in millennial Sài Gòn.

Chung's focus on the abiding impacts of natural disasters, climate change, and urban development compel her to work through expanded spatial and temporal scales that often "exceed human comprehension, and thereby present major challenges to representation systems."[21] In maps, videos, and installations, she begins to address what environmental humanities scholar Rob Nixon identifies as the central questions in the strategic and representational presentation of climate change:

> How can we convert into image and narrative the disasters that are slow moving and long in the making, disasters that are anonymous and that star nobody, disasters that are attritional and of indifferent interest to the sensation-driven technologies of our image-world? How can we turn the long emergencies of slow violence into stories dramatic enough to rouse public sentiment and warrant political interventions, these emergencies whose repercussions have given rise to some of the most critical challenges of our time?[22]

Counterintuitively, Chung resists the urge to dramatize these "long emergencies," and instead creates new systems of representation that bridge multiple temporalities, such as her excavations in Thủ Thiêm or houseboats that can float on a rising river. Here, she follows Edward Said, who described geography as "not only about soldiers and cannons but also about ideas, about forms, about images and imaginings."[23] Importantly, working within an expanded temporal and representational scale allows her to envision a different future. It is precisely this form of imaginative speculation that is at once catalyzing and hopeful.

In recent projects, Chung entwines excavation and speculation to poetically investigate expansive spatial and temporal scales. In the series *Terra Rouge: circles, traces of time, rebellious solitude* (see pp. 158–159), quivering lines form concentric circles on fine sheets of stacked vellum. More circles bleed through the translucent layers, revealing traces below the surface of the finely rendered drawings, as if stratigraphic layers. For Chung, these repeated circles allude to the Neolithic circular earthworks (CEW) found in multiple archaeological sites throughout the red earth plateaus in eastern Cambodia and around Bình Long–Phước Long in southwestern Việt Nam, where the brutal 1972 Easter Offensive was staged. Conceptually, however, they trace four entangled historical periods marked upon the topography of the site: Chung's recent attempts to locate the airfields where her father served as a South Vietnamese helicopter pilot before being captured as a prisoner of war, her father's experience during the war in Việt Nam, the establishment of rubber plantations during the French Colonial period, and prehistoric human settlements built between 2300 and 300 BCE. In repeating the concentric circles, Chung excavates the faint footprints left by the ancient inhabitants as a means to recuperate what was hidden beneath the scarred landscapes of colonialism, war, and nation building. The colored ground in her drawings leaves open a space to consider a world in which the original inhabitants never left.

Conversely, Chung looks to movements and migrations as another response to climatic and economic change, auguring a postindustrial world simultaneously in the past and yet to come. The video *Thousands of Years Before and After* (2012, fig. 11) responds to deindustrialization, depression, and deluge by following a group of displaced farmers and coalminers reimagined as "white-robed 'nomads'"[24] or, as Chung calls them, "postapocalyptic human drifters" through a barren landscape. Loosely inspired by research Chung conducted into the 1930s Dust Bowl that displaced farmers in the United States during the Great Depression, as well as the decline of small agricultural and industrial towns in Yamaguchi Prefecture in postwar Japan, the nomads' search for a new dwelling place draws together multiple temporalities and geographic spaces. In *The Galápagos Project* (fig. 12), Chung renders this transitory experience concrete, arraying thousands of meticulously crafted miniature glass bison into a potent, moving herd. Based, like the white-robed nomads, on research into the Dust Bowl, these horned animals

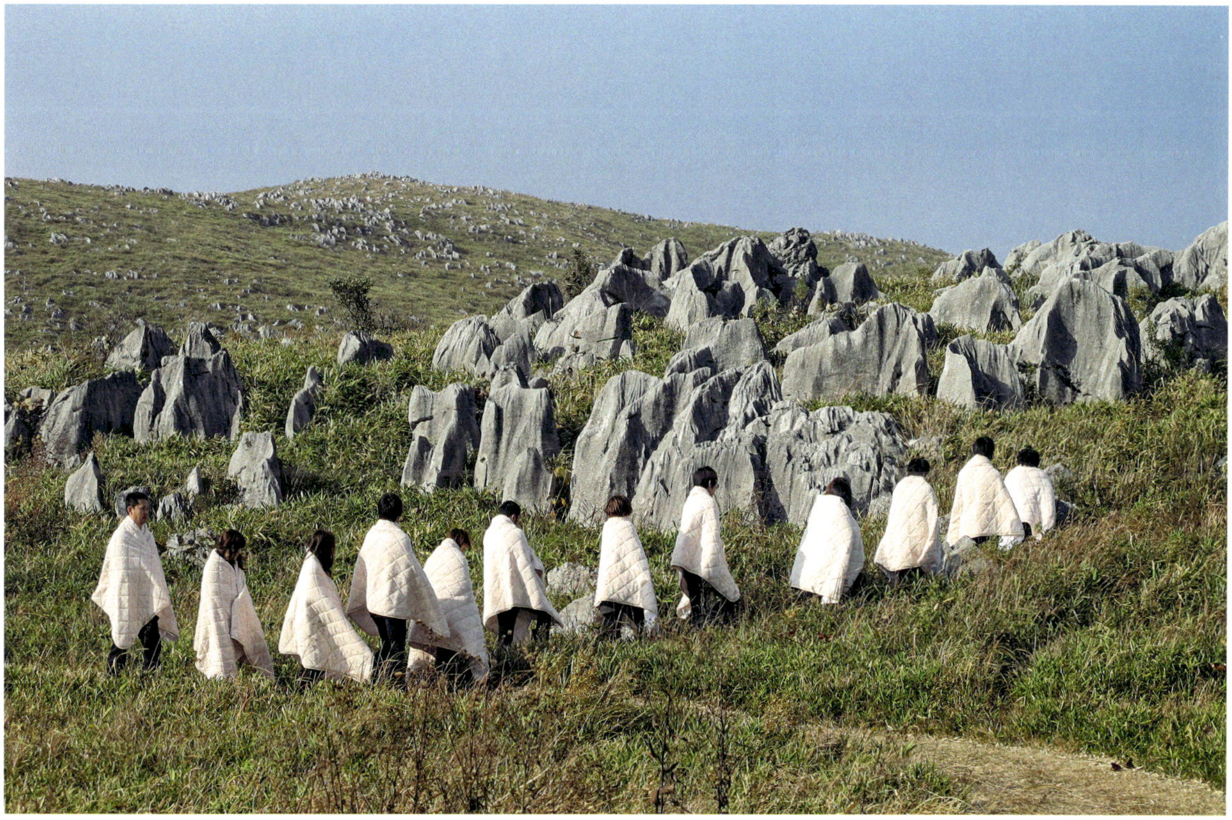

FIGURE 11 Tiffany Chung, *Thousands of Years Before and After*, 2012. Video still. HD, sound, 8:30 mins.

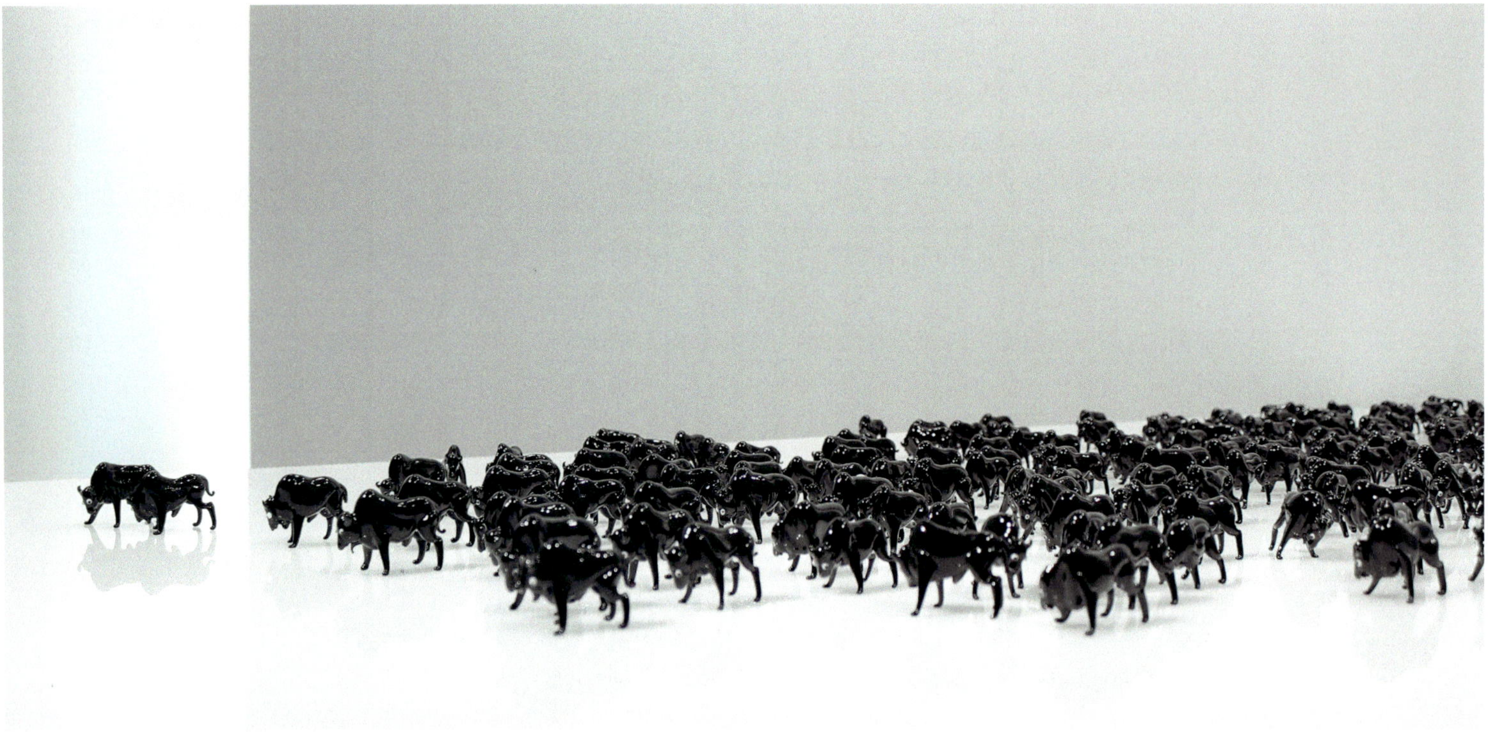

FIGURE 12 Tiffany Chung, *in between foraging sites, first raindrops and the Big .50,* 2012. 2,000 handcrafted glass bison and base, dimensions variable. Installation view, *Tomorrow Isn't Here: 1930s Dust Bowl of the Great Plains*, Tyler Rollins Fine Art, New York, 2012.

might be considered climate refugees, threatened by extinction but traveling together without a destination in sight. Yet the sheer number of bison in the herd suggests they are moving toward a new beginning.[25] Here, Chung bridges a divide between human and nonhuman animals, presenting migration as a primal urge for survival, as animals and insects, cultures and religions, spices and plants, diseases and germs all travel around the world.

Migration is a recurring theme in Chung's practice. Beyond the imagined, white-robed drifters, she has researched the exoduses of Vietnamese and Syrian refugees as well as the unprecedented displacement of people through the nexus of the climate-conflict crisis—a perspective that views climate change and armed conflict as the root causes of forced migration (see pp. 126–27). Since 2015, she has investigated migration from Western Asia and Africa to Europe and from Central America to the United States, in addition to human trafficking routes and the deaths of migrants at sea. She has also worked with young refugees, organizing map-making workshops that allow them to document their own experiences of migration. Chung's studies of migration distill complex conflicts into aesthetic systems that draw together diverse sources and forms of knowledge—archival, statistical, documentary, and testimonial—in order to make apparent the gaps in official records and documentation. Here, she employs *ma* as a method of reading between the lines and seeing what is missing, and also as an aesthetic quality manifested physically on the sheets of vellum. Her hand-drawn lines rarely touch the paper's edges. Only a few of her maps have keys that identify the graphic system she employs. Blank spaces often seem to overwhelm her renderings, as exemplified in the great blue expanses in *NYT: National Route 1, Diffa–fleeing Boko Haram and a road to nowhere* (2017, fig. 13). This leaves the onus of making sense of these maps on the viewer. Importantly, in Chung's renderings, migrations emerge as patterns of movement that contest, counterbalance, and counteract the naturalization and consolidation of national borders: dotted lines of flight traverse boundaries, countries or regions dissolve into blank spaces, proliferating dots marking the numbers of internally displaced people overtake locations. Her maps draw out the contradiction between the lived experience of refugees and the imagined boundaries of nation states, intervening at the intersection of situated and migratory histories, drawing out complex forms of relationality as they overlap with each other. Here, mobility is placed in tense opposition with grand historical narratives that centralize the stories of civilizations, places, and peoples tied to specific landscapes.

More recently, Chung has taken up the movements of plants and spices from the ancient silk routes to contemporary global commerce. *Global Spice Trade: routes from ancient times to the age of exploration/exploitation* (2024–25, see pp. 146–149) traces fourteen different trade routes in vibrant colors of thread, mapping the evolution from Austronesian protohistoric and historic maritime routes to the Incense Roads and the later Spice Trails and to Spanish and Portuguese Colonial trade networks, and finally to the Dutch, French, and British East India Companies. Charting the movement of spices as far back as 3,500 years, this map potently connects the origins of globalization to the first exchanges of spices. *Global Spread of Saffron* (2024, fig. 14) tracks the global dispersion of saffron from its native environment in present-day Iran. Chung renders each country in metallic ink, alluding to when saffron was valued more highly than gold. In *Studies of exotic botanical organisms and spices from the ends of the earth in quest of market dominance* (2024–25, see pp. 150–153), embroidered botanical illustrations of the trees and plants that produce spices are juxtaposed with samples of the dried and often processed seasonings purchased in grocery stores around the world. Each spice—including saffron, cumin, cinnamon, nutmeg, clove, vanilla, and pepper—bears witness to the colonial and imperial violence

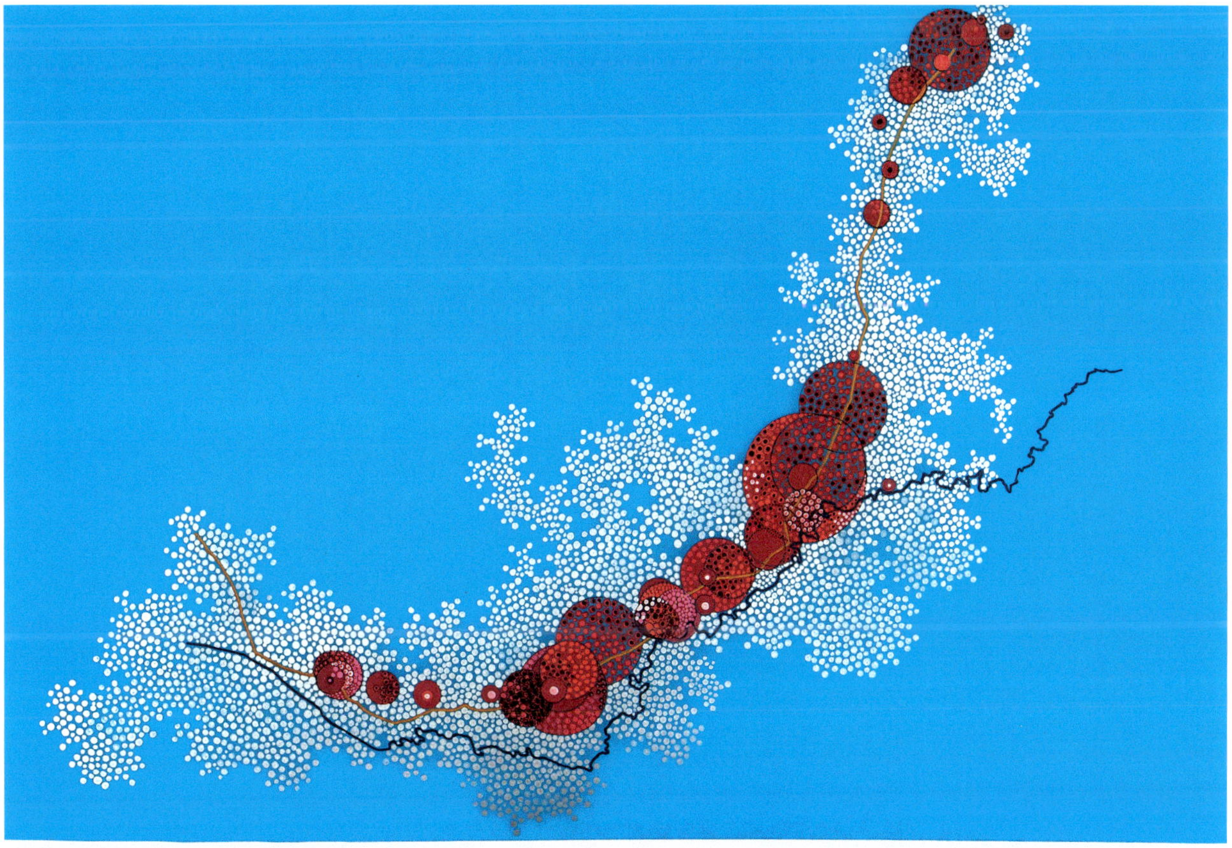

FIGURE 13 Tiffany Chung, *NYT: National Route 1, Diffa—fleeing Boko Haram and a road to nowhere*, 2017. Ink and oil on vellum and paper, 38 × 50 cm (15 × 19 ⅝ in.). Photograph by Nam Bui.

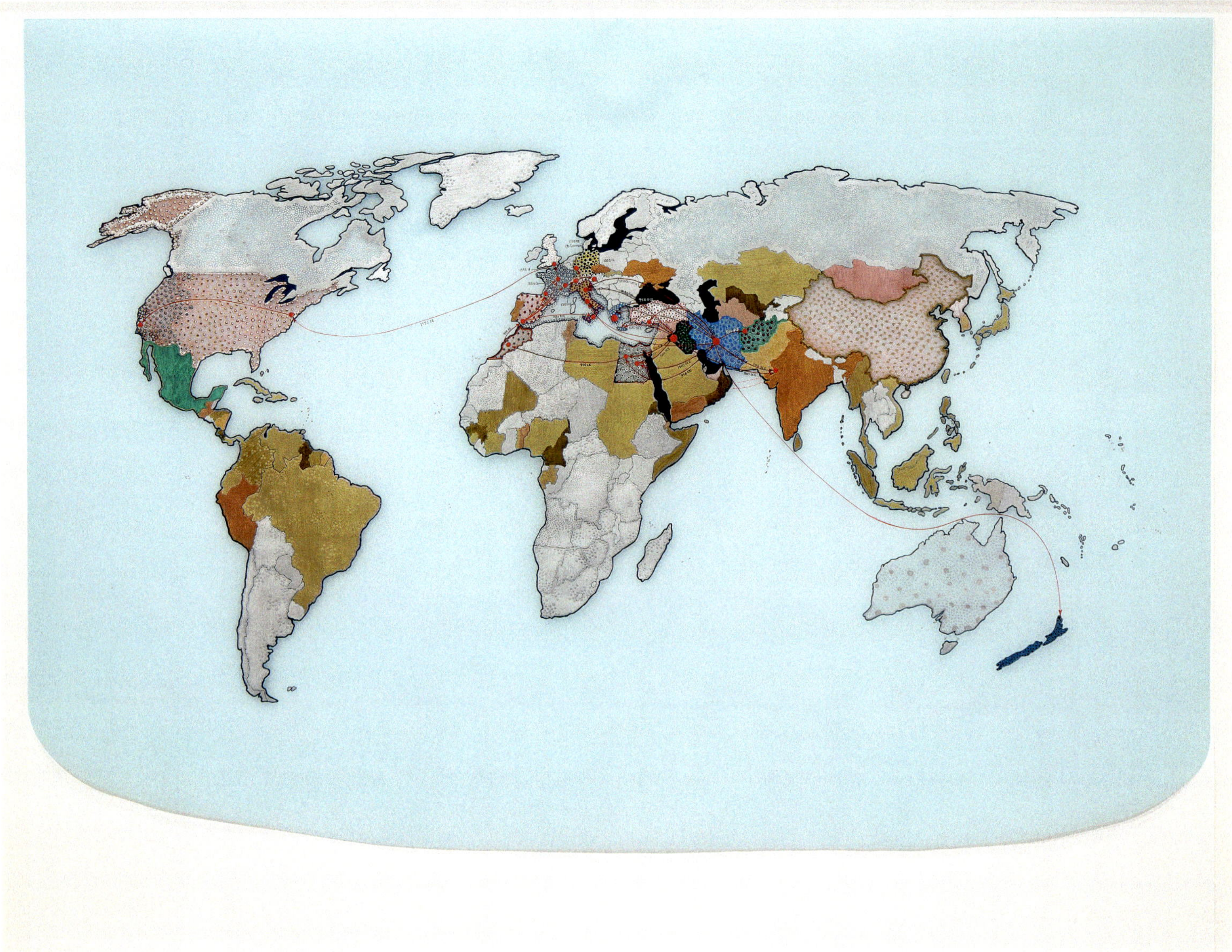

FIGURE 14 Tiffany Chung, *Global Spread of Saffron*, 2024. Ink and oil on vellum and paper, 77 × 100 cm (30 ⅜ × 39 ⅜ in.). Courtesy of the artist and Galería Max Estrella.

undertaken to control its market, the impacts of climate change on its cultivation, and its use in contemporary life. Connecting climate change to colonialism, global trade, and large-scale agriculture, Chung's artworks point to emerging scholarship on the Capitalocene or "the age of capital." As defined by T. J. Demos, the Capitalocene is an alternative to the Anthropocene, which is often used to describe the most recent period in the earth's history, characterized by the substantial and irrevocable human impact on the planet. For Demos, the Capitalocene names "the complex and interrelated process of the global-scale, world historical, and politico-economic organization of modern capitalism stretched over centuries of enclosures, colonialisms, industrializations, and globalizations" as the main culprit of climate change and planetary impact, as opposed to just human activity.[26] Within Chung's practice, migrations arise as traces of this transformation. *cracked heels and spices beyond my father's shoreline* (2025, see pp. 154–155) collapses the paths that four refugees took to get to the United States and the commercial trade routes of spices that remind them of home with the number of registered refugees from their native countries. Written into the migratory histories of peoples and spices are the seeds of globalization, interconnectivity, adaptation, and, ultimately, global imbalances of power.

For Chung, food and spices hold hidden histories of violence concealed by subsequent narratives and commodifications that are ripe to unveil. This is connected to research she conducted as part of *The Guatemala Project* with Stuardo A. Mejia in 2019 and 2020, which unpacked the exploitation of the United Fruit Company's (UFCo) monopoly across Central America and the Caribbean, and the United States government policy to intervene throughout the region on behalf of the company's interests. In bold white lines, *El Pulpo: UFCo's Great White Fleet routes and properties in Central America & the Caribbean* (2019, see pp. 140–141) plots the United Fruit Company's shipping networks throughout the Gulf of Mexico, while small yellow embroidered bananas indicate the international plantations they control. *Guatemala: UFCo PBSUCCESS 06.1954* (2019, fig. 15) maps the successful defeat of rebel forces by the United Fruit Company as it built its banana monopoly in the country; hand-drawn lines and arrows document planned and actual invasion routes from staging areas in El Salvador and Honduras into the country. *A Banana's Journey* (2019) illustrates the cultivation and harvesting of unripe fruit on banana plantations, the export and shipping of the bananas, the transfer of the green bananas to ripening facilities, and their eventual distribution to grocery store shelves. These illustrations are augmented with texts narrating this flow of goods alongside charts showing decreasing retail prices. Other artworks investigate the 1954 CIA-engineered coup d'etat into Guatemala (fig. 16, see also p.141) in elegant illustrations that are based on CIA stick figure drawn plans; the civil war period including the massacre of Indigenous people in 1982 and extrajudicial disappearances of Guatemalans by the National Police's Death Squad from 1983 to 1985; and the continued violence

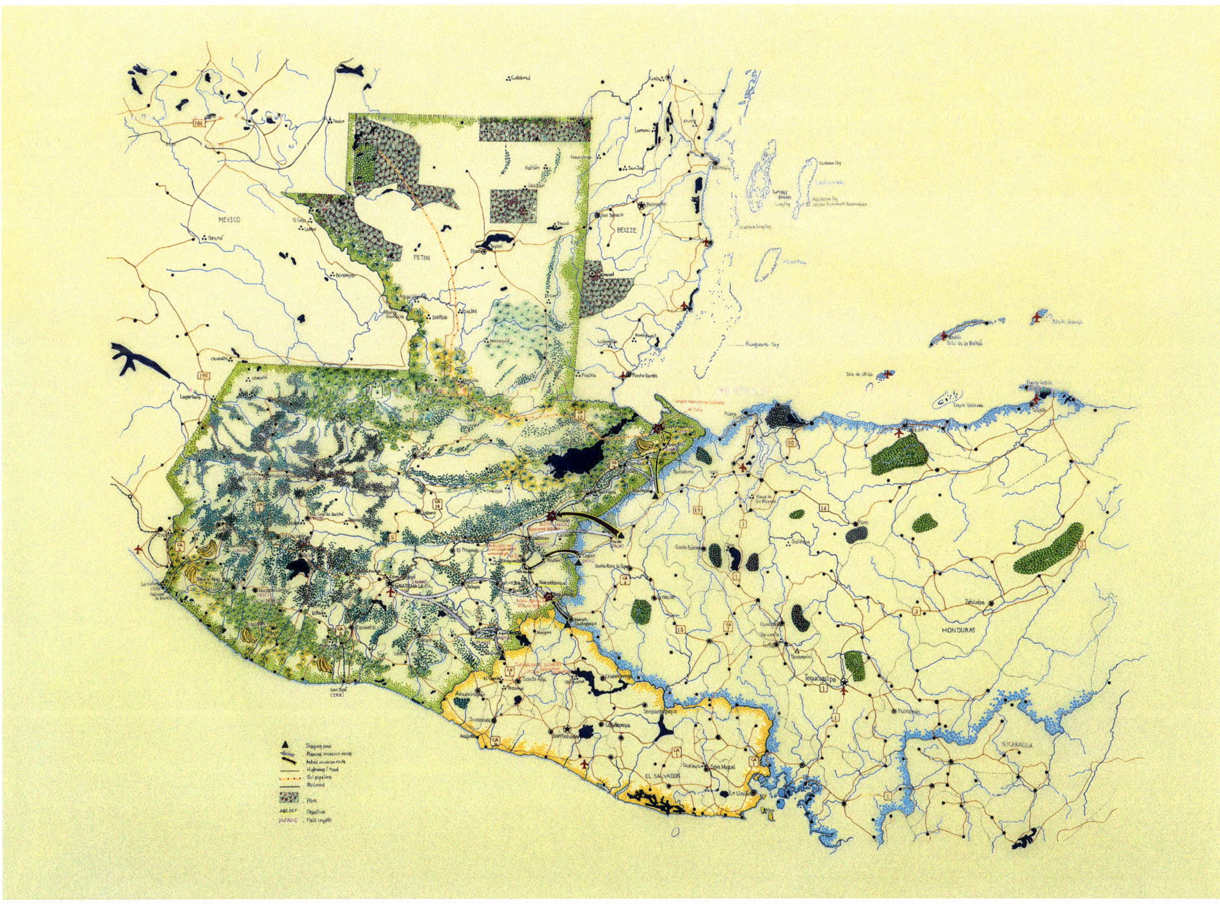

FIGURE 15 Tiffany Chung, *Guatemala: UFCo PBSUCCESS 06.1954*, 2019. Ink and oil on vellum and paper, 76.2 × 100.3 cm (30 × 39 ½ in.). Photograph by Nash Baker.

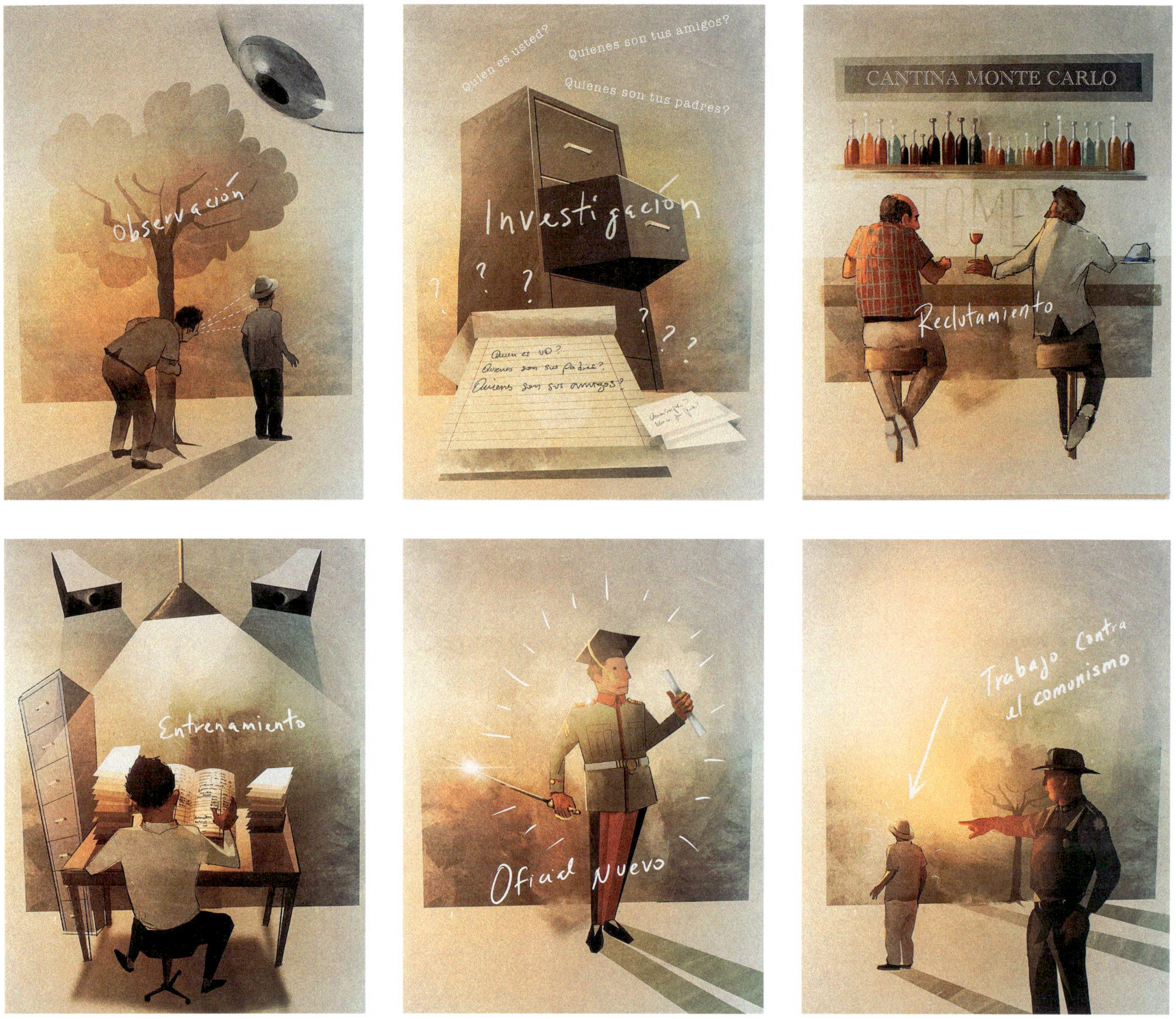

FIGURE 16 Tiffany Chung, *Ministry of Propaganda, Guatemala: steps towards a new intelligence system*, 2019. Giclée prints, each 28 × 37.34 cm (11 × 14 ⅝ in.). Digital illustrations by Jorge Hurtado based on archival CIA stick figure sketch.

caused by the development of transnational mega-projects (see pp. 142–143). Importantly, through these interrelated maps and drawings, Chung unravels the complex interconnection of commercial interests, American imperialism, unspeakable violence, and international development, showing the dispossession of Guatemalan land by corporate, state, and foreign interests.

In the related drawing, *from faraway lands to dust we return: Ewa Plantation Community Cemetery's Ledger Book* (2018, see pp. 144–145), Chung investigates the history of sugar plantations in Hawai'i, foreign labor, and the impacts of early free trade agreements. Faintly outlined rectangles are inscribed with the names and *bango* (identification numbers) of Japanese laborers who died while working on the sugar plantations. Multicolored dots seemingly overtake the cemetery plot, a record of overgrown foliage at the now-forgotten cemetery. Fueled by increasing US sugar consumption, Hawai'i and the US signed a reciprocity treaty guaranteeing a tariff-free market in 1875, which led to the increasing demand for cheap, often indentured, labor on the island plantations filled by Japanese immigrants. This map and *The Guatemala Project* artworks resist what literary scholar Lisa Lowe, in recent scholarship on the erasure of colonial histories of indentureship throughout North and South America, identifies as the naturalization of "the forgetting of the violent encounter" in the archive and subsequent narrative histories.[27] For Lowe, the archive's imperative is to separate—classify, collect, and document—information instead of making connections or identifying convergences.[28] In *from faraway lands to dust we return*, Chung reconnects the ledger book from the archive to the actual cemetery as a way of reading between the lines of the ledger and overgrowth among the plots. Chung turns to the concept of *ma* as a method to seek out the relationships between the archive, lived experience, and imperial and commercial interests in order to resist the eradication of these histories.

Here, the power of memory takes on potent force in Chung's work, acting as an antidote to forgetting as an intentional strategy of colonial and imperial authority, military victory, and nationalism. For Lowe, "forgetting reveals the politics of memory itself, and is a reminder that the constitution of knowledge often obscures the conditions of its own making."[29] Chung's project thus recuperates memory as a strategy for writing, in Lowe's words, "new narratives of affirmation and presence."[30] Chung works beyond archives alone, conducting extensive fieldwork, visiting the sites she is researching, engaging with the people impacted, listening closely and documenting their stories. *Remapping History: an autopsy of a battle, an excavation of a man's past* (2015–19, see pp. 80–81) is one of the rare works in which she directly references her own biography. Maps detailing the movement of troops in Operation Lam Sơn, an offensive campaign launched by the Southern Army of the Republic of Vietnam without US help and the battles of the counter Easter Offensive launched by the Northern People's Army of Vietnam are interspersed with photographs of Chung's father in uniform, the battlefields, international events, Chung's writing, and short videos to create an incomplete timeline. The work itself emphasizes the physical and temporal distance between Chung and her father, the images, and the viewer. At one point, she writes on the wall "with no maps in hand/I just know-/ he was somewhere not too far from here." Chung's limited use of autobiography becomes tenuous. Mirroring Chung's inability to trace her father's exact footsteps, the viewer cannot fully grasp what is happening, drawing out instead what is unknowable in another person's experience. The work replicates the ways memory is experienced—appearing in bursts, images, and fragments—while challenging the ways that knowledge is produced and codified.

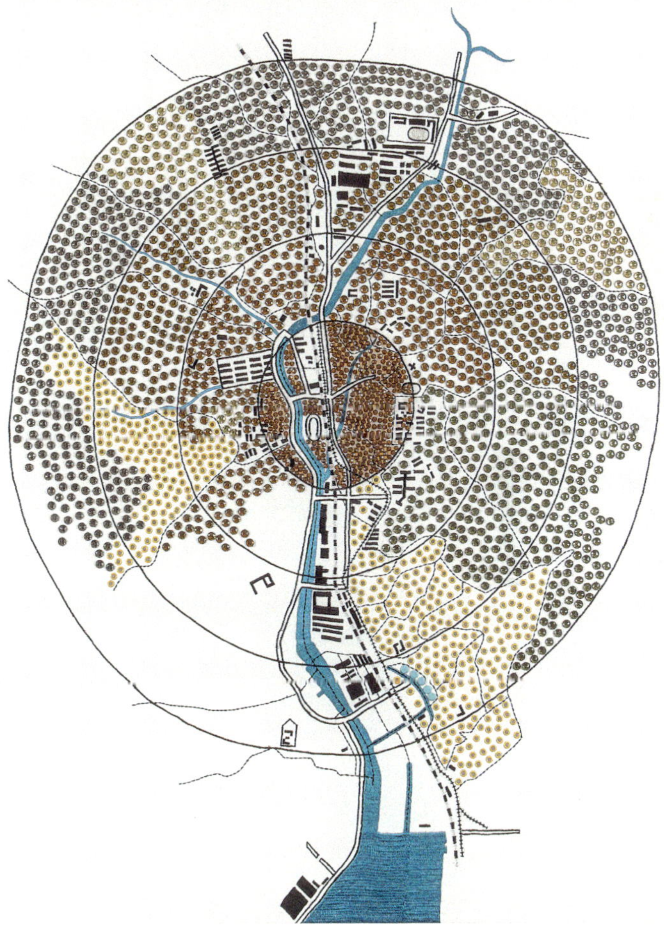

FIGURE 17 Tiffany Chung, *Nagasaki*, 2010. Embroidery, beads, metal grommets, buttons on canvas, 111 × 84 cm (43 ¾ × 33 in.).

Thinking of the physical and intangible walls that separate people and nation-states, *Scratching the Walls of Memory* (2010, see pp. 70–71) supplements histories of trauma and displacement in the twentieth century with personal memories. Inspired by the inscriptions left by survivors of the atomic bomb found on the walls of an elementary school in Hiroshima, Chung wrote excerpts of survivor accounts, messages, and news articles on chalkboards and bags sewn from used army tents in order to bring "forth the lost voices of the victims"[31] and bear witness to their memories. Curator Zoe Butt has described this installation as a "re-evaluated history class,"[32] where Chung provides an entry point for viewers to begin their research into these histories. In exhibitions, she pairs this installation with carefully embroidered maps that represent military conflicts and Cold War politics throughout the twentieth century: the end of World War II (see fig. 17), the wars in Korea and Việt Nam, and multiple border disputes, including those between Thailand and Cambodia, Tibet and China. Yet Chung does not readily connect specific maps and thus specific conflicts to the words of individual survivors. Instead, viewers must draw both together, speculating on who experienced which traumatic event. Chung withholds the possibility of experiencing a full, complete understanding, instead emphasizing the space between the viewer's and survivor's experiences—a moment of empathetic speculation. It is in this space that Chung resists the reduction of knowledge to consumable bits. Instead, she draws out complexities, contradictions, and what remains unknowable. Chung is attuned to the ways that knowledge replicates power, erasing as much as it records. Colonial and imperial powers used cartography as a method of control and domination, where maps allowed them to record the territory they controlled, expunging the existing peoples, cultures, and polities. Instead, Chung transforms cartography to create new systems of representation that incorporate indelible traces as a means of resisting erasure.

Tiffany Chung: indelible traces considers Tiffany Chung's practice from multiple disciplinary standpoints to provide not only a comprehensive understanding of her extraordinary career, but also a grounding in the specific histories and themes with which her artworks engage. In her own words, Chung elucidates the ideas, memories, stories, and scholarship that are embedded in her artworks. Her writing provides a poetic foundation that undergirds the complex representational systems she creates. Anthropologist Erik Harms delves into the history of millennial Sài Gòn, positioning Chung's early artworks in the context of the frenzied urban development and economic expansion at that moment. Turning to the wars in Việt Nam, historian Mark Bradley looks at her artworks through the lens of traumatic displacement. Next, literary scholar Heidi Amin-Hong investigates how Chung excavates the traces of environmental change, human migration, and resource exploitation through deep time. Finally, curator Sarah Newman considers the artist's strategic deployment of research in her practice, focusing on the roles of the archive and the atlas. The artworks that illustrate this catalog are arranged according to the loose but entangled themes that repeat and overlap among her different projects: shifting waterscapes and landscapes, war and memory, home and elsewhere, and currents of trade and imperialism. Taken together, these artworks and essays demonstrate Chung's ability to pointedly reveal histories that have too often been overlooked or intentionally ignored. In questioning not only how history is told but also who tells a given history, who is included, and who and what is excluded, her artworks ask us to imagine new ways of both chronicling our world and imagining the future.

NOTES

1 Meiko Sano, "TIFFANY CHUNG—Excavating and Remapping Erased Histories: an artistic practice on protesting against historical amnesia," Japan Foundation, https://asiawa.jpf.go.jp/en/culture/features/asiahundreds-tiffany-chung/4/.

2 Sylvia Tsai, "Tiffany Chung: To Be Remembered," *Art Asia Pacific* 100 (September/October 2016): 131.

3 Sano, "Excavating and Remapping Erased Histories."

4 Tsai, "To Be Remembered," 136.

5 Benjamin H. D. Buchloh, "Venice 2015: Biennale on the Brink," *Artforum* 54, no. 1 (September 2015), https://www.artforum.com/features/benjamin-h-d-buchloh-9-225379/.

6 T. J. Demos, *The Migrant Image: The Art and Politics of Documentary during Global Crisis* (Duke University Press, 2013), xviii.

7 Nato Thompson, "In Two Directions: Geography as Art, Art as Geography," in *Experimental Geography: Radical Approaches to Landscape, Cartography, and Urbanism*, ed. Nato Thompson and Independent Curators International (iCI and Melville House, 2008), 15.

8 Nigel Thrift, "Intensities of Feeling: Towards a Spatial Politics of Affect," *Geografiska Annaler, Series B: Human Geography* 86, no. 1 (2004): 57.

9 Pamela N. Corey, *The City in Time: Contemporary Art and Urban Form in Vietnam and Cambodia* (University of Washington Press, 2021), 52.

10 Việt Lê, *Return Engagements: Contemporary Art's Traumas of Modernity and History in Sài Gòn and Phnom Penh* (Duke University Press, 2021), 108.

11 Matthew Fuller and Eyal Weizman, *Investigative Aesthetics: Conflicts and Commons in the Politics of Truth* (Verso, 2021), 2.

12 Fuller and Weizman, *Investigative Aesthetics*, 12.

13 Lê, *Return Engagements*, 111.

14 Sano, "Excavating and Remapping Erased Histories."

15 Tsai, "To Be Remembered," 132.

16 Colin Gardner, "Probeheads of Resistance and the Heterotopic Mirror: Tiffany Chung and Dinh Q. Lê's Stratigraphic Cartographies," in *Arts, Pedagogy and Cultural Resistance: New Materialisms*, ed. Anna Hickey-Moody and Tara Page (Rowman and Littlefield, 2015), 46.

17 Lê, *Return Engagements*, 126.

18 Erik Harms, "Tiffany Chung – an archaeology project for future remembrance," in *Tiffany Chung* (Galerie Quynh and Tyler Rollins Fine Art, 2015), 121.

19 Corey, *The City in Time*, 51.

20 Tiffany Chung, "stored in a jar: monsoon, drowning fish, color of water, and the floating world [2010-2011]," in *Tiffany Chung*, 76.

21 T. J. Demos, *Against the Anthropocene: Visual Culture and Environment Today* (Sternberg Press, 2017), 12–13.

22 Rob Nixon as quoted in Demos, *Against the Anthropocene*, 13.

23 Edward W. Said, *Culture and Imperialism* (Knopf, 1993), 7.

24 Gardner, "Probeheads of Resistance," 49.

25 Tiffany Chung, "The Galápagos Project [2009-present]," in *Tiffany Chung*, 55.

26 Demos, *Against the Anthropocene*, 86.

27 Lisa Lowe, *The Intimacies of Four Continents* (Duke University Press, 2015), 2–3.

28 Lowe, *Intimacies of Four Continents*, 5.

29 Lowe, *Intimacies of Four Continents*, 38–39.

30 Lowe, *Intimacies of Four Continents*, 40.

31 Tiffany Chung, "August 2009," in *Tiffany Chung*, 98.

32 Zoe Butt, "scratching the walls of memory," in *Tiffany Chung: Scratching the Walls of Memory* (Tyler Rollins Fine Art, 2010).

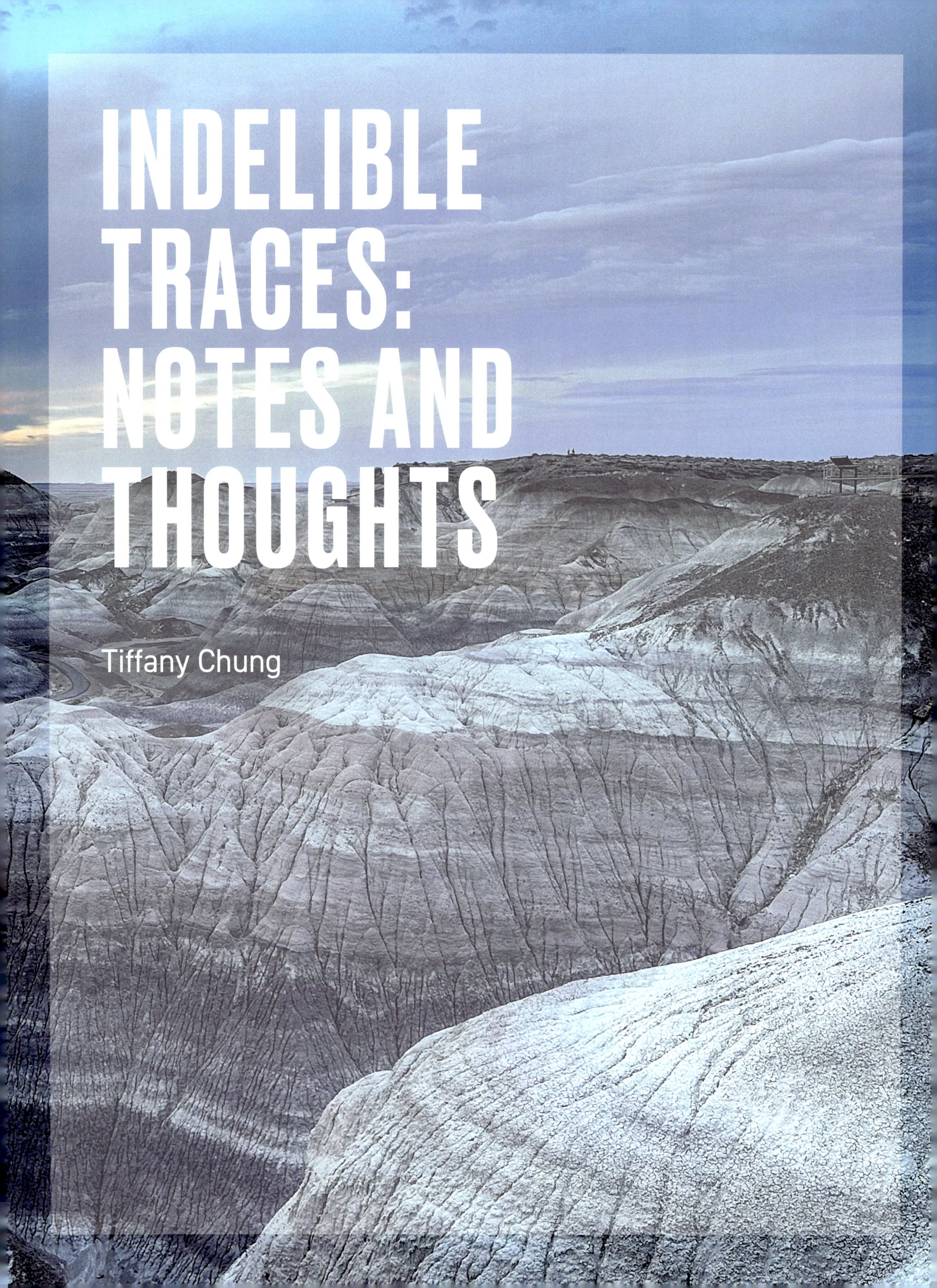

INDELIBLE TRACES: NOTES AND THOUGHTS

Tiffany Chung

. . . ma (間)

My late maternal grandparents taught me to see things in the in-between space through the stories they told, which were often magical and metaphorical. Actions they took reflected quiet love and understated emotion. When I was eight, my sister and I were taken away from our grandparents' home as my mother was forcibly relocated to a New Economic Zone.[1] We were moved around a bit and, through our mother, became keenly observant of life's hardship, of injustice and new social order, of mental stress and its manifestation. My sister and I were always together despite our different personalities. As a child, I learned to swim in the river using a floater made by tying two coconuts together; my sister was afraid of water and nearly drowned several times. My sister would sit quietly watching me fish in the river streams. She would follow me and watch me play jump rope with my classmates. I would come to her defense against school bullies. As time passed, we silently mourned the loss of innocence. We learned to float through the emptiness, the nothingness, the void of our childhood—alone and together, without confiding in each other through words. We raised each other that way until adolescence, until my sister left home.

While living in Japan in my thirties, I began to learn how the concept of *ma* is central in Eastern cultures. Written in Kanji, *ma* (間) is composed of two parts, a door or gate (門) and the sun (日); together these etymologically describe a door being slightly open to let in the sunlight. In Japanese culture, *ma* is an "interval," "gap," or "emptiness" that occupies the space between things, events, moments, words, or people. *Ma* denotes spatial or temporal extension, like the silence between the music notes that evokes sounds. While *ma* goes beyond Japan's sphere of influence[2] and is universally used in art, architecture, music, and poetry, it is the philosophy that informs the way in which many of us from East Asian cultures move through life. We learn to find solace in *ma*, in the silent presence and absence of those we love. When a close friend's father suddenly passed away, I returned to Fukuoka to pay respect. We sat on the tatami with our bodies slightly close to each other, enough to feel the warmness at a time of sadness. Together, we ate a simple meal I had prepared. Together, we breathed quietly and pausingly, embracing the presence of one another. As I said goodbye to Okasan ("mother" in Japanese), her cat held onto my legs as though asking me to stay. I left town for good very soon after, taking with me a pause in time and an expanse of emotion that could only be conveyed in *ma*.

. . . words and worlds

My curiosity about the world began with words. The worlds of others are captured in words. Words encourage us to imagine. As a child, I wanted to be a writer. Living in a crowded household in Sài Gòn for school and away from my mother, who had to stay in a post-1975 New Economic Zone, I sought solitude in literature. With tropical monsoon rains pounding on tin roofs, I hid in a corner reading Gabriel García Márquez's *One Hundred Years of Solitude*. It was my first introduction to Latin America, providing an alternative and unofficial history of the region, a place so far away from everything a child in Việt Nam could have ever imagined, and one that perhaps I could not fully comprehend. It was during the period after the war in my ravaged home country on the other side of the Pacific. Today I can transport myself back in time and see that little girl quietly reading Colombia's finest novel of magic realism, pondering a village called Macondo.

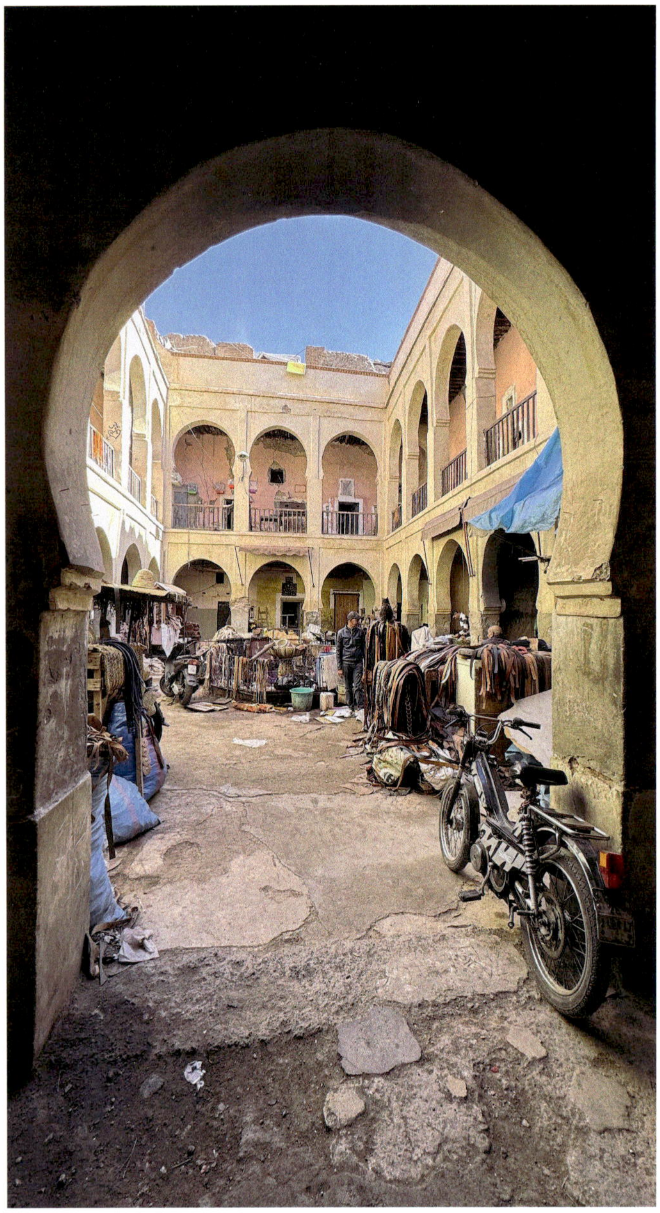

FIGURE 1 A former *fondouk* (caravanserai) in the Medina, Marrakesh, 2025.

The classic literature that I read during those childhood years by Leo Tolstoy, Victor Hugo, and Margaret Mitchell, among others was certainly my refuge in the war's aftermath and it shaped my curiosity of the world beyond my country's turbulent history. Decades after reading *One Thousand and One Nights*, without remembering much of it, my work brought me to the Mediterranean crossroads again. For years I wanted to learn about the Silk Road but found myself unable to disentangle such a complex network of routes, literally and figuratively. Walking around the old town of Diriyah on the outskirts of Riyadh, Saudi Arabia, sparked my desire to anchor my focus in the ancient spice routes. As if a massive piece of fabric, the global history of the spice trade is interwoven with culinary, economic, cultural, and political threads that held it in place for several millennia. The spices' trajectories across time and space link commerce, maritime development, conflict, and colonialism, which led to modern capitalism. They tell stories of how globalization began—through trade, migration, linguistic movements, culinary and cultural adaptation—and how it is inevitably intertwined with wars.

Continuing to follow the spices in my research, I wandered around the labyrinth of small alleys in the Medina of Marrakesh, once part of the ancient caravan routes. I imagined the courtyards and fruit trees behind all the closed doors in the old town. I walked into former *fondouks* (fig. 1), imagining the atmosphere of the caravanserais that had once hosted merchants on their stops along the caravan routes but are now abandoned or turned into craftsman workshops and stores. Finding myself on the top of a building surrounded by Marrakesh rooftops, with the vast Atlas Mountains in the background, I felt in awe of the place etched with memories of human connections and of ancient nature. Real places put things in perspective, temporally and spatially. Visiting places where we can see and touch and smell and listen to life makes us aware of other histories—those less visible, written by now-unknown people such as the unnamed spice traders.

. . . history

My passage through life in the war's aftermath taught me that the history we learned in school did not reflect multiple perspectives. As we recited rhetorical tales of the revolution in class and at weekly flag salutes, I imagined that unwritten personal memories of historical events were hidden in the blank space between pages of school textbooks. What I was not taught in school has become the knowledge that I seek through academic research and oral histories. These microhistories began with the family stories that I was told and the events that followed. The lived experiences and cultural memories that remain unrecorded across different times and terrains are witnesses of history—occupying the in-between and intangible spheres of the past. In that *ma* space, the omitted and the disremembered can be seen and heard. We can question and challenge what is said and unsaid, for there is nothing absolute regarding history: it is always told or written through someone's perspective. Through time, memories can be distorted and manipulated. Trying to access the past, we become aware of its inaccessibility. This does not mean there is no truth in what took place for certain events, but rather, historical truth might be relative—it depends on who remembers and for what purposes. This awareness is critical when delving into history—especially when a grand narrative does not allow multiple interpretations—as it leads to considering the creative means through which one can intervene and add layers to the dominant or official account. As the invisible sonic fields of a music composition conjure up a range of emotions and memories, the aesthetic fields enable an abstract space, which can breathe life into statistics and stories collected from research and data mining. This space can weave various lines of inquiry with visual elements, giving forms to the fragmented, the incomprehensible, and the unfinished [hi]stories.

. . . home, conflict, and arts

The experience of living through war, being displaced, and rebuilding one's life elsewhere is often interwoven with memories of home—its landscapes, cultures, sounds, and smells—with dreams and hopes for our ruined cities and fractured countries. Distance fosters our relationships with one another and our longing for home and its comforts: the fragrance of the freshly picked herbs from my mom's garden, her cooking, the clanking of pots and pans in her kitchen, the clatter of dinnerware at the dinner table—the unspoken love given and felt with food. When I visited home while living abroad, time dripped slowly. I would rummage aimlessly through my father's cabinets to find random tools and gadgets. I would flip the changing pages of my little brother's books to see him growing up. Home enables us to slow down and breathe.

For many of us who have lived through wars, the home that we grew up in only lingers in memories. Walking down an alleyway in another country, my heart sinks as the houses and atmosphere transport me back to the city where I was born—and a wave of bittersweet warmth sweeps over me. Home lives within us, in our minds and hearts. Tracking conflicts and forced displacement around the world in my work (fig. 2), Syria to me is a place that is both haunting and inspiring. For many Syrians, home is in the memories of those who could not come back, and of those who stay behind without the people they once knew. I often imagine and remember Syria, a place I have only seen in pictures and read about, with poignant nostalgia imagined through the sense of smell and taste. Such a tender moment is profoundly captured in the poem "Damascus—The Festival of Water and Jasmine" by Syrian poet and diplomat Nizar Qabbani:

> I cannot write Damascus, without feeling the jasmines on my fingers.
> And I cannot say her name, without my tongue blazing with the juices
> of apricots, pomegranates, berries and quince.
> And I cannot mention her without a thousand doves landing on the walls
> of memory, and a thousand doves taking off.[3]

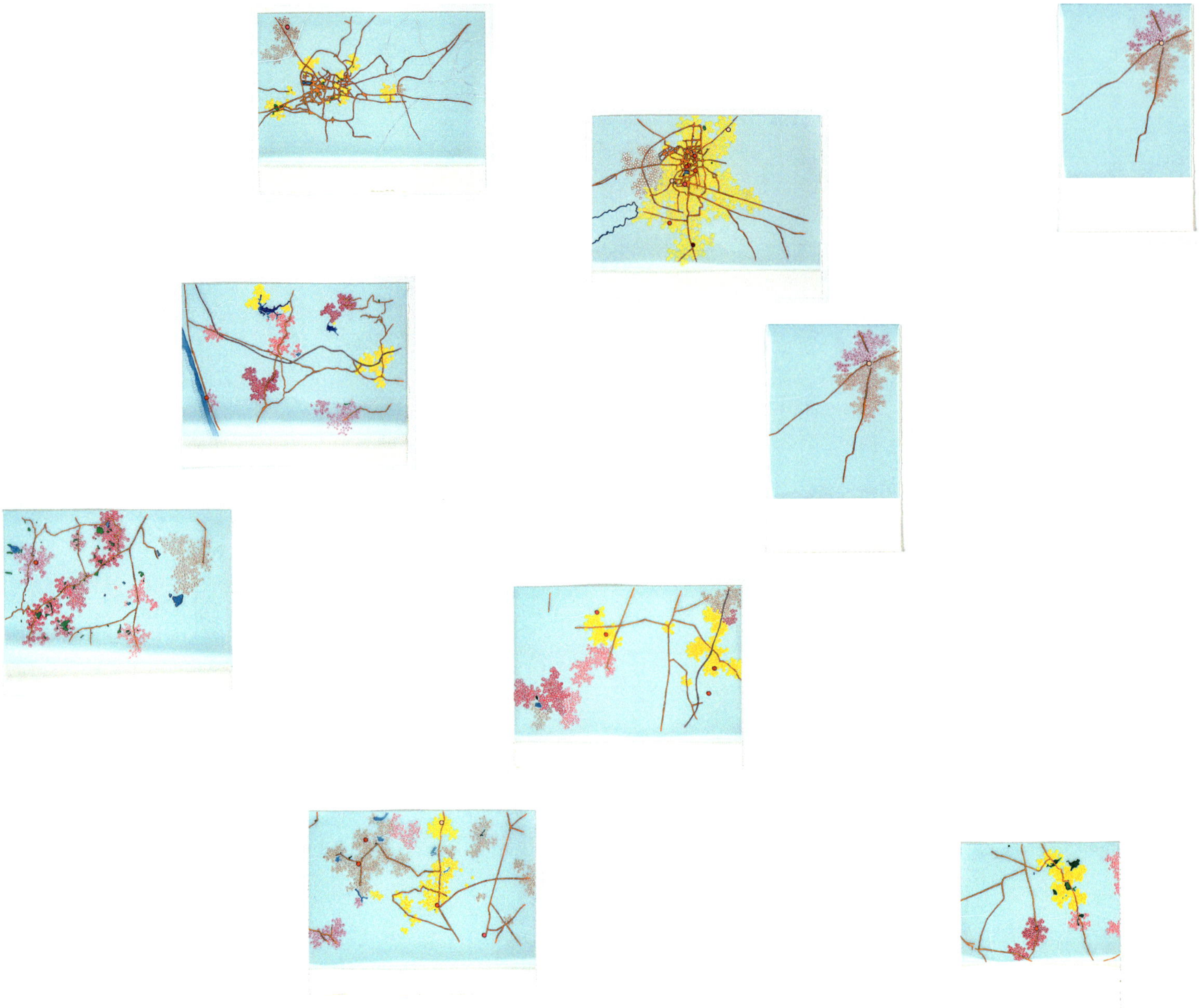

FIGURE 2 Tiffany Chung, *Syria Tracker: numbers of children killed in different governorates, March 2011–November 2014*, 2014–2015. Ink and oil on vellum and paper, dimensions variable.

Among the architectural ruins of Syria's war-torn heritage sites, one could still hear ancient Syriac hymns passed down orally through the centuries and Sufi invocations echoed over the stone walled courtyards of homes. One would be aware that faith and spiritual health can offer immense comfort and restore hope and optimism in such dark times.

> We have fallen into the place
> where everything is music.
> The strumming and the flute notes
> rise into the atmosphere,
> and even if the whole world's harp
> should burn up, there will still be
> hidden instruments playing.[4]

This excerpt from Rumi's poem "Where Everything Is Music" is also profoundly uplifting, evoking the spirit of resilience amid an upside-down world. Beneath the images of death and destruction from places known as "conflict zones," we can still find strength, beauty, hope, and humanity. The abstract, atmospheric, and ephemeral sensory effects of music, poetry, and visual art linger mesmerizingly and tap into our senses. The intangible sounds and memories depicted through arts can give forms and textures to the seemingly imperceptible lifeworld of people in unimaginable circumstances. In these spheres, one might find home again (fig. 3).

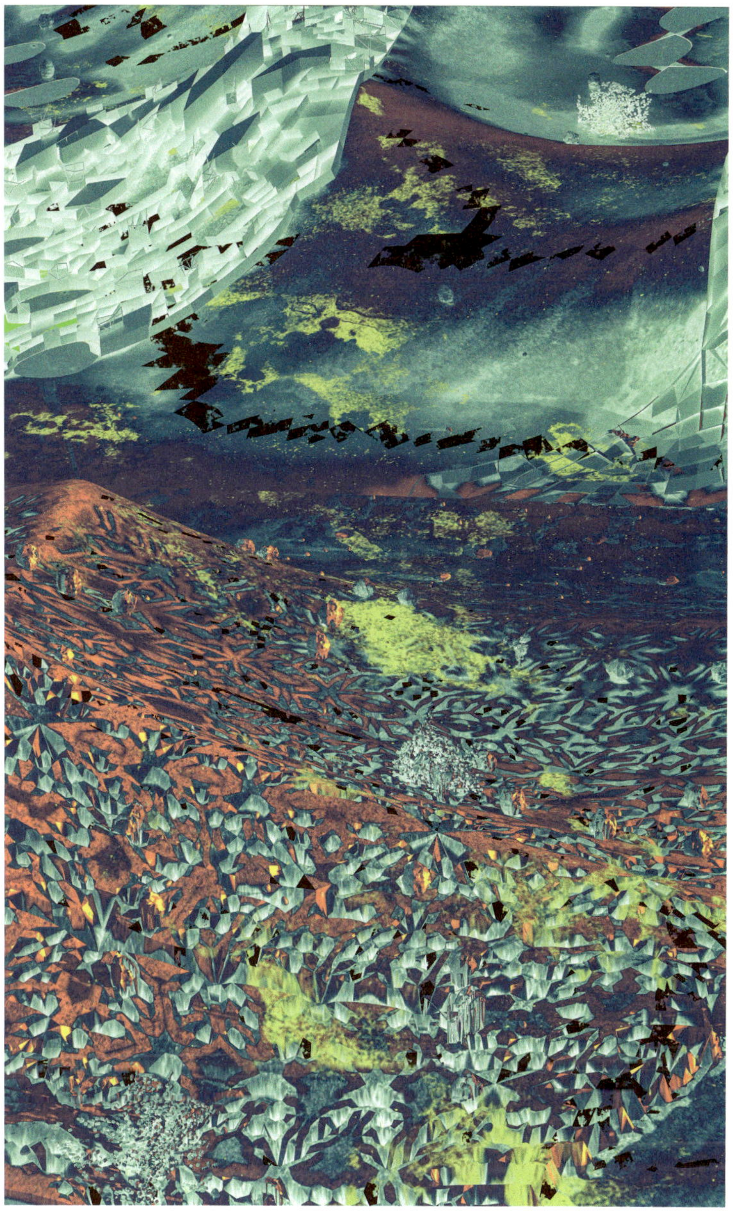

FIGURE 3 Tiffany Chung, *Poetic Landscapes Remembered*, 2023. Printed vinyl decals distilled from video animation, approx. length 45 m (150 ft.). Installation view, *Tiffany Chung: Rise Into the Atmosphere*, Dallas Museum of Art, Texas, 2023–2025.

. . . from dry lands to the deep seas and sky

Our movements from one place to another are inextricably linked to our desire and search for home. Being away from home, we come to understand what home means. Looking at the sky full of stars at night, we contemplate the mysterious universe beyond Earth's magnetic field. As space exploration launches us far throughout the solar system, into solar orbit and interstellar space, we use the science to observe, study, and collect data for Earth—for the understanding of terrestrial phenomena taking place on our home planet. But before the 1969 moon landing, Continental Shelf Station missions supported by the French Navy and the US Navy's Man-in-the-Sea project, both started in 1962, explored the ocean as inner space and led to the Sealab program's subsea exploration and human habitation project.[5] While we constantly meander across unknown and newfound territories, we regularly leave our marks in passing.

Throughout history, human-driven alterations of landscapes, of flora and fauna, are often indelible. Evidence of transhumance—pastoral and nomadic societies—during the Chalcolithic period have been recognized in Neolithic circular ditched enclosures dating from 5000 BCE found across Central Europe and the Iberian Peninsula. The ancient nomadic populations that frequented the Iberian enclosures during the period around 3000 BCE used some of the sites as social and meeting places, adding further concentric rings to them and carrying out depositional practices. As a result, significant *recintos de fosos* (ditched enclosures) in the southern Iberian Peninsula such as Perdigões (fig. 4), La Pijotilla, Marroquíes, or Valencina continued to pop up on an enormous scale, resulting in wider and deeper ditches and pits filled with various materials, including human remains, though without evidence of traditional funerary rituals.[6] Although some traces of prehistoric material cultures are less visible than others, they remain. Circular earthworks in Cambodia and Việt Nam (2300–300 BCE) with similar features in morphology were found, along with stone tools, potsherds, and glass bangles at excavation sites.[7] Scientists presumed that because fewer marks were left, the settlements in Việt Nam and Cambodia had managed sustainable ecological relationships with the environment until they integrated into floodplain settlements. I would argue that subtle traces do not necessarily indicate that these early inhabitants lived in harmony with nature. The fact of the matter is that these sites are understudied; many are concealed under rubber plantations or dense vegetations such as old forests, and are in danger of being built over.

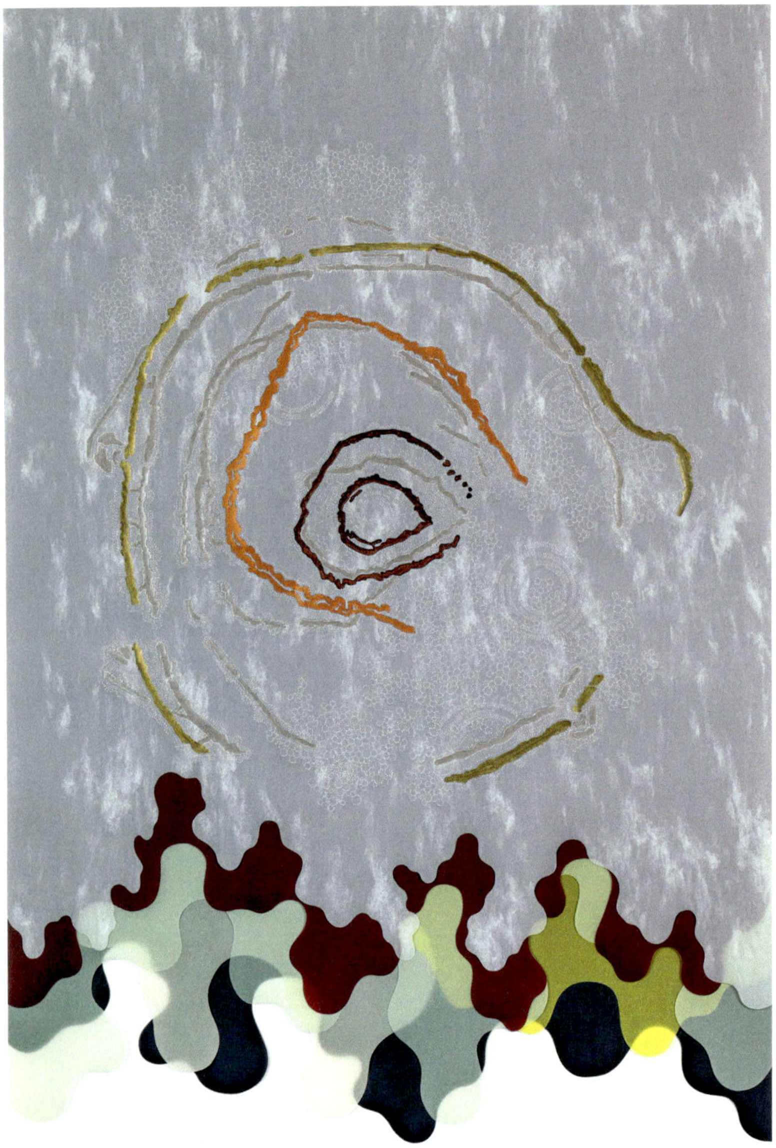

FIGURE 4 Tiffany Chung, *Ditch Enclosure Perdigões, Portugal*, 2025. Ink, oil, and hand perforating on vellum and paper, 112 × 70.5 cm (44 × 27 ¾ in.). Courtesy of the artist and Galería Max Estrella.

Exchange, trade, migration, and colonization in ancient times were evidenced by the archaeobotanical remains of spices, grains, and tools found across the world. Black pepper was among the spices traded by Babylonia and Assyria with the Malabar region of Kerala in India as early as 3000 BCE; pepper was contained in the mummy of Ramesses II in ancient Egypt, dating back at least to the thirteenth century BCE.[8] Cinnamon traces were found in 3,000-year-old Phoenician vessels located in today's northern coast of Israel.[9] At the archaeological site of Óc Eo, the entrepôt of the Funan Kingdom in today's southern Việt Nam, microremains of turmeric, ginger, fingerroot, sand ginger, galangal, clove, nutmeg, and cinnamon—the ingredients used in making South Asian curry—were recovered from stone grinding tools.[10] Scientists believe that such spices were introduced to Việt Nam

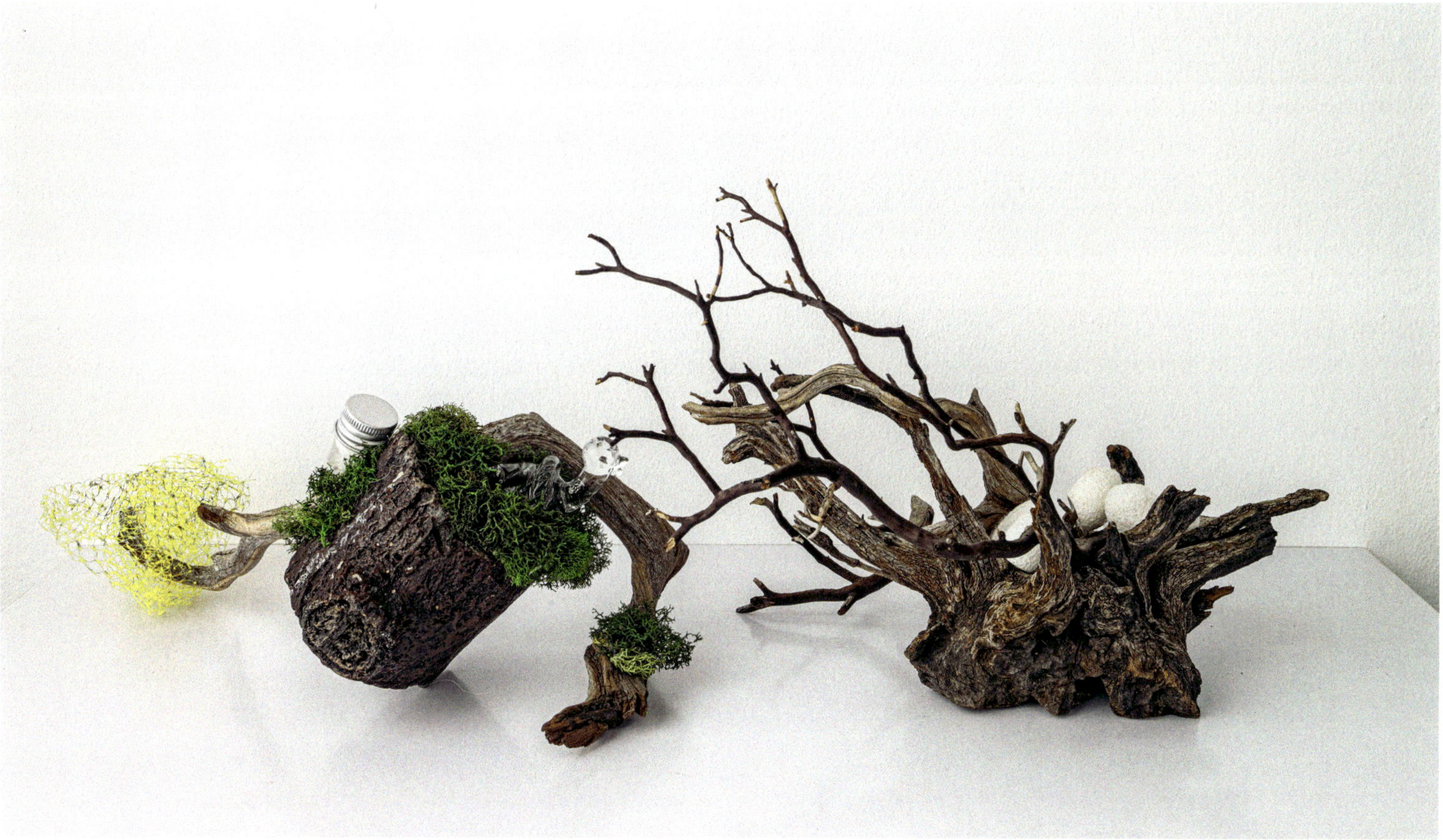

via the Indian Ocean trade 2,000 years ago, while historical texts from China, Roman Europe, and India noted more exotic spices that originated in Southeast Asia. Situated 6,000 km from Southeast Asia, Madagascar Island's language is part of the Austronesian language family unique to Southeast Asia and the Pacific,[11] pointing to the Austronesian expansion that started from Taiwan 4,000 years ago. Besides linguistic, ethnographic, and genetic evidence, archaeobotanical assemblages dating from the eighth to the tenth centuries CE found in Comoros and Madagascar are dominantly Asian crops (e.g., rice, mungbean, cotton). The transplanting of botanical organisms from their native environments to all corners of the Earth indicates the extent of human migration as well as our colonization of nature (fig. 5), resulting in significant changes in various forms of biodiversity. We have made profound impacts on creation, on the natural world that provides for and enables our survival. In turn we are responsible for the sustainability of ecologies to maintain life on Earth. I feel determined to stay committed so that even if the world will go to pieces tomorrow, I still want to plant a tree or two today, to borrow a quote attributed to Martin Luther, as taking one small step in the right direction can begin a new cycle of life.

FIGURE 5 Tiffany Chung, *the world through my mother's cabinets of curiosities,* 2025. Detail. Multiple miniature sculptures made from repurposed materials, approx. installation length 15 m (49 ¼ ft.), dimensions of sculptures variable. Courtesy of the artist and Kiang Malingue Gallery, Hong Kong | New York. Photo by Francisco Ramos.

. . . Earth

Sometimes when I look at trees, I think of my grandparents' backyard, where I spent many an afternoon staring at leaves swaying in the wind, with fleeting moments of shimmering light and shadows. I remember the well that was tucked away in a back corner, where my mom washed our clothes. As a child, I often looked down into it to see a tiny sliver of the sky reflected in the water. Years later, work took me to the Petrified Forest National Park in northeastern Arizona, where the sky is expansive in every direction. At the end of a hike through the Blue Mesa, I climbed up to higher ground to take in the full view of the breathtakingly multi-hued, layered

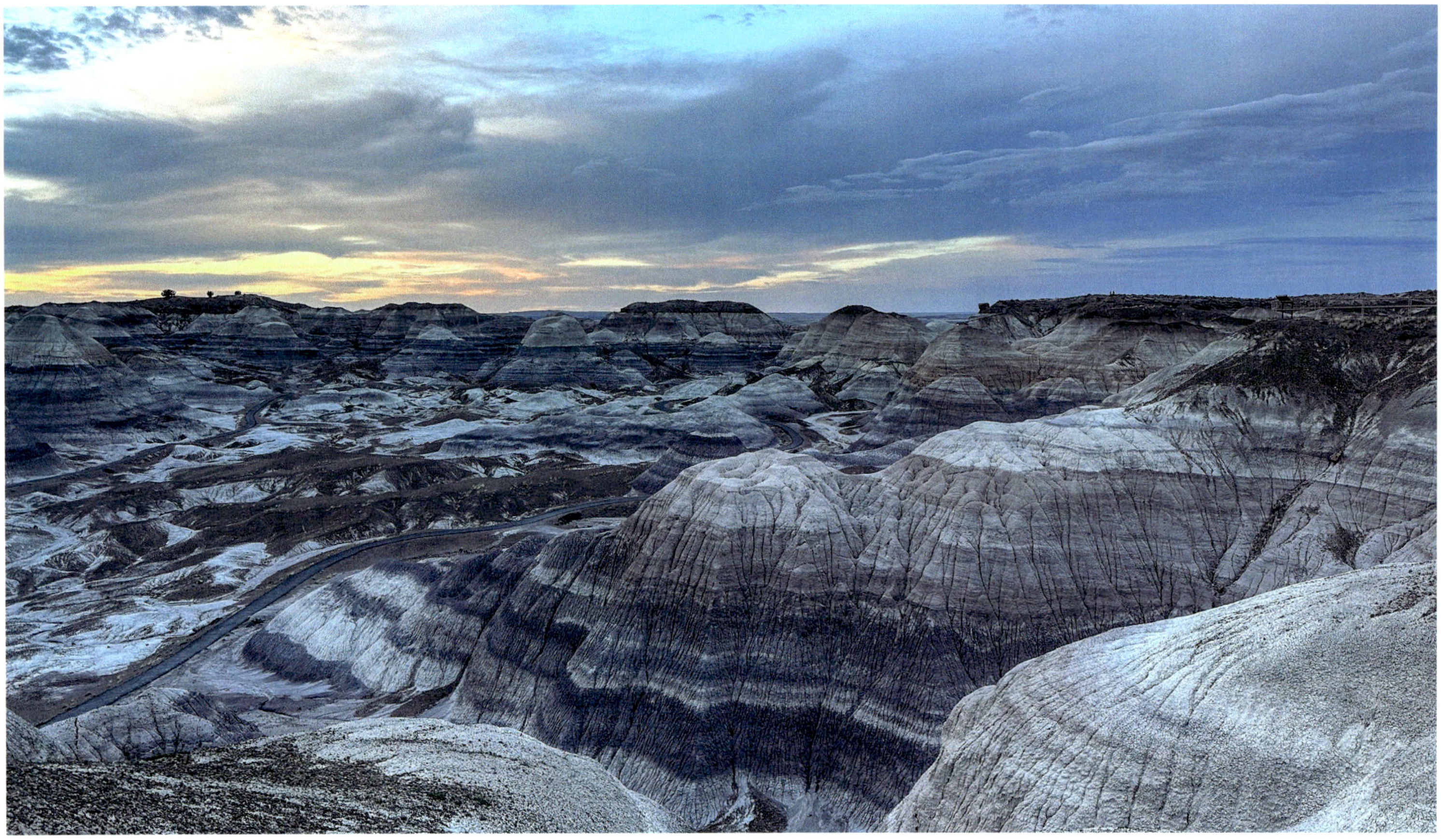

FIGURE 6 Blue Mesa at the Petrified Forest National Park, Arizona, 2023.

badlands that are part of this vast landscape (fig. 6), as the sun was setting against the orange-purple sky. This 225-million-year-old petrified forest from the Late Triassic Chinle Formation and the Mio-Pliocene Formation had been part of the supercontinent Pangaea—where traces of ancient tropical environments can still be seen through the eroded sediments, the rich-mineral, colorful cross-section of petrified logs, and the diverse ecosystem. I felt a sense of comfort being surrounded by Earth's ancient remnants, the same way my memories of my grandparents persist over the years.

Knowledge can be found in depositional environments of Earth. Buried in stratigraphic records of the Earth's crust, this evolving and incomplete information indicates processes and climate events that took place in deep geological time. To cast a glimpse of a glimpse of the intact Permian world alive 291 million years ago, 40 million years before the world's greatest mass extinction, I traveled to two archaeological excavation sites of the Chemnitz petrified forest in eastern Germany, where the diverse ecosystem of the Permian forest was preserved by explosive volcanism and buried under Chemnitz City. This forest is one of the most important Fossil-Lagerstätte for the Permian period, with fully terrestrial deposits of flora and fauna fossilized into small, intricate details. These traces are hidden but indelible—they teach us what the living Earth has embodied over millions of years. As I consider our human history within the Earth's expansive record that spans geologic eras, our civilizations and societies feel humble and microscopic. We are just a mere speck within the Earth's sediments. However, the imprints of our progress and our alterations of the natural world have left and will continue to leave consequential impacts for the future. Learning about both petrified forests and the Permian-Triassic extinction, which scientists postulate was caused by the release of sulfur dioxide and carbon dioxide into the atmosphere, remind me of the unimaginable, catastrophic effects of carbon dioxide and greenhouse gases in massive quantities today. Although the continuity of life on Earth from pre-human times and throughout several mass extinctions gives me the hope that nature will eventually bounce back, I am also reminded that Earth took at least ten million years to recover from the Great Dying. This truly goes beyond the human timescale and existence. Looking at the Permian and Triassic traces contained within petrified woods, fossilized specimens, and rock formations, I wonder what memories and legacies we are leaving for tomorrow, in and beyond this world.

NOTES

1 For more information on New Economic Zones in Việt Nam, see "New Economic Zones program," Wikipedia, accessed 10 August 2025, https://en.wikipedia.org/wiki/New_Economic_Zones_program.

2 See Michael Lucken and Miriam Rosen, "The Limits of ma: Retracing the Emergence of a 'Japanese' Concept," *Journal of World Philosophies* 6, no. 1 (2021): 38–57.

3 As quoted in Lubna Safi, "Jasmine Fingers," *Guernica*, 22 August 2019, https://www.guernicamag.com/jasmine-fingers/.

4 Rumi, "Where Everything Is Music," *Poet Seers*, trans. Coleman Barks with John Moyne, https://www.poetseers.org/spiritual-and-devotional-poets/contemp/rumibarks/4-2/.

5 See Phil Short, "The history of subsea human habitation," *Deep*, 31 January 2025, https://www.deep.com/article/the-history-of-subsea-human-habitation/.

6 See Marta Díaz-Zorita Bonilla, et al., "The Deposition of Human Remains Inside Chalcolithic Ditched Enclosures: Ditch 5 at Marroquíes (Jaén, Spain)," *European Journal of Archaeology* 23, no. 3 (2020): 330–55.

7 See Miriam Haidle, Udo Neumann, and Alfred Pawlik, "Variety and Absence: A Cambodian Stone Tool Assemblage at the Dawn of the Metal Ages," in *Lithic Technology in Metal Using Societies: Proceedings of a UISPP Workshop, Lisbon, September 2006*, ed. B. V. Eriksen (Archaeological Society Publications, 2010), 247–58.

8 See Belkheir Hammouti, et al., "Black Pepper, the 'King of Spices': Chemical Composition to Applications," *Arabian Journal of Chemical and Environmental Research* 6, no. 1 (2019):12–56.

9 "Traces of Cinnamon Found in 3,000-Year-Old Vessels," *Archaeology Magazine*, 22 August 2013, https://archaeology.org/news/2013/08/22/130822-israel-cinnamon-spice-trade/.

10 See Weiwei Wang, et al., "Earliest curry in Southeast Asia and the global spice trade 2000 years ago," *Science Advances* 9, no. 29 (2023), https://www.science.org/doi/10.1126/sciadv.adh5517.

11 See Alison Crowther, et al., "Ancient crops provide first archaeological signature of the westward Austronesian expansion," *Proceedings of the National Academy of Science of the United States of America* 113, no. 24 (2016): 6635–40.

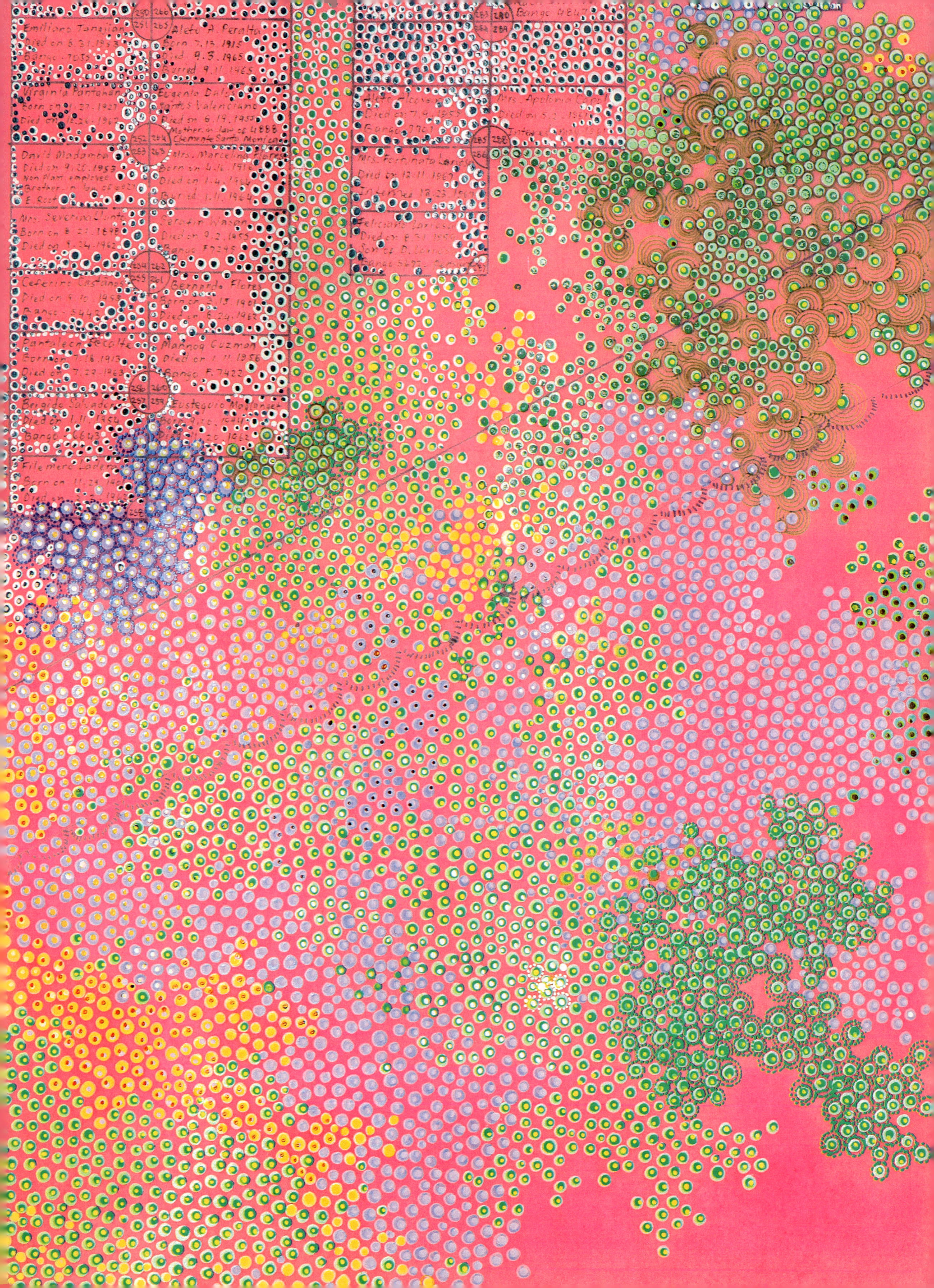
Emiliano Tanajion
Bango 7035
Aleto A. Peralta
Born 7.13.1915
Died 9.3.1965
Buried 9.11.1965
Virginia Pantahan
Born on 1.27.1927
Eugenio Dalos
Santos Valenciano
Died on 6.19.1955
Mother-in-law of 4888
Clemente Santa Monica
David Madamba
Died on 9.20.1953
Non Plant employee
Mrs. Marcelina Flores
Born on 6.16.1916
Buried 1.11.1964
Mrs. Severina Llanto
Died on 9.24.1962
Serafin Wasan
Died on 9.2.1955
Ceferino Castaños
Bernardo Flores
Born on 3.15.1901
Died on 6.24.1962
Pantaleon Ecolte
Born on 7.16.1913
Died on 7.29.1963
Mannoq Guzman
Died on 1.11.1956
Bango F.7422
Bergido Salvador
Died on 1.11.1954
Eustequio Maglanget
Filemero Ladera
Born on 11.24.1901

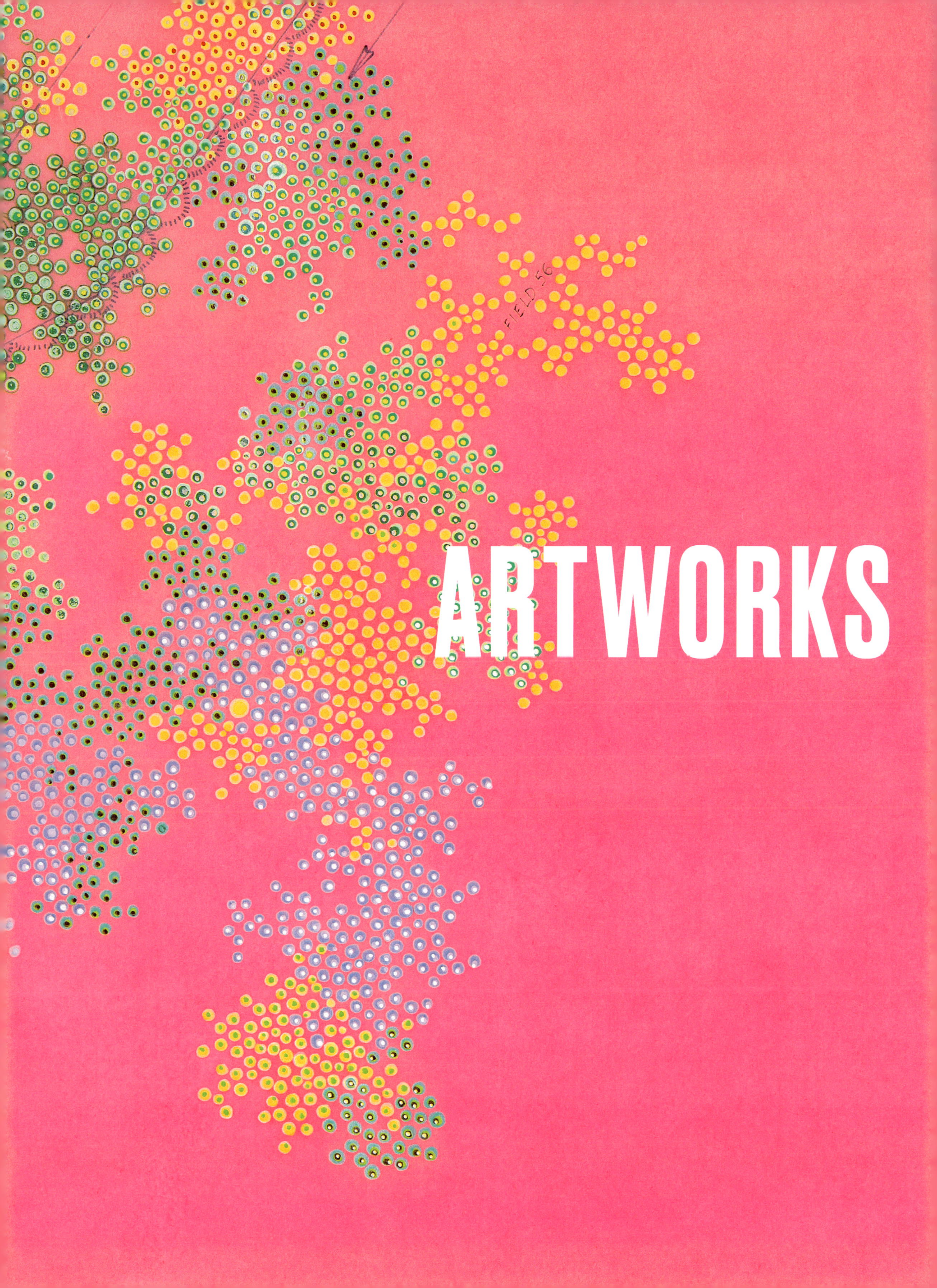

ARTWORKS

HCMC extreme flood prediction 2050–ADB & ICEM reports, 2013
Ink and oil on vellum and paper
110 × 70 cm (43 ¼ × 27 ½ in.)

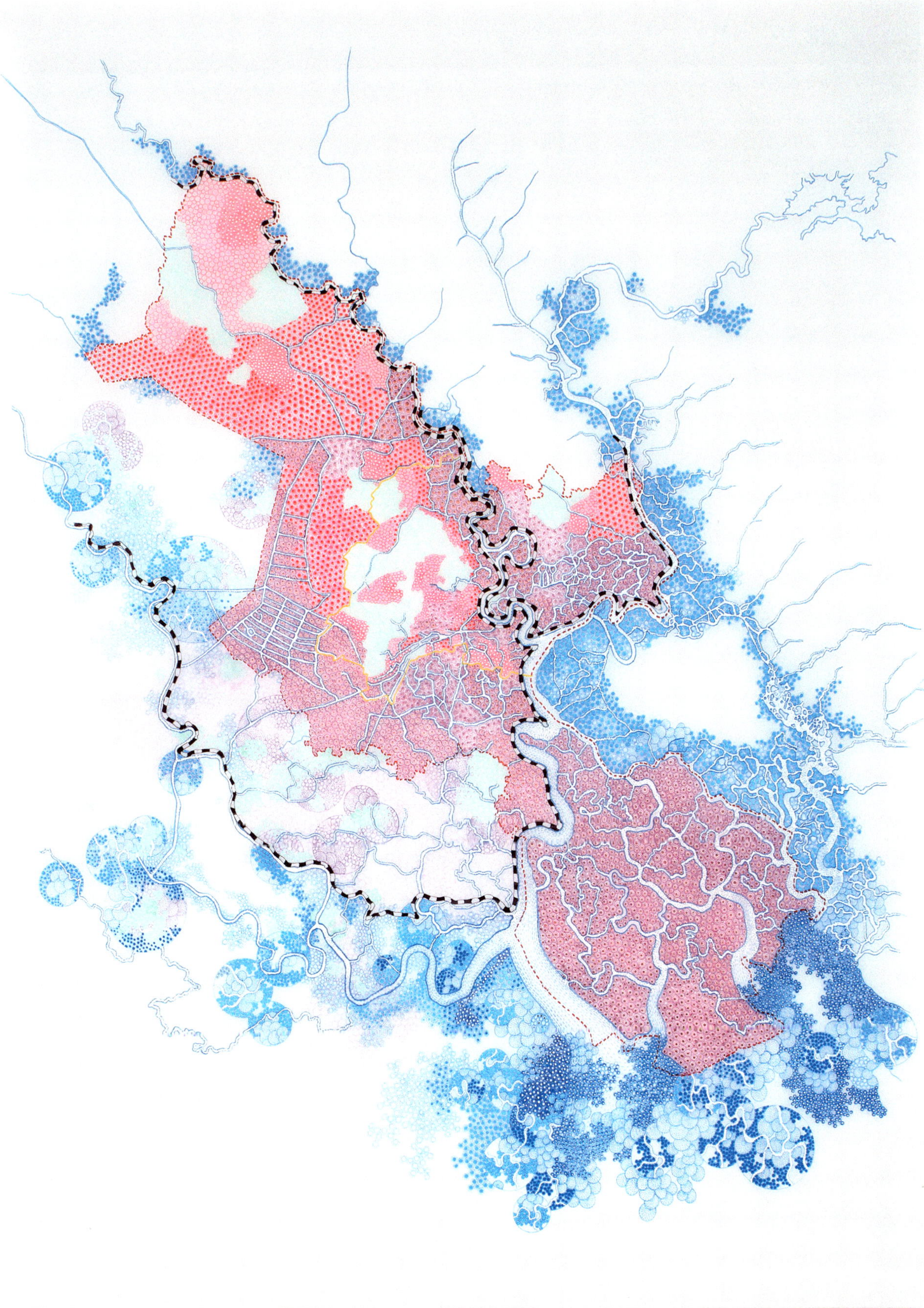

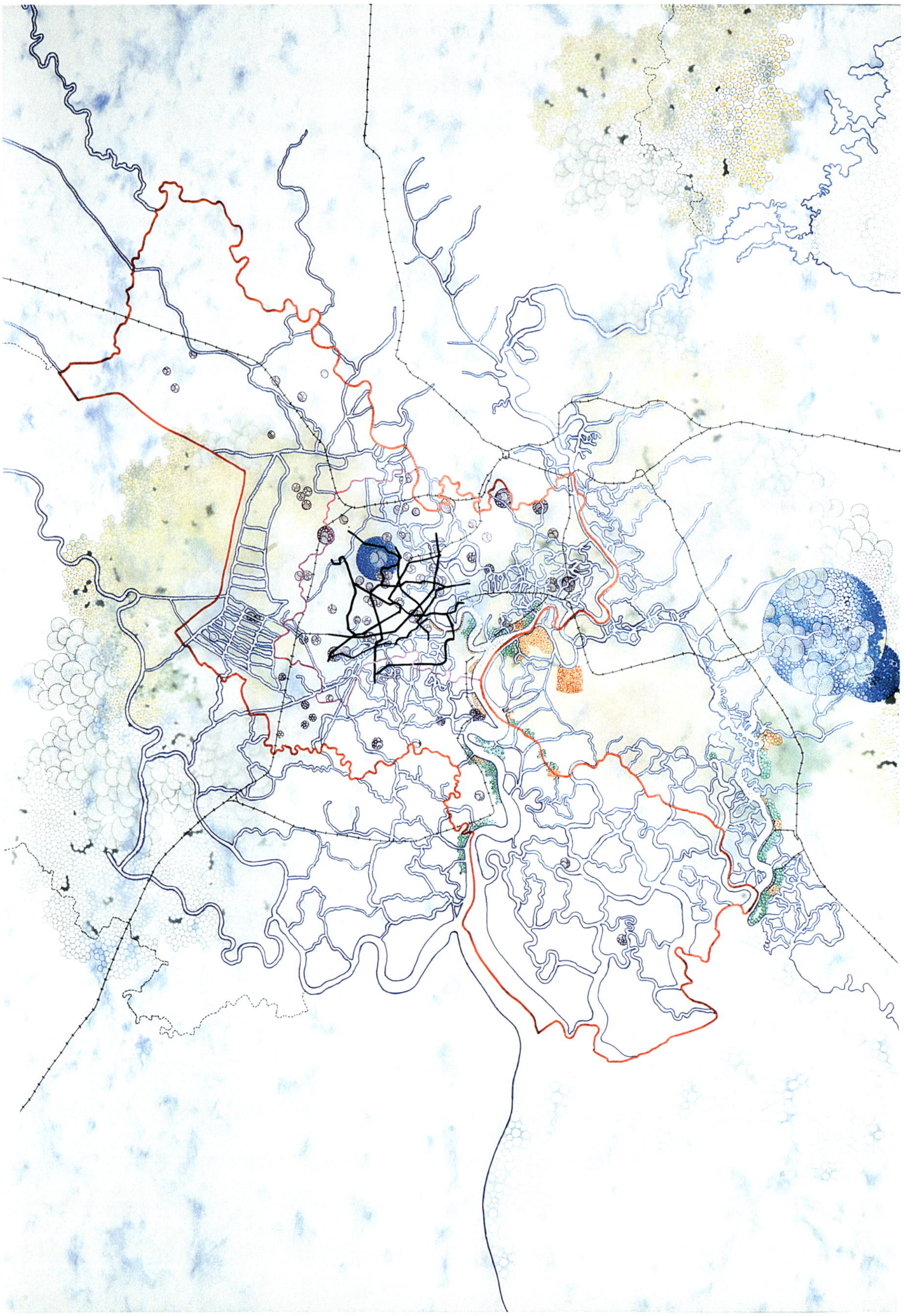

Flora and Fauna Outgrowing the Future, 2010
Ink and oil on vellum and paper
110 × 70 cm (43 ¼ × 27 ½ in.)

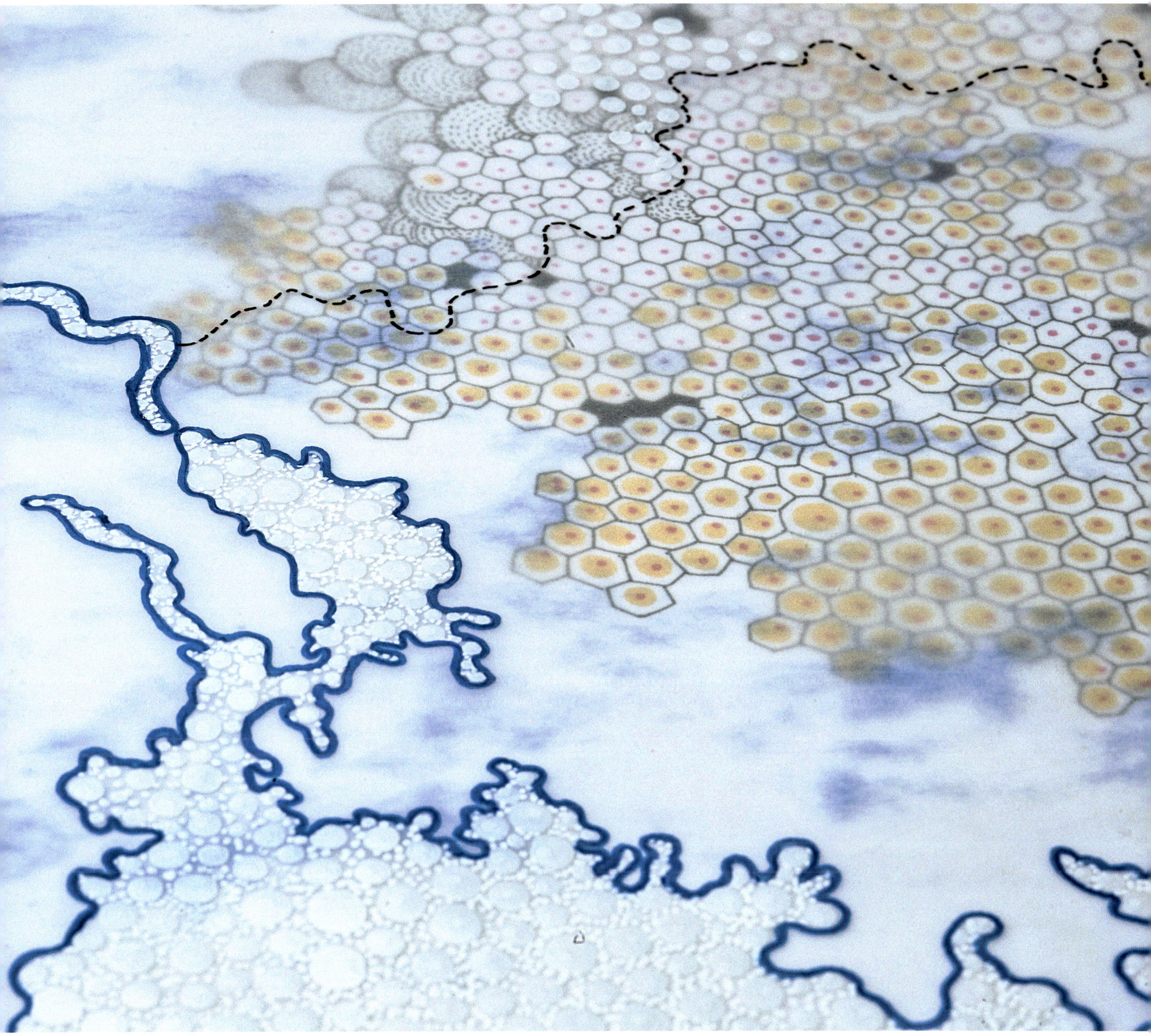

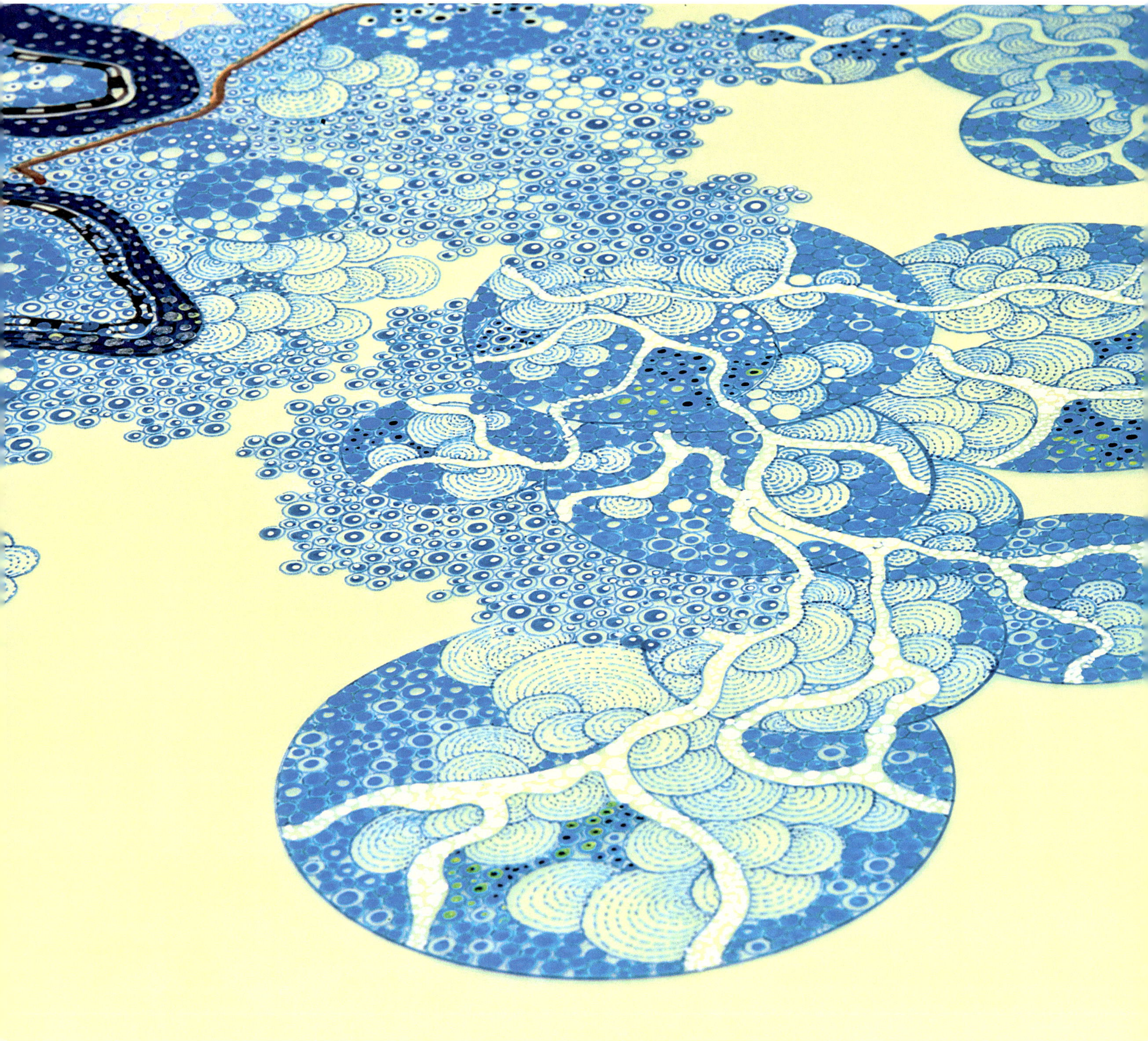

One Giant Great Flood
2050, 2010
Ink and oil on vellum and paper
110 × 70 cm (43 ¼ × 27 ½ in.)

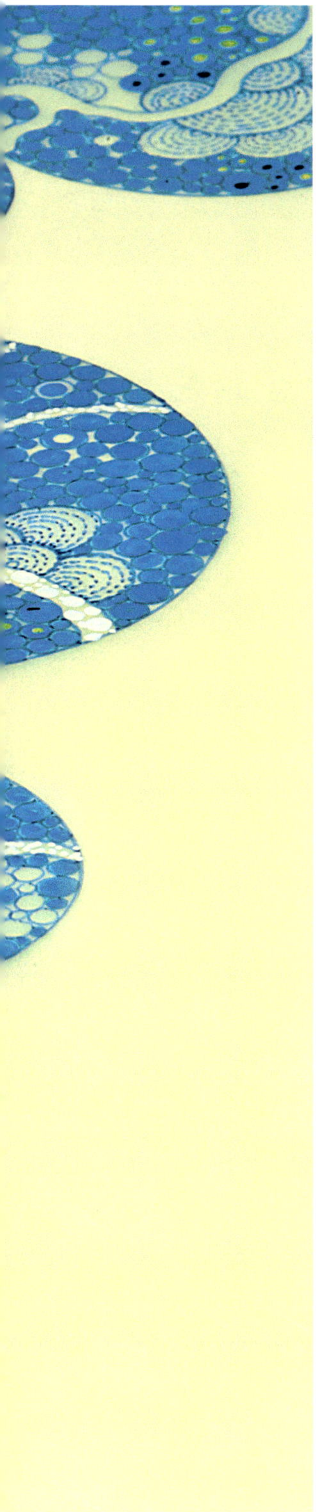

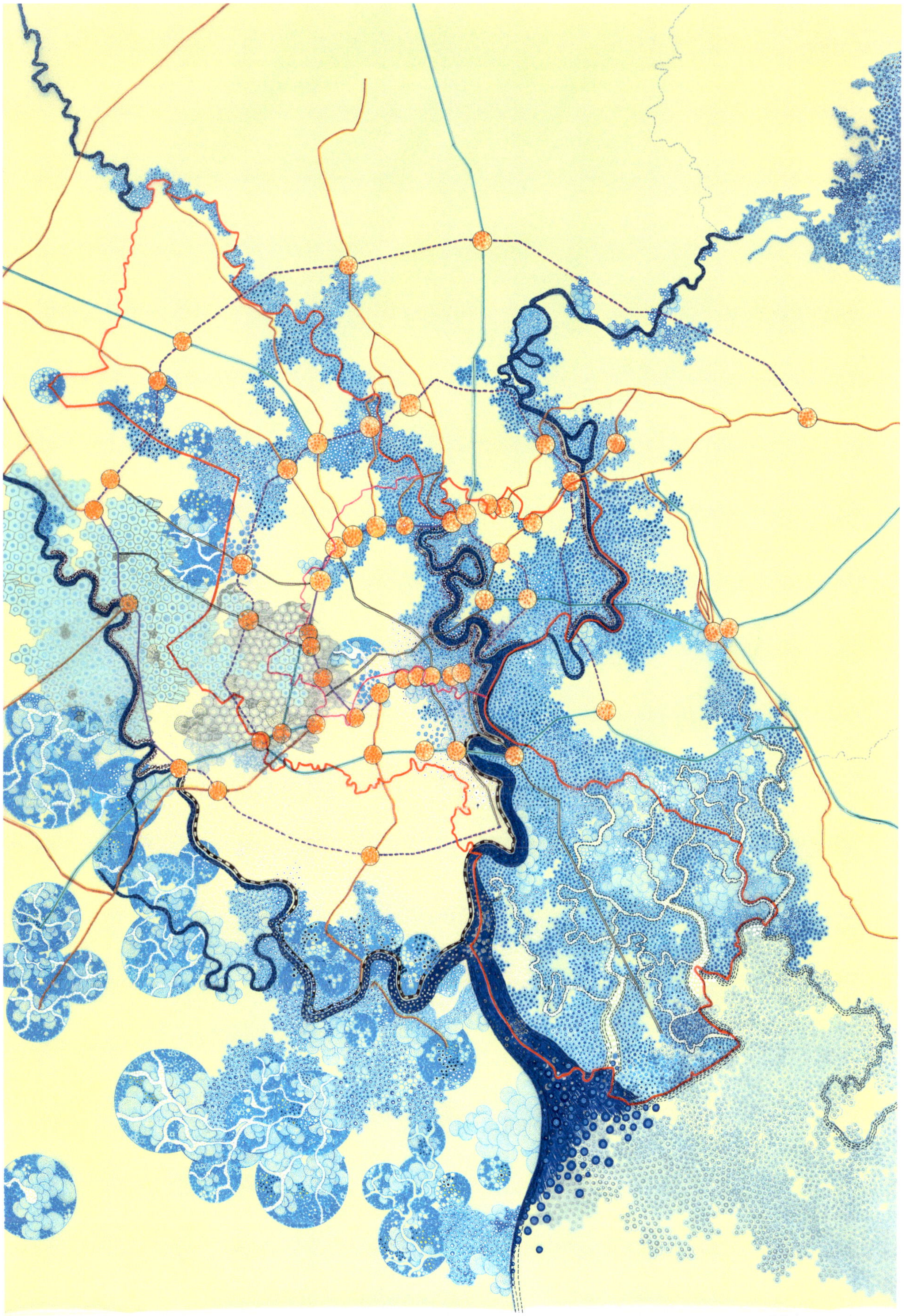

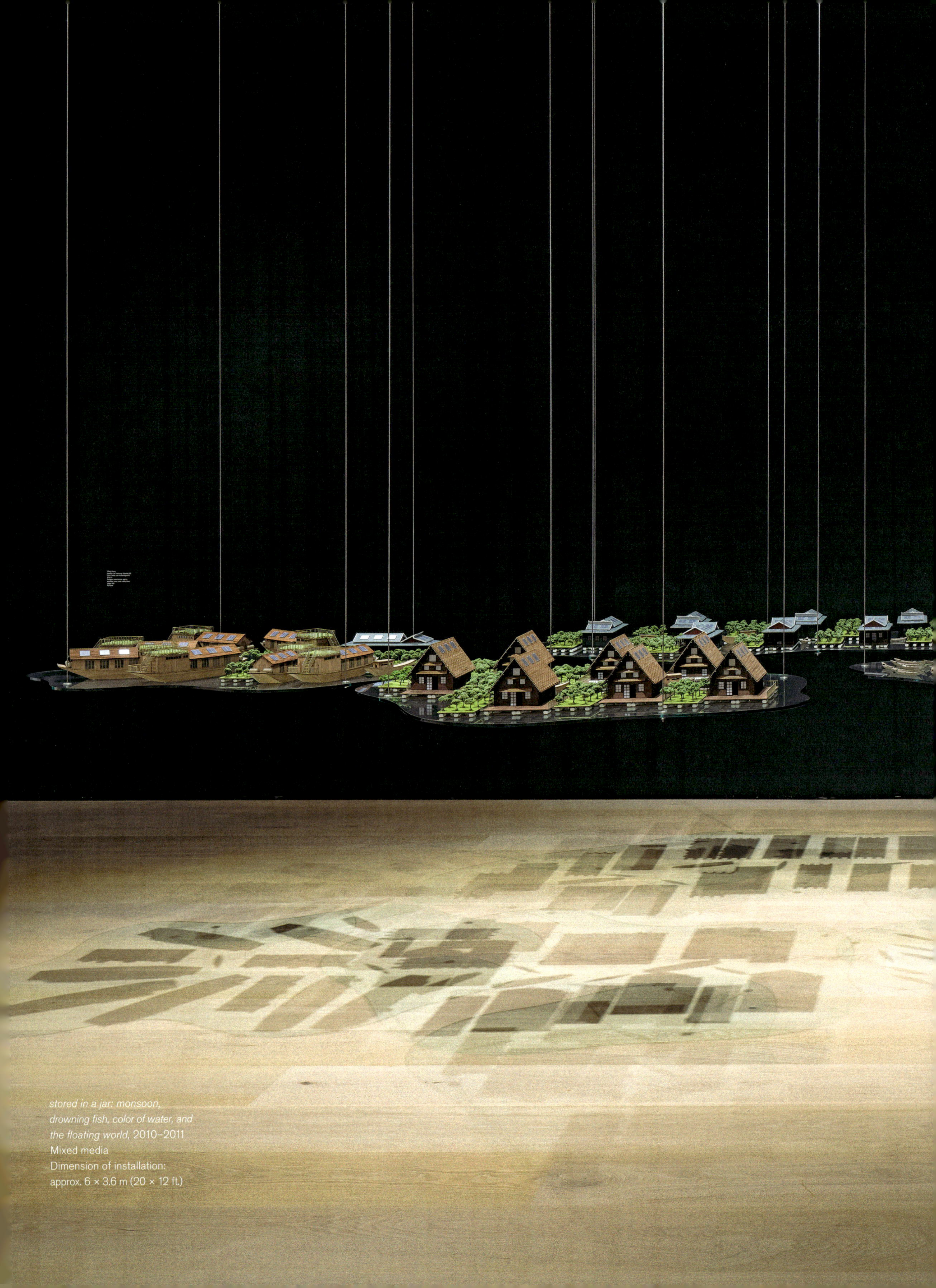

stored in a jar: monsoon, drowning fish, color of water, and the floating world, 2010–2011
Mixed media
Dimension of installation:
approx. 6 × 3.6 m (20 × 12 ft.)

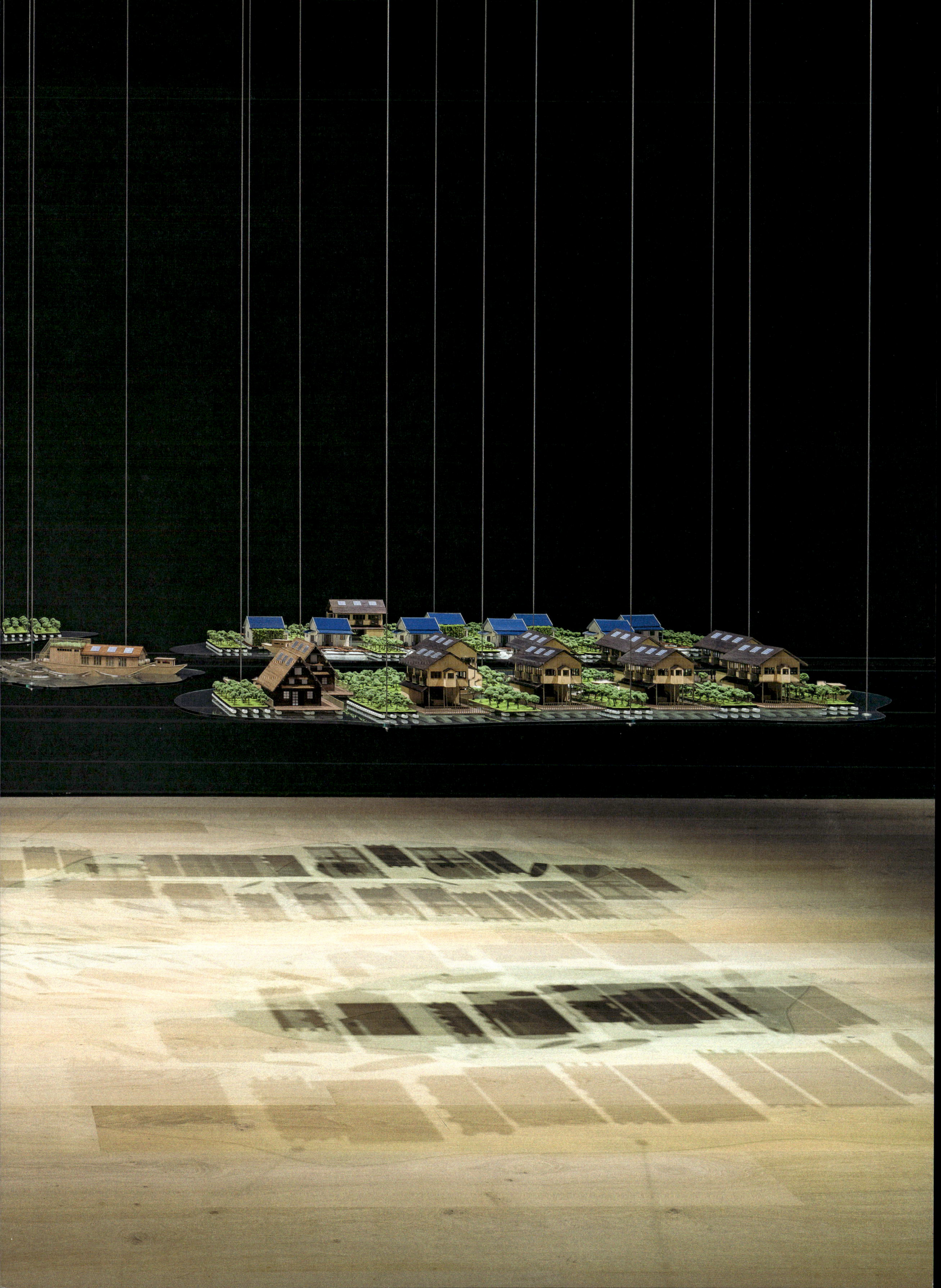

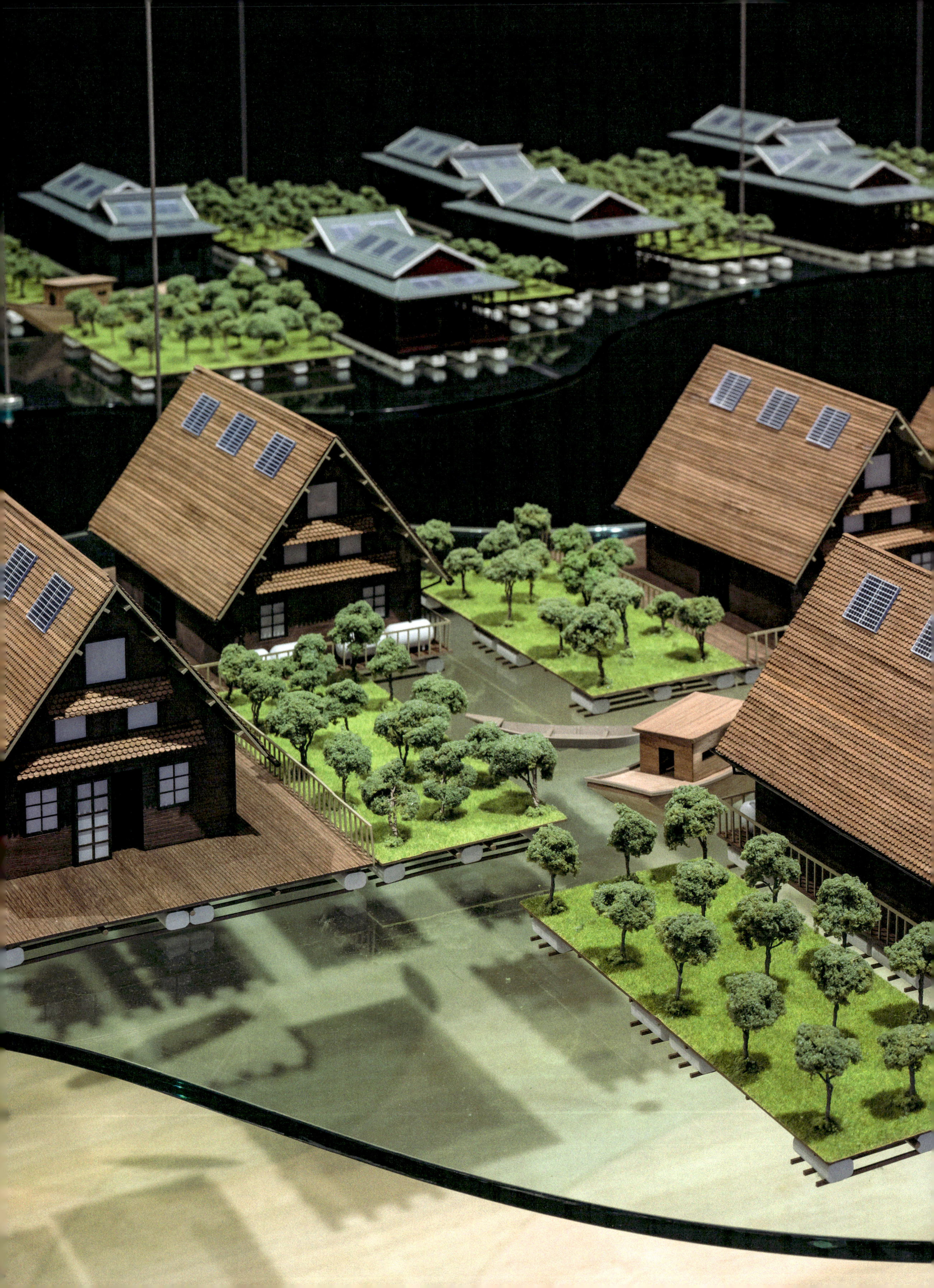

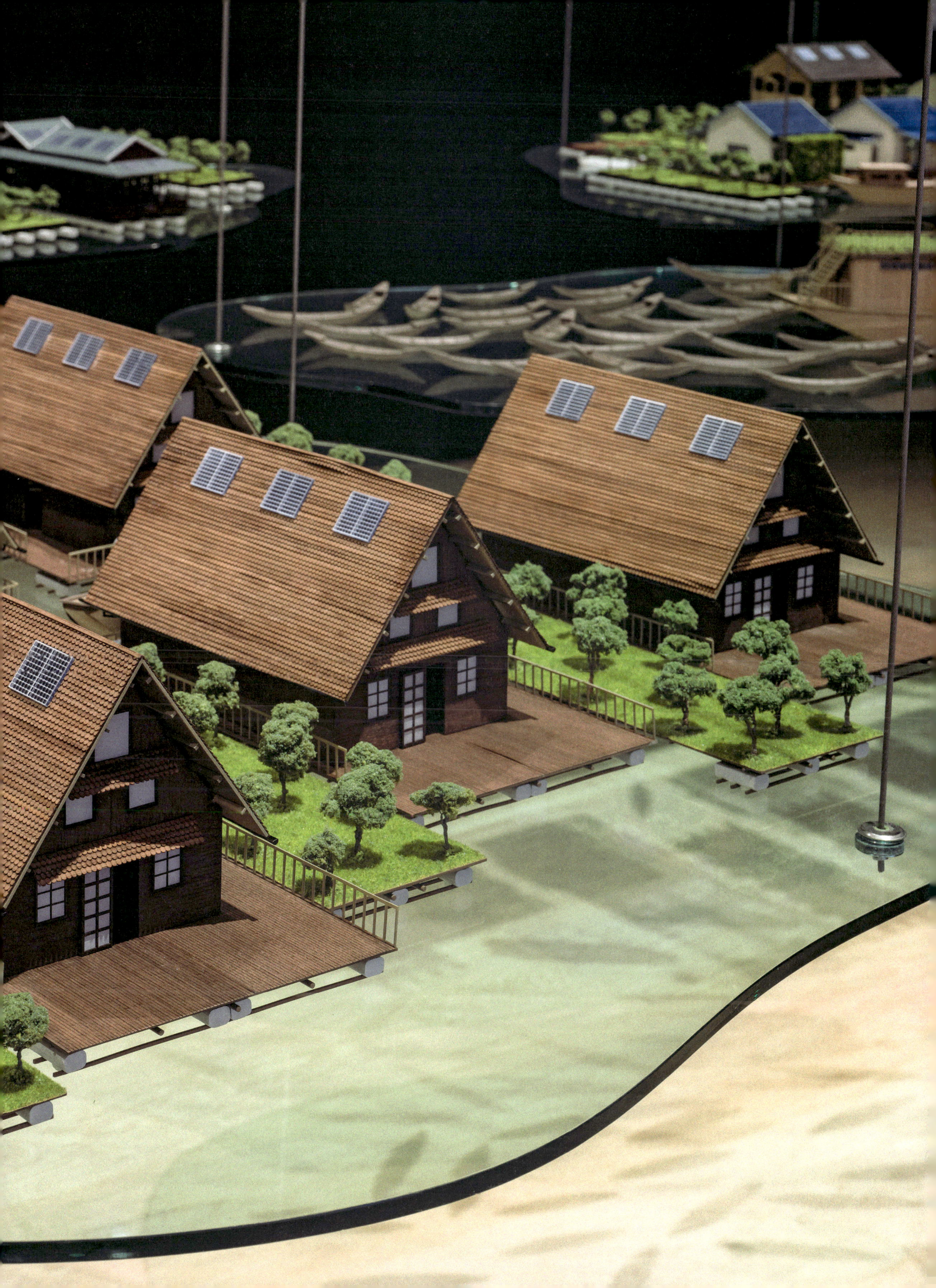

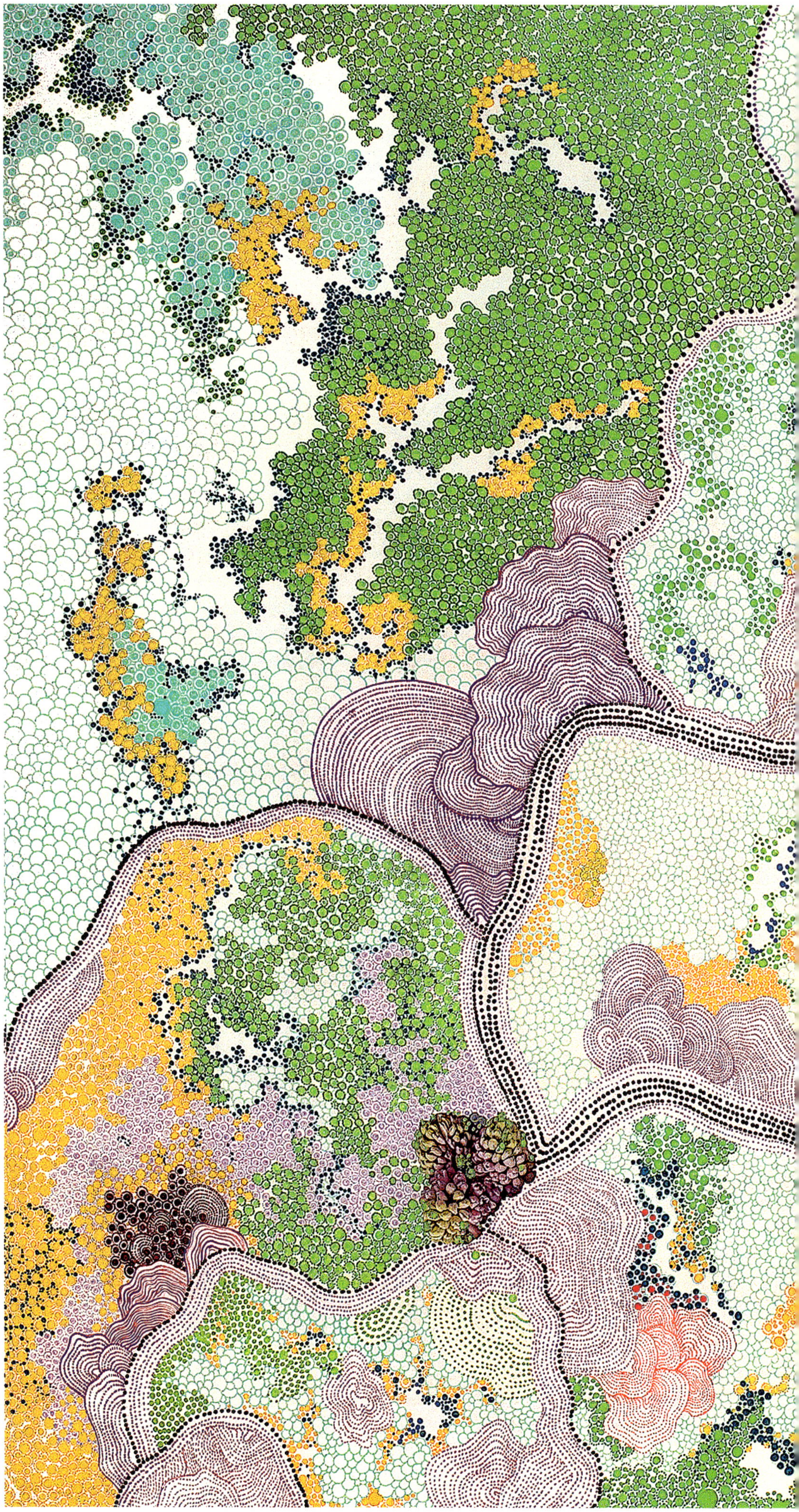

10.9677°N 106.4667°E, 2007
Ink, oil, and collage on paper
79 × 109 cm (31 ⅛ × 43 in.)

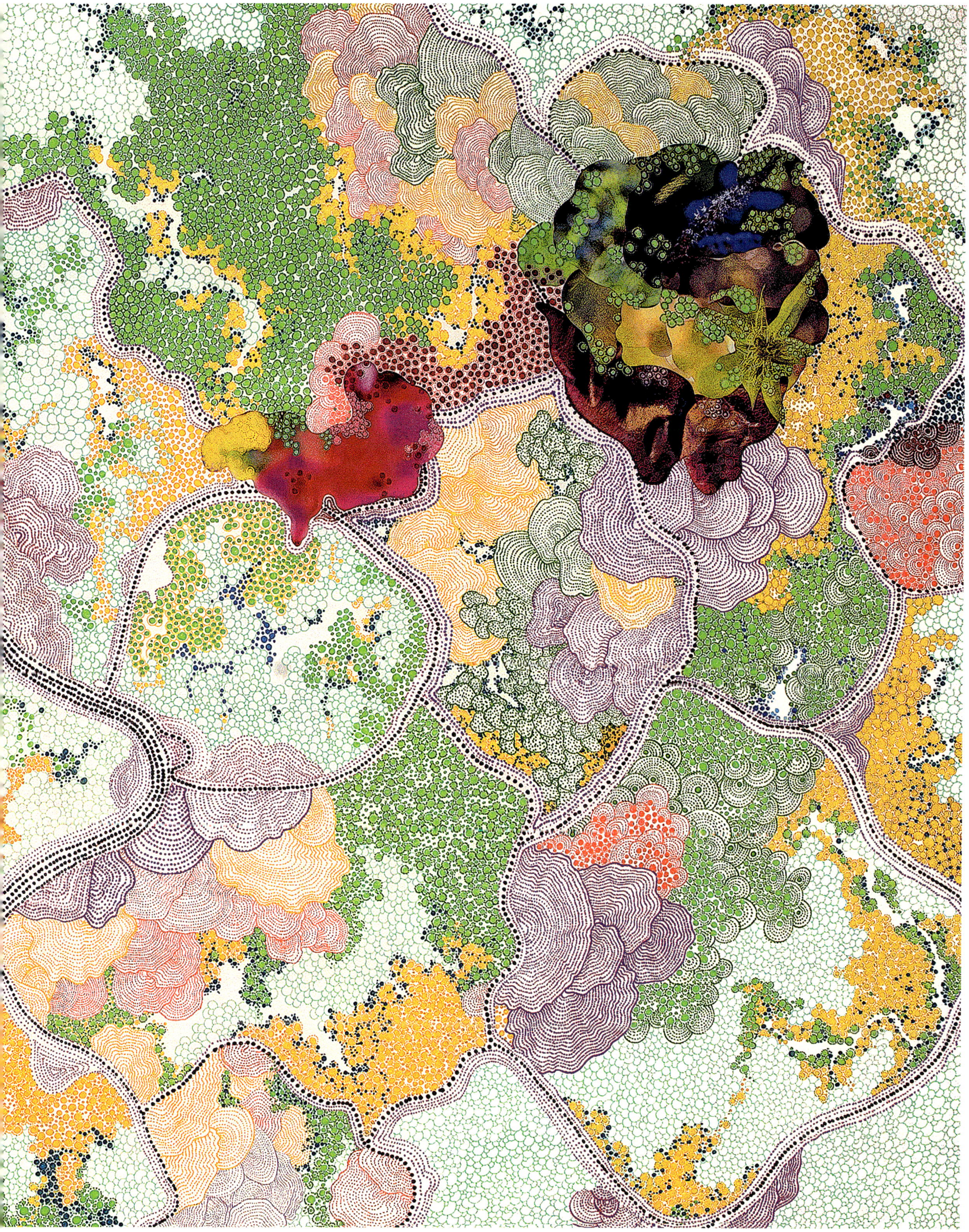

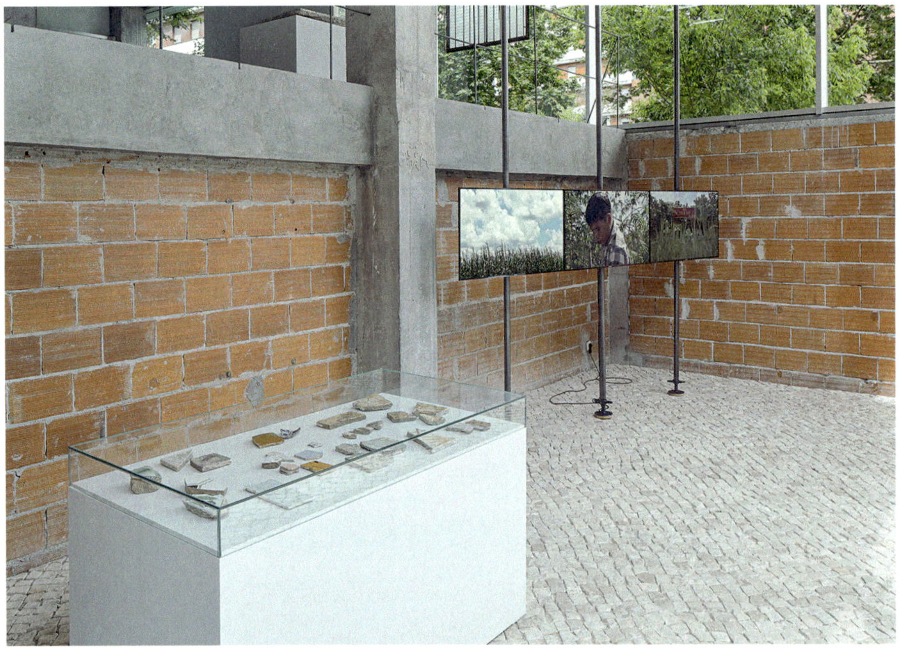

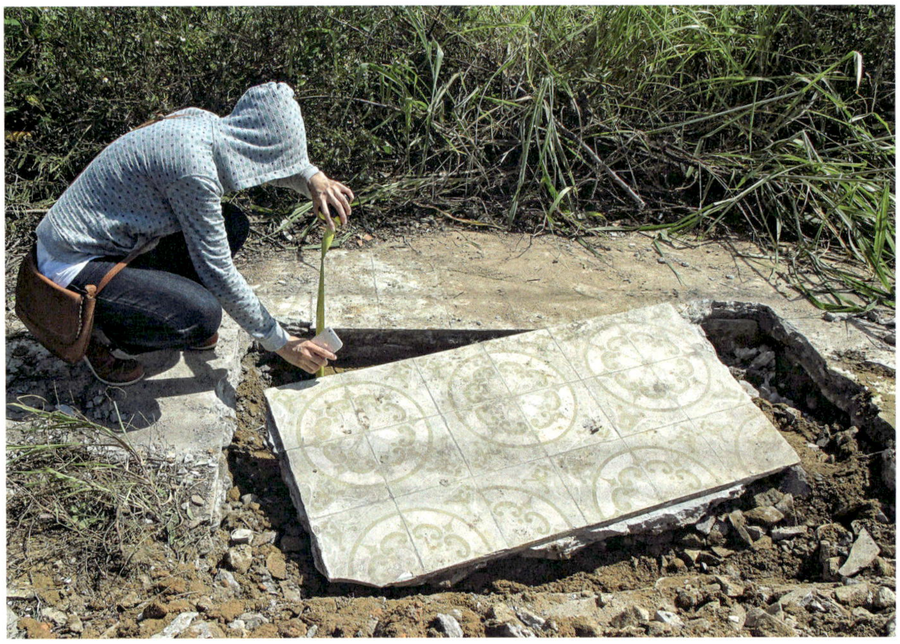

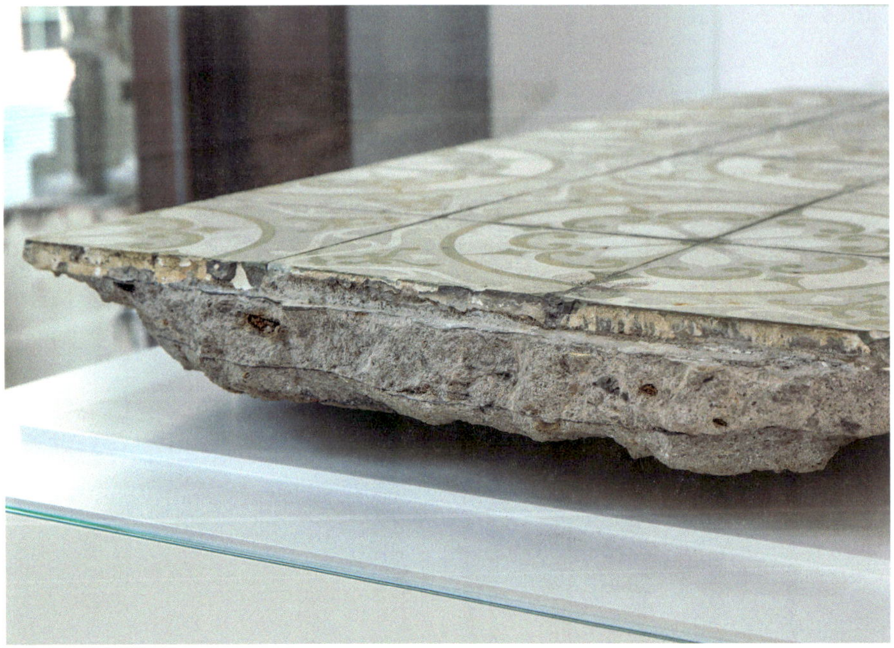

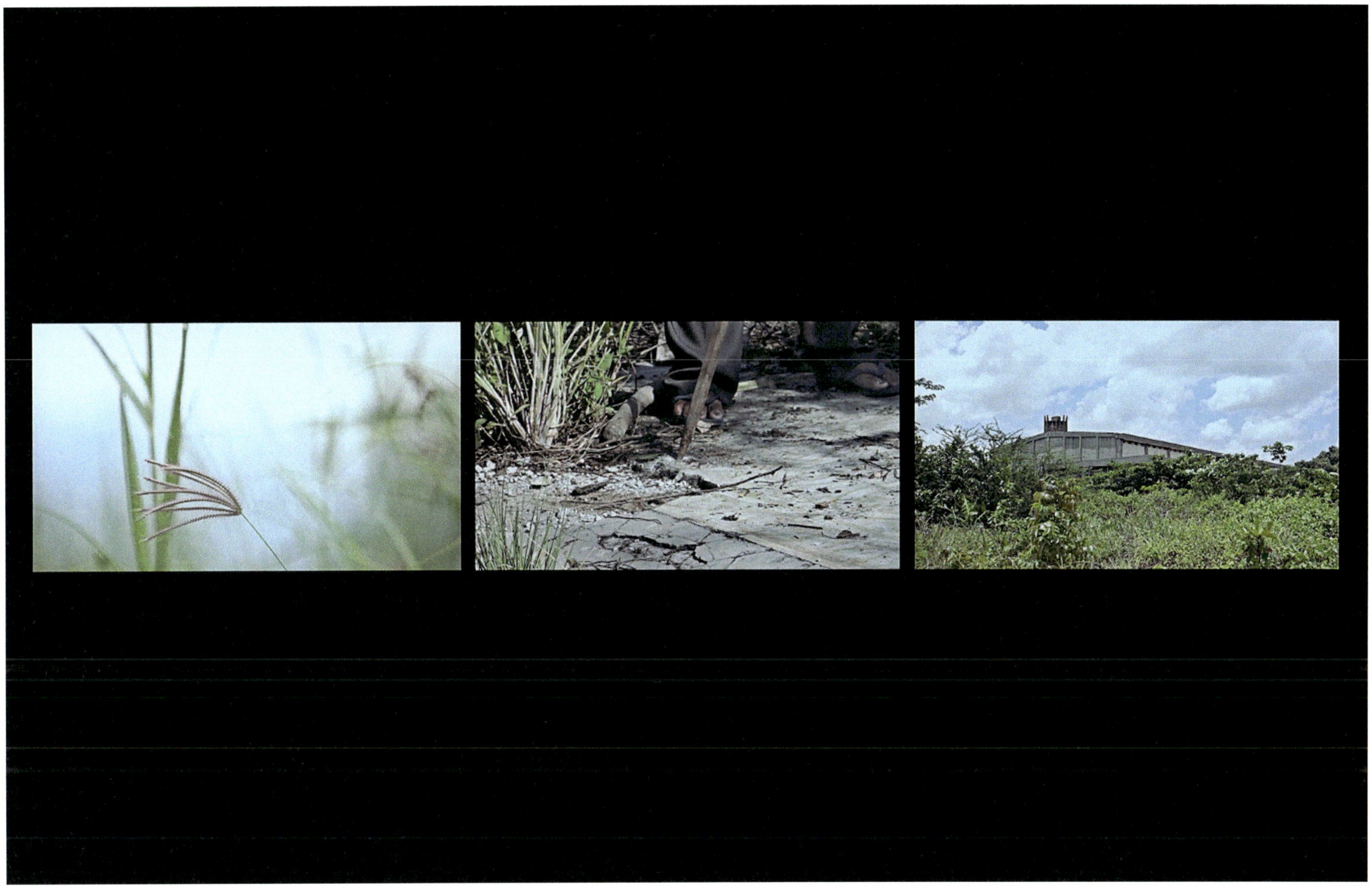

10°45'39"N 106°43'23"E, 2013
Excavated concrete slab
with ceramic tiles
128 × 64 × 30 cm
(50 ⅜ × 25 ⅛ × 11 ¾ in.)

landscapes and traces of a people yet to come, 2013
3-channel video, HD, color, sound
6:26 minutes

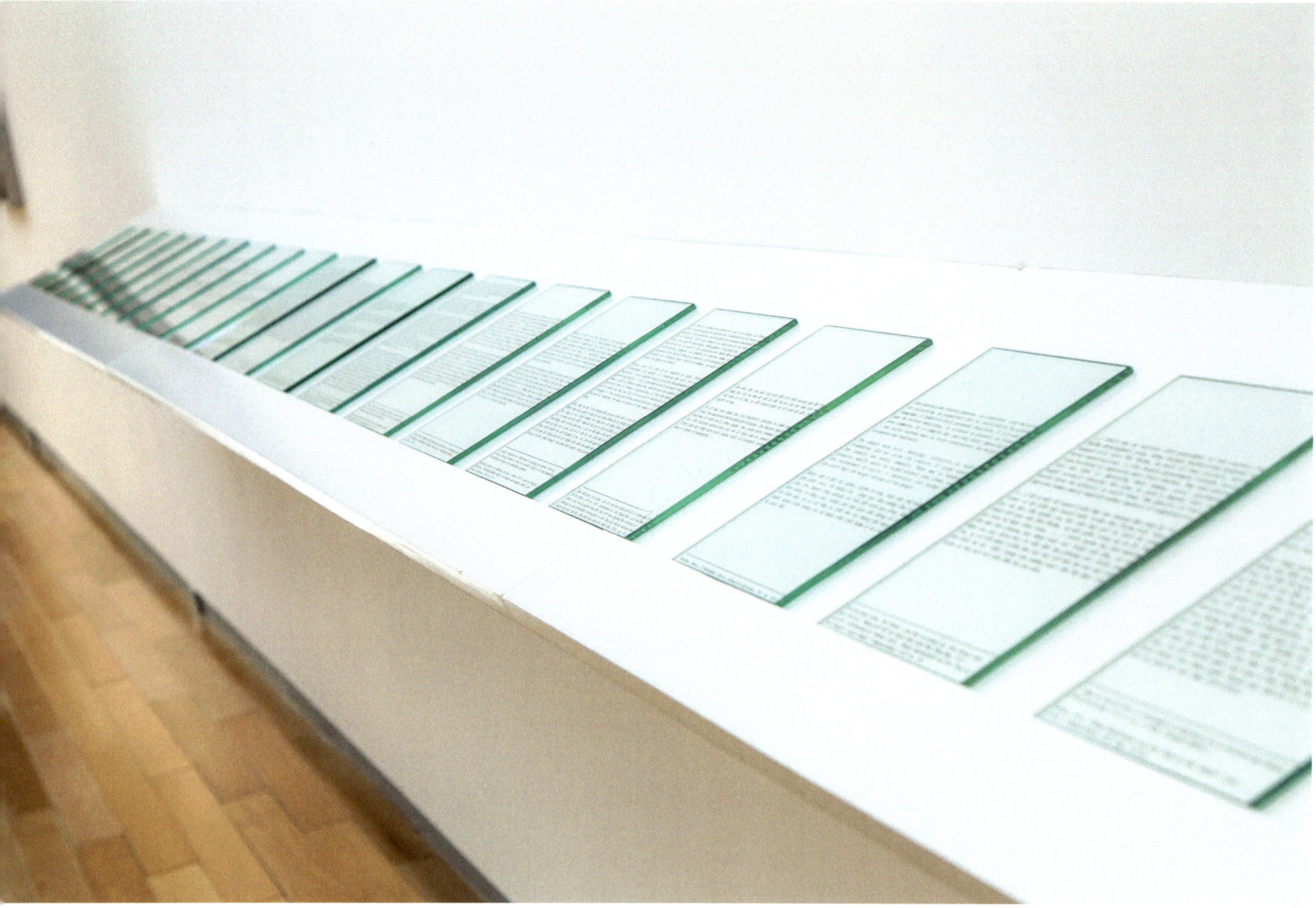

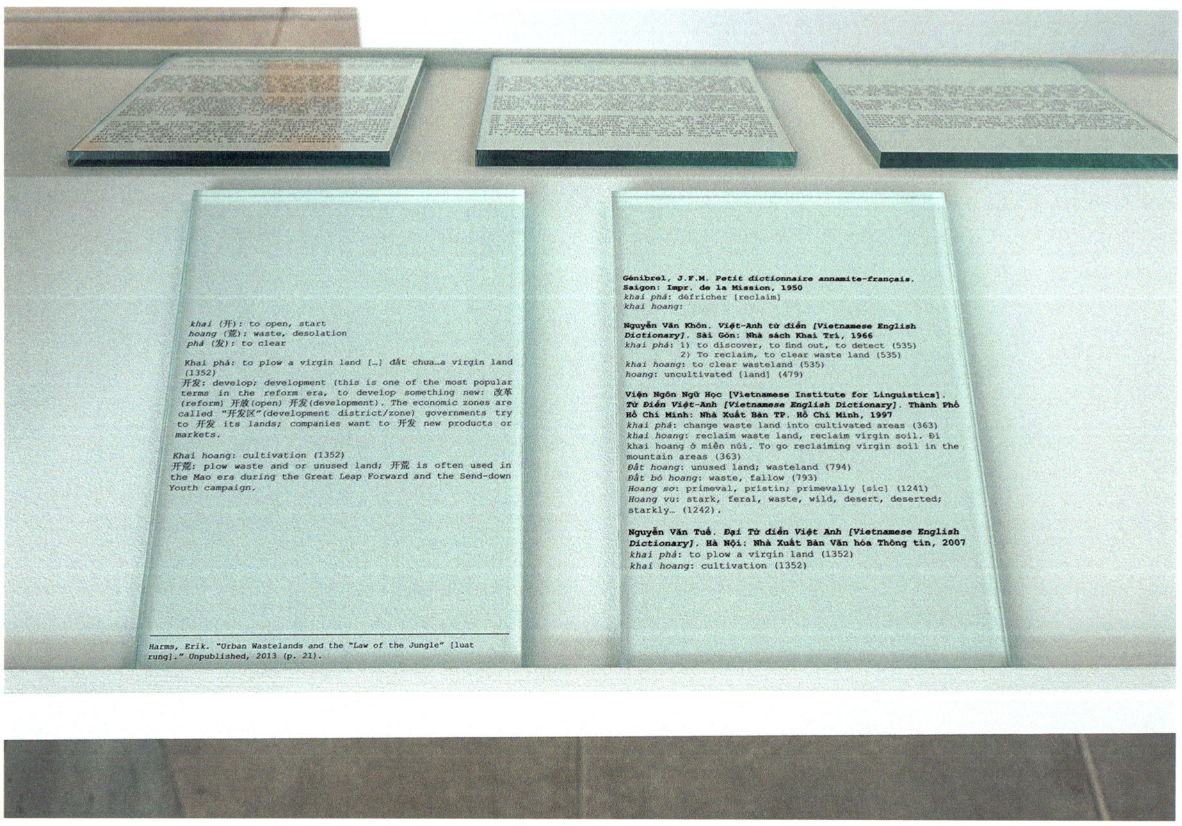

knowing into oblivion, 2013
Digital C-type printing on
26 glass plates
16 × 23.4 cm (6 ¼ × 9 ¼ in.) each

While readers may be inclined to link this trend in urbanization to the introduction of European and colonial models of development, colonial construction was situated within a landscape already subject to earlier trends of urbanization and land reclamation that followed Vietnamese and Chinese models. Since the late 1600s, Chinese settlers has been establishing trading posts along the main rivers; and since the 1750s, the Nguyễn dynasty had struggled to extend its control over the delta region through campaigns to construct forts, granaries, and canals in what had formerly been Khmer territory.

Trong khi bạn đọc có chiều hướng liên kết cái xu hướng trong đô thị hóa này với sự giới thiệu các mô hình của Châu Âu và thực dân trong sự phát triển, sự xây dựng thuộc địa được đặt vào trong một vùng đất đã lệ thuộc vào những xu hướng trước đây của đô thị hóa và khai hoang dựa theo mô hình Việt Nam và Trung Hoa. Từ cuối thế kỷ 17, những người định cư Trung Hoa đã thiết lập những trạm thông thương buôn bán dọc theo những con sông chính, và từ thập kỷ 50 của thế kỷ 18, triều nhà Nguyễn đã cố gắng mở rộng sự kiểm soát vùng châu thổ qua những chiến dịch xây dựng đồn bốt, kho thóc và kênh đào ở nơi từng là lãnh thổ của người Khơ-me.

Biggs, David. *Quagmire: Nation-Building and Nature in the Mekong Delta* (Weyerhaeuser Environmental Books): University of Washington Press, 2010. (p, 56).

Mise en valeur is a term which connotes not only economic development of the kind pursued by other capitalist imperial nations, but also the moral and cultural improvement to be wrought in the colonies. … *Mise en valeur* could be put forward as an example of the beneficial value of French colonial action, and thus served as a form of autolegitimation for imperial France. *Mise en valeur* came to be one of the pillars of French colonial ideology, a touchstone, and a means through which to measure and display the beneficial impact of the French enterprise abroad. It was the policy through which France quite literally constructed Indochina.

Mise en valeur [khẩn hoang][1] là một thuật ngữ bao hàm không chỉ là sự phát triển kinh tế được theo đuổi bởi các quố gia tư bản thực dân, mà còn là sự cải thiện tinh thần và văn hóa được rèn ở các thuộc địa. ... *Mise en valeur* có thể được xem như một thí dụ của giá trị lợi ích từ ảnh hưởng thực dân Pháp, và được dùng như một hình thức của sự tự động hợp pháp hóa cho đế quốc Pháp. *Mise en valeur* trở thành một tr những cột trụ của hệ tư tưởng thực dân Pháp, một tiêu chuẩn và một phương cách mà thông qua nó để đo lường và phô bày tác động ích lợi của ý đồ của Pháp ở nước ngoài. Nó là chính sách mà Pháp đã xây dựng Đông Dương.

---

[1] Loosely translated as 'khẩn hoang' according to context. *Mise en valeur* literally means to "put into value", which is to turn something considered valueless into something valuable.

Cooper, Nicola. *France in Indochina: Colonial Encounters*. Oxford: Berg. Douglass, Mike, and Liling Huang, 2001. (p. 29).

Erasure builds n t e will to discover and then to improve the very spaces th re erased. Erasure begins not from a lack of knowledge but from the will to knowledge itself. Erasure is the aftereffect of discovery, a kind of disappearing act.

Sự xóa bỏ được xây dựng trên một ý chí quyết khám phá, và tiếp theo đó là cải tạo những không gian đã được xóa bỏ. Sự xóa bỏ không phải bắt đầu từ sự thiếu hiểu biết, nhưng từ ý chí tìm kiếm tri thức. Sự xóa bỏ là hiệu quả sau cùng của sự khám phá, là một loại hành động biến mất.

Knowing into oblivion can be understood as an act of knowing peoples and the places they live so that they can be cleared and civilized, and then, in the process of clearing them, obliterating all that was known about them.

Hiểu biết vào trong quên lãng có thể được hiểu như một cách tìm hiểu về con người ta và nơi sinh sống của họ để rồi những nơi đó có thể được giải tỏa và khai hóa, và trong quy trình giải tỏa, xóa sạch hết những điều đã biết về những nơi chốn ấy.

Harms, Erik. "Urban Wastelands and the "Law of the Jungle" [lu t rung]." Unpublished, 2013 (pp. 5,7)

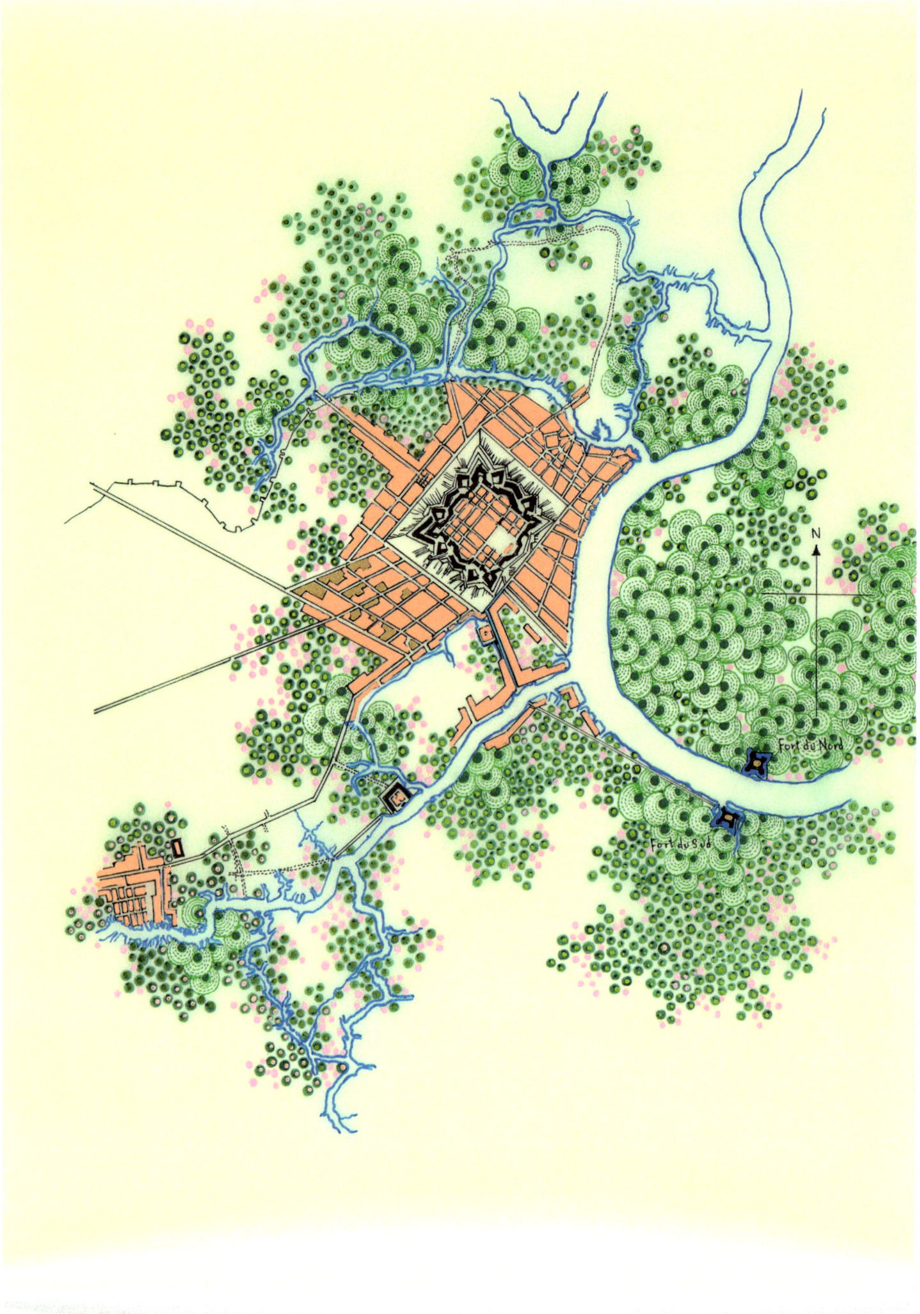

Saigon en 1795–On aperçoit le tracé de la Citadelle de Gia-Long et des Forts du Nord et du Sud, 2016
Ink and oil on vellum and paper
35 × 23 cm (13 ¾ × 9 in.)

After 1972 USAID Thu Thiem Development Plan, 2013
Ink and oil on vellum and paper
110 × 70 cm (43 ¼ × 27 ½ in.)

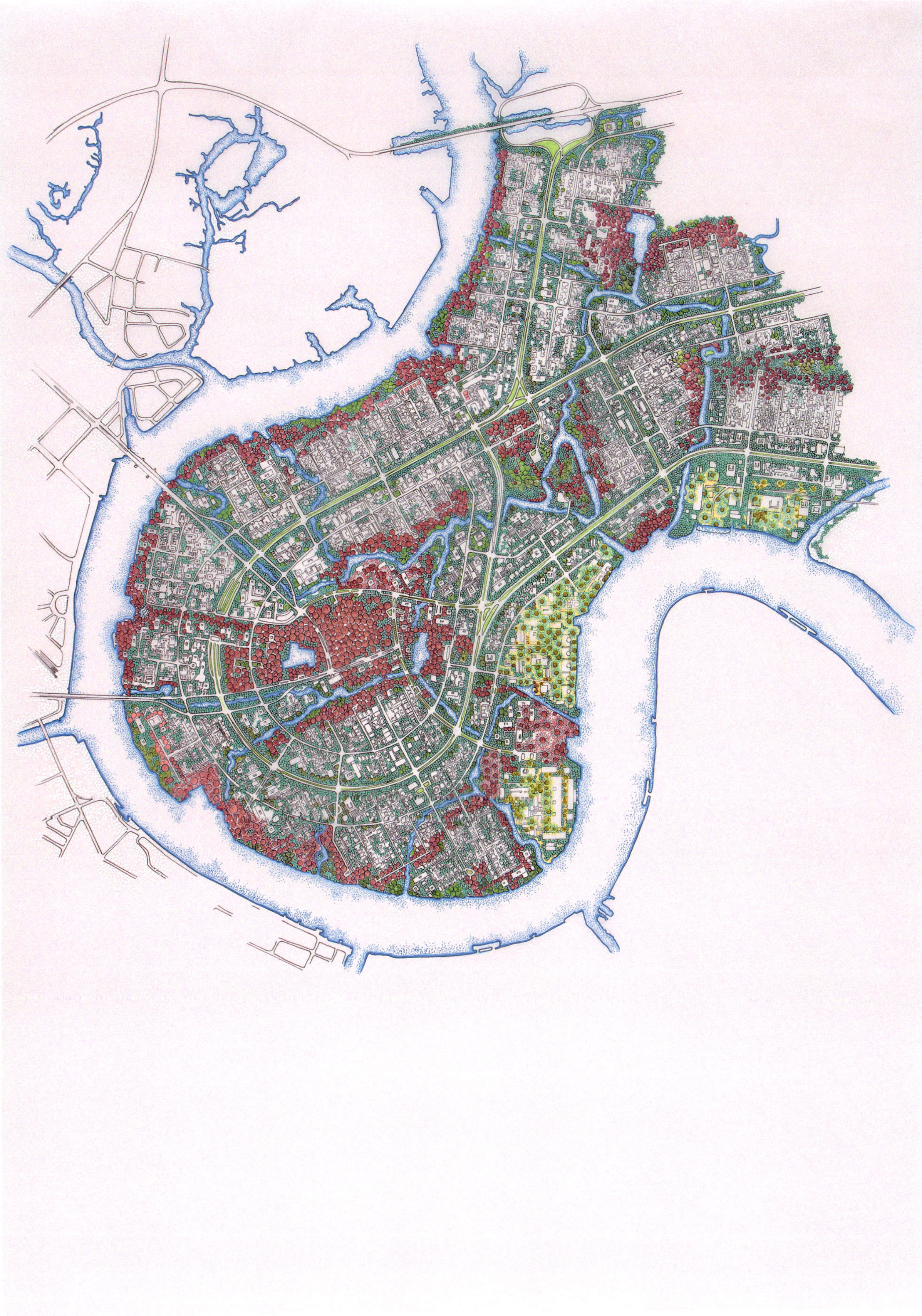

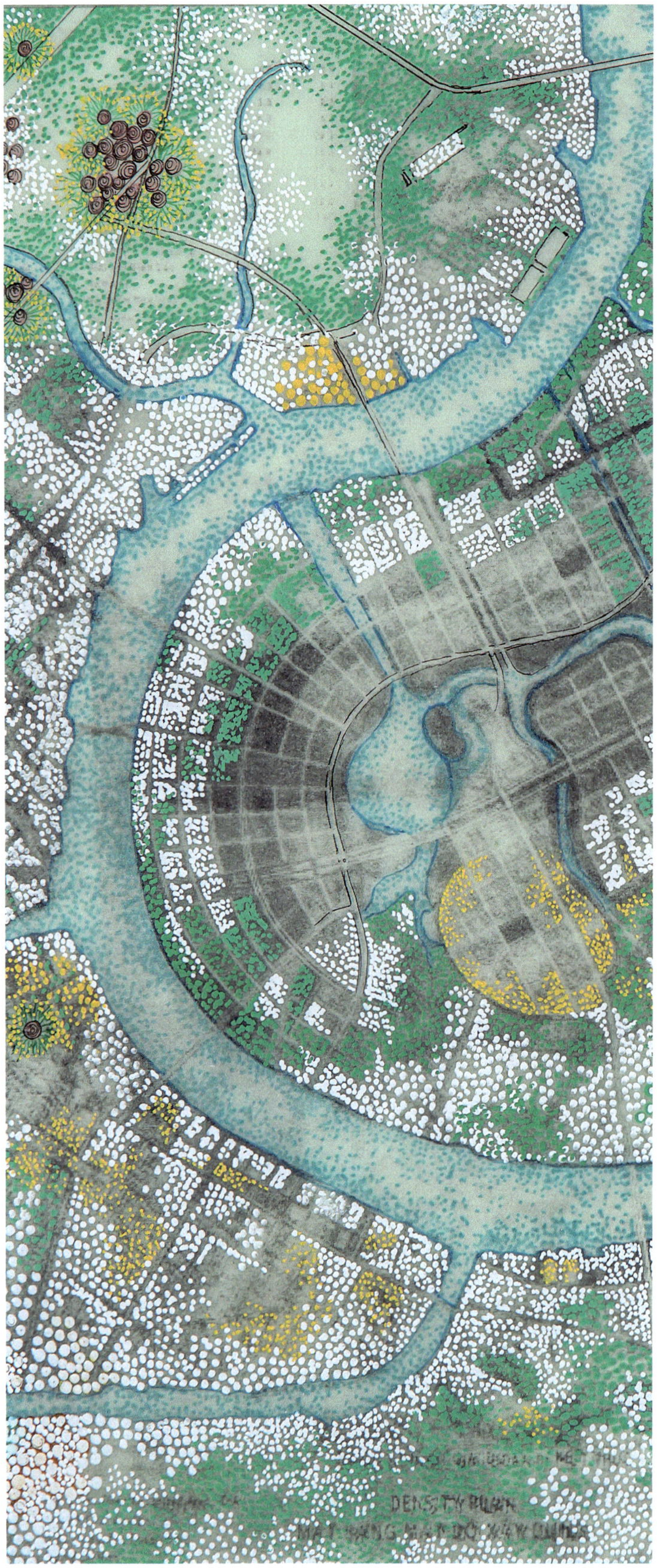

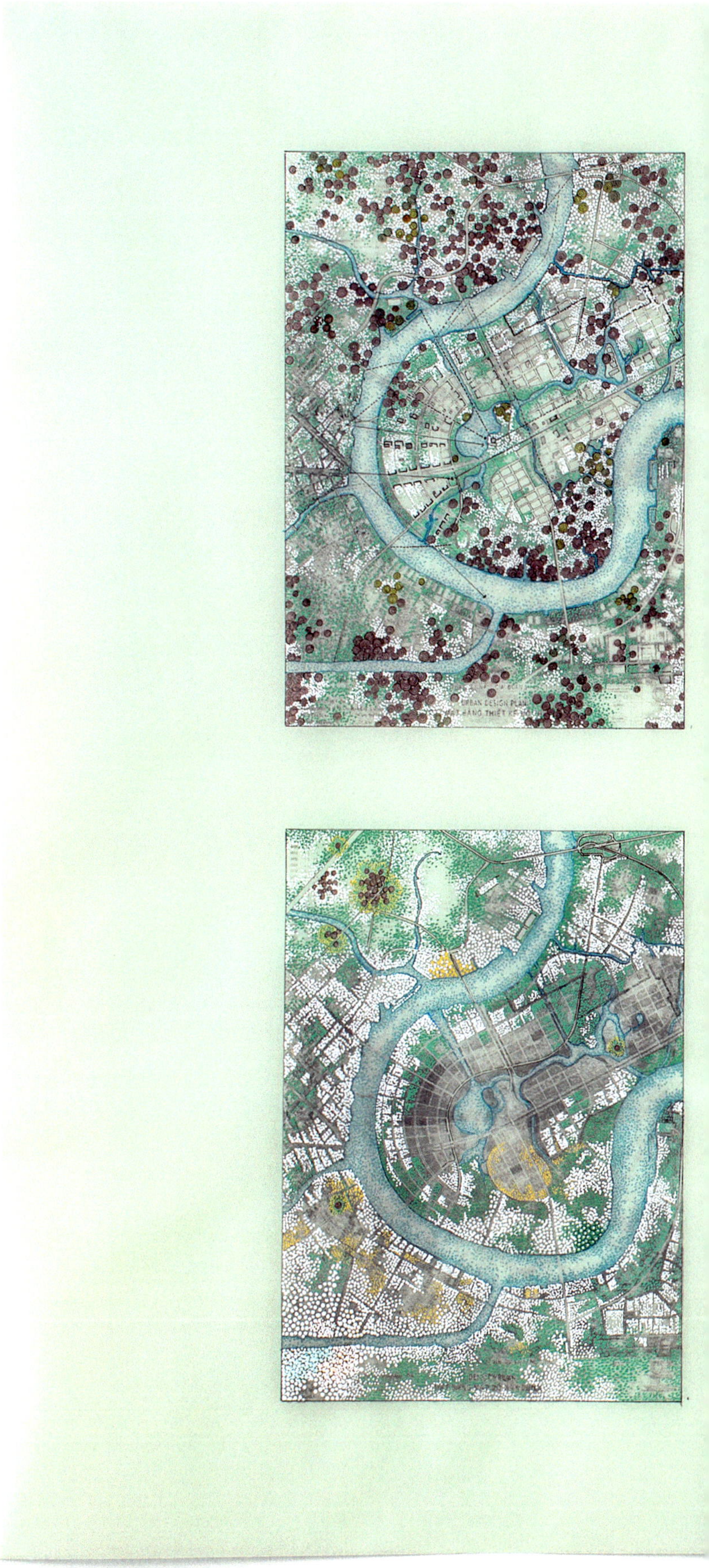

landscapes of a people yet to come–HCMC ICA plans for New Thu Thiem Urban Area, 2013
Ink, oil, pencil, and image transfer on vellum and paper
79 × 100 cm (31 ⅛ × 39 ⅜ in.)

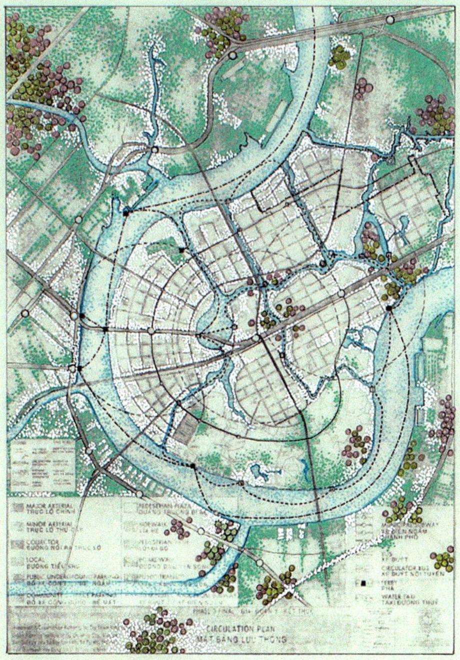
MAJOR ARTERIAL
MINOR ARTERIAL
COLLECTOR
LOCAL
BUS
FERRY
WATER TAXI
CIRCULATION PLAN
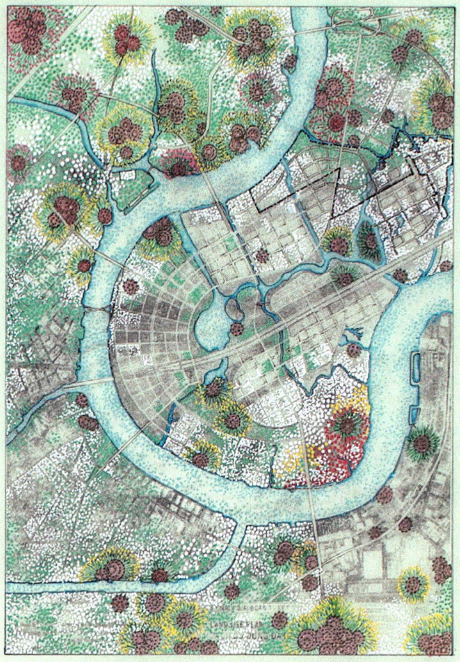
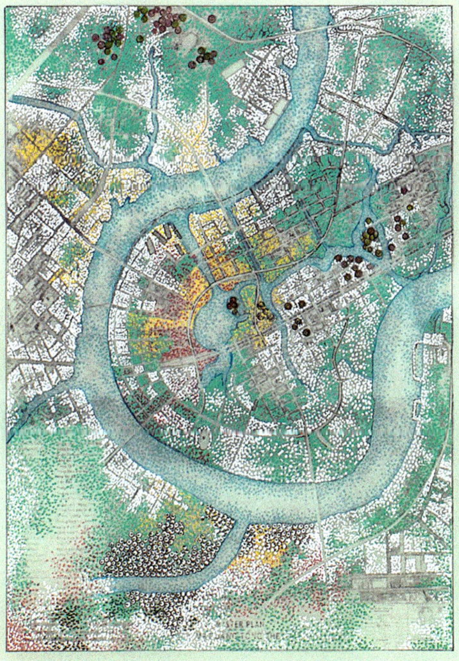
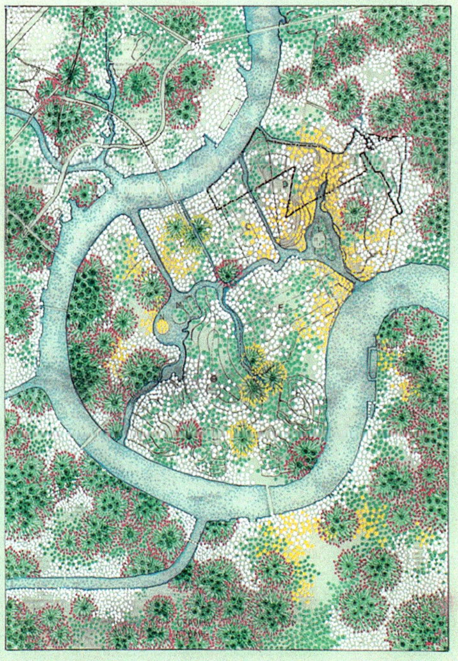

snow covered paths, winter evergreens and defunct coal mines in Yamaguchi, 2012–2013
Ink and oil on vellum and paper
110 × 70 cm (43 ¼ × 27 ½ in.)

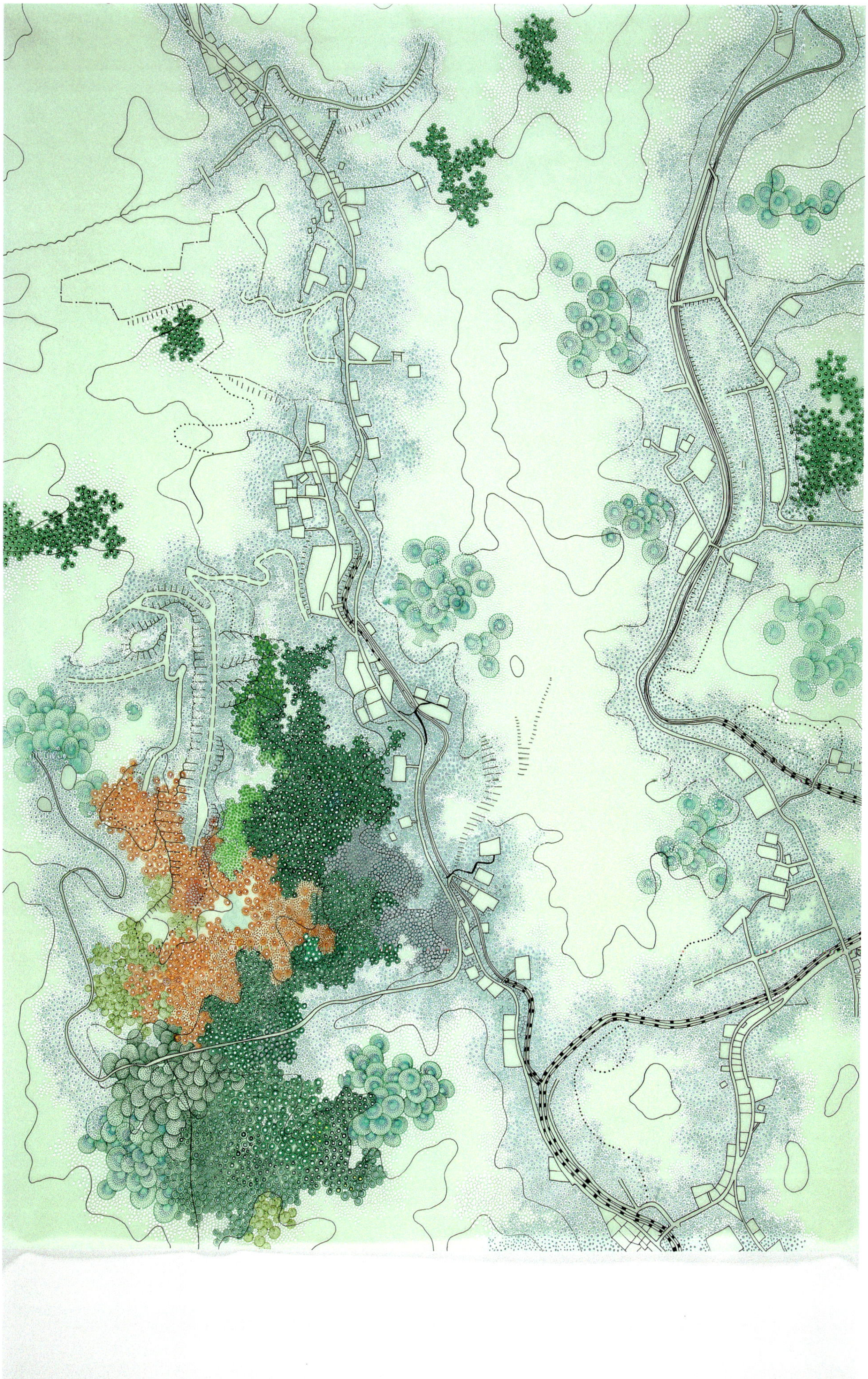

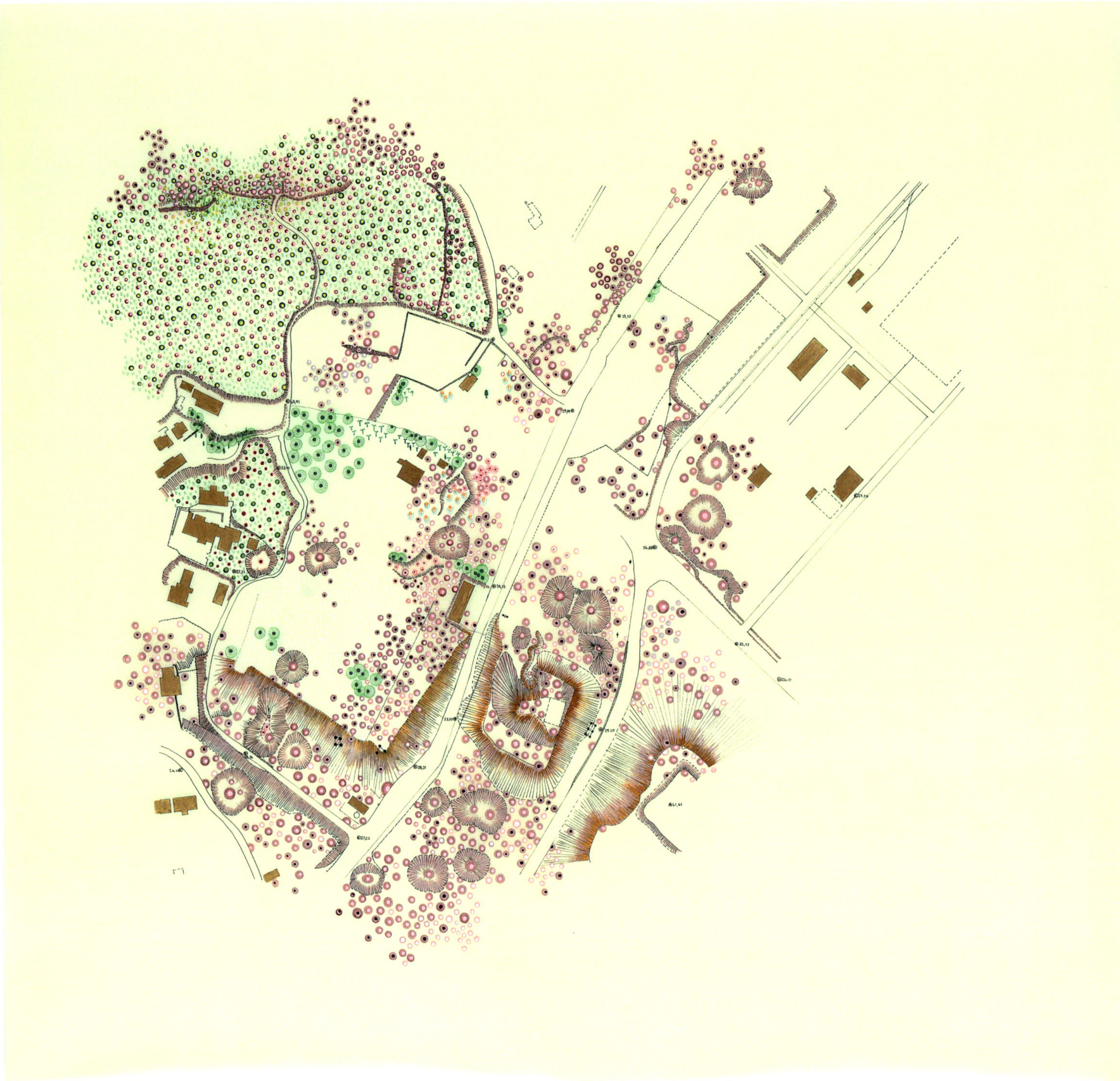

1946 survey #37–semi-blank space: Hitachi Factory, 2016
Acrylic, ink, and oil on vellum and paper
65 x 64.7 cm (25 ⅝ × 25 ½ in.)

1946 survey: Hitachi Urban Damage Plan, 2016
Acrylic, ink, and oil on vellum and paper
75 × 62.5 cm (29 ½ × 24 ⅝ in.)

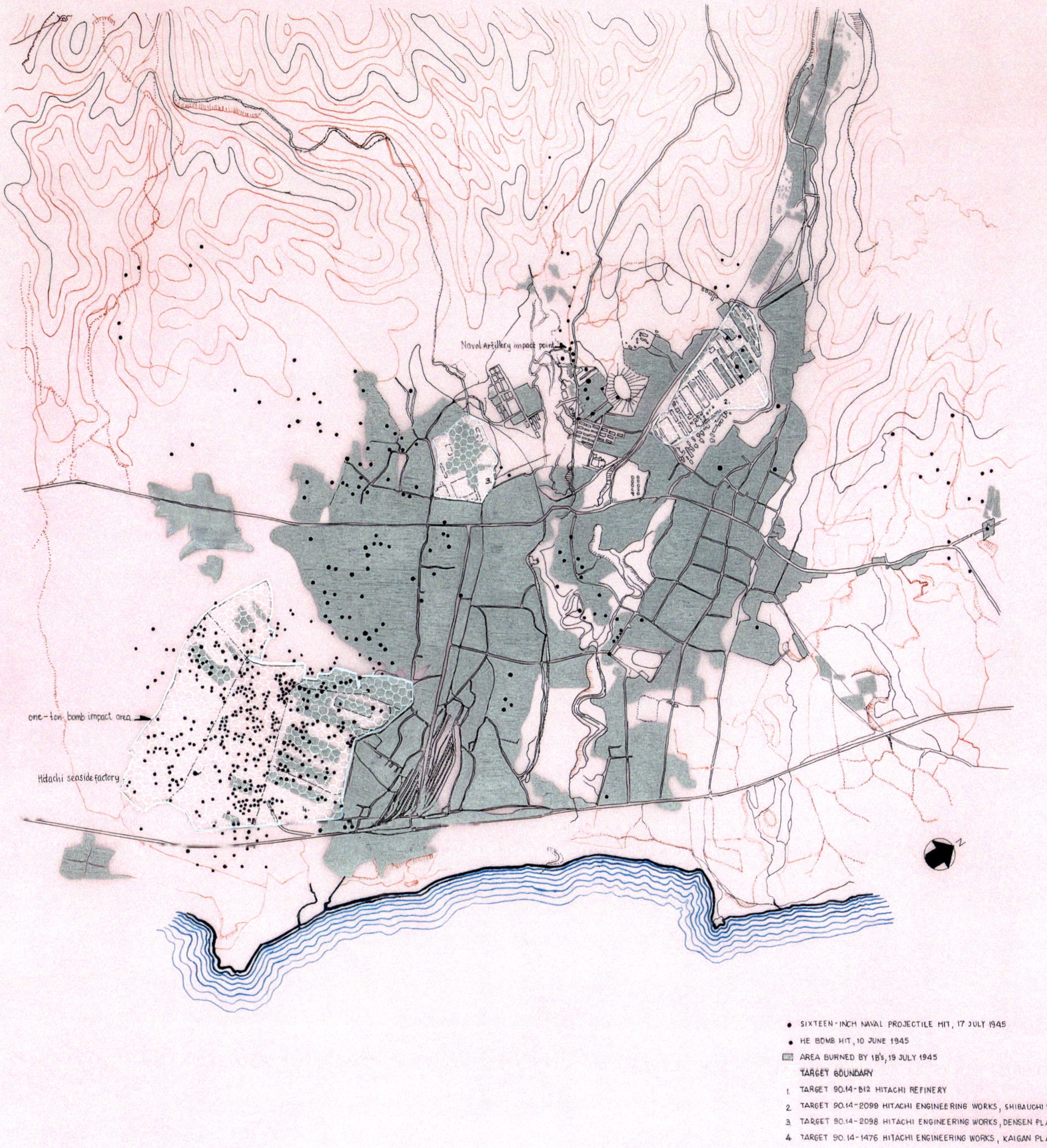

Naval Artillery impact point
one-ton-bomb impact area
Hitachi seaside factory
SIXTEEN-INCH NAVAL PROJECTILE HIT, 17 JULY 1945
HE BOMB HIT, 10 JUNE 1945
AREA BURNED BY 1B's, 19 JULY 1945
TARGET BOUNDARY
1. TARGET 90.14-812 HITACHI REFINERY
2. TARGET 90.14-2099 HITACHI ENGINEERING WORKS, SHIBAUCHI PLANT
3. TARGET 90.14-2098 HITACHI ENGINEERING WORKS, DENSEN PLANT
4. TARGET 90.14-1476 HITACHI ENGINEERING WORKS, KAIGAN PLANT

1946 survey #28–blank space: Hitachi Factory, seaside, 2016
Acrylic, ink, and oil on vellum and paper
70 × 47.5 cm (27 ½ × 18 ¾ in.)

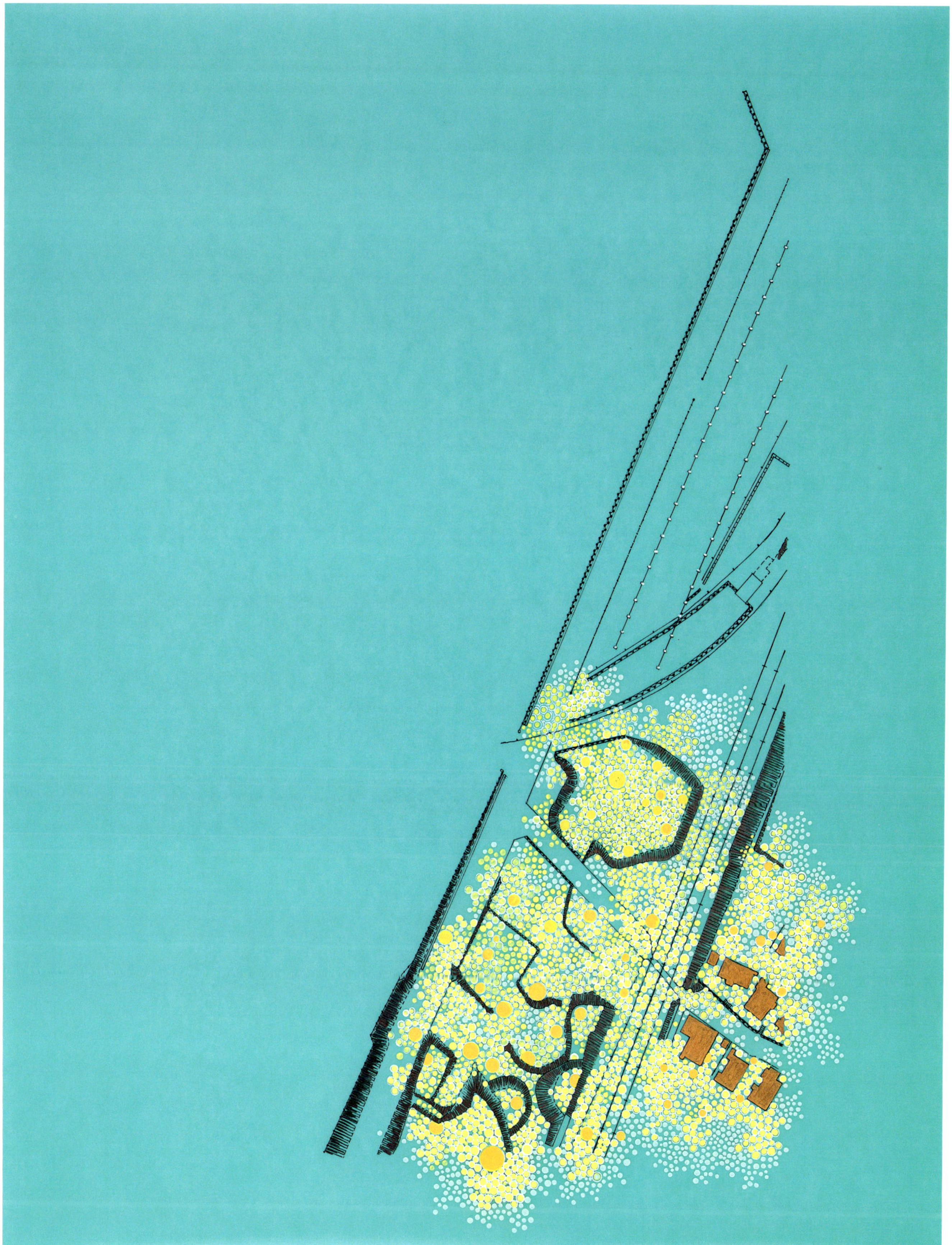

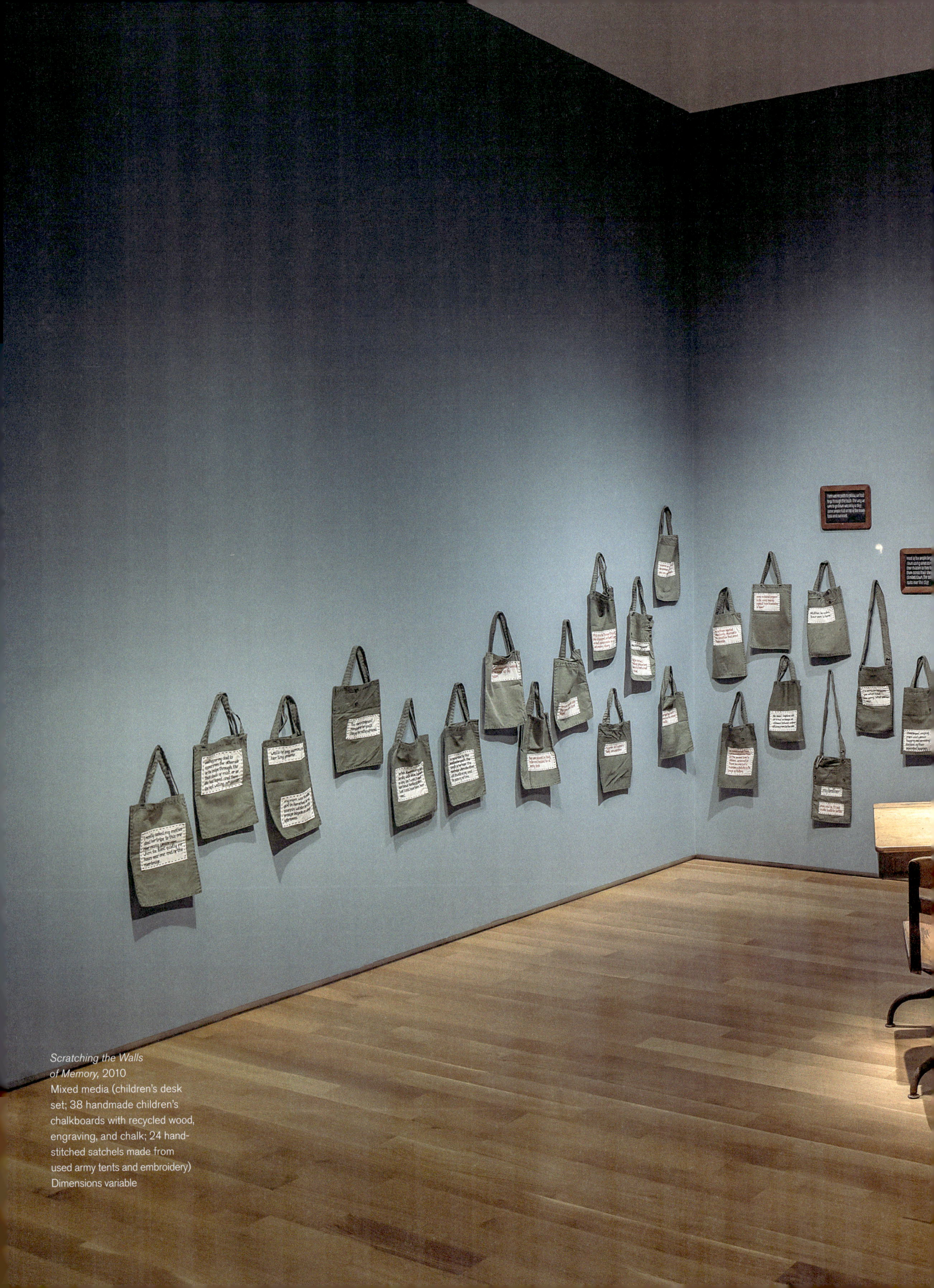

Scratching the Walls of Memory, 2010
Mixed media (children's desk set; 38 handmade children's chalkboards with recycled wood, engraving, and chalk; 24 hand-stitched satchels made from used army tents and embroidery)
Dimensions variable

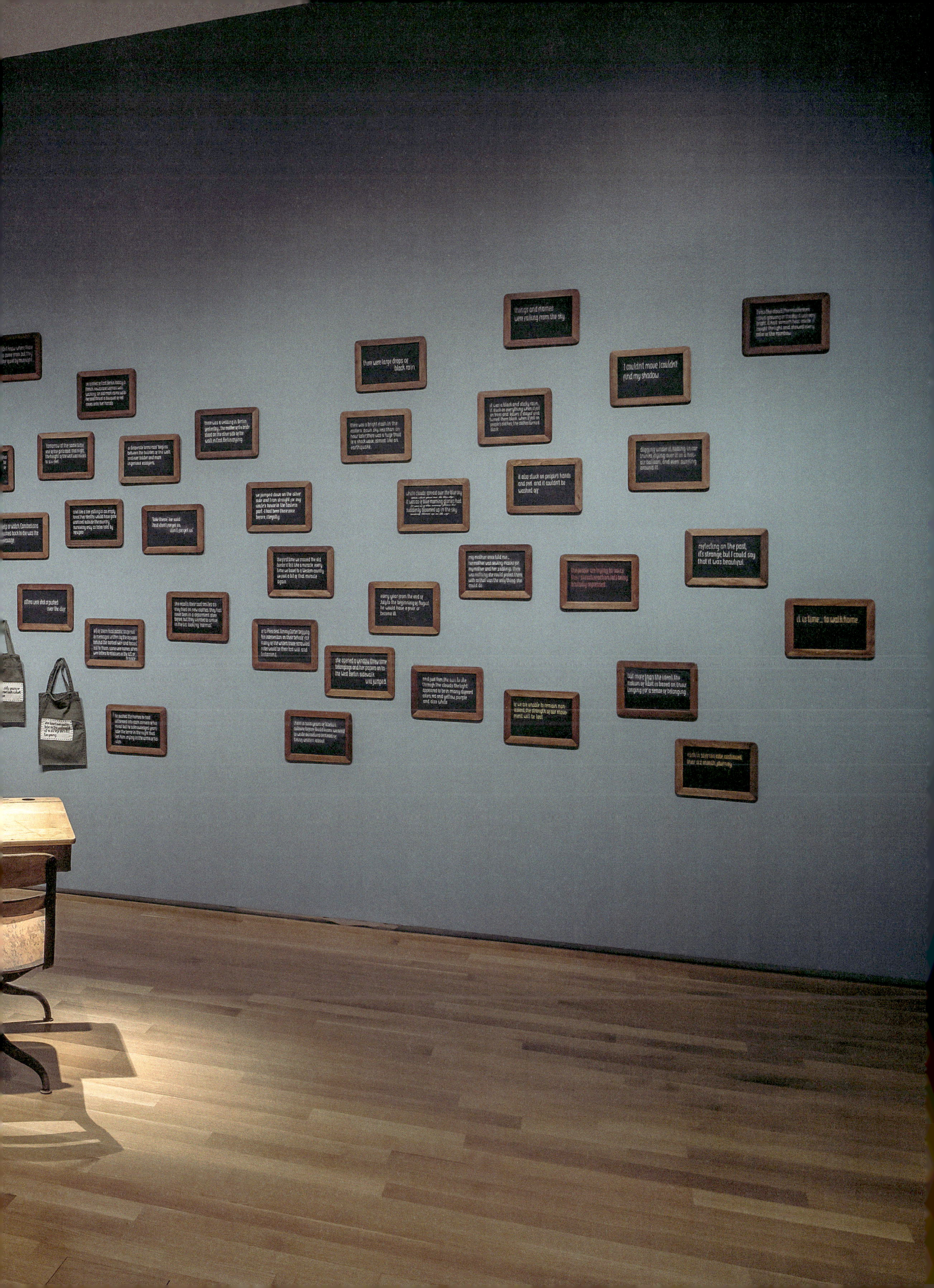
things and flames
were falling from the sky
I couldn't move I couldn't
find my shadow
there were large drops of
black rain
it also stuck on people's hands
and feet, and it couldn't be
washed off
reflecting on the past,
it's strange but I could say
that it was beautiful
it is time... to walk home

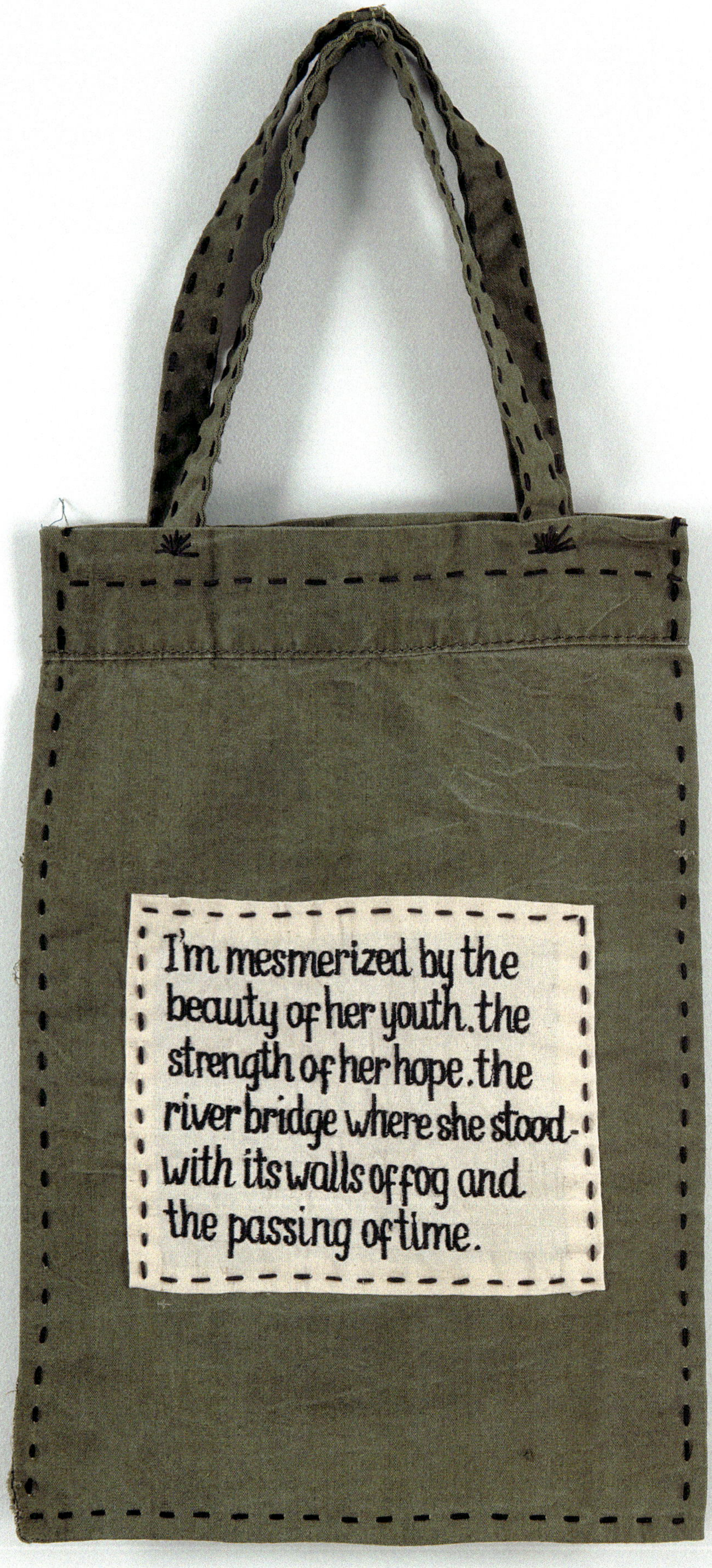
I'm mesmerized by the beauty of her youth. the strength of her hope. the river bridge where she stood- with its walls of fog and the passing of time.

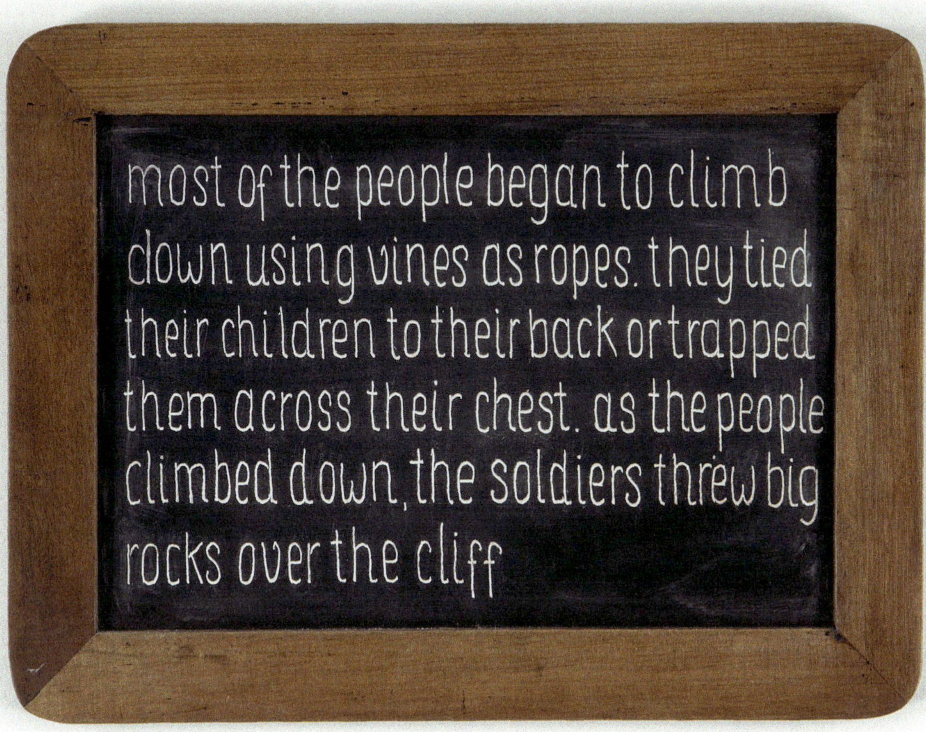
most of the people began to climb
down using vines as ropes. they tied
their children to their back or trapped
them across their chest. as the people
climbed down, the soldiers threw big
rocks over the cliff

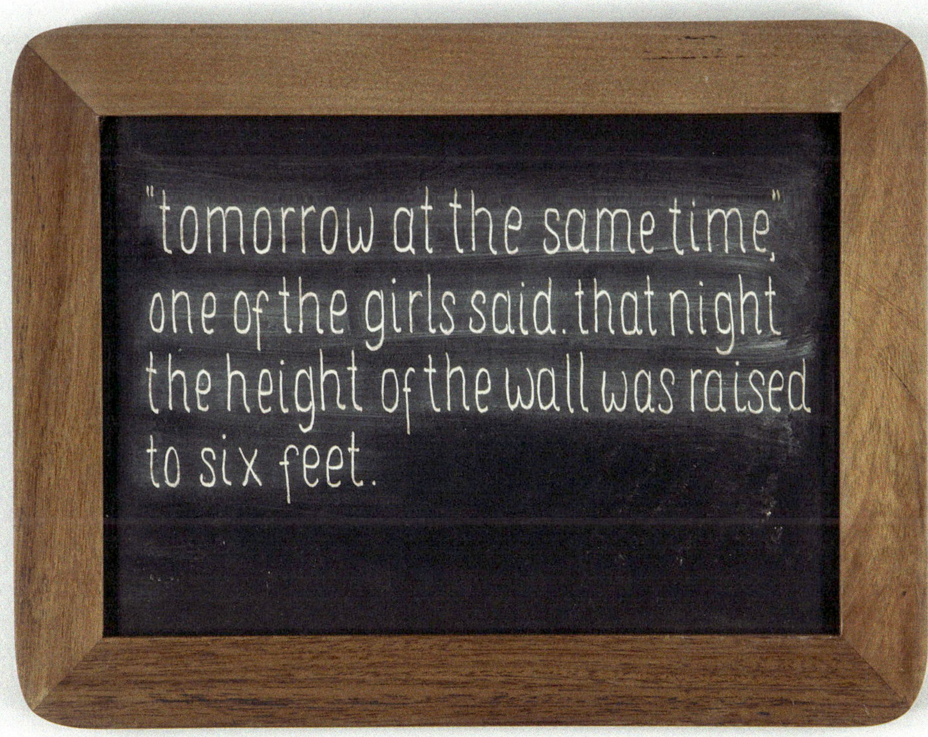
"tomorrow at the same time",
one of the girls said. that night
the height of the wall was raised
to six feet.

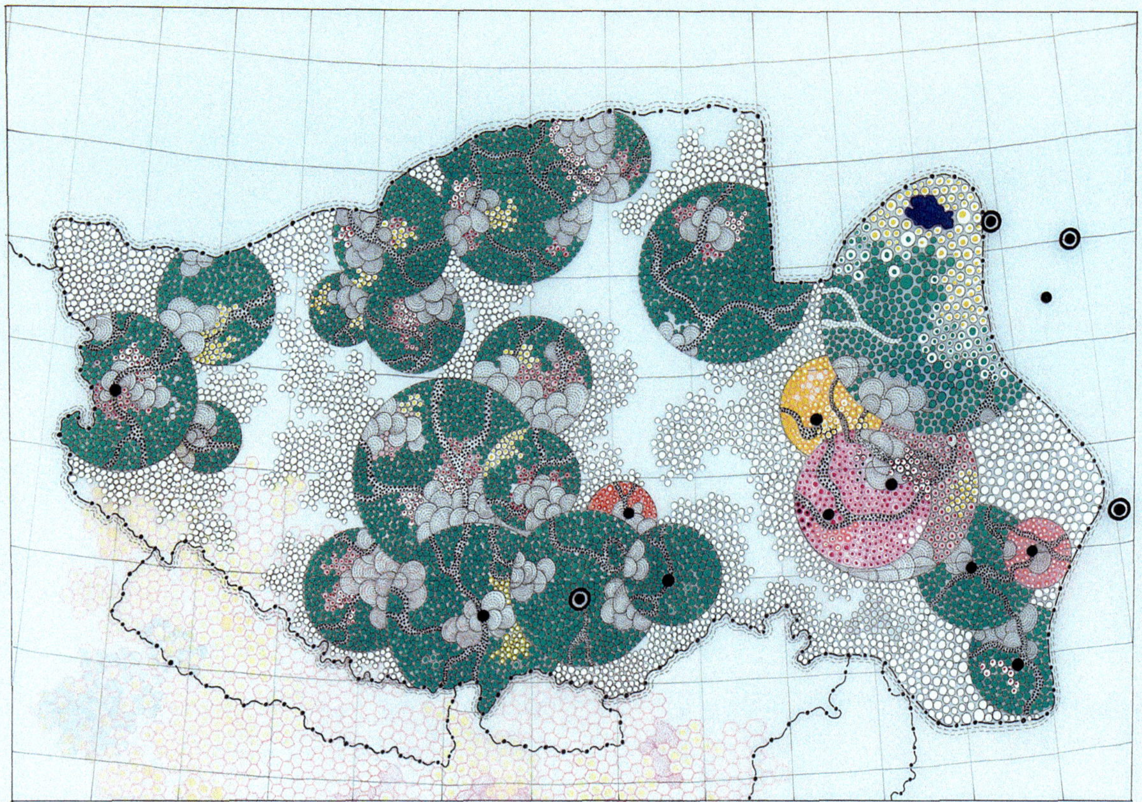

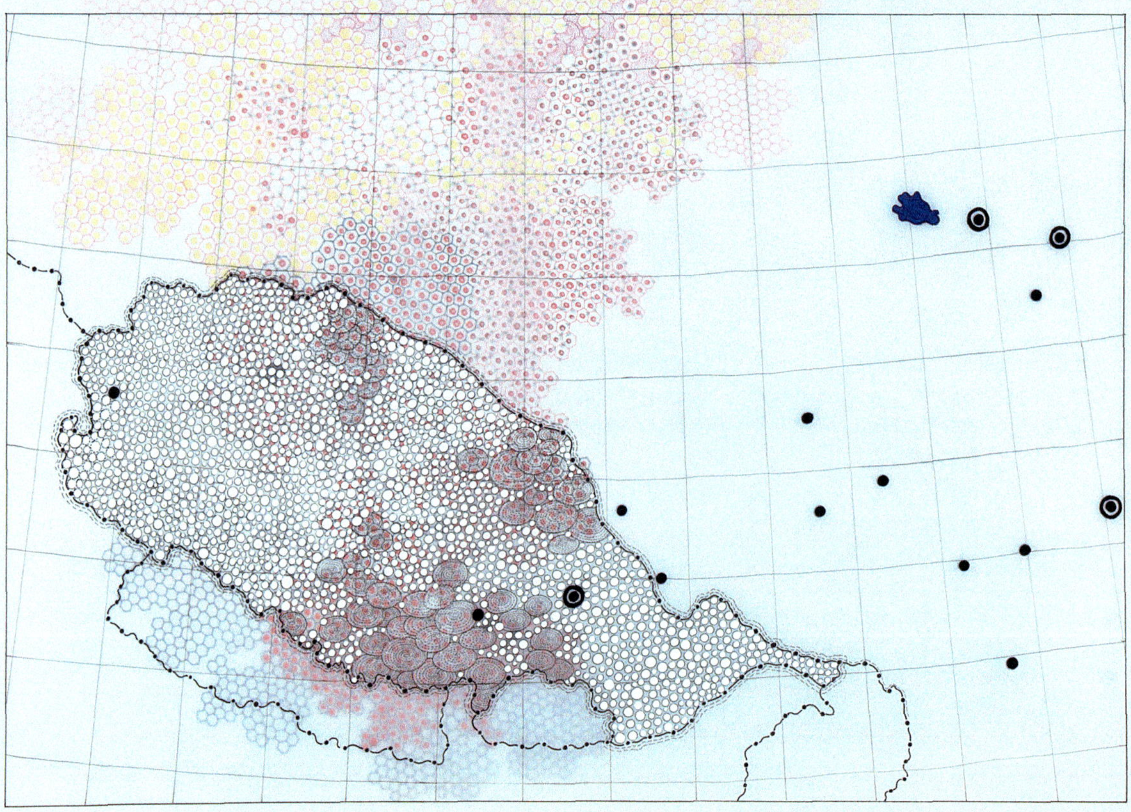

Frontier of Tibet as claimed by Tibetans in 1914/Frontier of Tibet as claimed by Nationalist Chinese in 1914, 2010
Ink and oil on vellum and paper
100 × 62.8 cm (39 ⅜ × 24 ¾ in.)

Frontier of Tibet as proposed at the Tripartie Simla Conference in 1914/Territories under the control of the Dalai Lama's Government (1918–1950), 2010
Ink and oil on vellum and paper
100 × 62.8 cm (39 ⅜ × 24 ¾ in.)

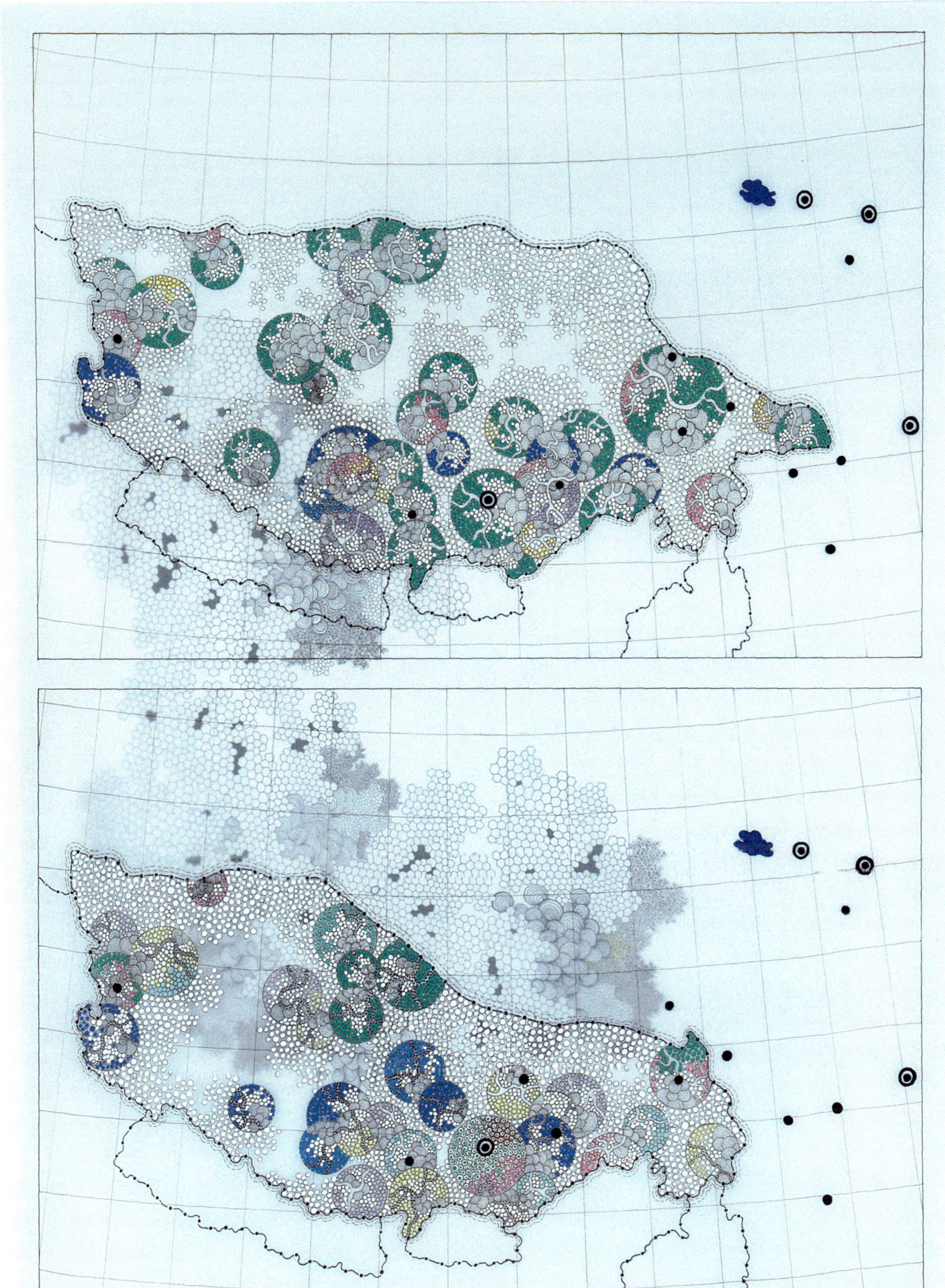

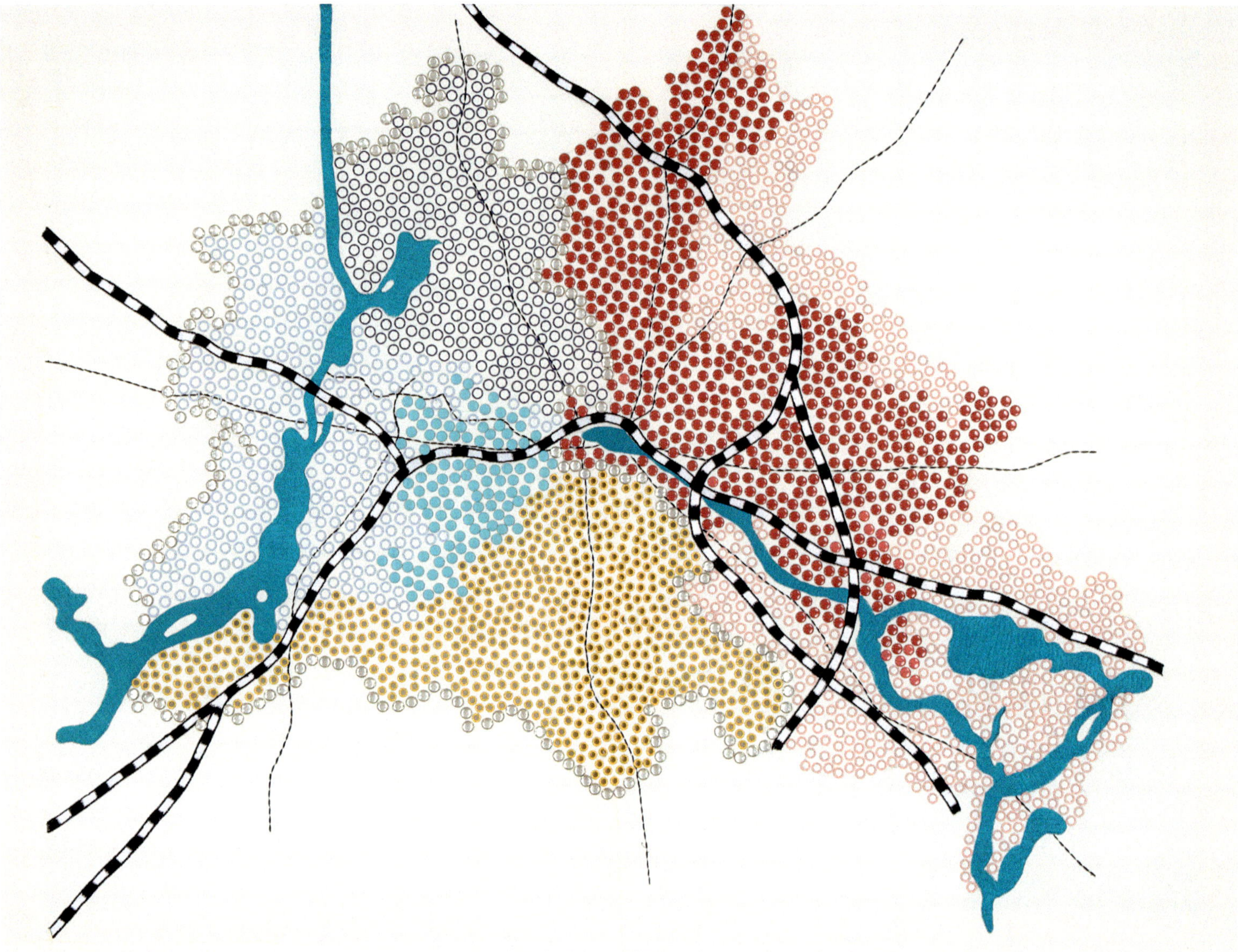

Berlin Wall, 2010
Embroidery, metal grommets, and buttons on canvas
84 × 112.5 cm (33 ⅛ × 44 ¼ in.)

Kaesong Armistice Conference Site 1951, 2010
Embroidery, beads, metal grommets, and buttons on canvas
112 × 86.5 cm (44 × 34 in.)

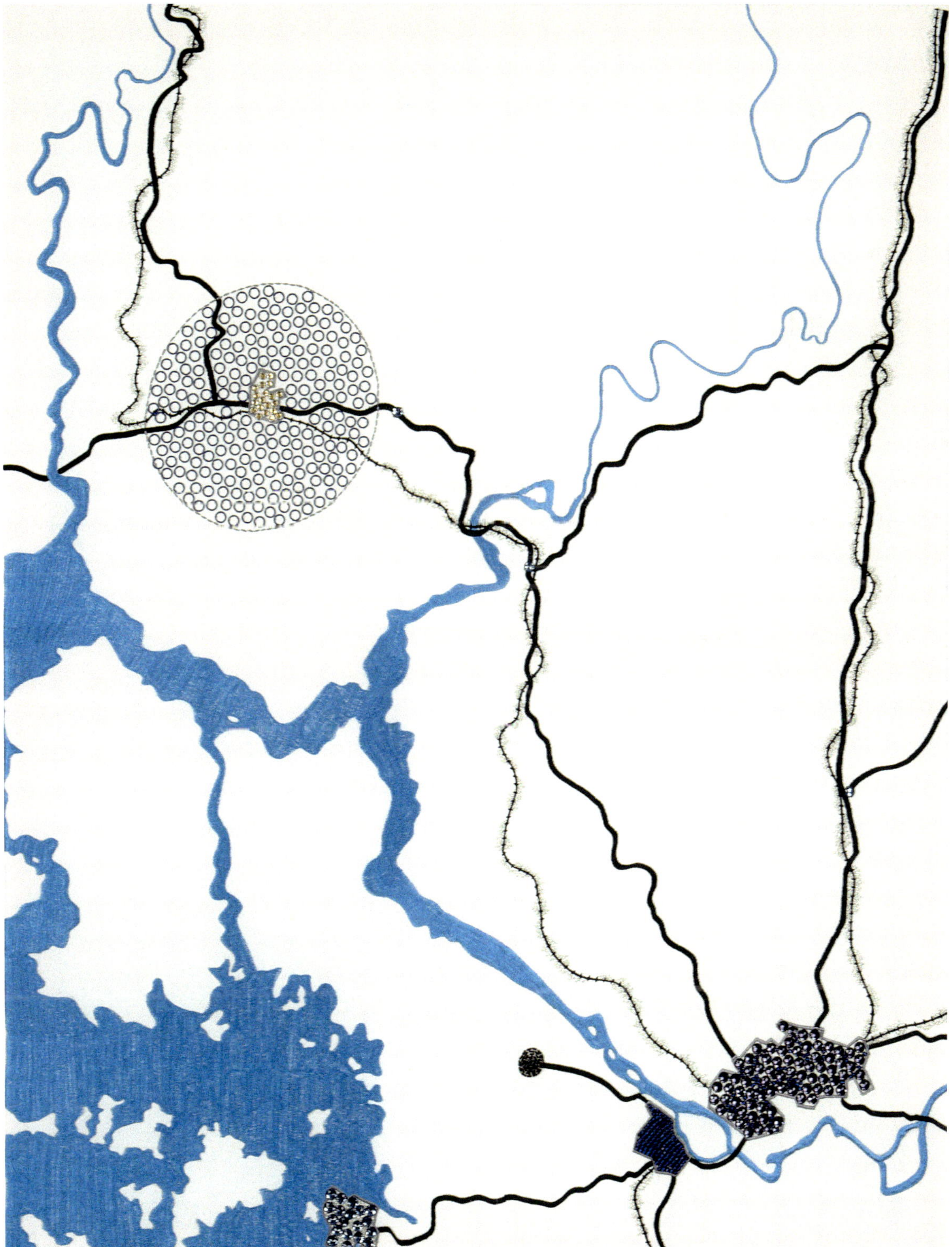

Iraqi State Railways after Anglo-Iraqi Treaty 1930 & Current Pipelines, 2010
Ink and oil on vellum and paper
100 × 63 cm (39 ⅜ × 24 ½ in.)

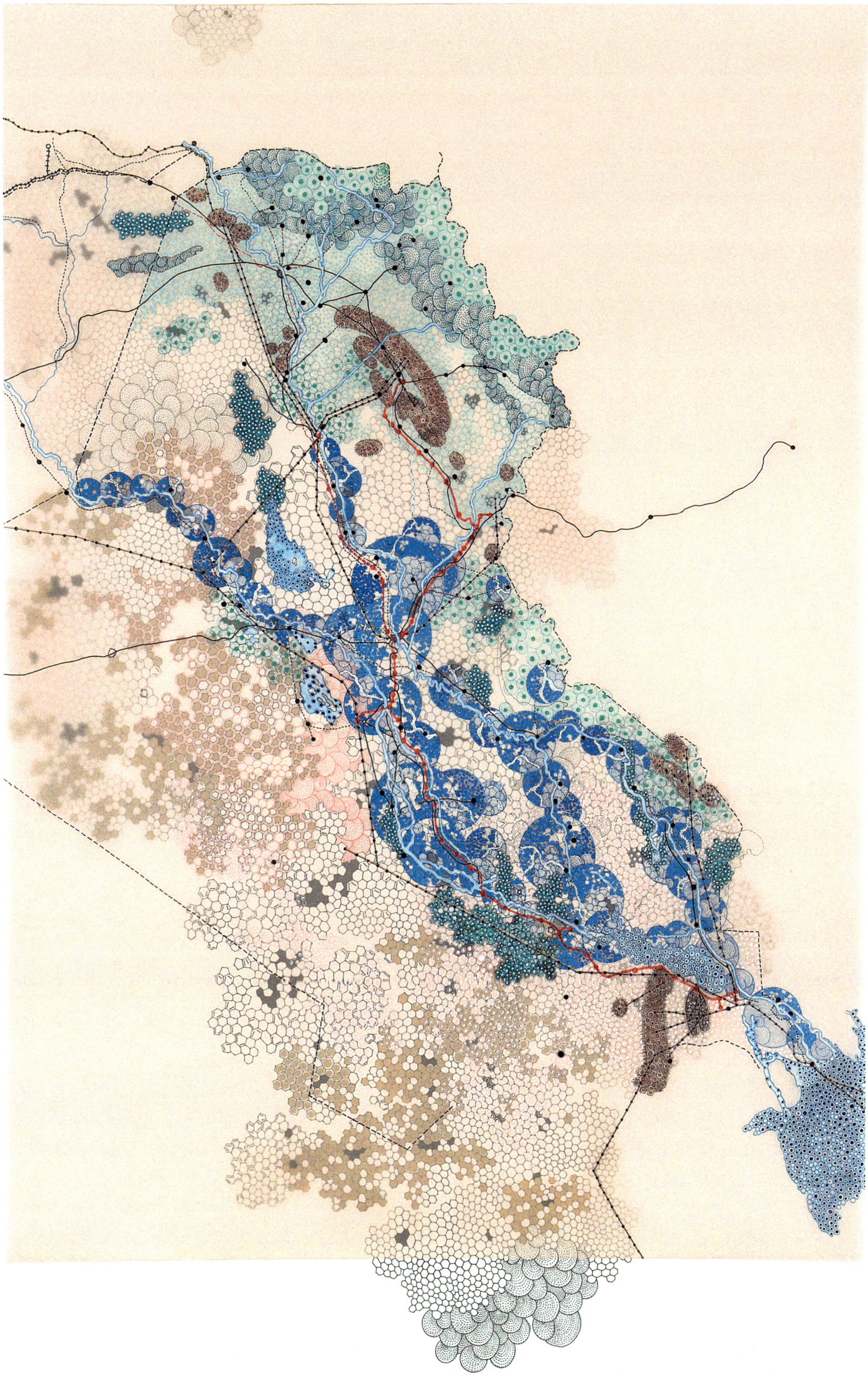

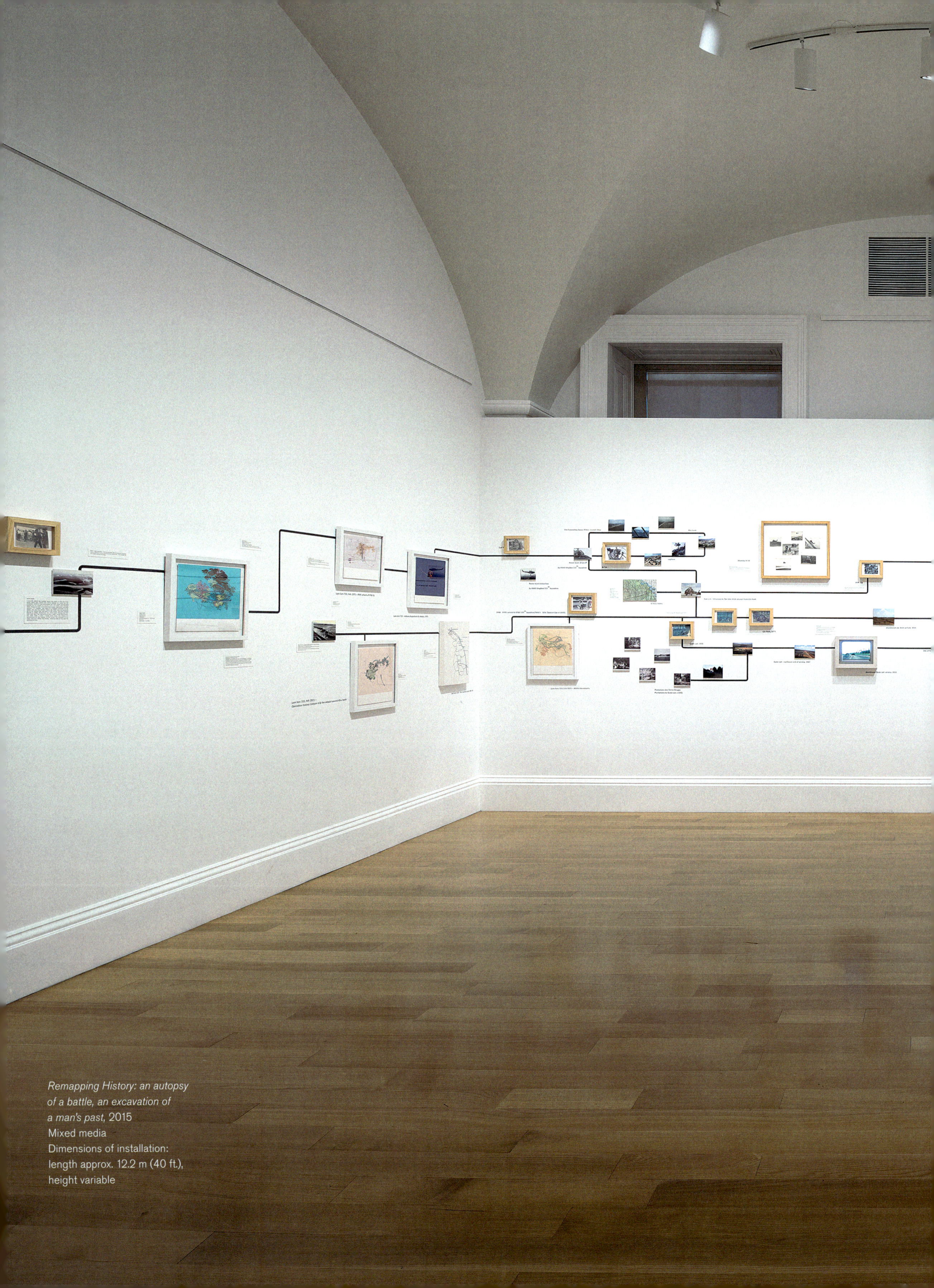

Remapping History: an autopsy of a battle, an excavation of a man's past, 2015
Mixed media
Dimensions of installation: length approx. 12.2 m (40 ft.), height variable

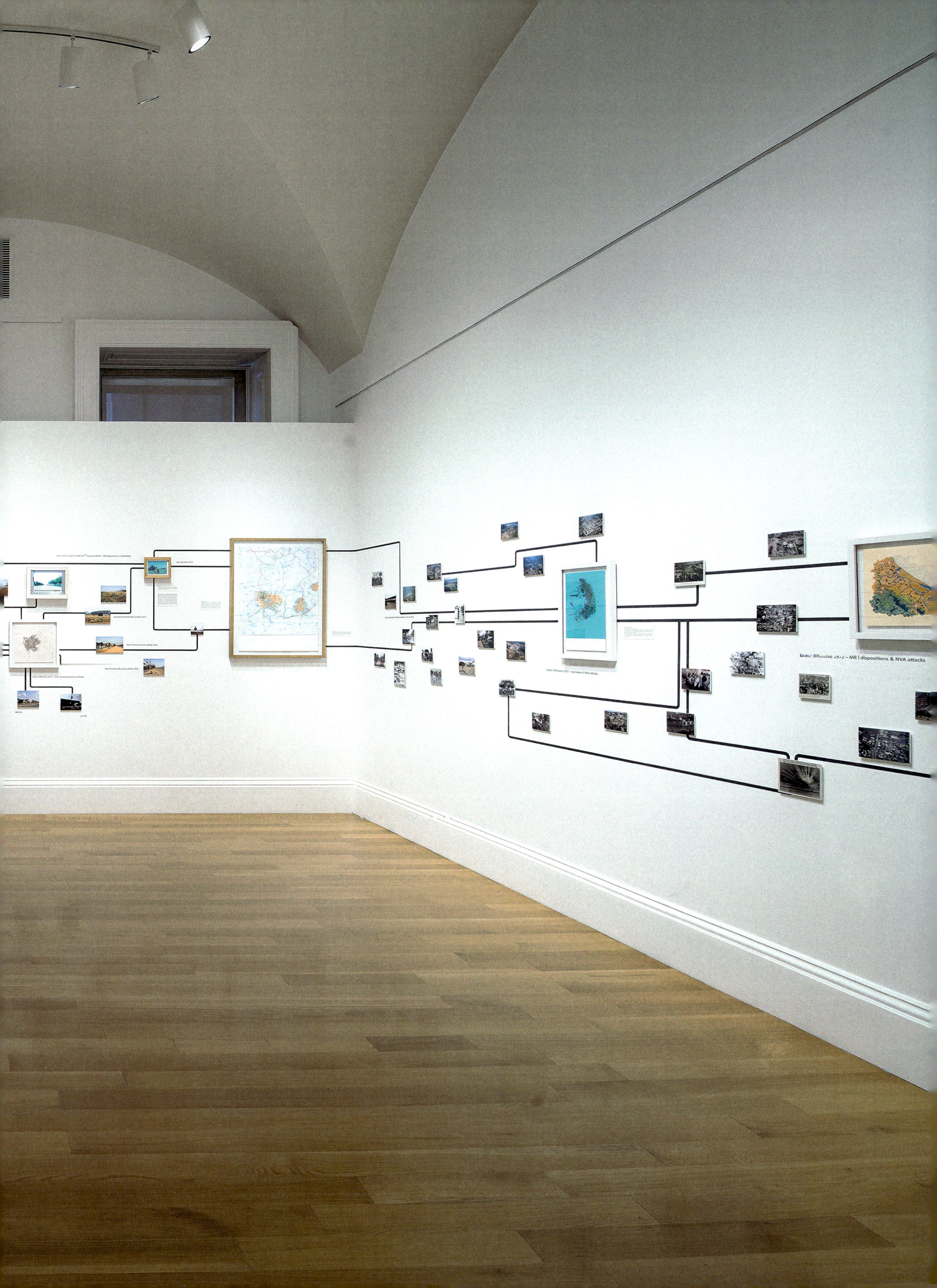
Easter Offensive 1972 – MR I dispositions & NVA attacks

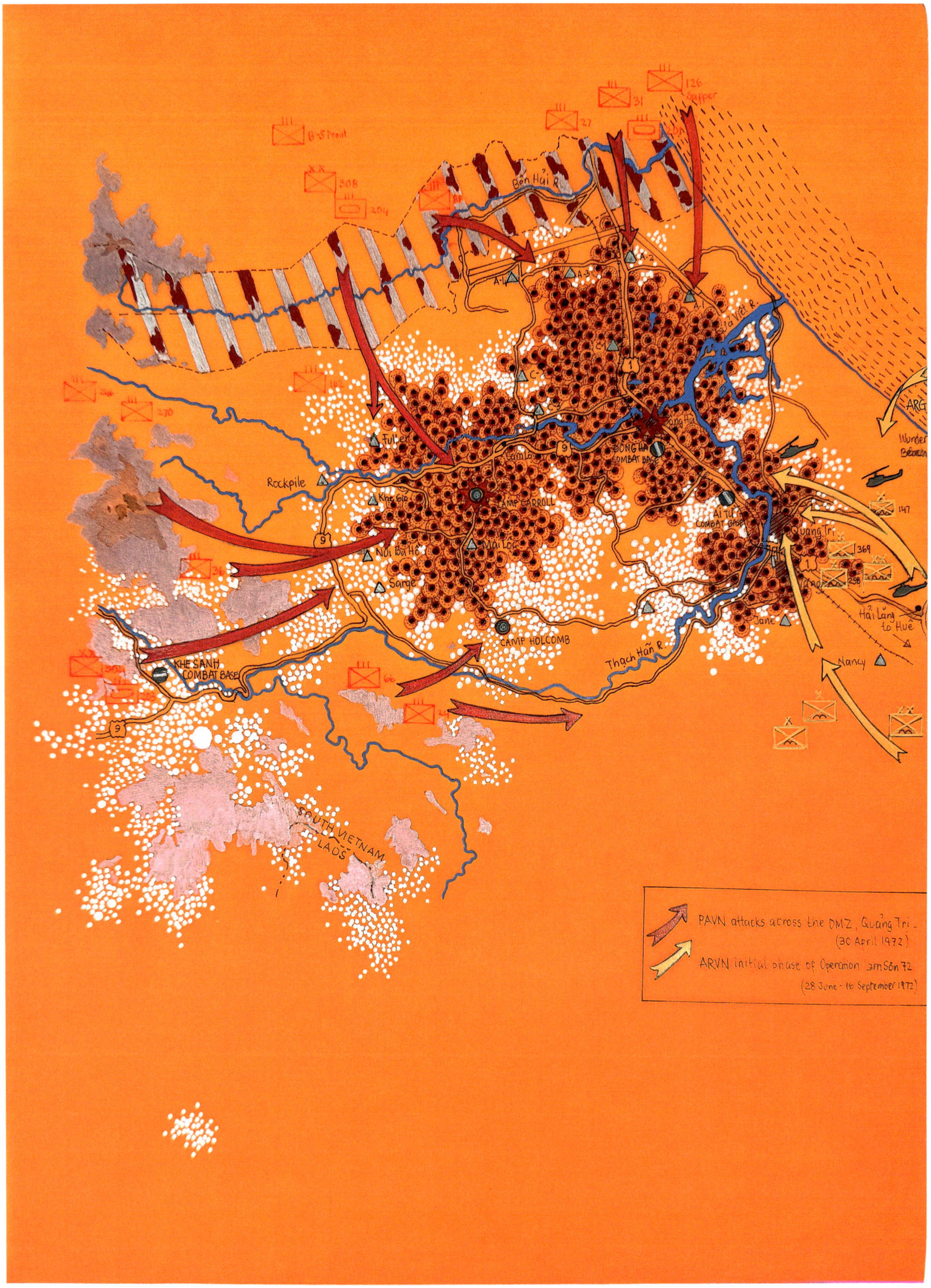
126 Sapper
B-5 Front
308
Bến Hải R.
A-1
A-2
A-3
A-4
C-1
C-2
Fuller
Rockpile
Cam Lộ
Khe Gió
CAMP CARROLL
Núi Bá Hô
Mai Lộc
Sarge
CAMP HOLCOMB
ĐÔNG HÀ COMBAT BASE
Đông Hà
Quảng Trị
Hải Lăng
to Huế
Jane
Nancy
Thạch Hãn R.
KHE SANH COMBAT BASE
SOUTH VIETNAM
LAOS
PAVN attacks across the DMZ, Quảng Trị
(30 April 1972)
ARVN initial phase of Operation Lam Sơn 72
(28 June - 16 September 1972)

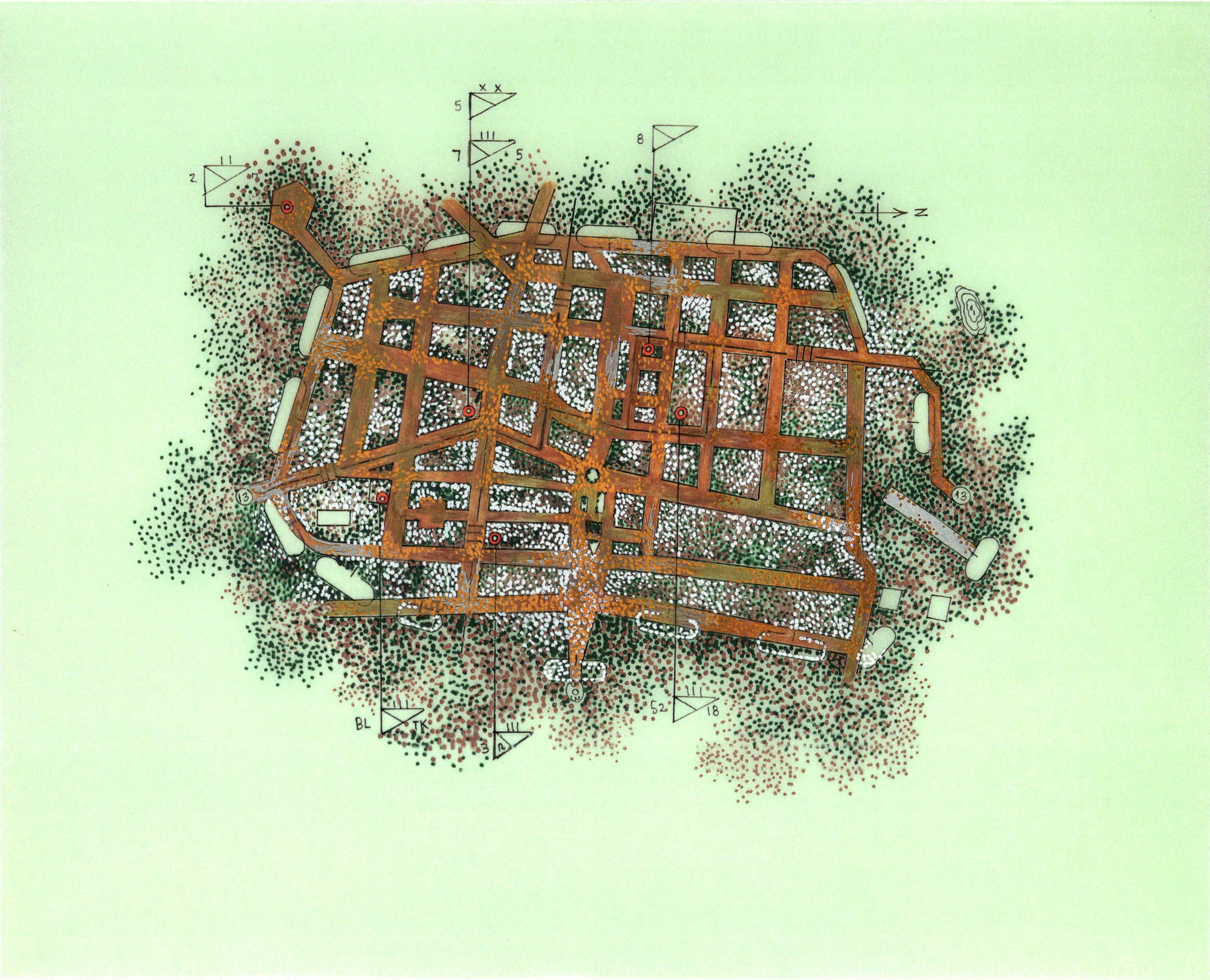

Crossing the DMZ–1972
Easter Offensive, 2022
Ink and oil on vellum and paper
38 × 25.5 cm (15 × 10 in.)

Easter Offensive 1972,
Defense of An Lộc, 2015
Ink and oil on vellum and paper
24 × 28 cm (9 ½ × 11 in.)

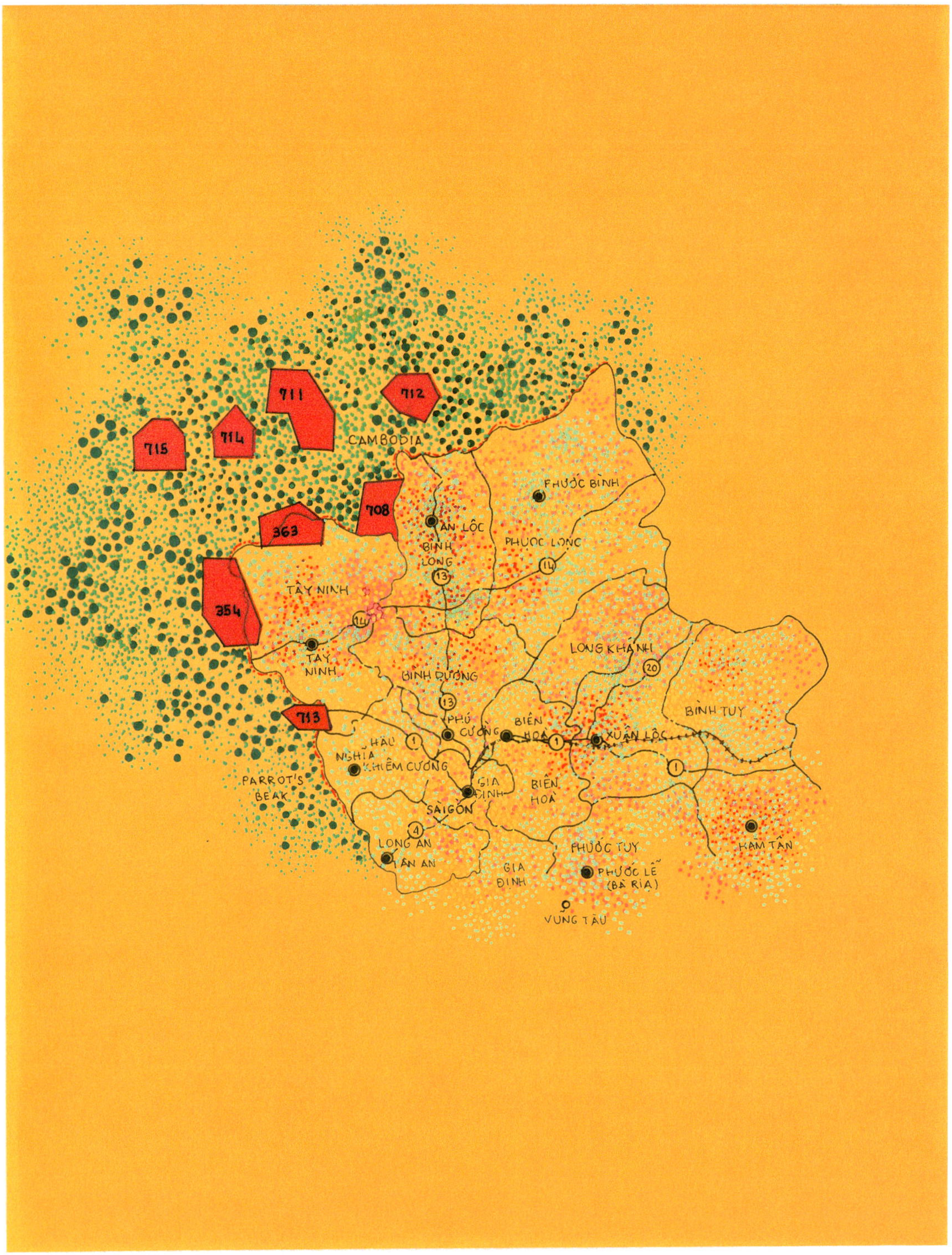

Easter Offensive 1972, NVA base areas on the Cambodian–RVN border, 2015
Ink and oil on vellum and paper
29.8 × 21 cm (11 ¾ × 8 ¼ in.)

Easter Offensive 1972, Battle for Kontum MR III, 2022
Ink and oil on vellum and paper
34.3 × 30.5 cm (13 ½ × 12 in.)

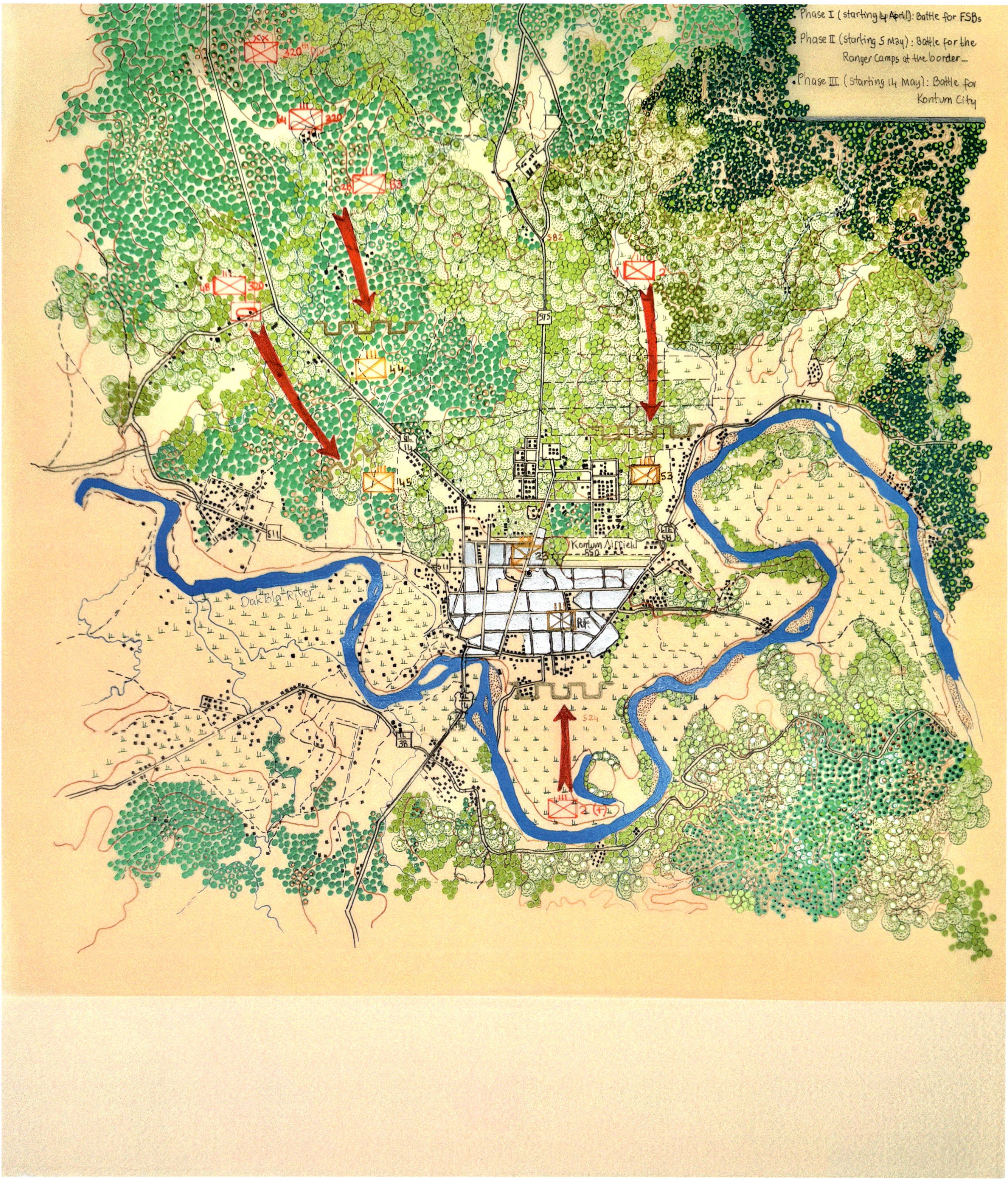
• Phase I (starting April): Battle for FSBs
• Phase II (starting 5 May): Battle for the Ranger Camps at the border
• Phase III (starting 14 May): Battle for Kontum City
Kontum Airfield
Dak Bla River

Easter Offensive 1972, NVA bases, regimental dispositions and attacks, MR-IV, 2015
Ink and oil on vellum and paper
42 x 29.7 cm (16 ½ x 11 ¾ in.)

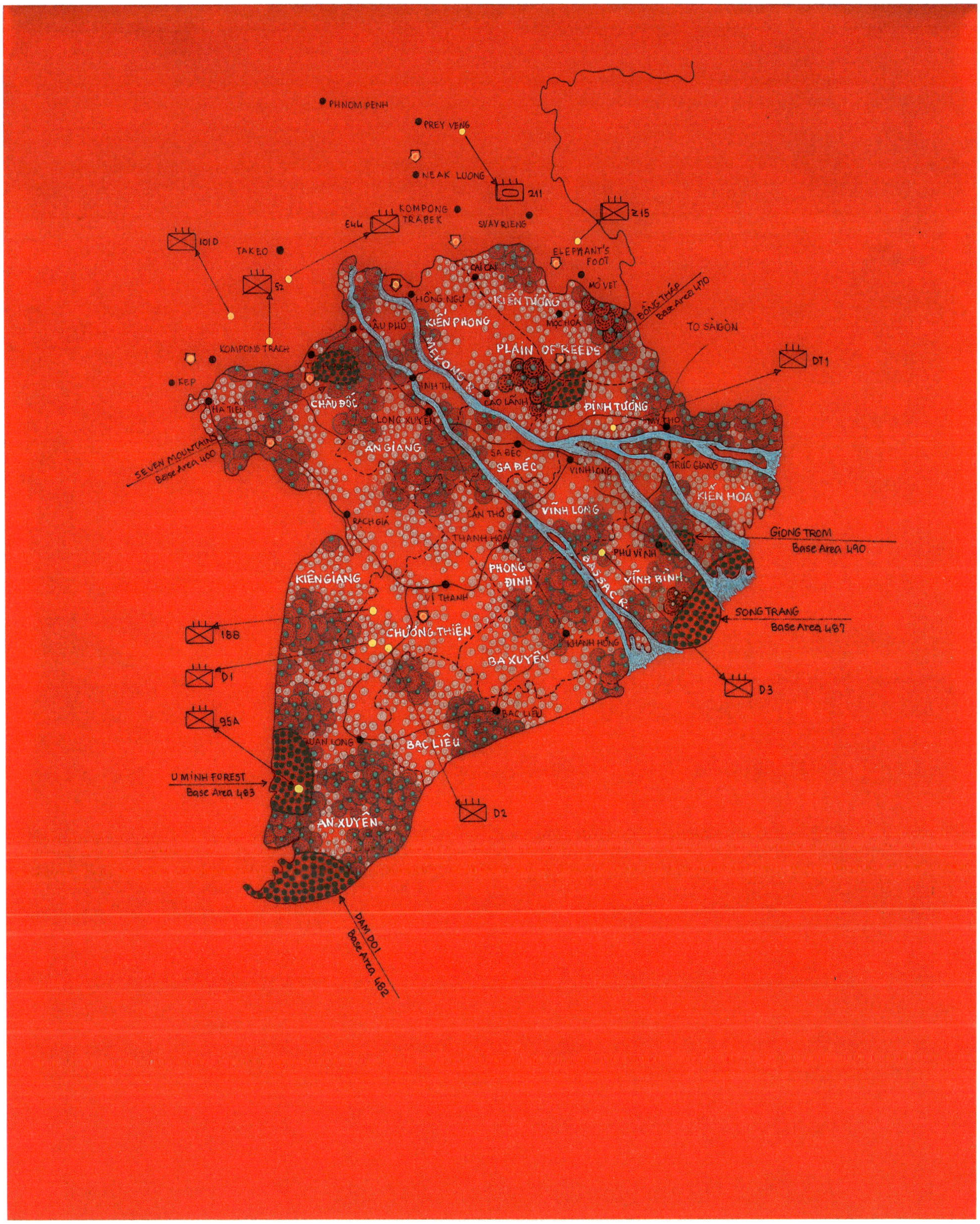
PHNOM PENH
PREY VENG
NEAK LUONG
211
Z15
KOMPONG TRABEK
E44
SVAY RIENG
101 D
TAKEO
52
ELEPHANT'S FOOT
CAI CAI
MỎ VẸT
HỒNG NGỰ
KIẾN TƯỜNG
KIẾN PHONG
ĐỒNG THÁP
Base Area 470
TO SÀIGÒN
PLAIN OF REEDS
MỘC HÓA
DT1
KOMPONG TRACH
KEP
HÀ TIÊN
CHÂU ĐỐC
MEKONG R.
LONG XUYÊN
CAO LÃNH
ĐỊNH TƯỜNG
MỸ THO
SEVEN MOUNTAINS
Base Area 400
AN GIANG
SA ĐÉC
VĨNH LONG
TRÚC GIANG
KIẾN HÒA
RẠCH GIÁ
CẦN THƠ
THANH HÓA
GIONG TROM
Base Area 490
PHONG ĐỊNH
PHÚ VINH
VĨNH BÌNH
BASSAC R.
KIÊN GIANG
18B
CHƯƠNG THIỆN
SONG TRANG
Base Area 487
D1
KHÁNH HƯNG
BA XUYÊN
D3
95A
BẠC LIÊU
QUẢN LONG
U MINH FOREST
Base Area 483
D2
AN XUYÊN
DAM DOI
Base Area 482

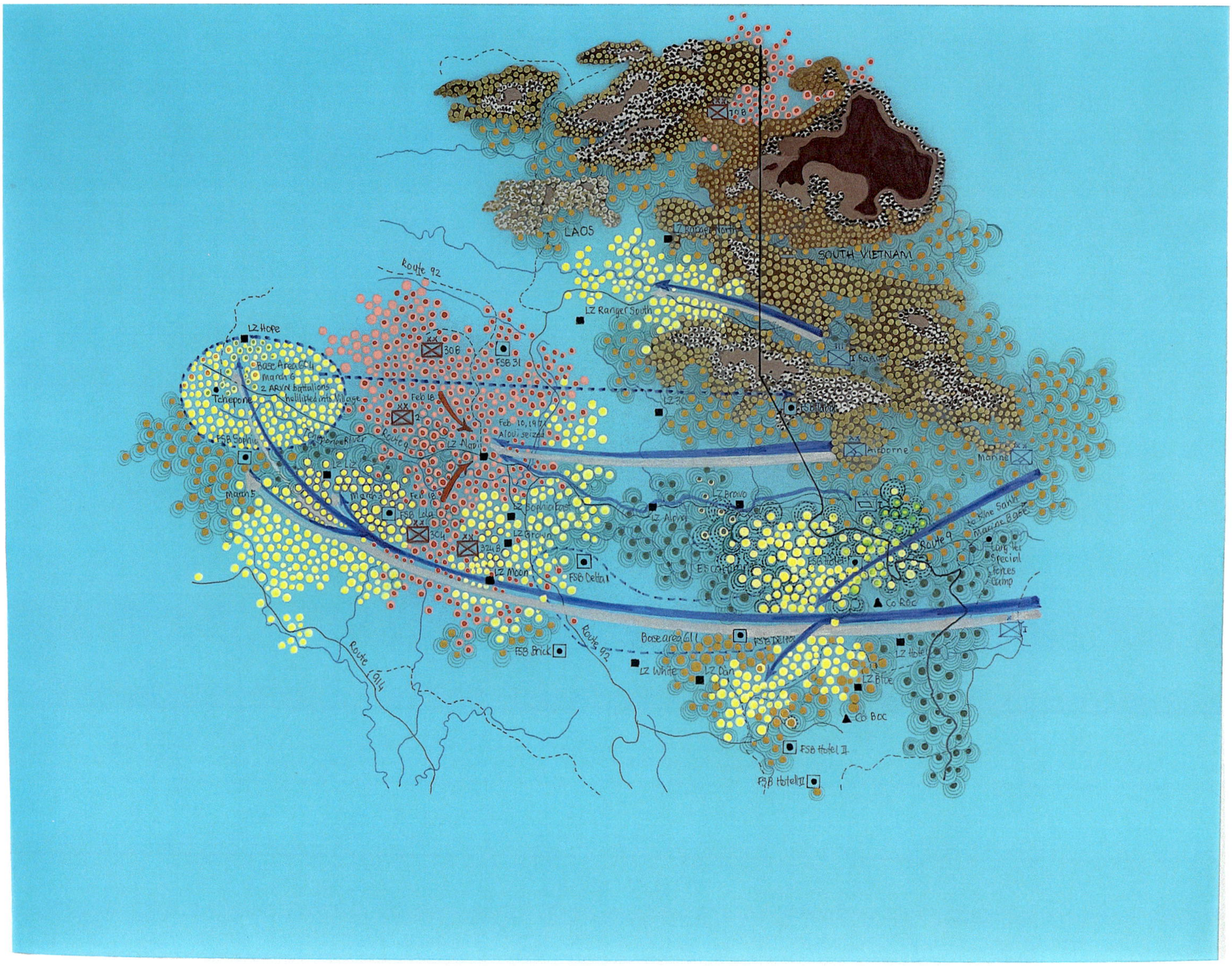

Operation Lam Sơn 719, 30 Jan–6 April 1971, 2018
Acrylic, ink, and oil on vellum, and paper
31.1 × 34.3 cm (12 ¼ × 13 ½ in.)

Operation Lam Sơn 719, Feb 1971–ARVN movements, 2018
Ink and oil on vellum and paper
34.3 × 30.8 cm (13 ½ × 12 ⅛ in.)

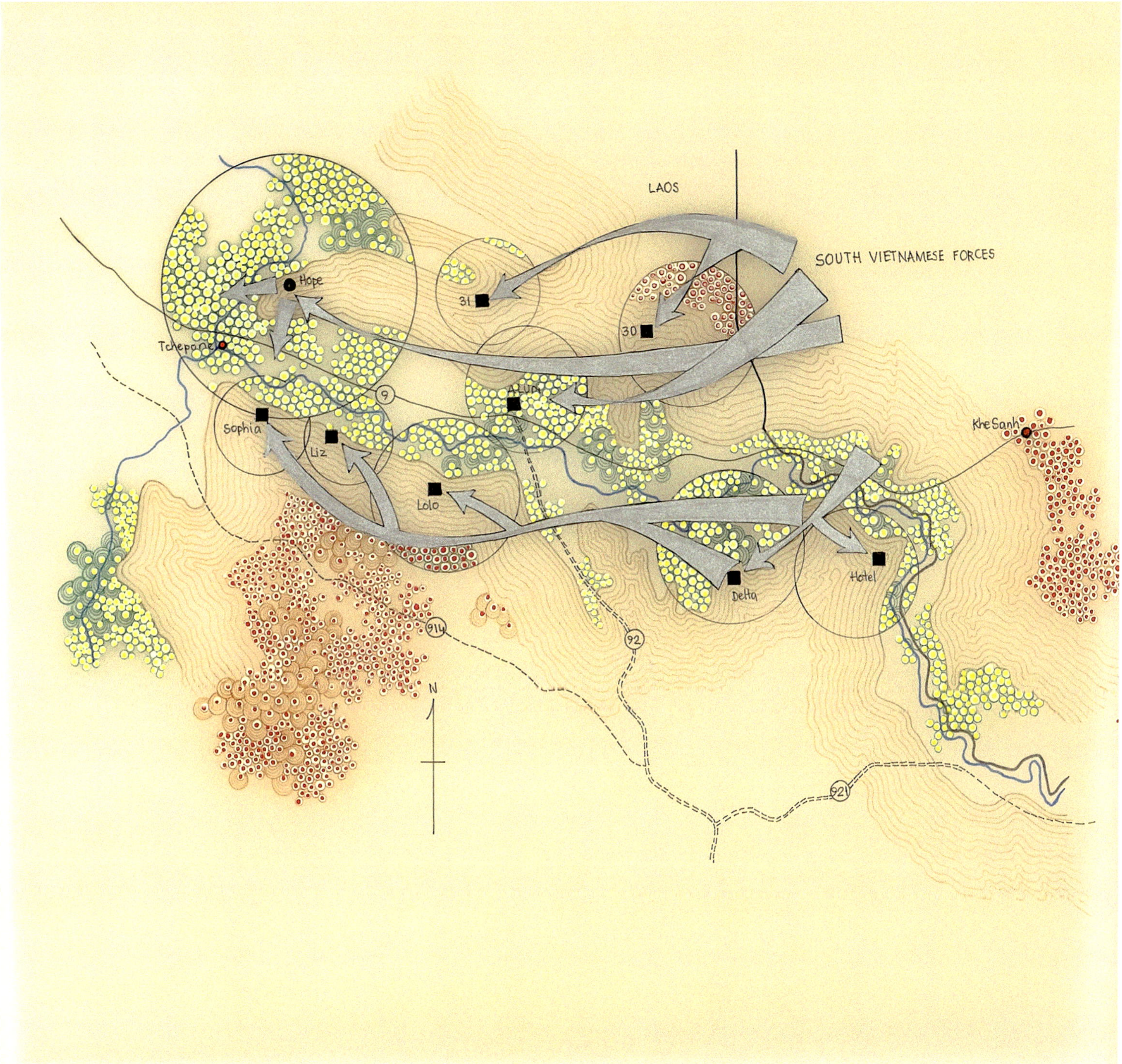
LAOS
SOUTH VIETNAMESE FORCES
Hope
31
30
Tchepone
9
Sophia
Liz
Lolo
Khe Sanh
Delta
Hotel
914
92
921
N

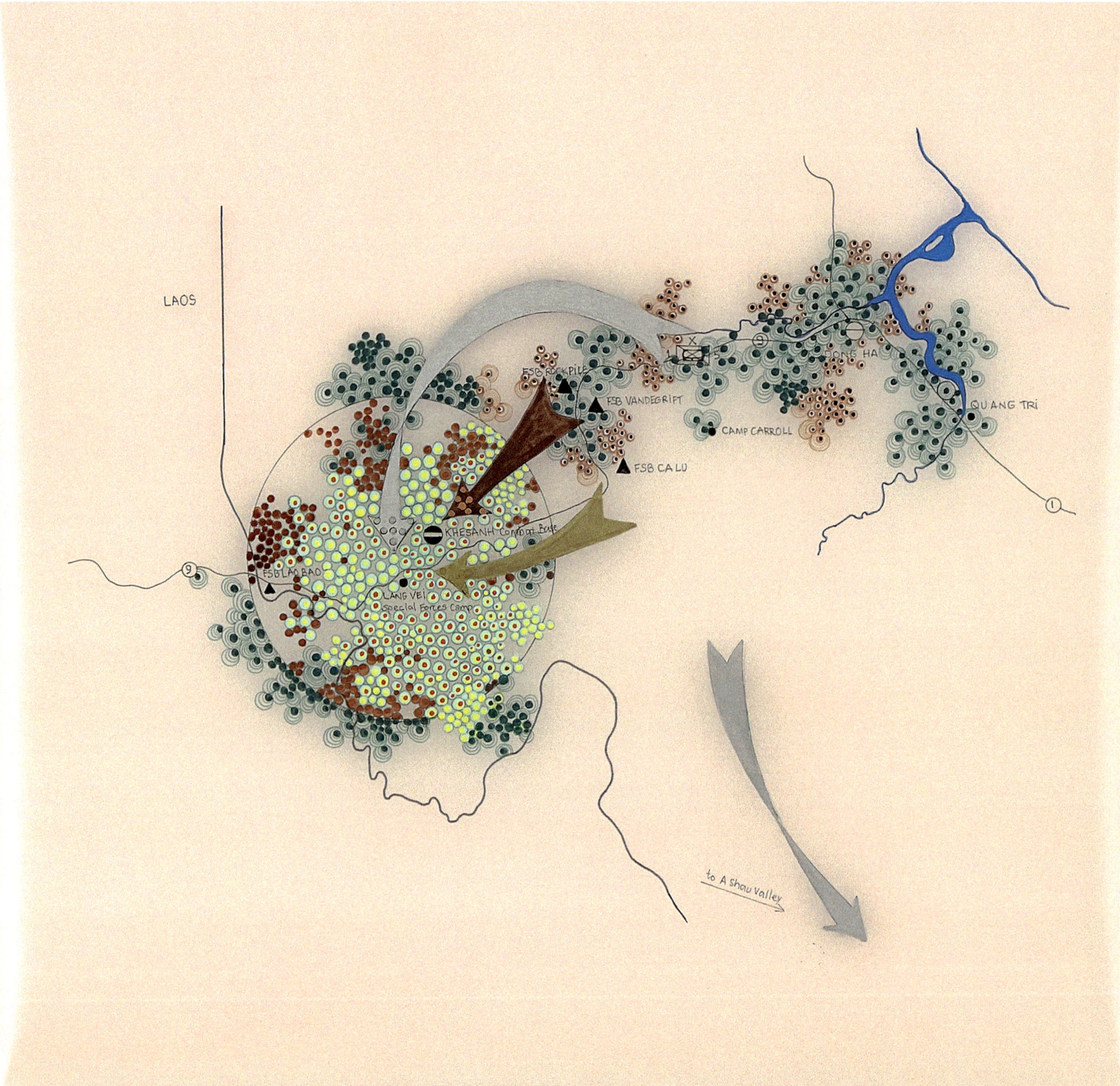
LAOS
FSB ROCKPILE
FSB VANDEGRIFT
FSB CA LU
CAMP CARROLL
DONG HA
QUANG TRI
9
1
KHESANH Combat Base
FSB LAO BAO
LANG VEI
Special Forces Camp
to A Shau Valley

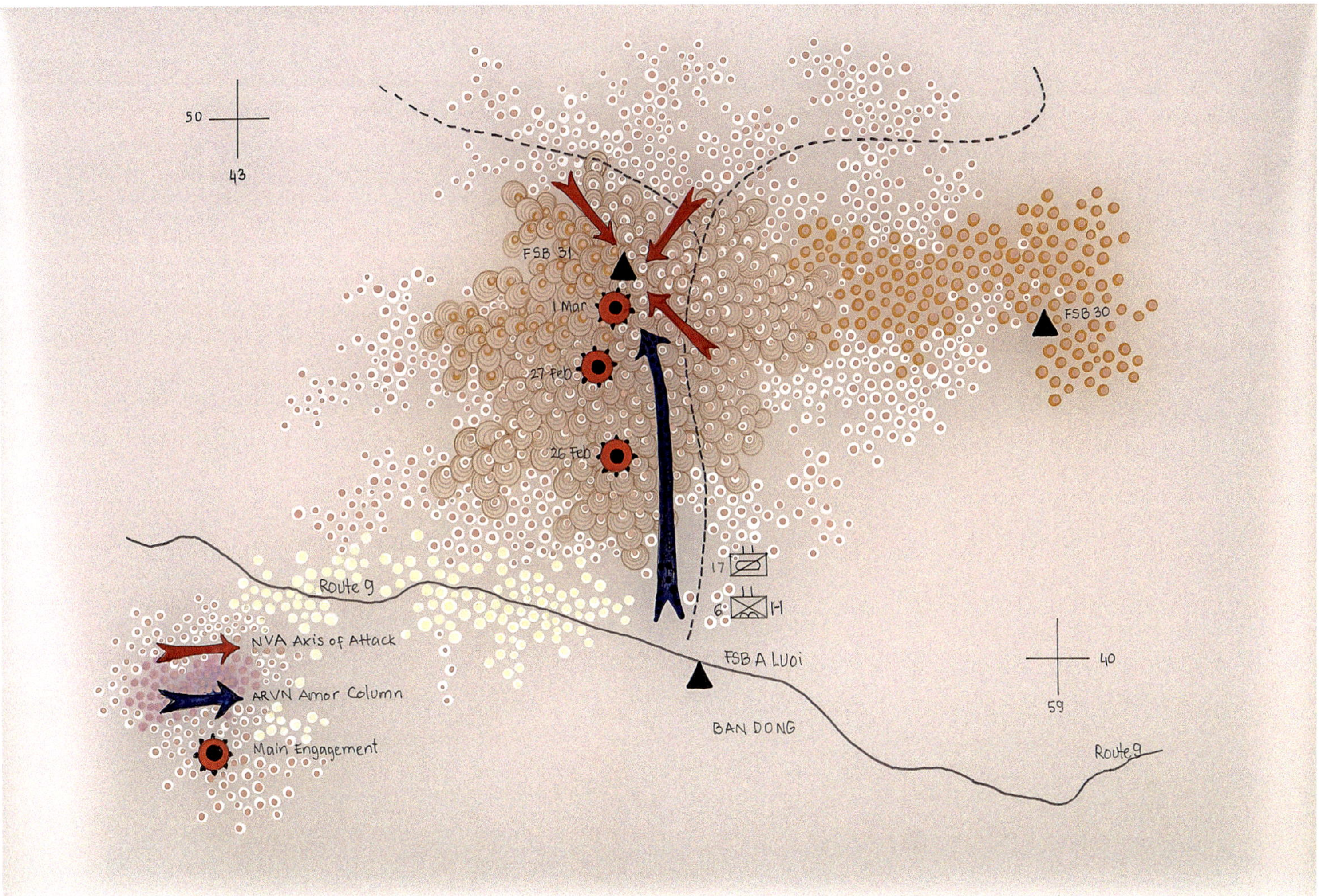

Operation Lam Sơn 719, Feb 1971–Operation Dewey Canyon II & the attack toward Khe Sanh, 2018
Acrylic, ink, and oil on vellum and paper
34.3 × 30.8 cm (13 ½ × 12 ⅛ in.)

Operation Lam Sơn 719, Feb 1971–NVA attack of FSB 31, 2018
Acrylic, ink, and oil on vellum and paper
25.4 × 29.8 cm (10 × 11 ¾ in.)

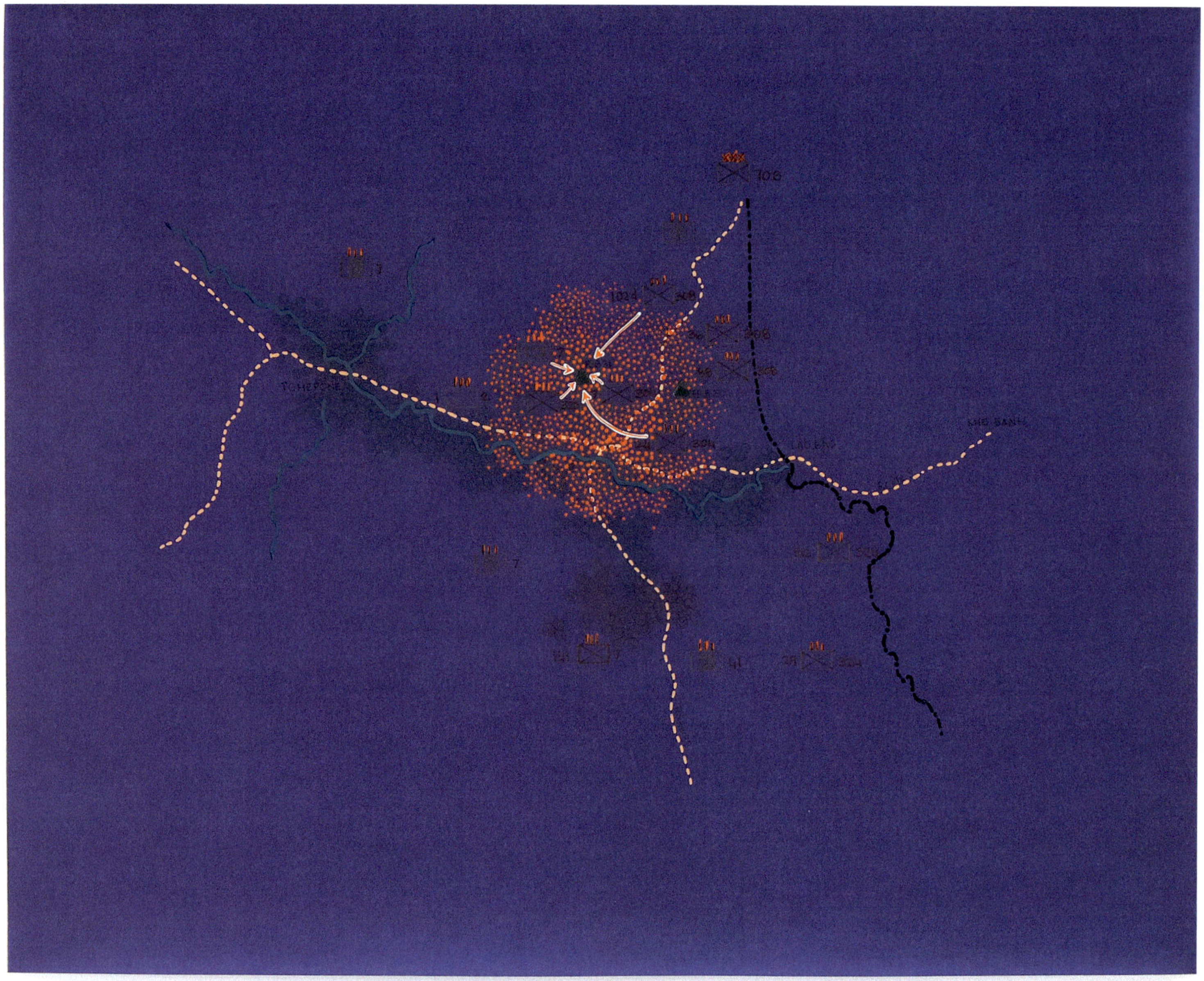

Operation Lam Sơn 719–military dispositions & attacks 1971, 2018
Acrylic, ink, and oil on vellum and paper
29.8 × 32.4 cm (11 ¾ × 12 ¾ in.)

Operation Lam Sơn 719–the border area, MR I-II, 2018
Embroidery on canvas
45.7 × 30.5 cm (18 × 12 in.)

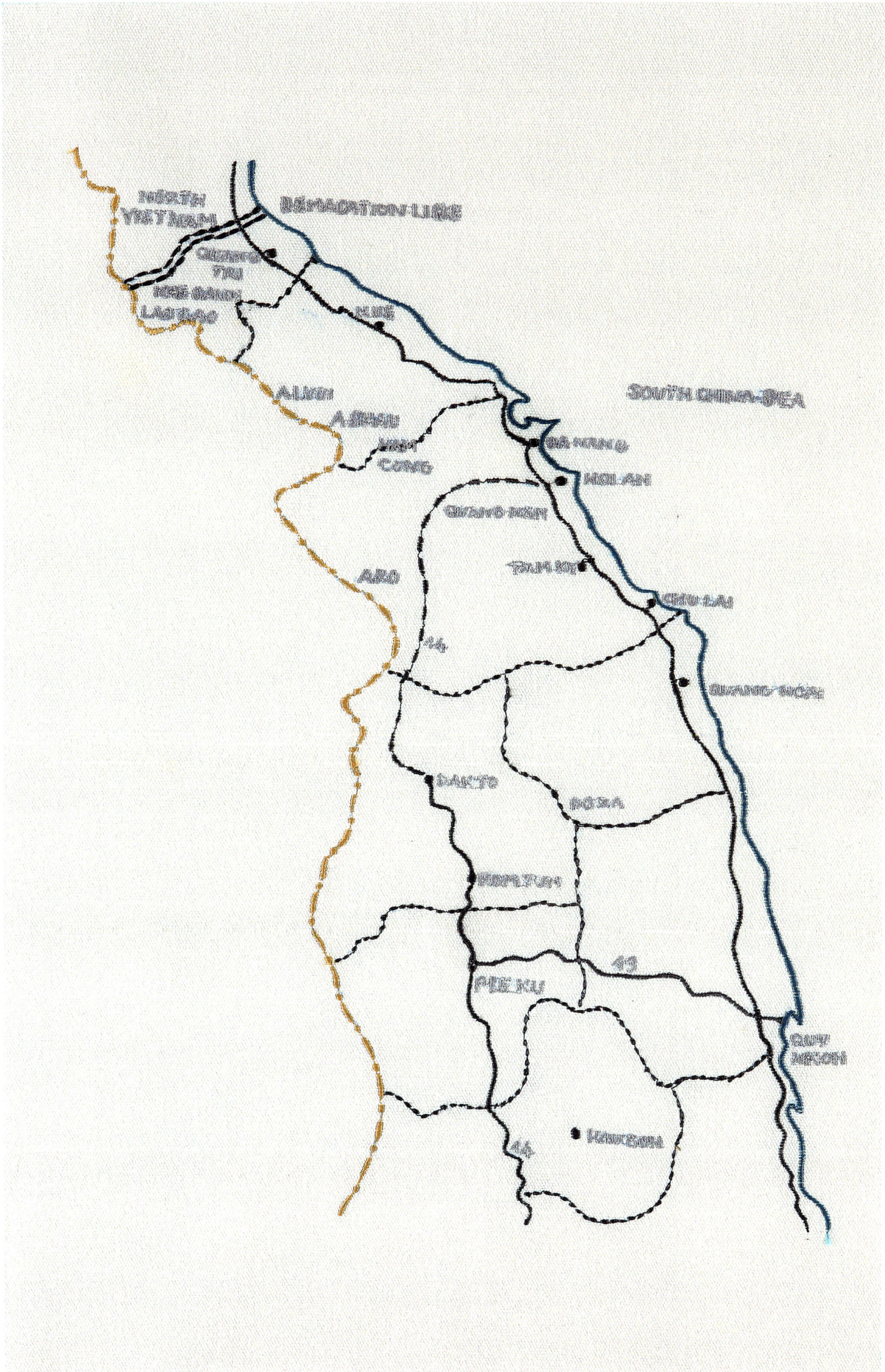
NORTH VIETNAM
DEMARCATION LINE
QUANG TRI
KHE SANH
LAO BAO
HUE
A LUOI
A SHAU
NAM DONG
SOUTH CHINA SEA
DA NANG
HOI AN
QUANG NAM
TAM KY
CHU LAI
14
QUANG NGAI
DAK TO
KONTUM
19
PLEIKU
QUY NHON
14

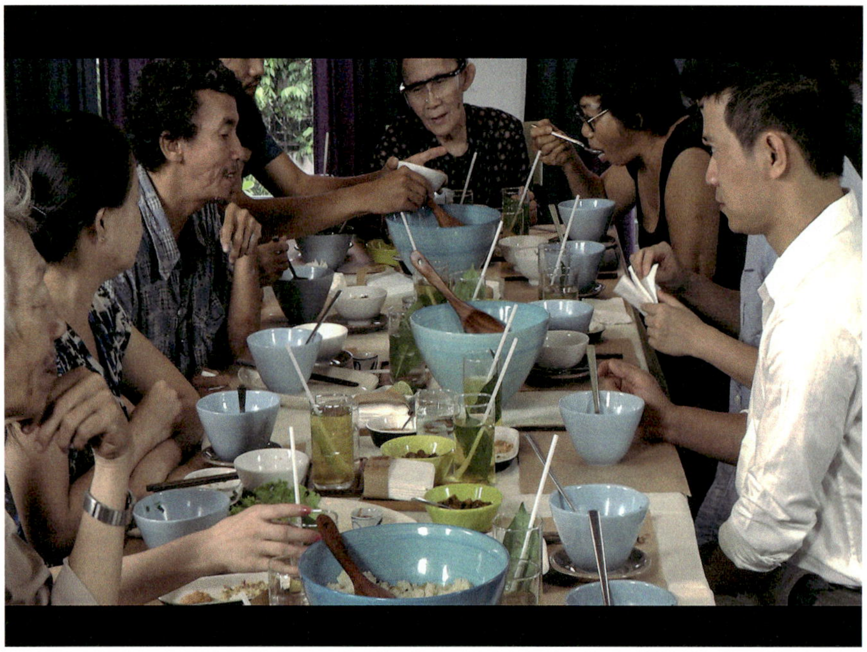

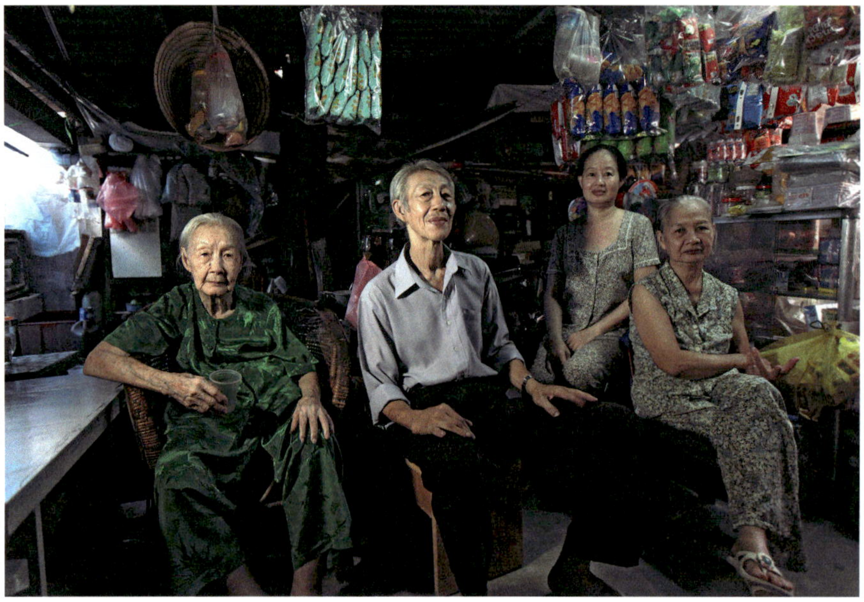

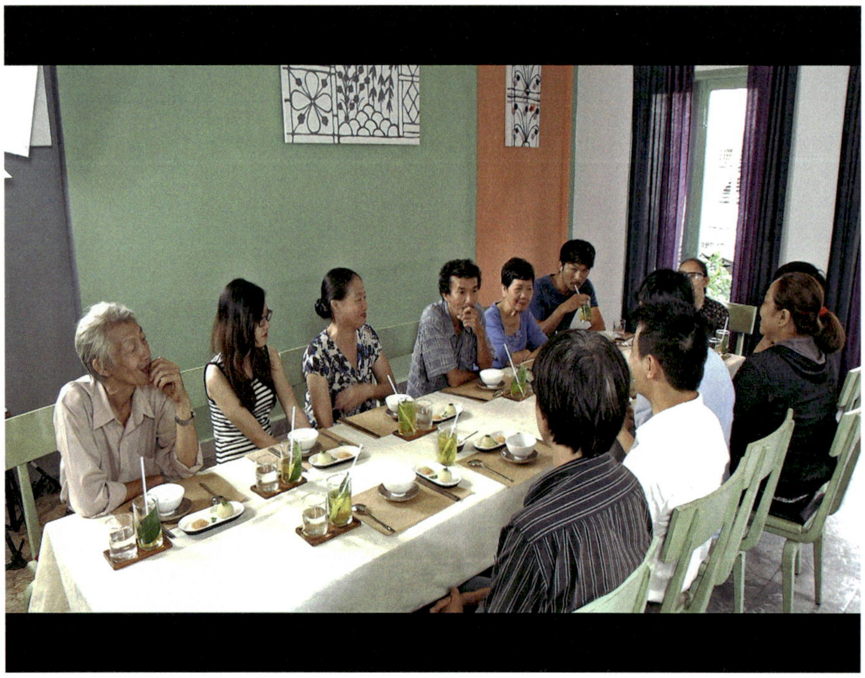

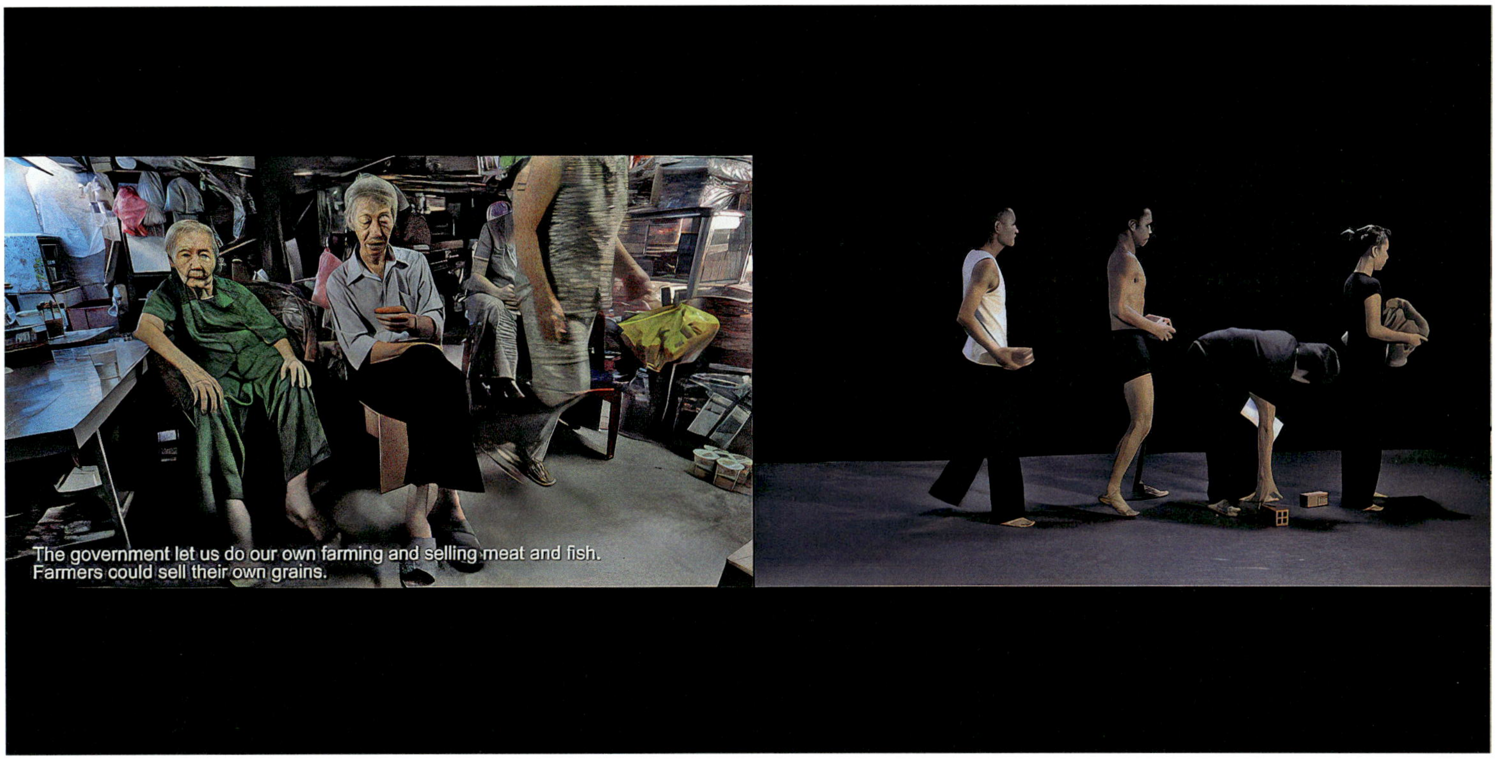

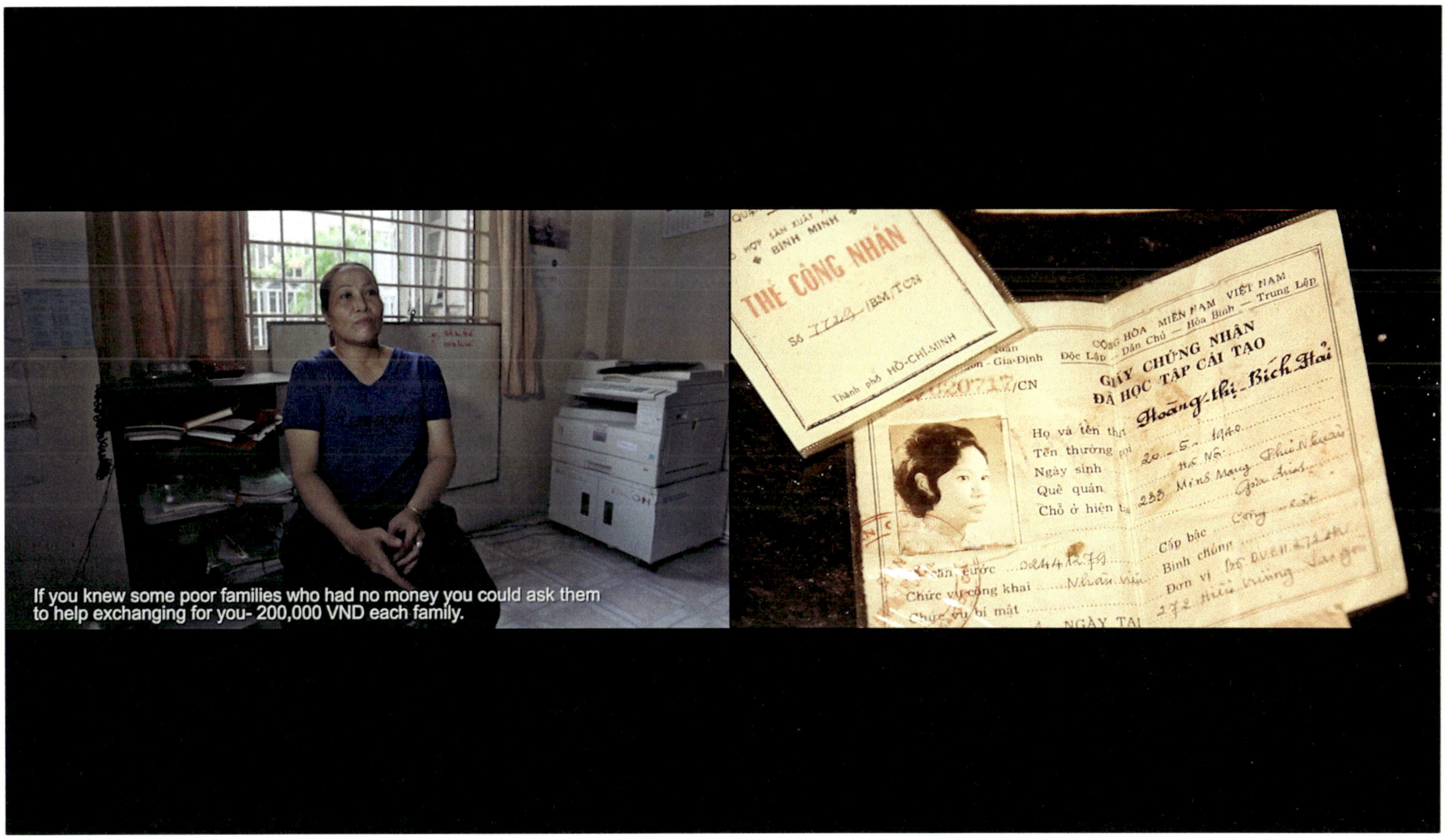

Recipes of Necessity, 2013
Single-channel video, HD,
color, sound, 33 minutes

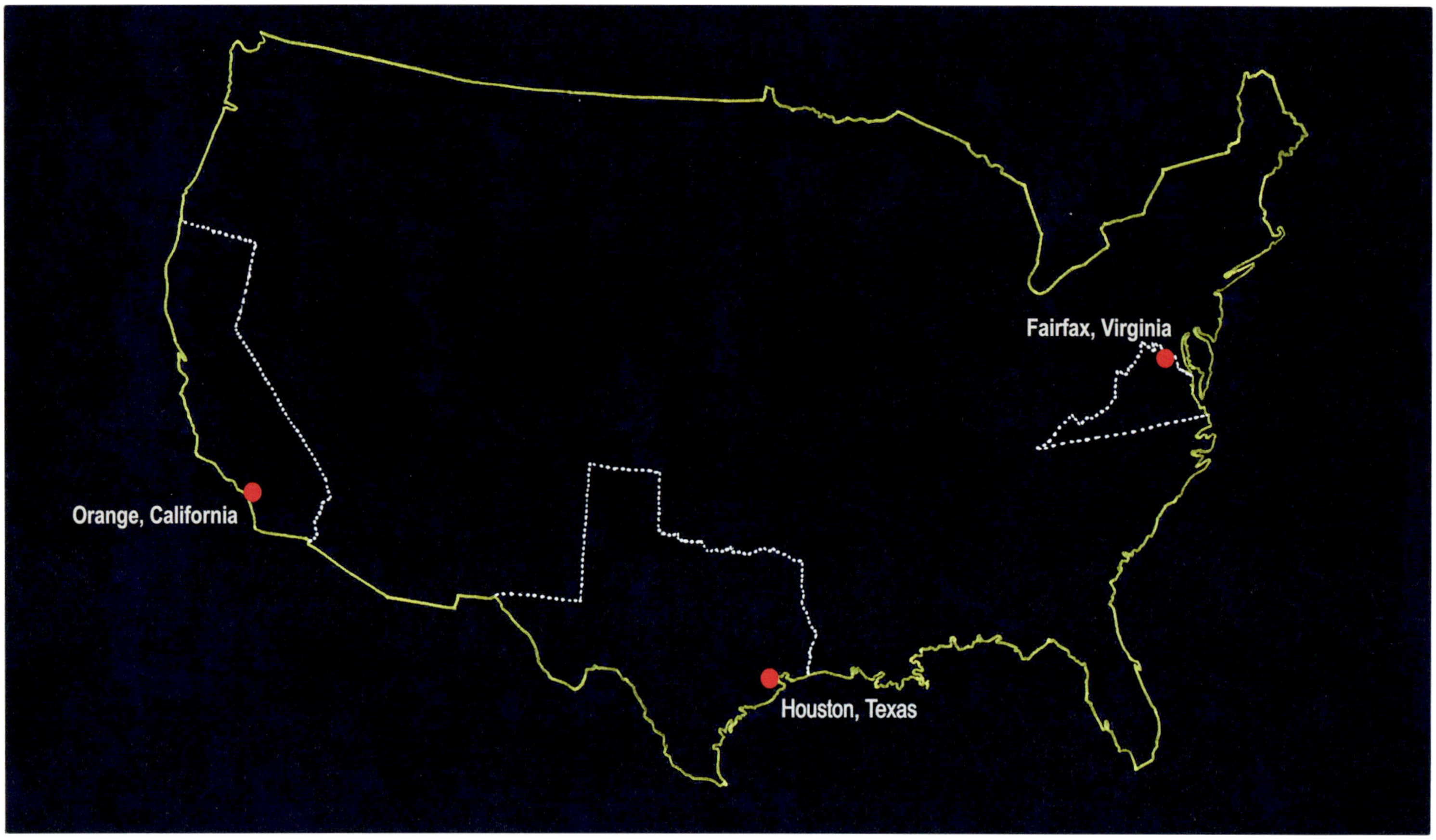

Collective Remembrance of the War: voices from the exiles, 2018–2019
HD, color, sound, [21 video interviews], durations variable

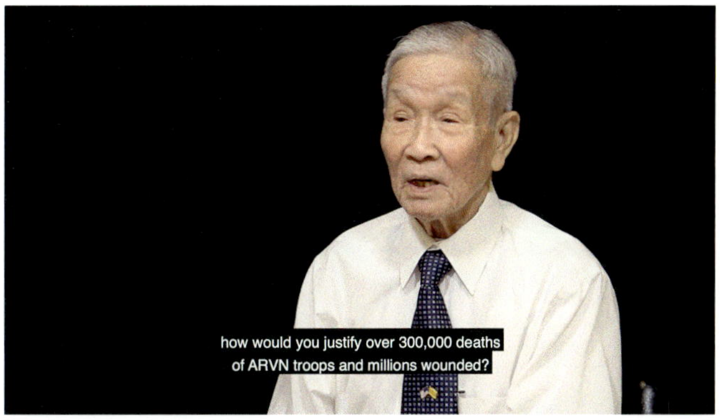
how would you justify over 300,000 deaths
of ARVN troops and millions wounded?

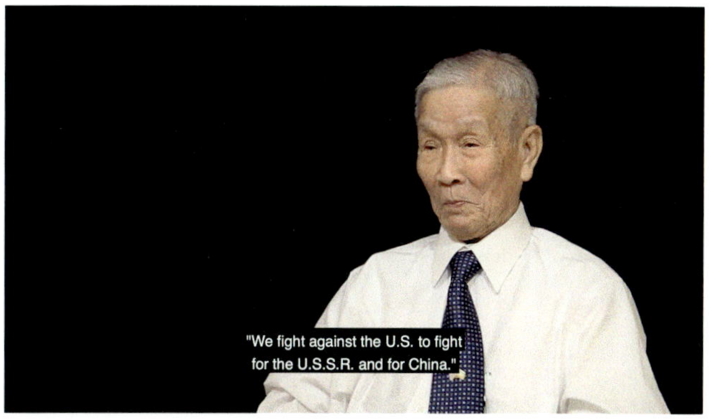
"We fight against the U.S. to fight
for the U.S.S.R. and for China."

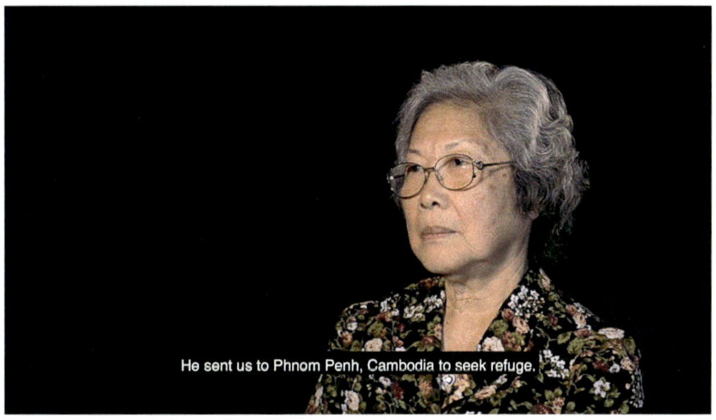
He sent us to Phnom Penh, Cambodia to seek refuge.

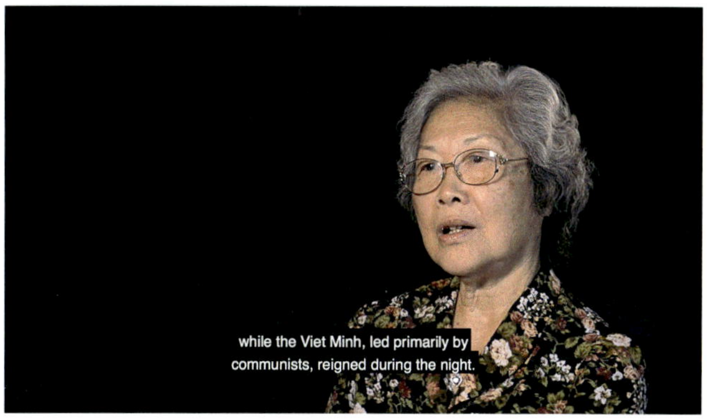
while the Viet Minh, led primarily by
communists, reigned during the night.

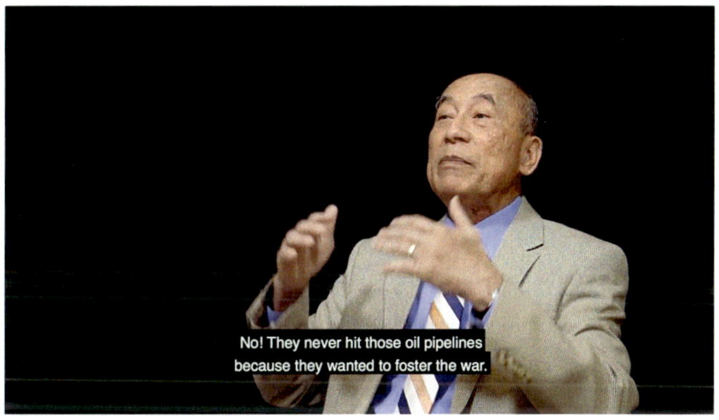
No! They never hit those oil pipelines
because they wanted to foster the war.

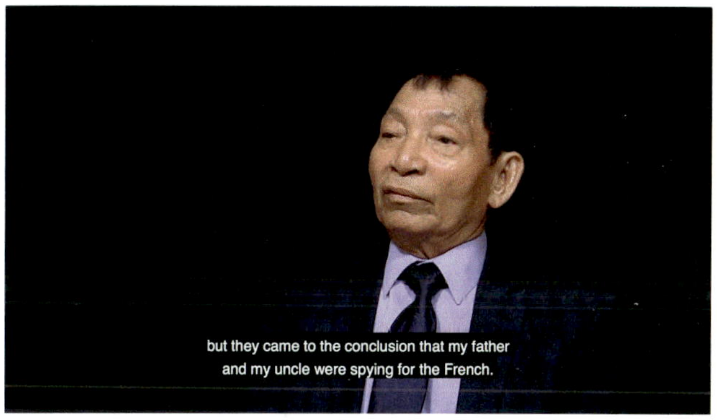
but they came to the conclusion that my father
and my uncle were spying for the French.

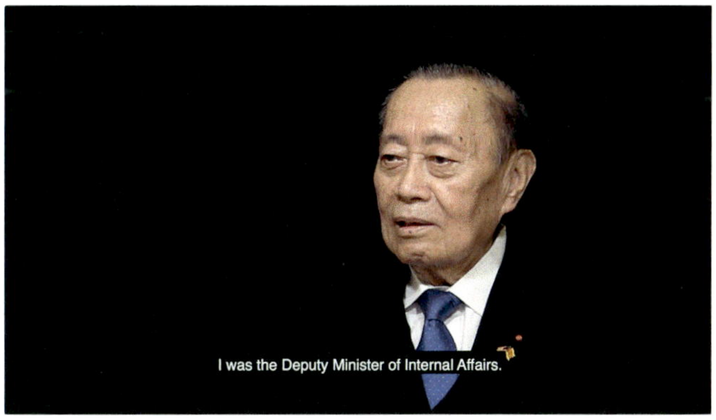
I was the Deputy Minister of Internal Affairs.

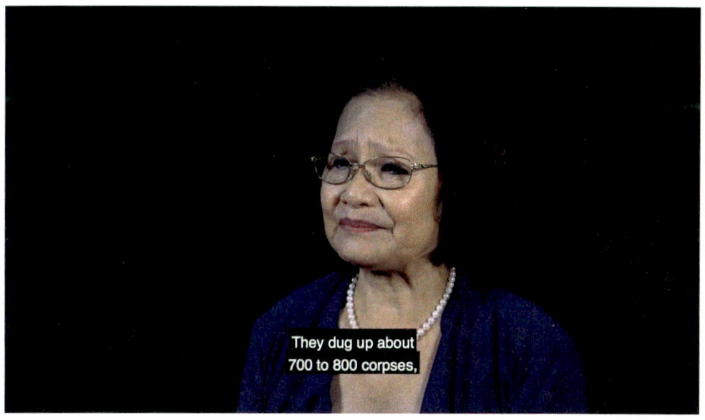
They dug up about
700 to 800 corpses,

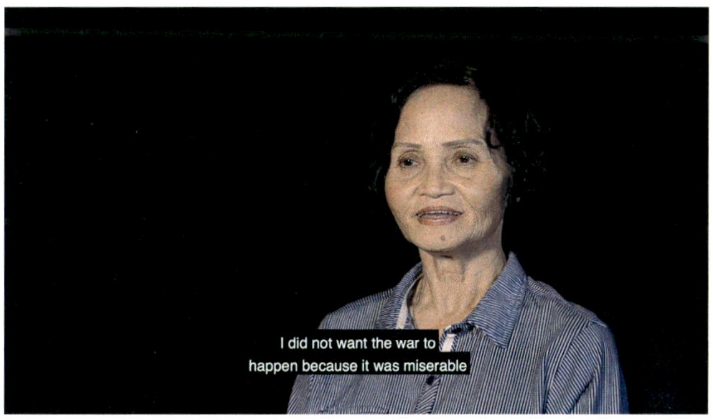
I did not want the war to
happen because it was miserable

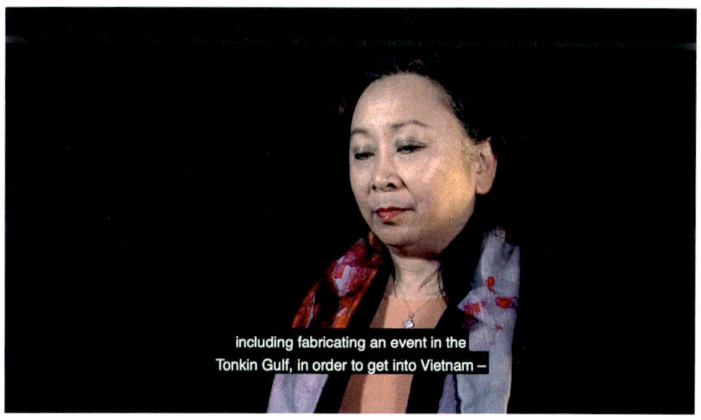
including fabricating an event in the
Tonkin Gulf, in order to get into Vietnam –

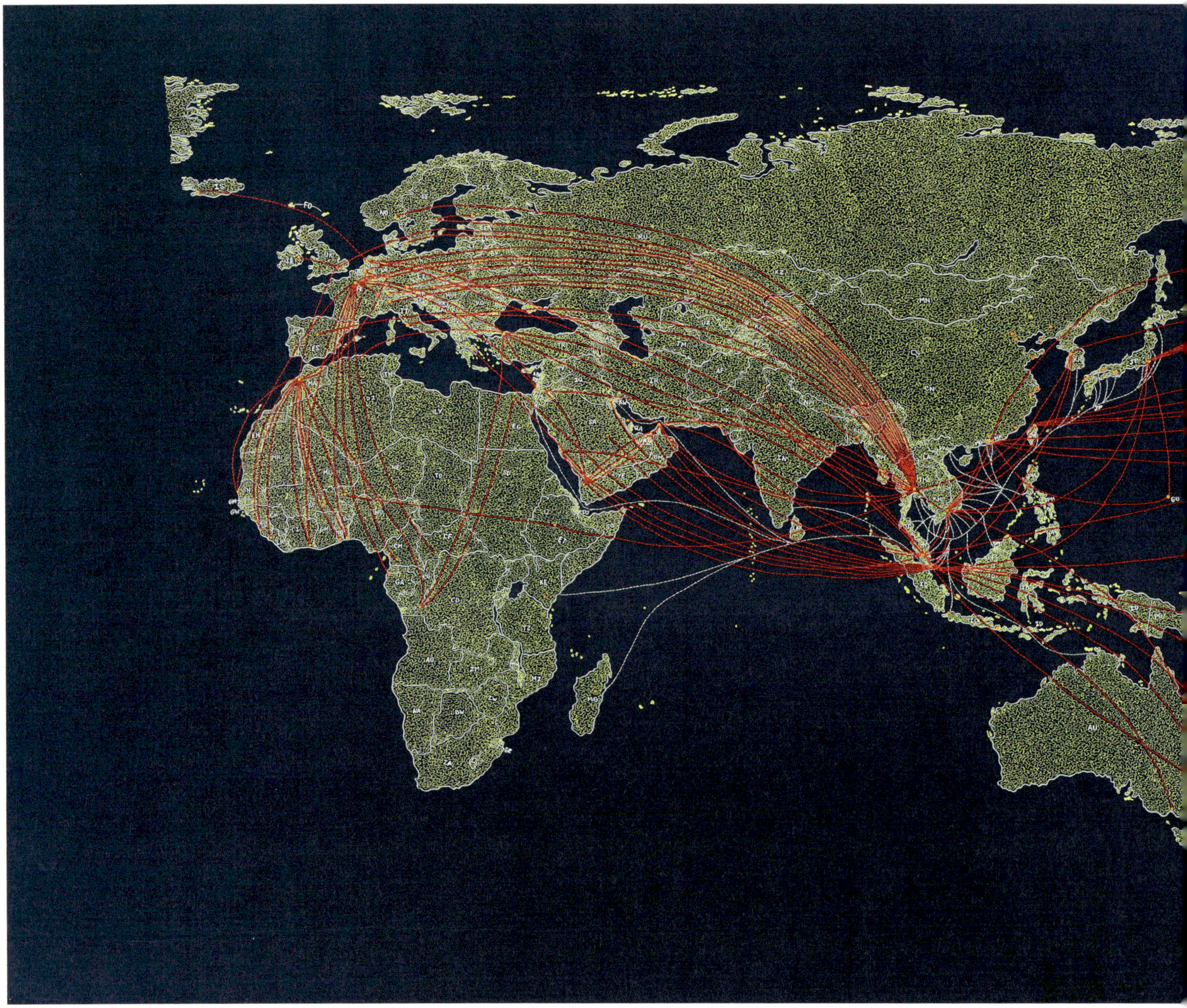

reconstructing an exodus history: boat trajectories from Vietnam and flight routes from refugee camps and of ODP cases, 2020
Embroidery on fabric
140 × 350 cm (55 × 137 ¾ in.)

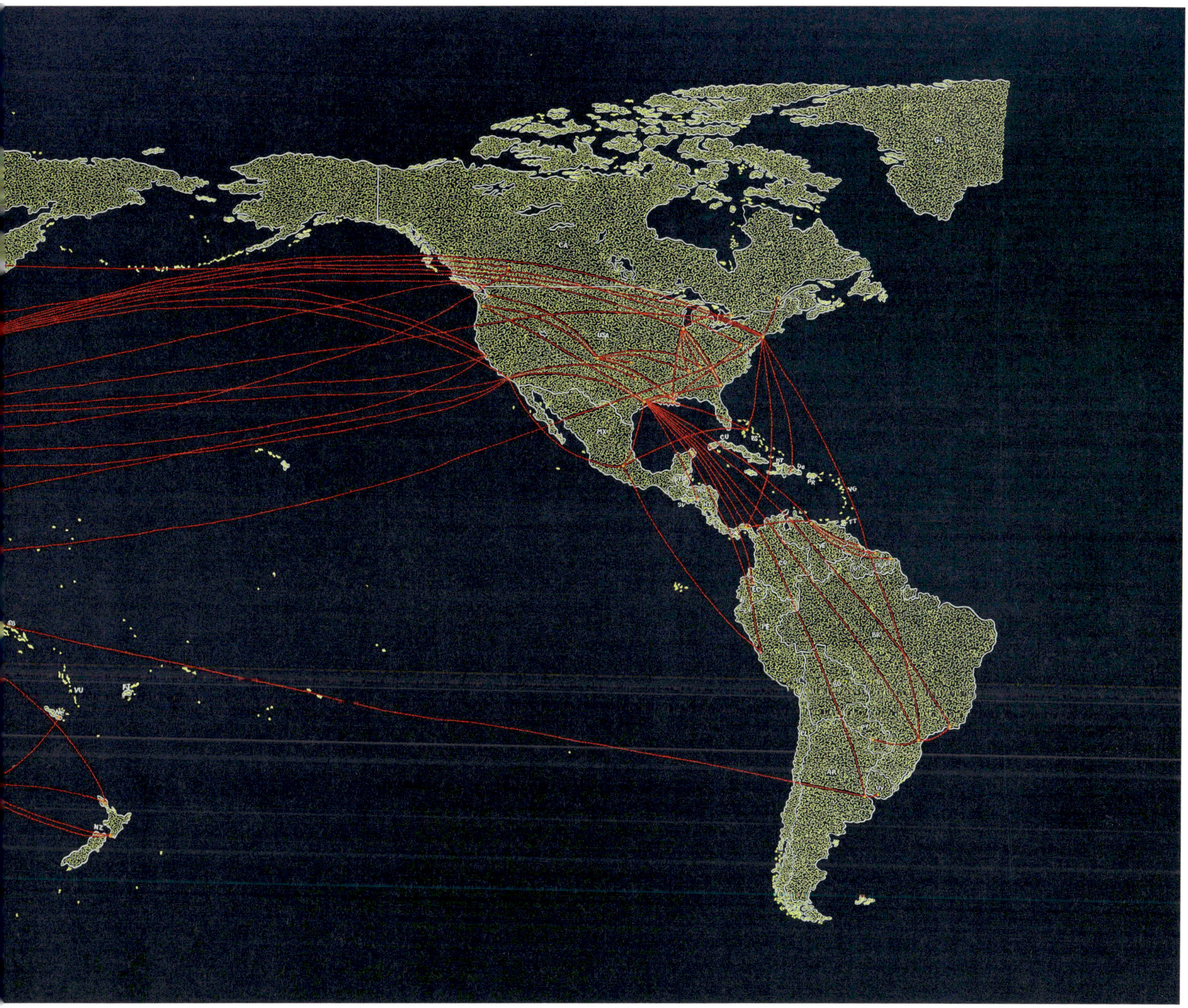
GL
CA
USA
MX
CU
VU
FJ
NZ

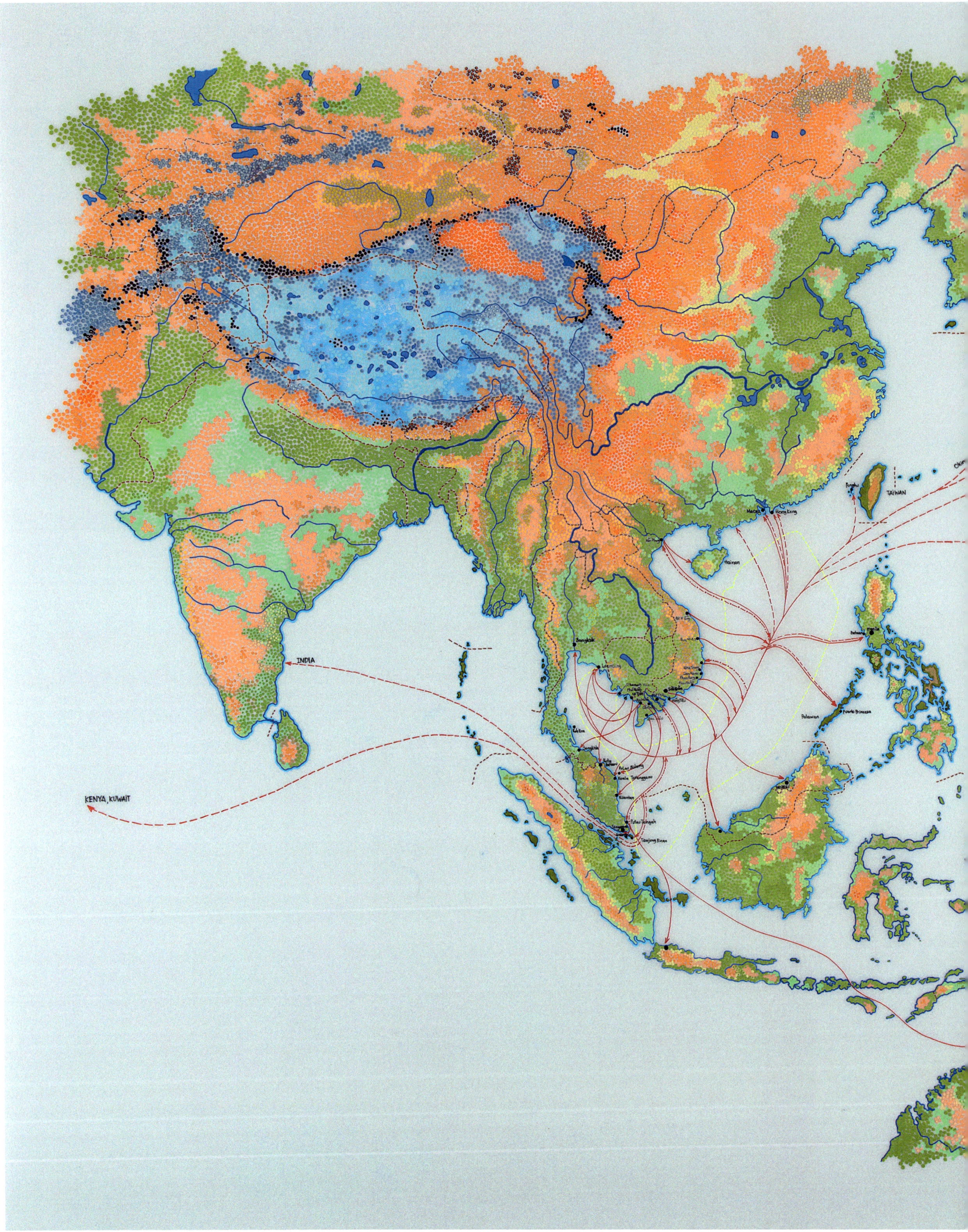
INDIA
KENYA, KUWAIT
Penghu
TAIWAN
Macau
Hong Kong
Hainan
Bangkok
Saigon
Manila
Palawan
Puerto Princesa
Songkhla
Pulau Bidong
Kuala Terengganu
Kelantan
Pulau Tengah
Tanjung Pinan
BRUNEI

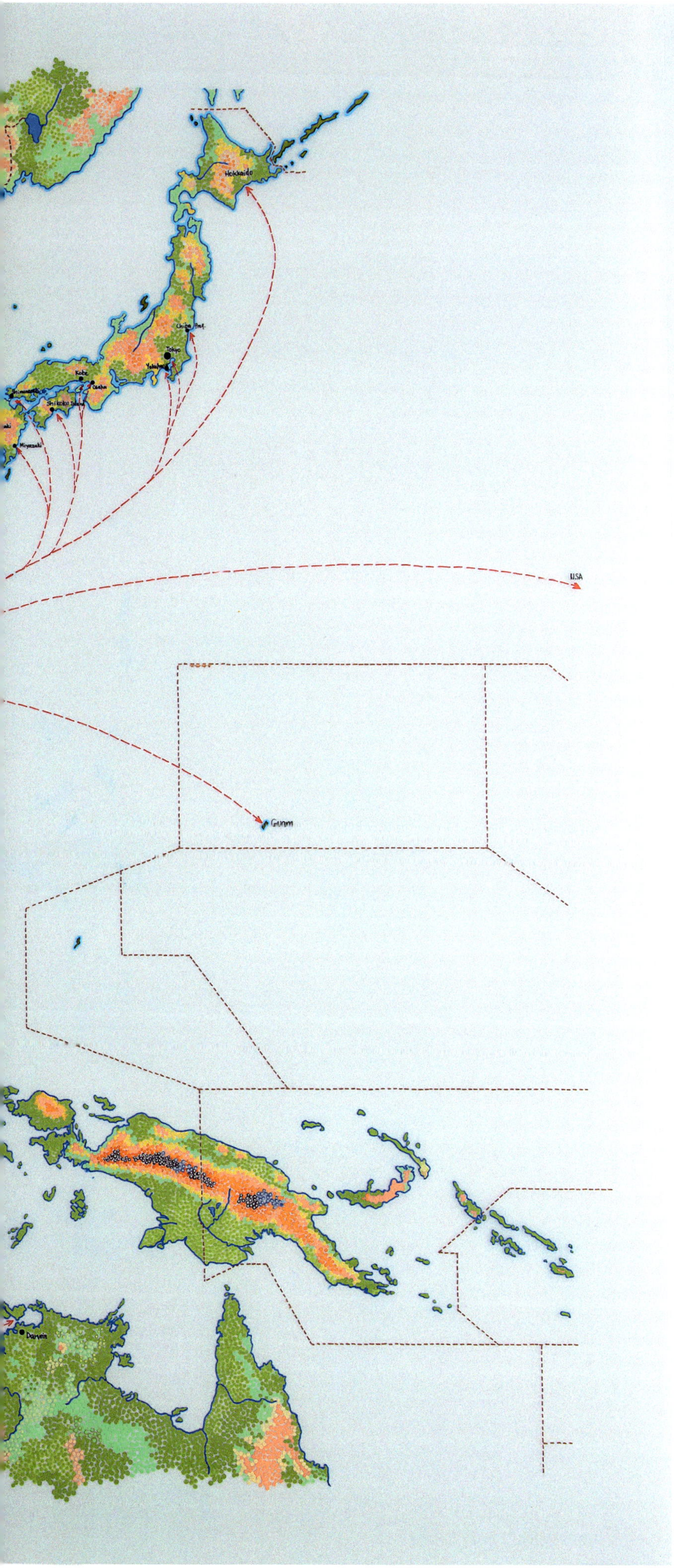

reconstructing an exodus history: boat trajectories in Asia, 2017
Acrylic, ink, and oil on drafting film
92 × 119 cm (36 ¼ × 46 ⅞ in.)

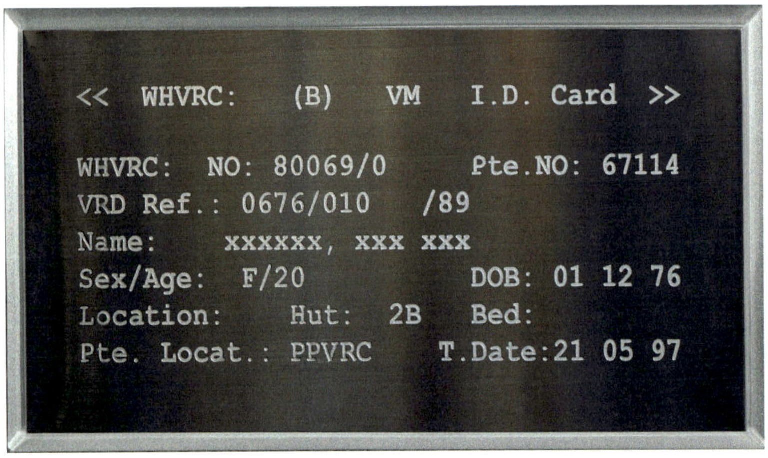

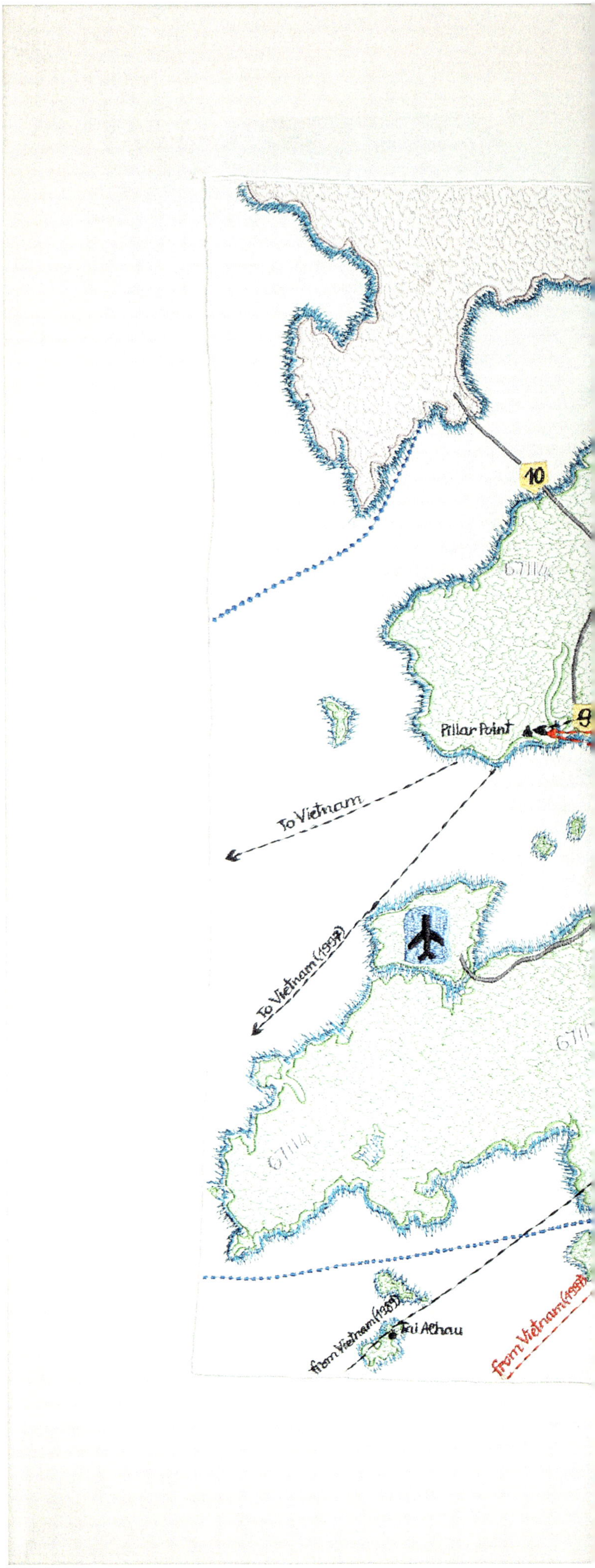

from the sea and back to the sea– the ten-year journey of a stateless, unaccompanied minor, 2016
Embroidery on canvas; etching on stainless steel plaque mounted on plexiglass
80 × 100 cm (31 ½ × 39 ⅜ in.); 20 × 34 cm (7 ⅞ × 13 ⅜ in.)

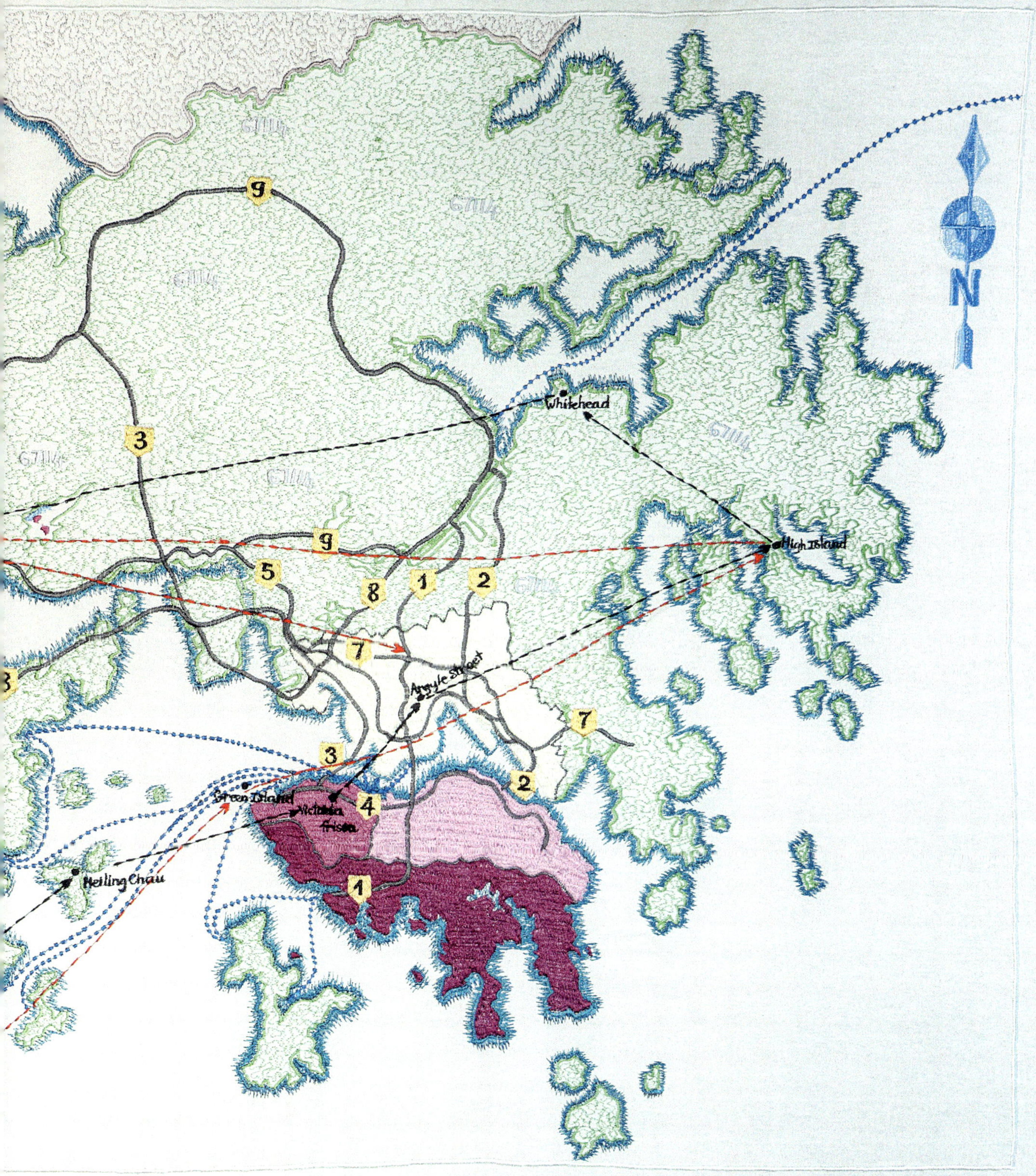
Whitehead
High Island
Argyle Street
Green Island
Hei Ling Chau

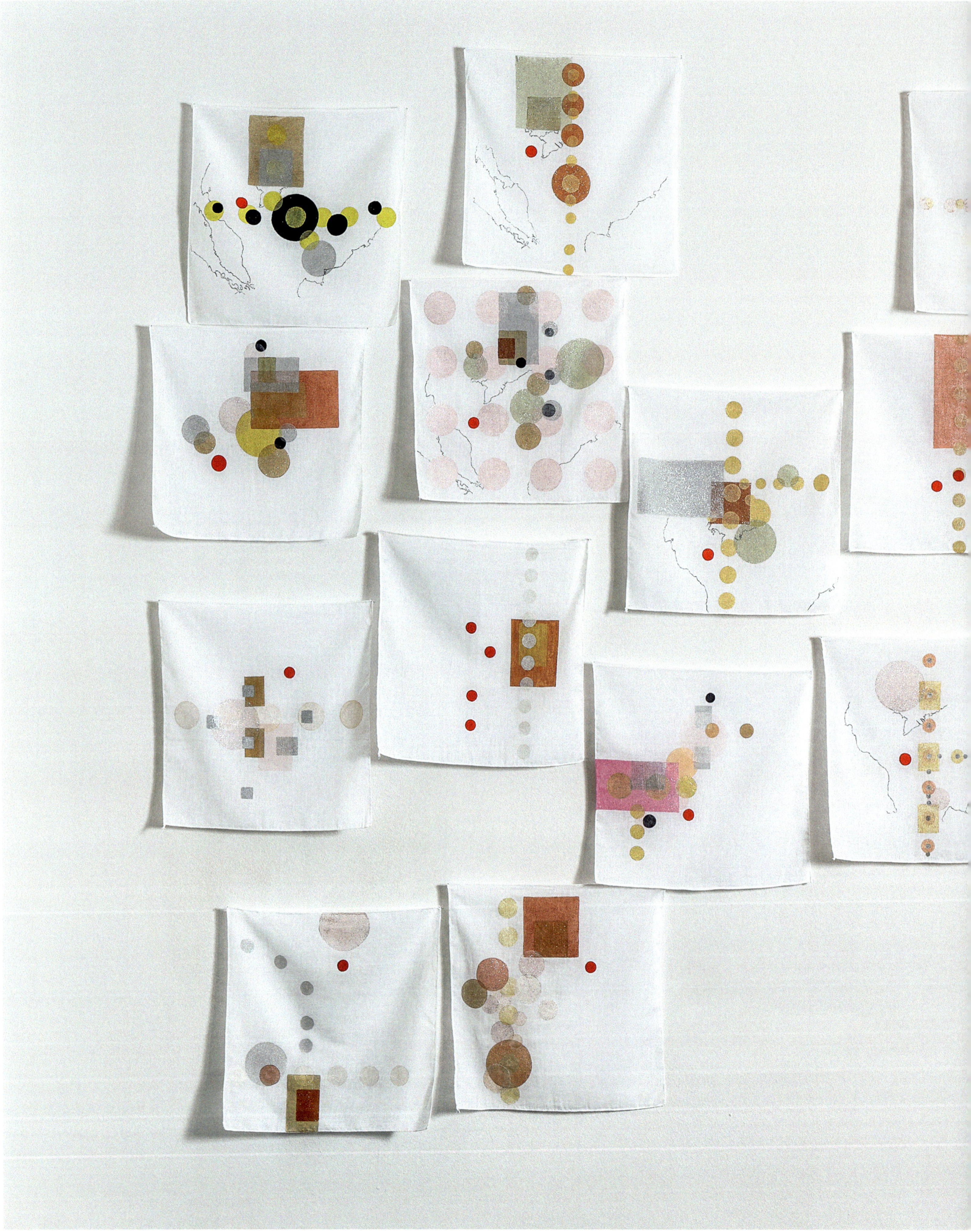

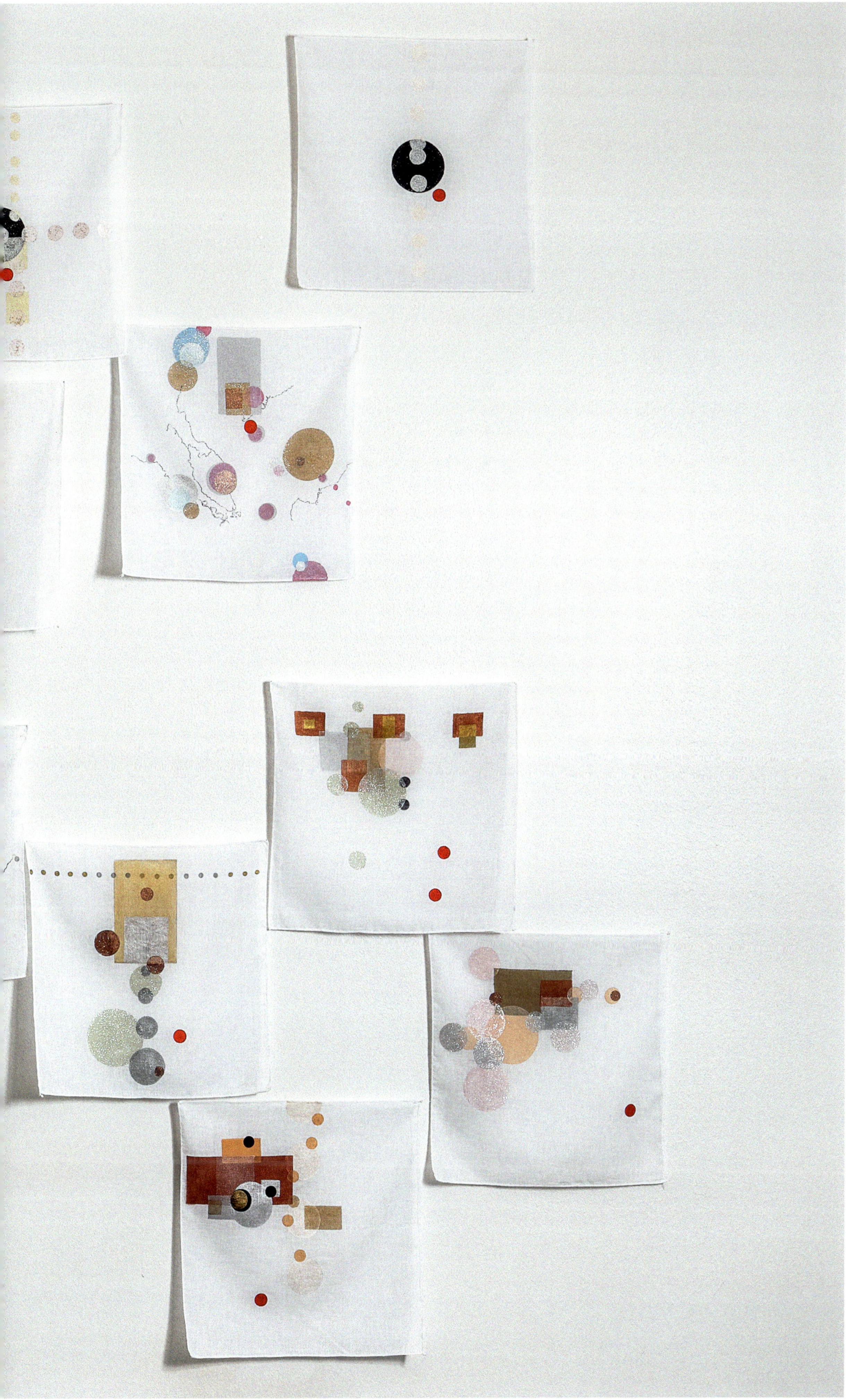

Destination Pulau Bidong, Dec 1985–June 1986, 1999/2019
Acrylic, glitter, fabric, and thread on 19 cotton handkerchiefs
39.4 × 39.4 cm
(15 ½ × 15 ½ in.) each

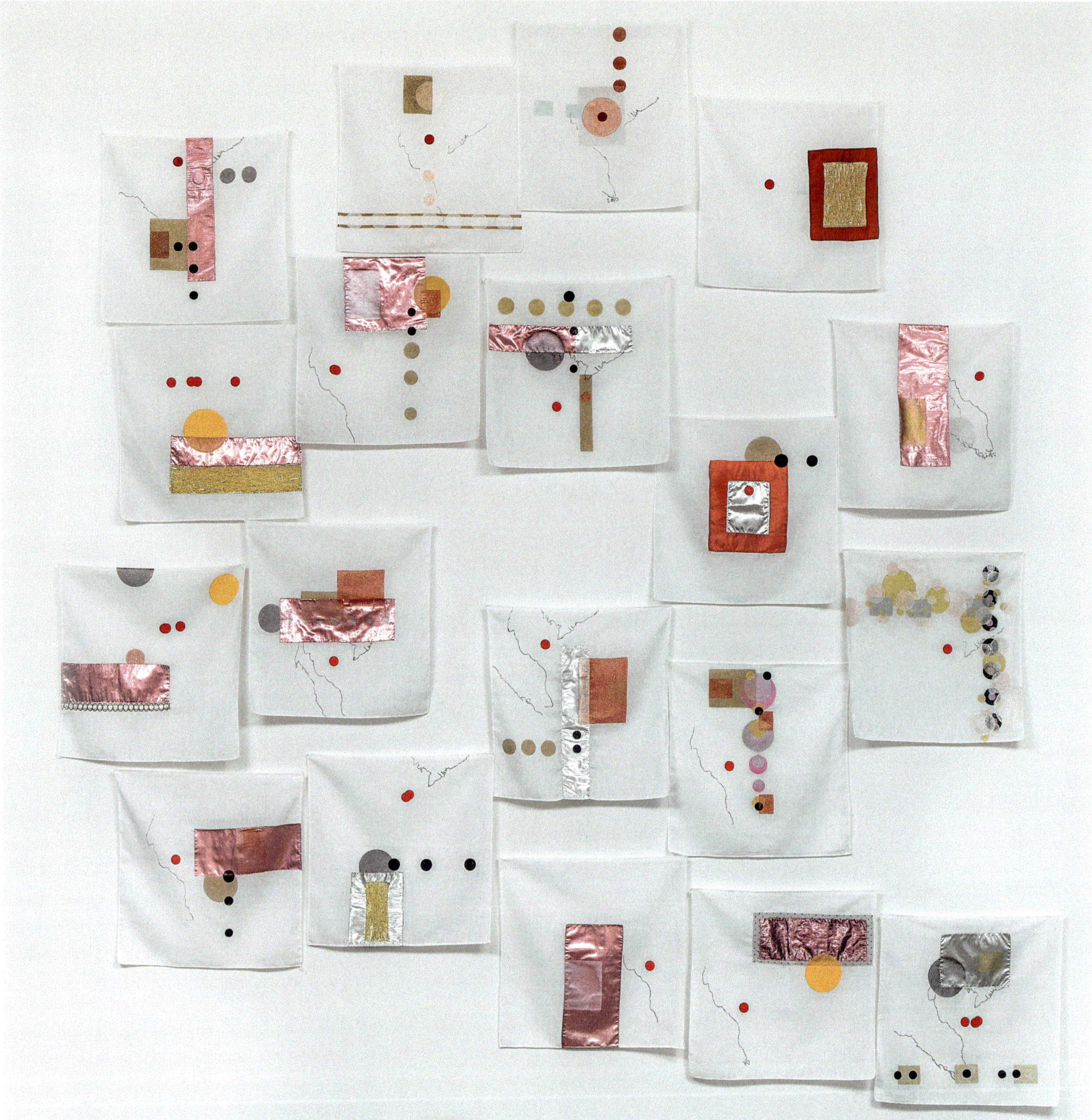

Destination Songkhla: pirate attacks in the Gulf of Thailand, Oct–Dec 1985, 1999/2019
Acrylic, glitter, and fabric on 19 cotton handkerchiefs
39.4 × 39.4 cm
(15 ½ × 15 ½ in.) each

selected cases of pirate attacks in the Gulf of Thailand, Oct 1985–June 1986, 2019
Ink and oil on vellum and paper
96.5 × 63 cm (38 × 24 ¾ in.)

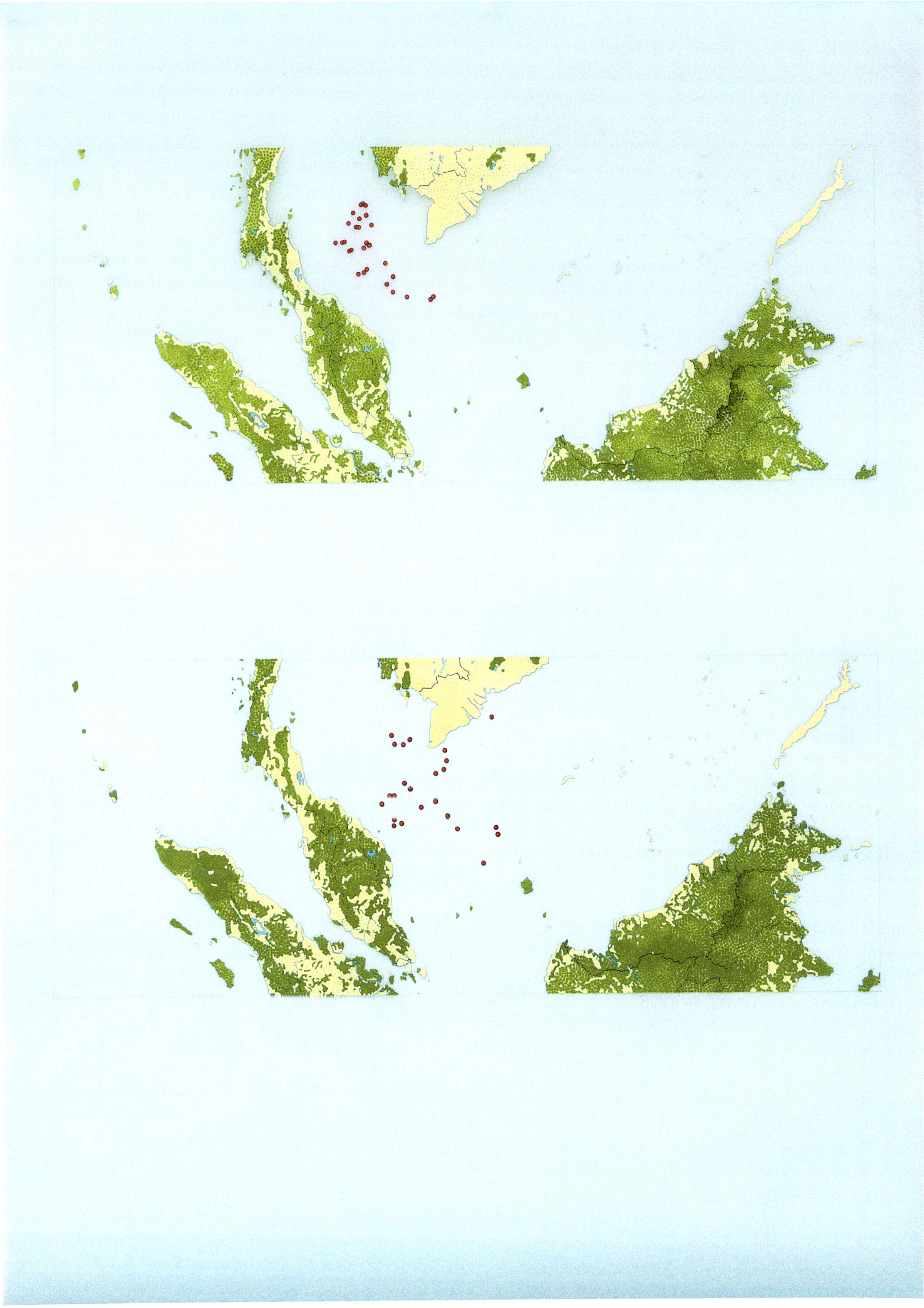

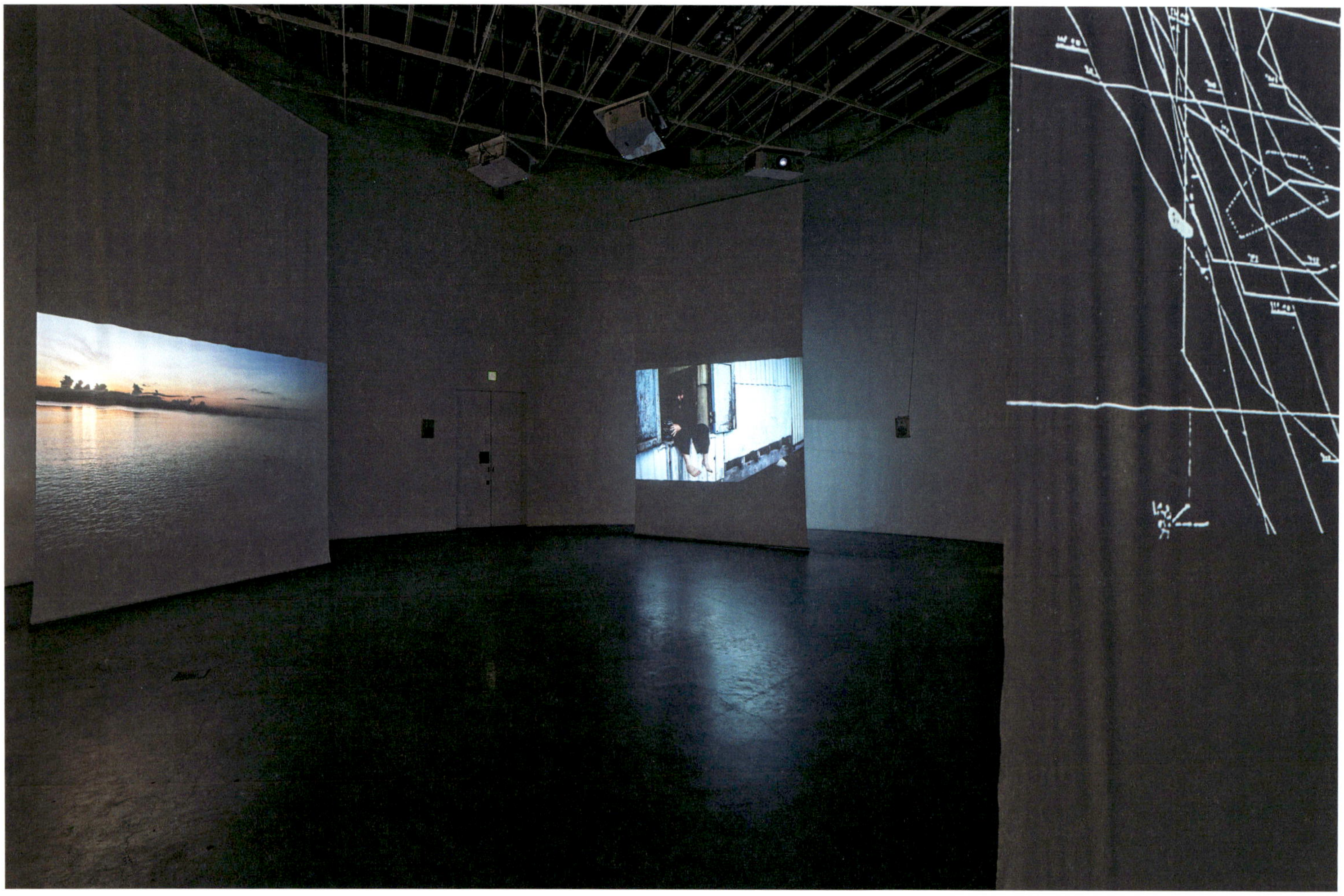

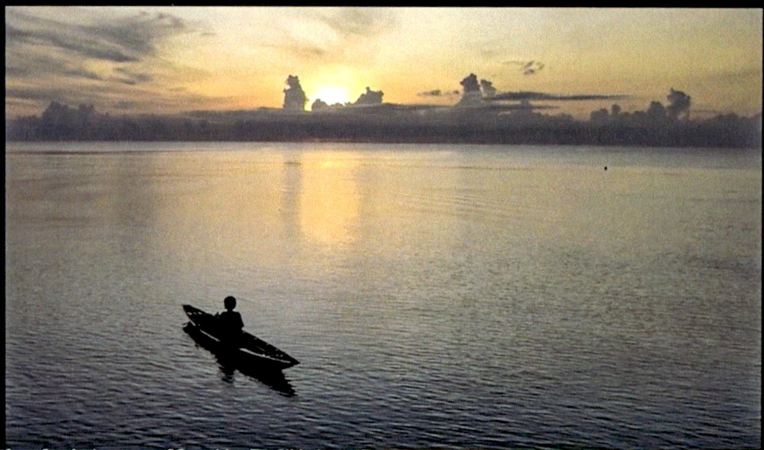

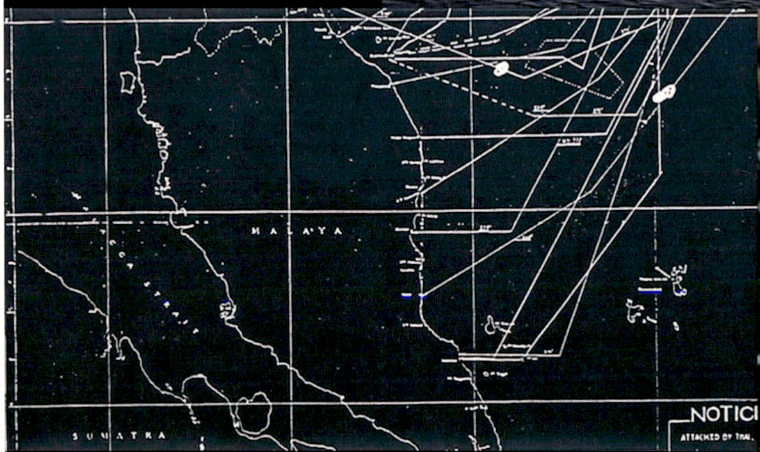
MALAYA
SUMATRA

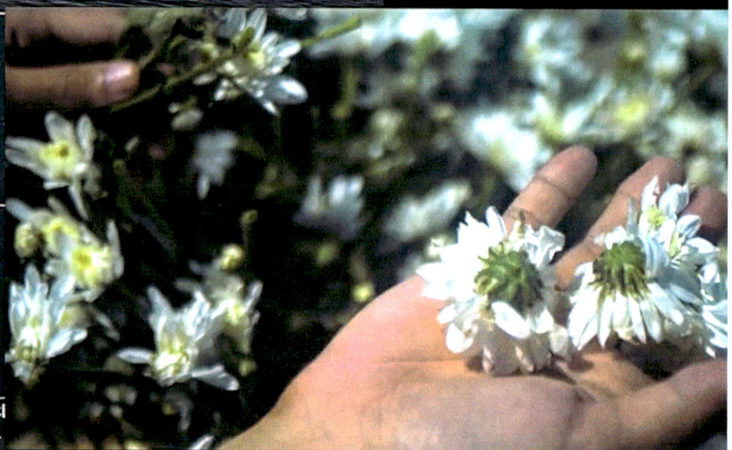

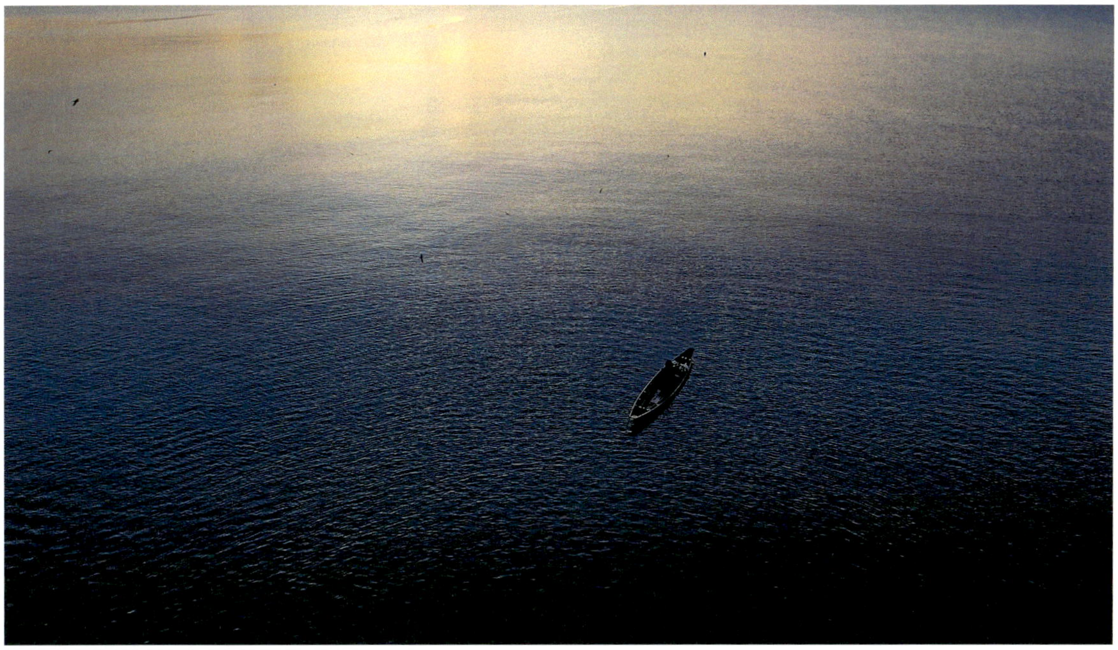

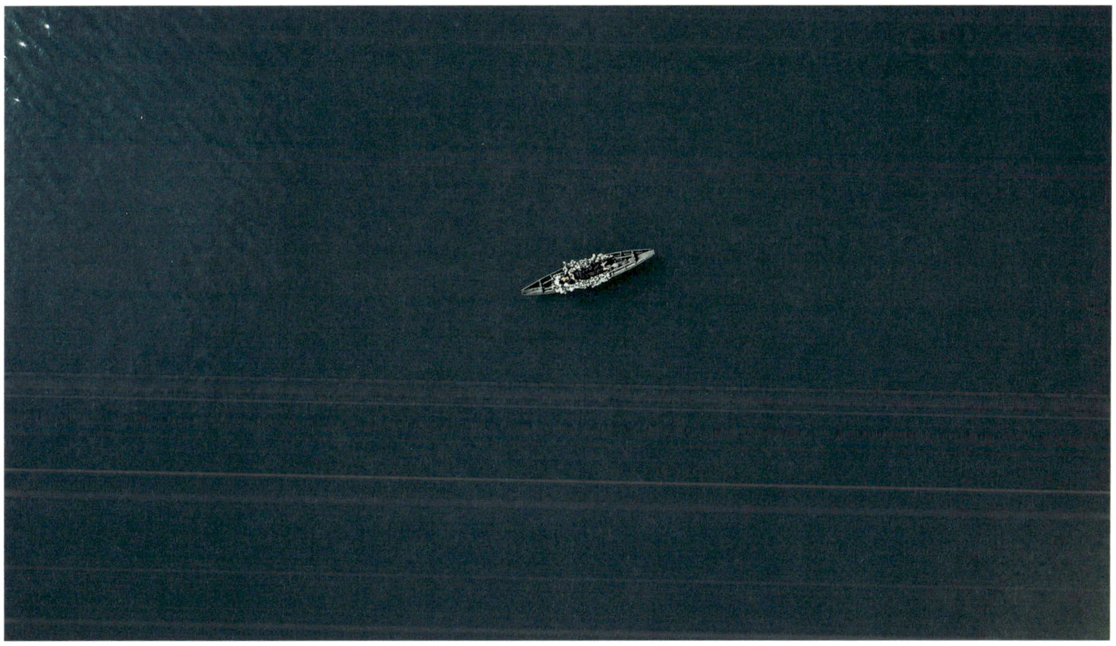

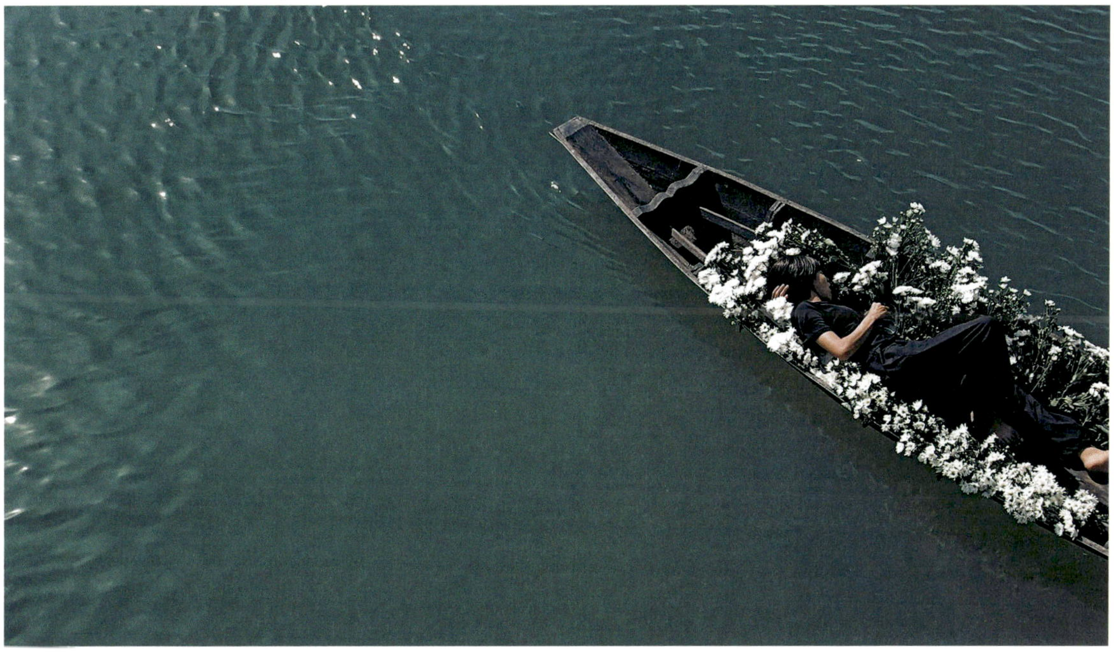

If Water Has Memories, 2022
3-channel video, HD, color,
5.1 sound, 6 minutes

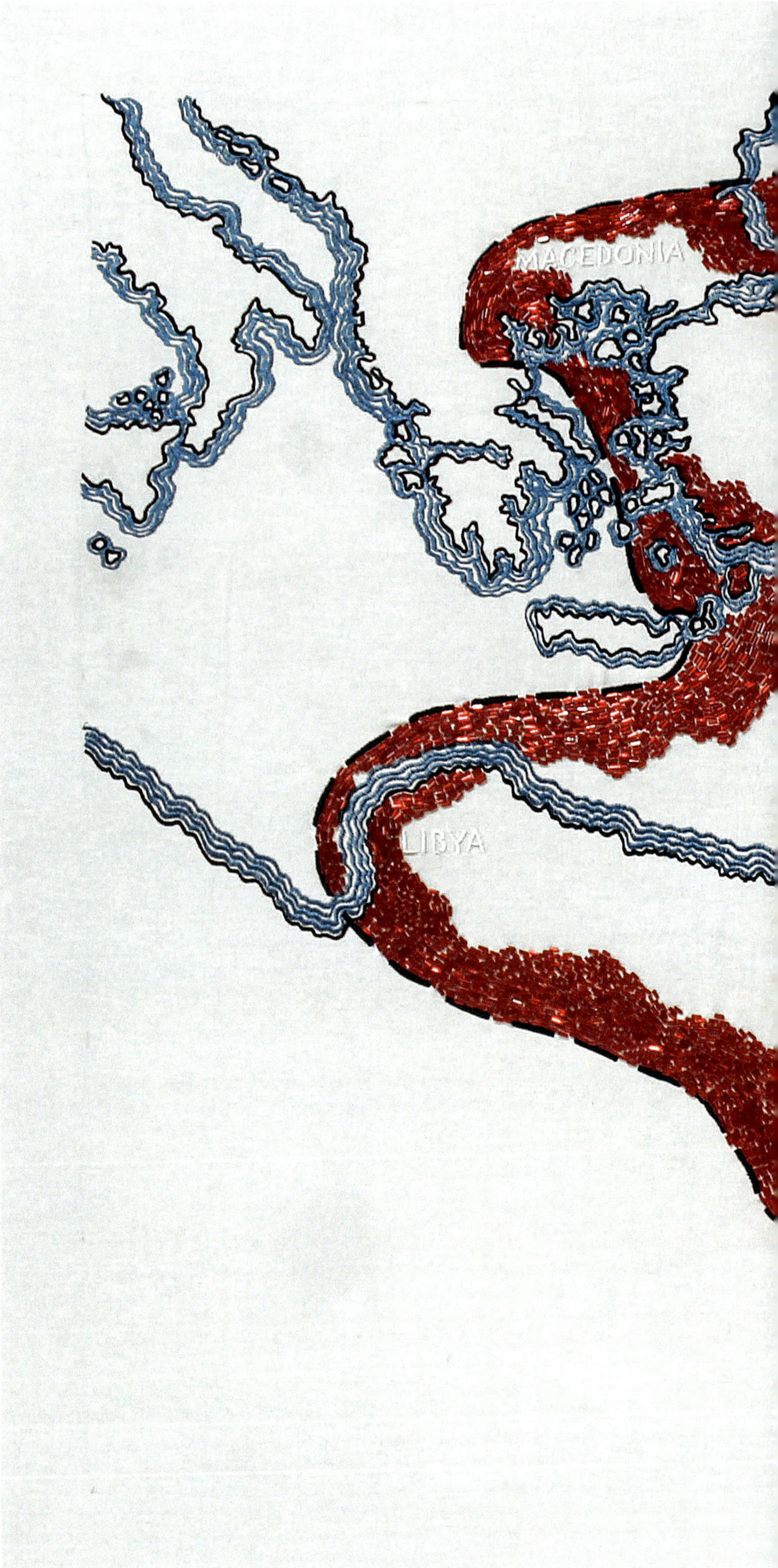

life, which you look for, you will never find–the ancient Near East, 2015
Embroidery, beads, and plastic gems on canvas
85 × 115 cm (33 ½ × 45 ¼ in.)

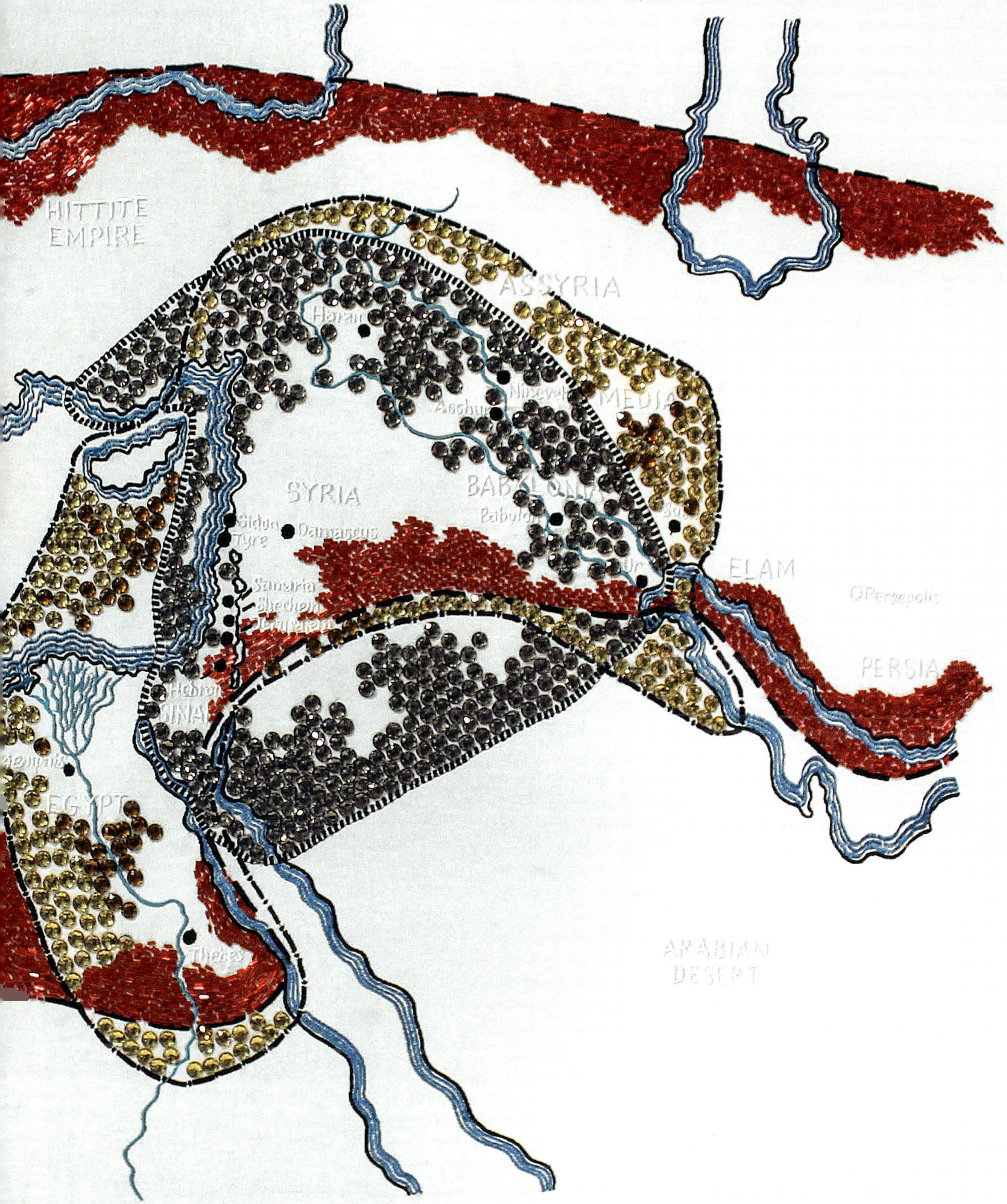
HITTITE EMPIRE
ASSYRIA
Haran
MEDIA
Asshur
SYRIA
Sidon
Tyre
Damascus
Samaria
Shechem
Hebron
ELAM
Persepolis
PERSIA
EGYPT
Thebes
ARABIAN DESERT

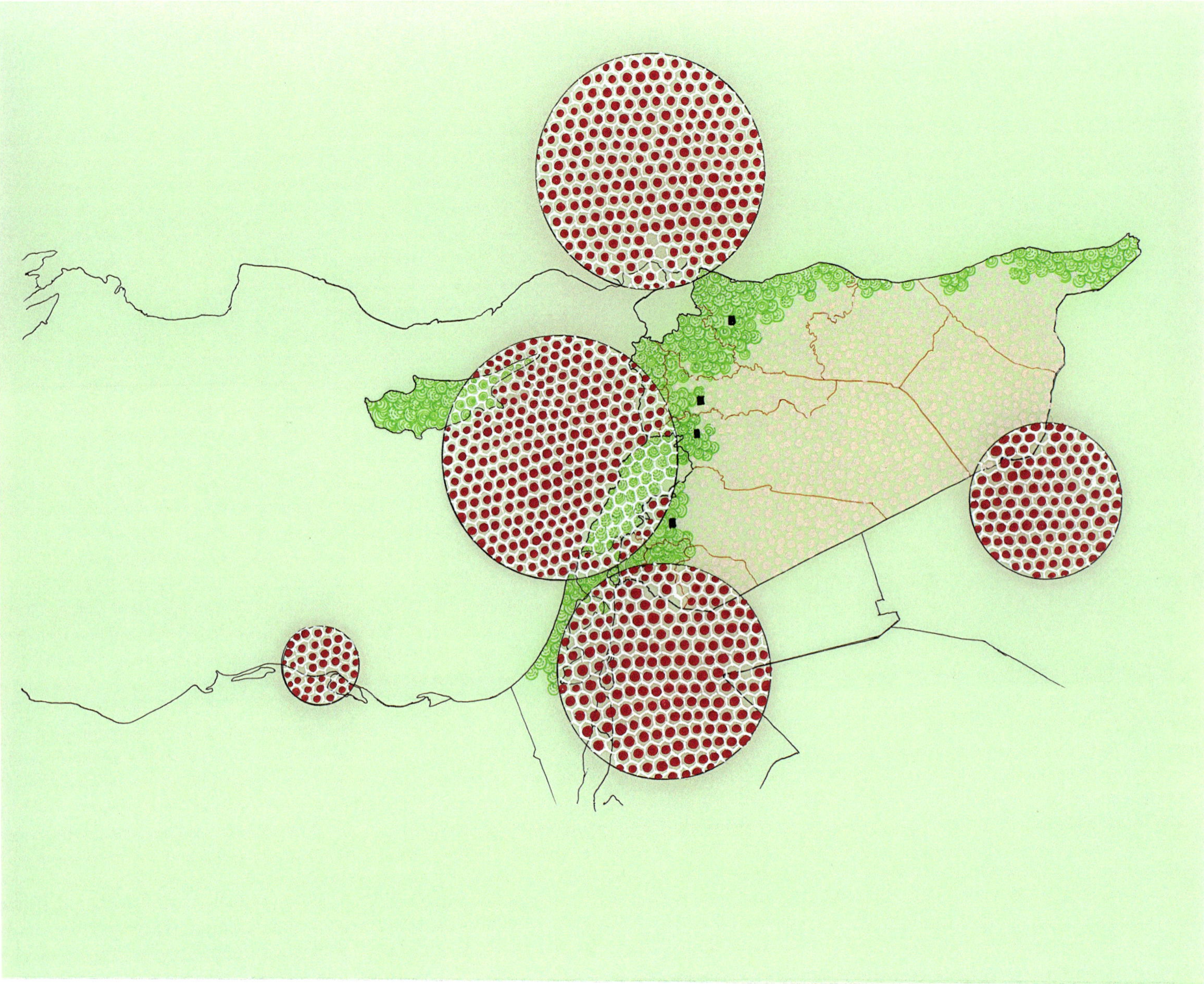

UNHCR/HIU/IDMC: Syria Crisis Displacement–686,851 refugees, camps and conflict areas, January 2013, 2015
Ink and oil on vellum and paper
36 × 29.8 cm (14 ⅜ × 11 ⅞ in.)

UNHCR Regional Data Analysis Group: 857,712 Syrian Refugees, February 2013, 2015
Ink and oil on vellum and paper
27 × 28 cm (10 ¼ × 11 ¼ in.)

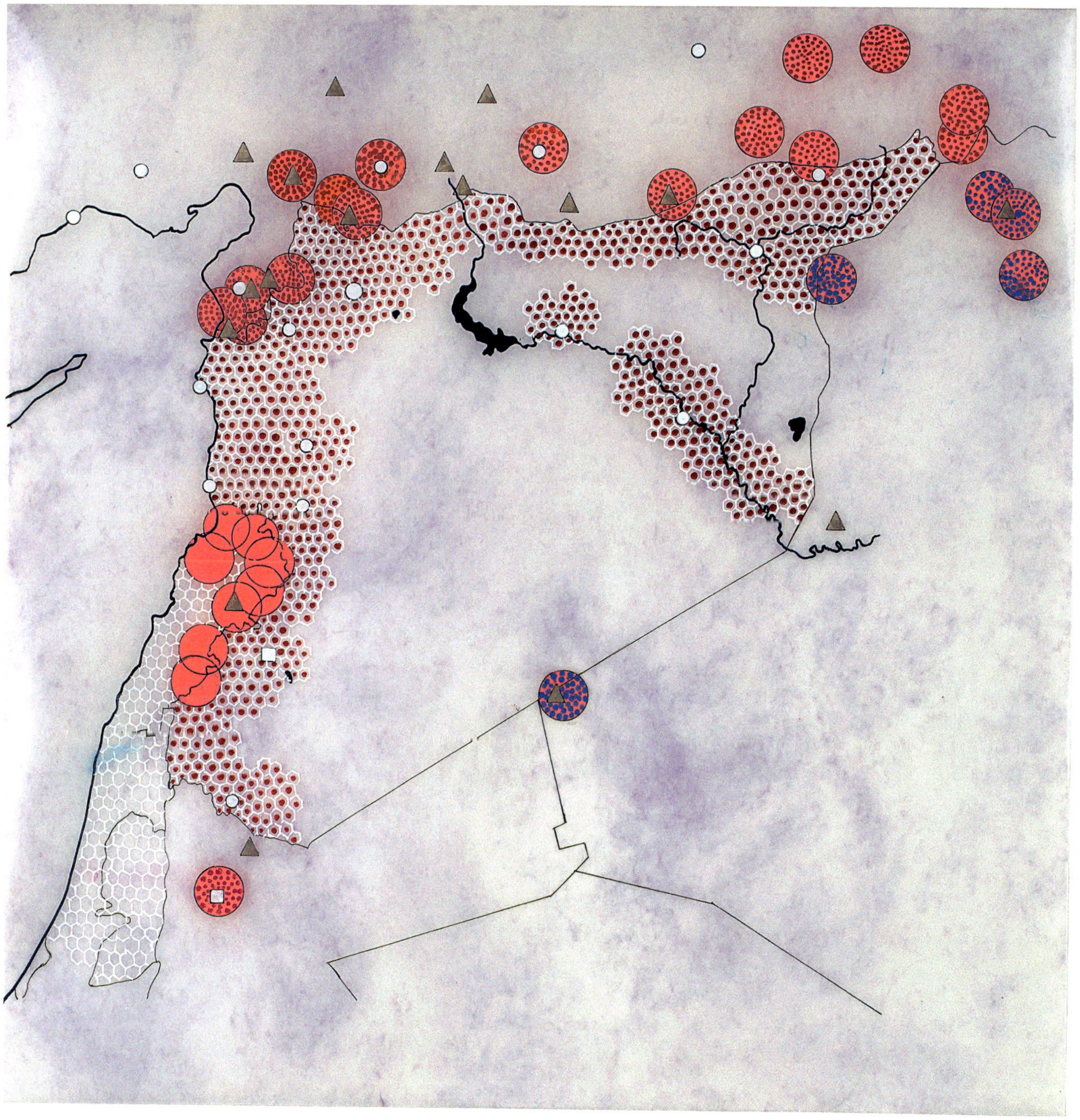

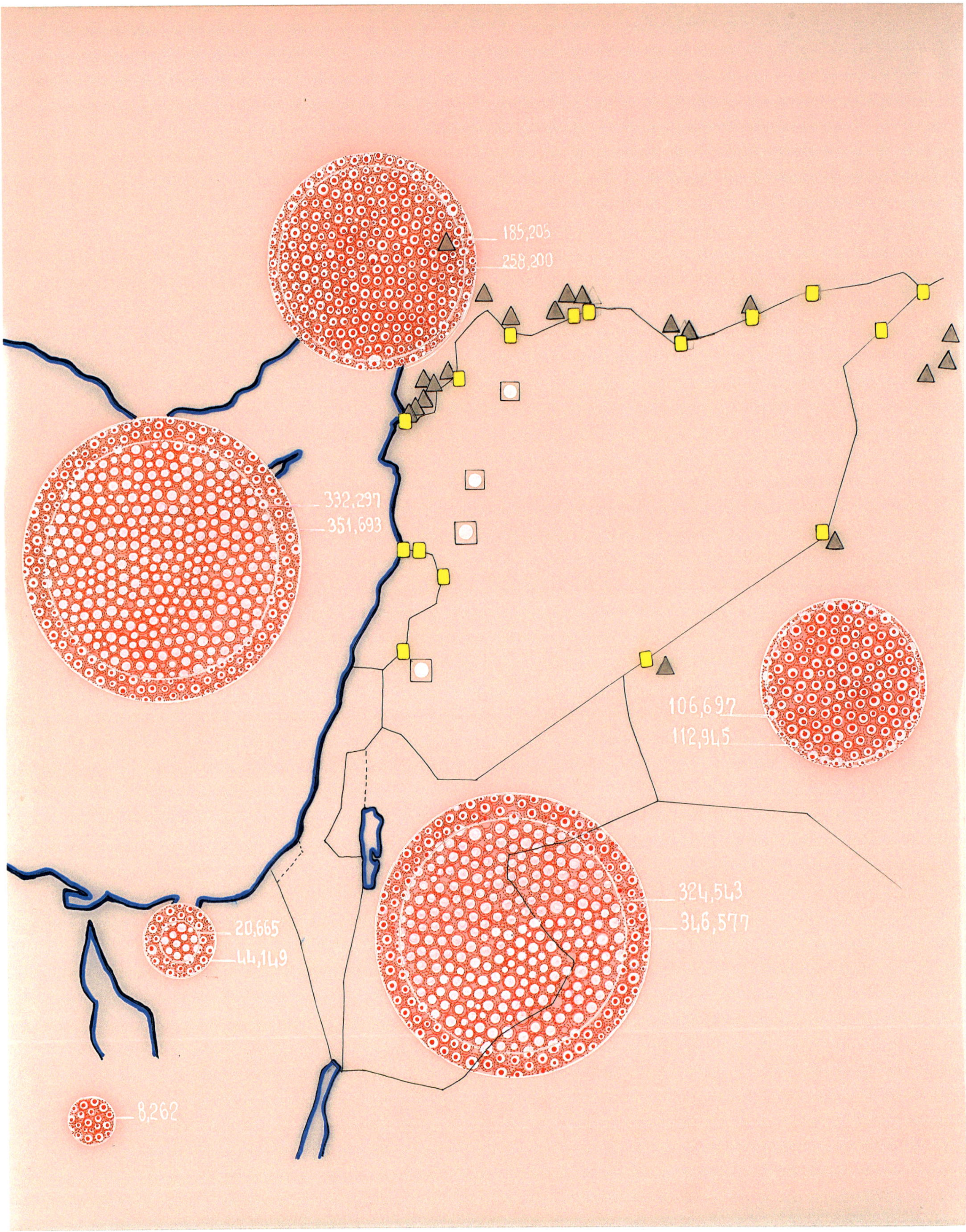
185,205
258,200
332,297
351,693
106,697
112,945
324,543
346,577
20,665
44,149
8,262

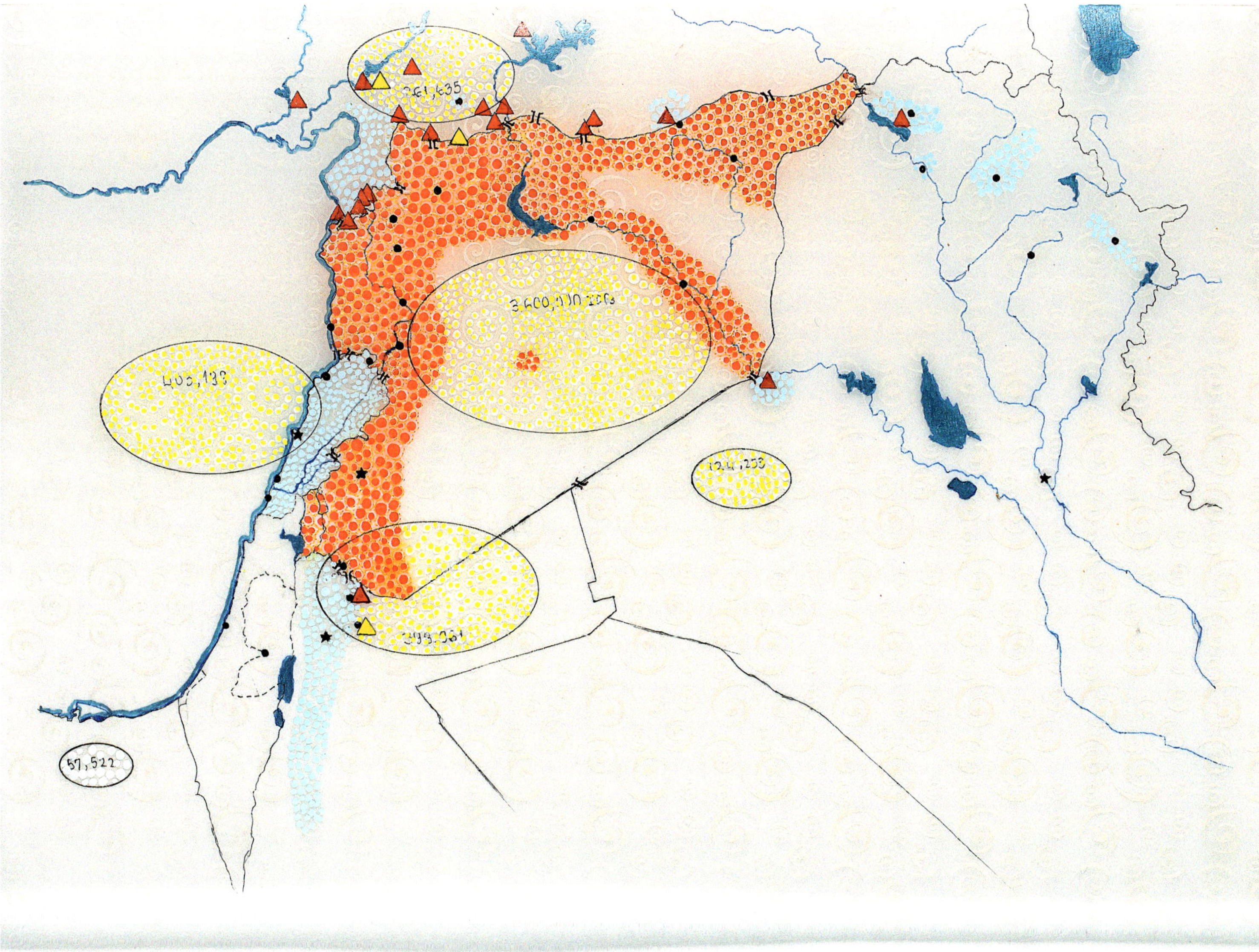

UNHCR/Guardians/Your Middle East: over 1 million Syrian refugees, camps and border crossings, March 2013, 2015
Ink and oil on vellum and paper
42 × 29.8 cm (16 ½ × 11 ⅞ in.)

HIU: 1,245,570 Syrian Refugees, 3.6 million IDPs, April 2013, 2015
Ink and oil on vellum and paper
21 × 28 cm (8 ⅜ × 11 ¼ in.)

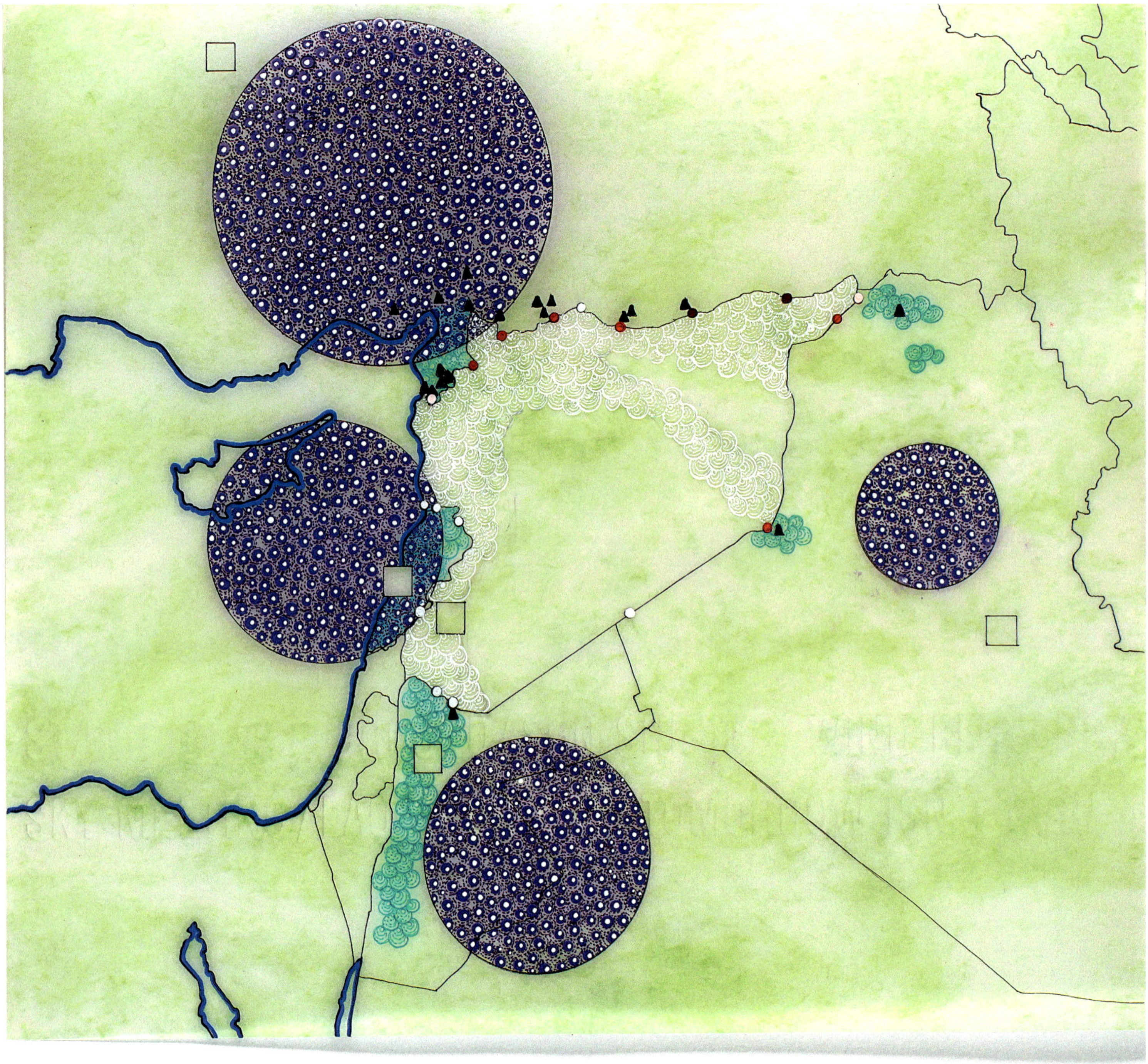

UNHCR/VOA/HIU:
1.5 million have fled Syria,
May 2013, 2015
Ink and oil on vellum and paper
30 × 29.8 cm (11 ⅞ × 11 in.)

UNHCR/HIU: Syria
Regional Crisis 1,658,177
camp and non-camp
refugees, June 2013, 2015
Ink, oil, and embossing on paper
42 × 29.8 cm (16 ½ × 11 ¾ in.)

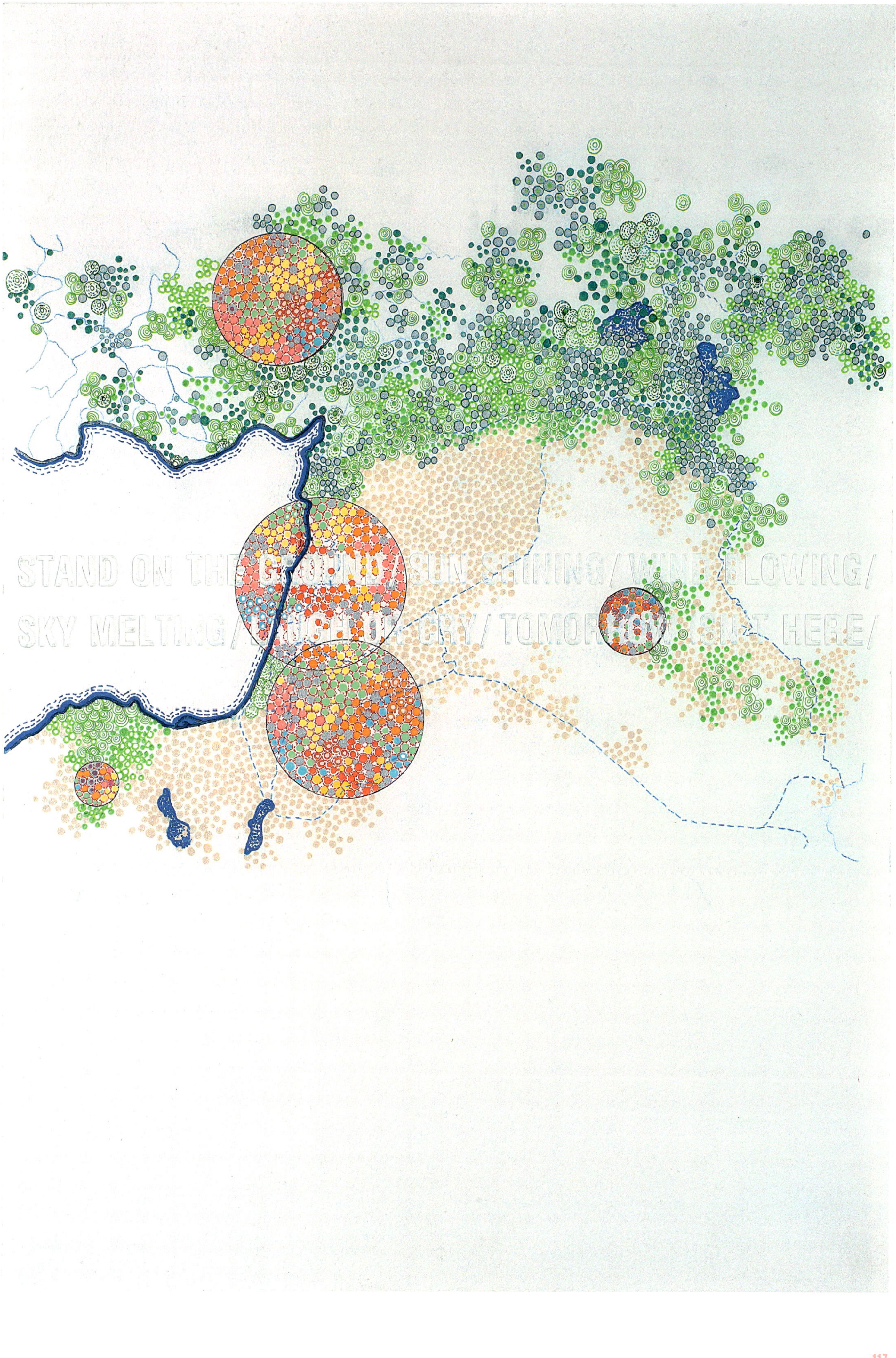
STAND ON THE GROUND/SUN SHINING/WIND BLOWING/
SKY MELTING/LAUGH OR CRY/TOMORROW ISN'T HERE/

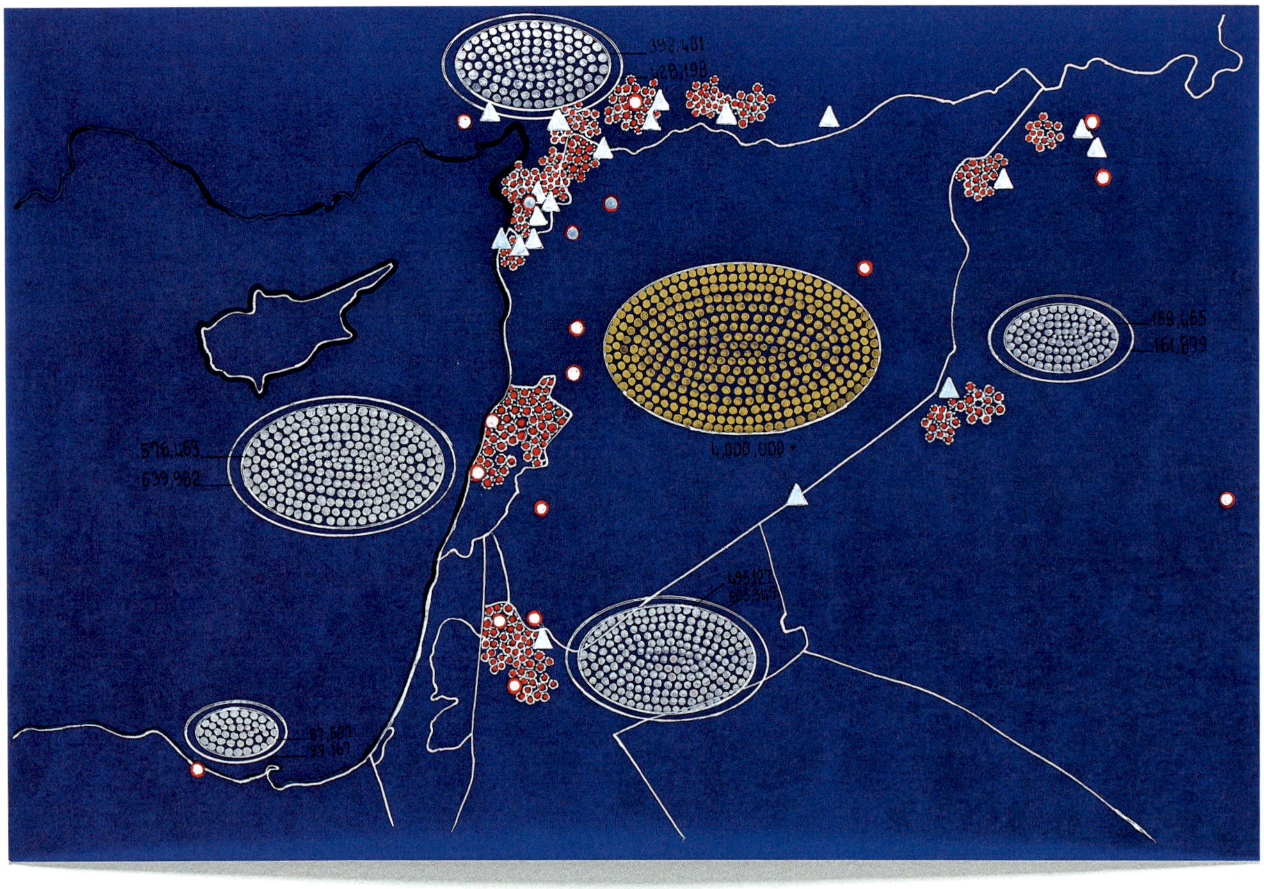
392,481
428,198
159,465
161,839
576,463
639,982
4,000,000+

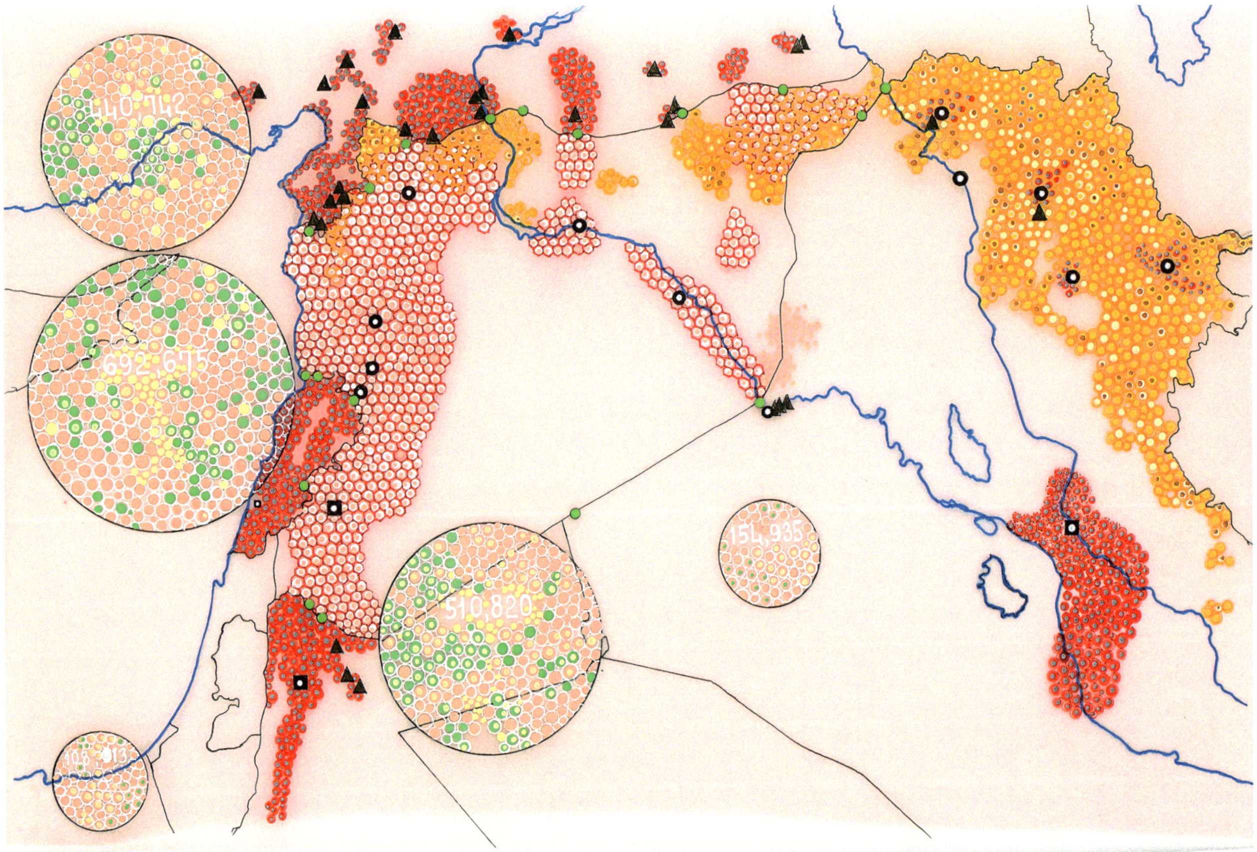
440,742
692,675
510,820
154,935

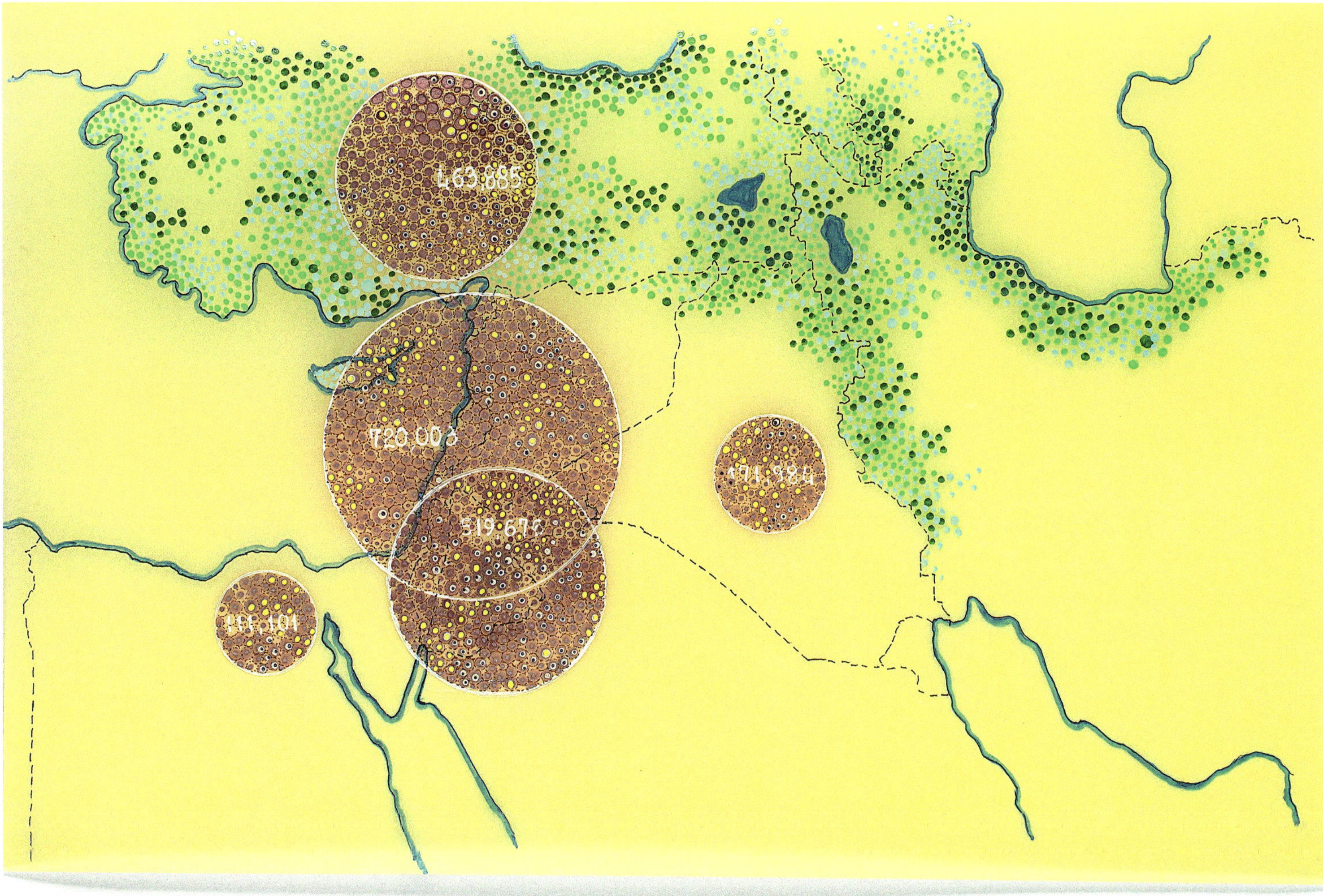

Focus on Syria: The humanitarian crisis, July 2013, 2015
Ink and oil on vellum and paper
21 × 30 cm (8 ⅜ × 11 ⅞ in.)

UNHCR/REUTERS: Syrian Refugee Crisis–1.9 million refugees in the region, August 2013, 2015
Ink and oil on vellum and paper
24 × 30 cm (9 ½ × 11 ⅞ in.)

UNHCR/WSJ: 4.25 million IDPs, 2 million Syrian Refugees–September 2013, 2015
Ink and oil on vellum and paper
21 × 30 cm (8 ⅜ × 11 ⅞ in.)

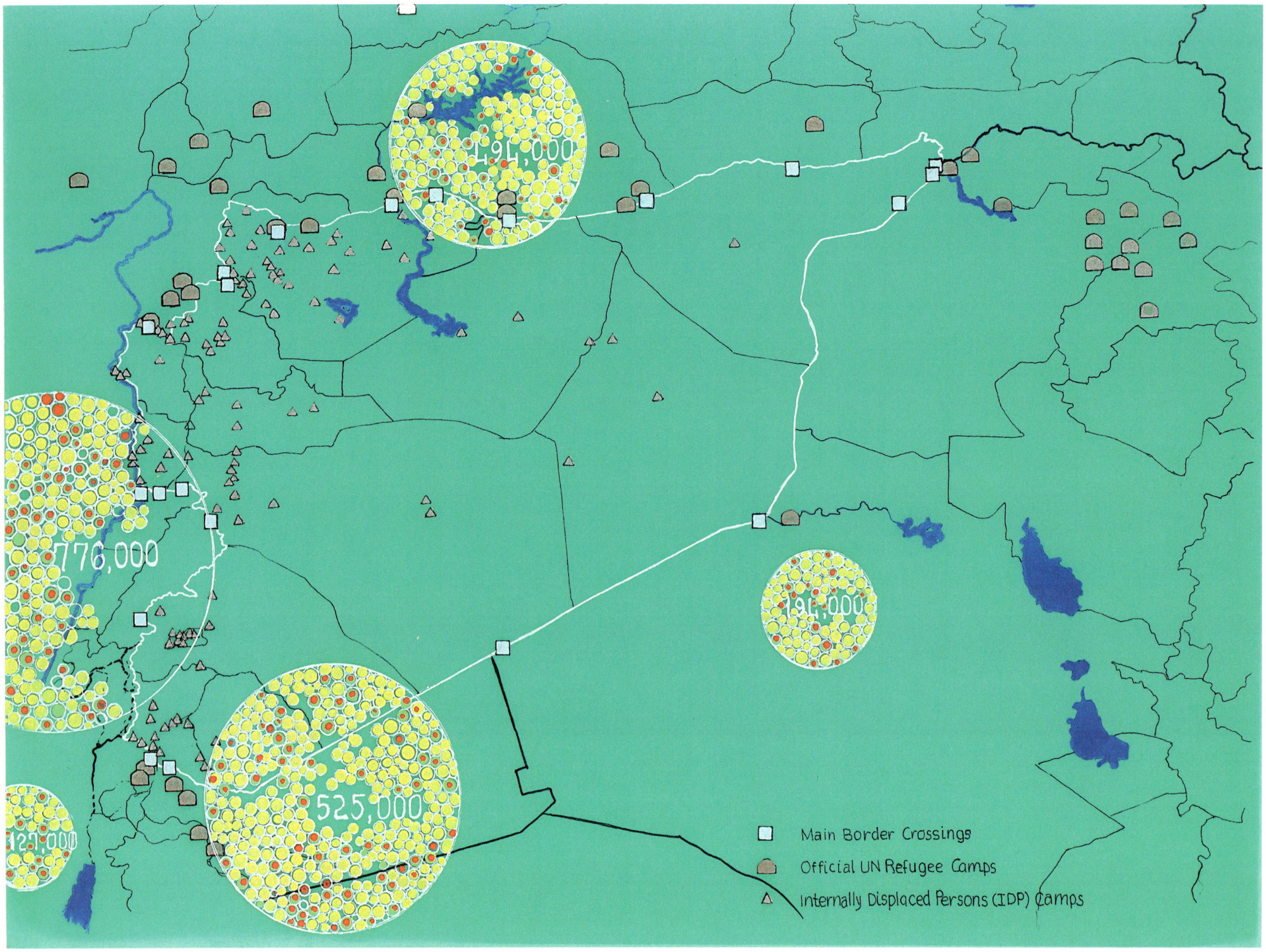

UNHCR/HIU/MERCY CORPS/OREGONIAN: Syrian Displacement–camps, refugees and IDPs, October 2013, 2015
Ink and oil on vellum and paper
21 × 29.8 cm (8 ³⁄₈ × 11 ⁷⁄₈ in.)

Syria Tracker: 92,120 Documented Killings in Syria, 18 March 2011–31 December 2013, 2015
Ink and oil on vellum and paper
21 × 30 cm (8 ³⁄₈ × 11 ⁷⁄₈ in.)

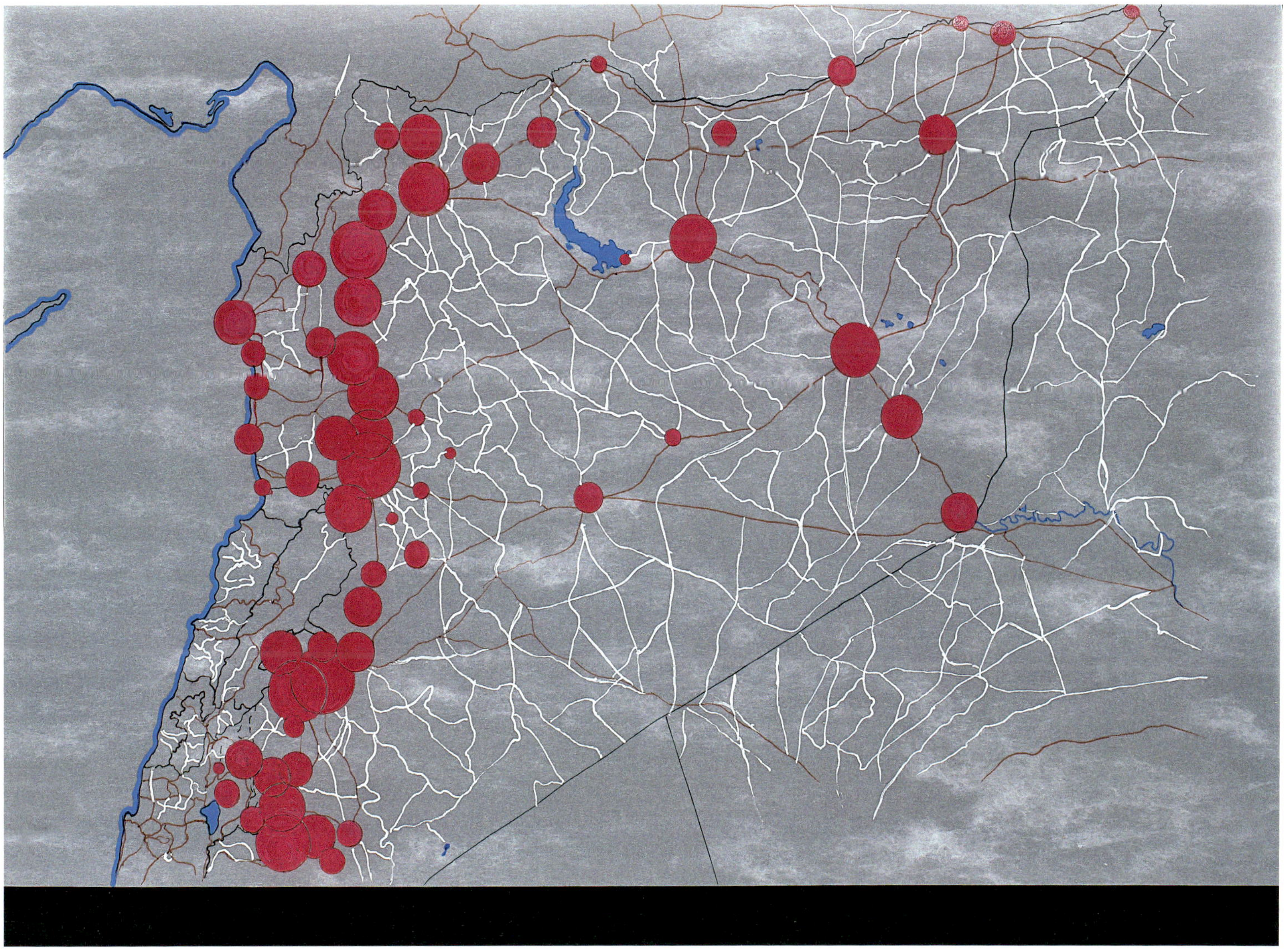

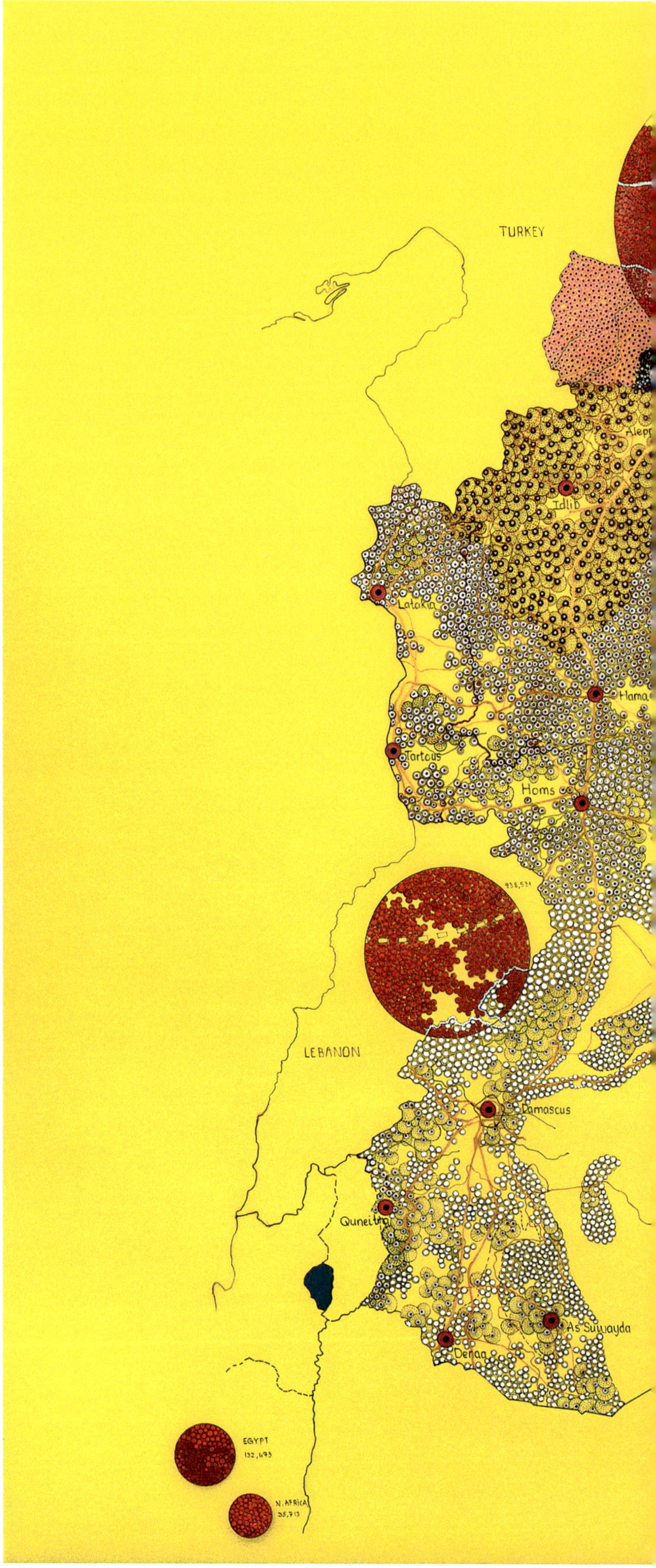

ISW: areas of control; UNHCR: numbers and locations of Syrian refugees and IDPs as of April 2019, 2019
Acrylic, ink, and oil on vellum and paper
76 × 93 cm (30 × 37 in.)

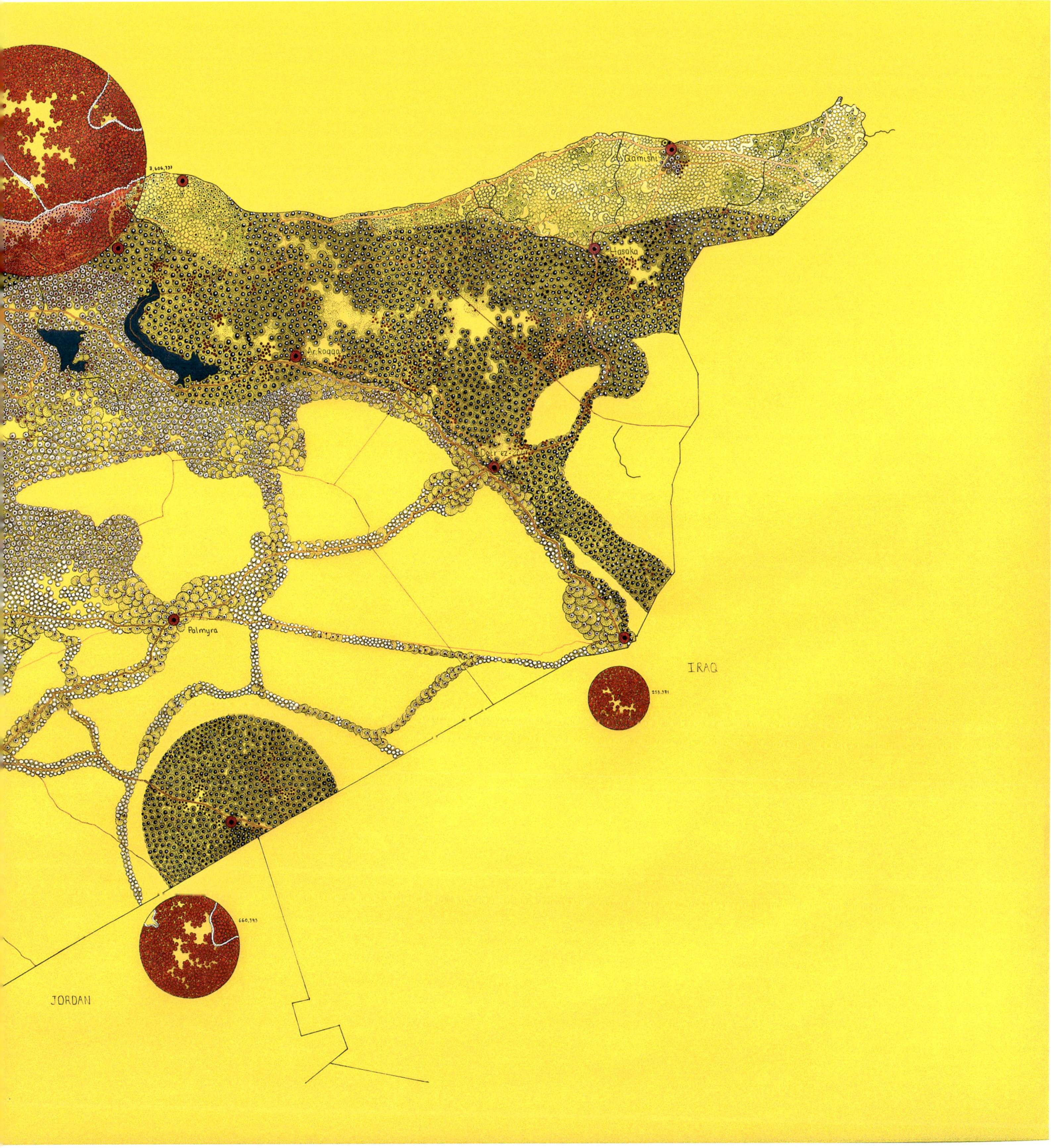
3,606,737
Qamishli
Hasaka
Ar Raqqa
Deir ez-Zour
Palmyra
IRAQ
253,371
660,393
JORDAN

Dignity Revolution, 2014–2020
Oil and hand perforating on
vellum and paper
76 × 52.5 cm (30 × 20 ⅝ in.)

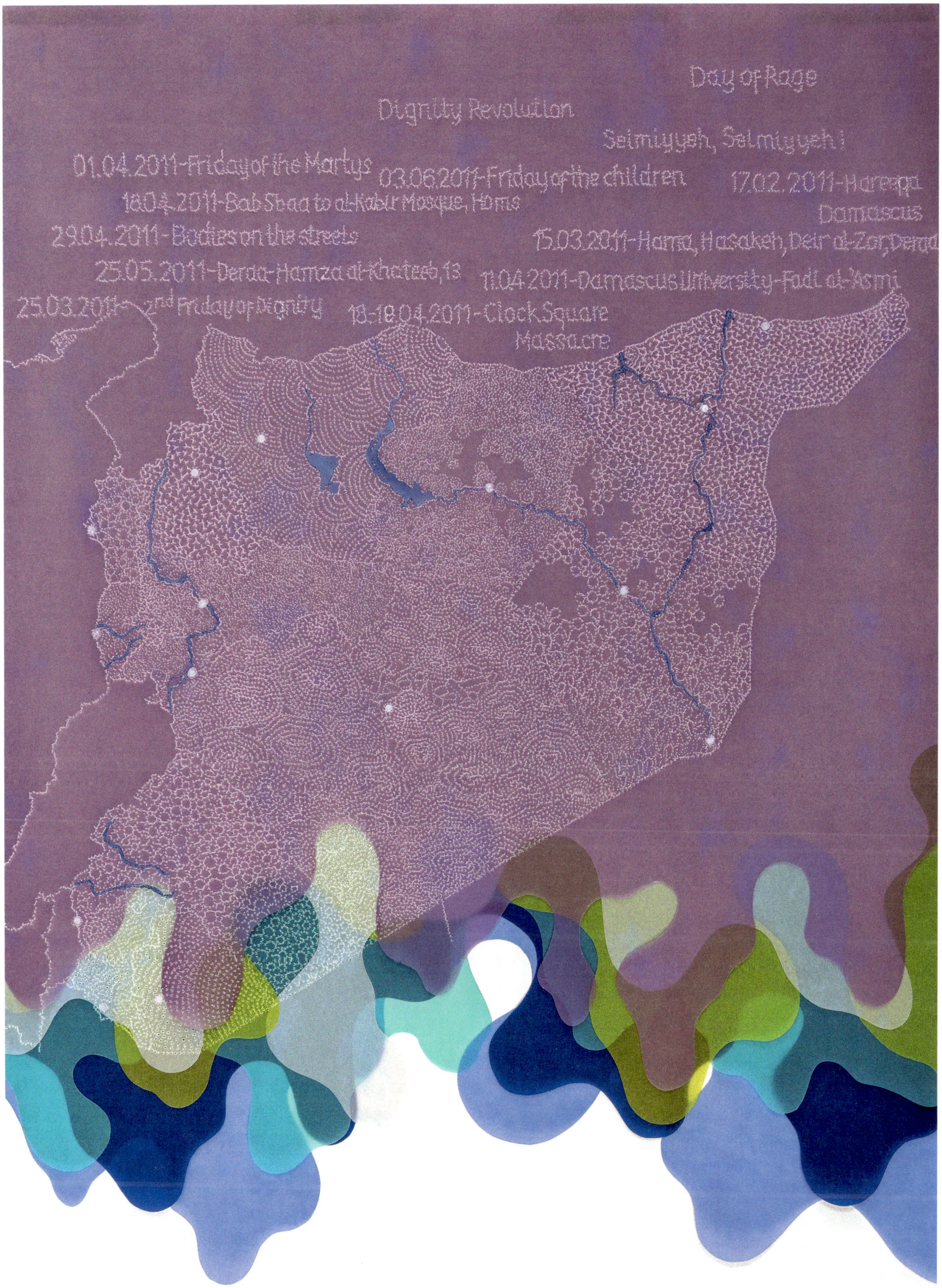
Day of Rage
Dignity Revolution
Selmiyyeh, Selmiyyeh!
01.04.2011-Friday of the Martys
03.06.2011-Friday of the children
17.02.2011-Hareeqa
18.04.2011-Bab Sbaa to al-Kabir Mosque, Homs
Damascus
29.04.2011-Bodies on the streets
15.03.2011-Hama, Hasakeh, Deir al-Zor, Deraa
25.05.2011-Deraa-Hamza al-Khateeb, 13
11.04.2011-Damascus University-Fadi al-'Asmi
25.03.2011-2nd Friday of Dignity
18-18.04.2011-Clock Square
Massacre

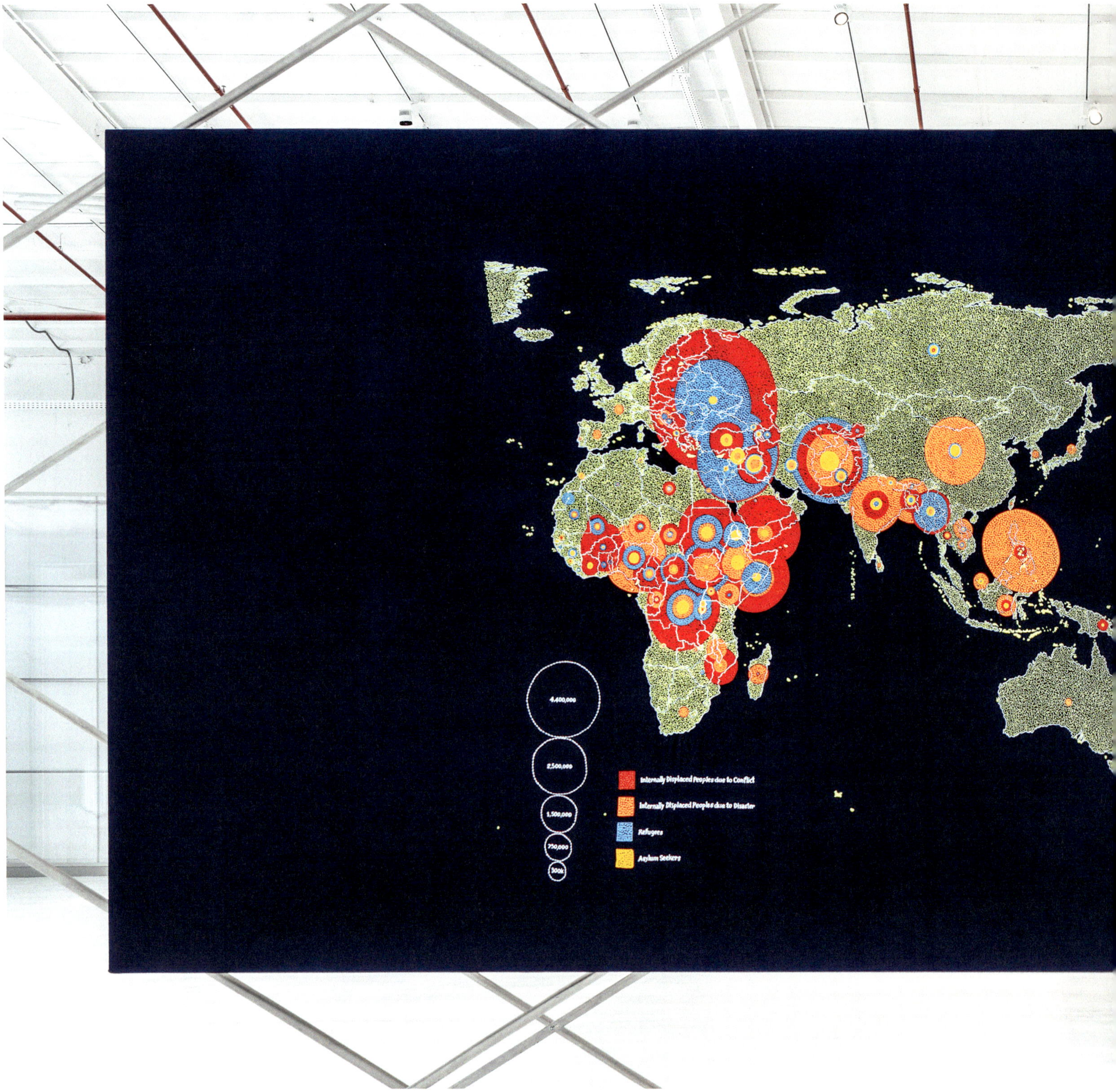

Mapping Global Displacement and Migration: nexus dynamics between conflict & violence and climate disaster [UNHCR, IDMC, EM-DAT: cross-border refugees, asylum-seekers, IDPs, and those affected in selected cases >2022<], 2023
Embroidery on fabric
140 × 350 cm (55 × 137 ¾ in.)

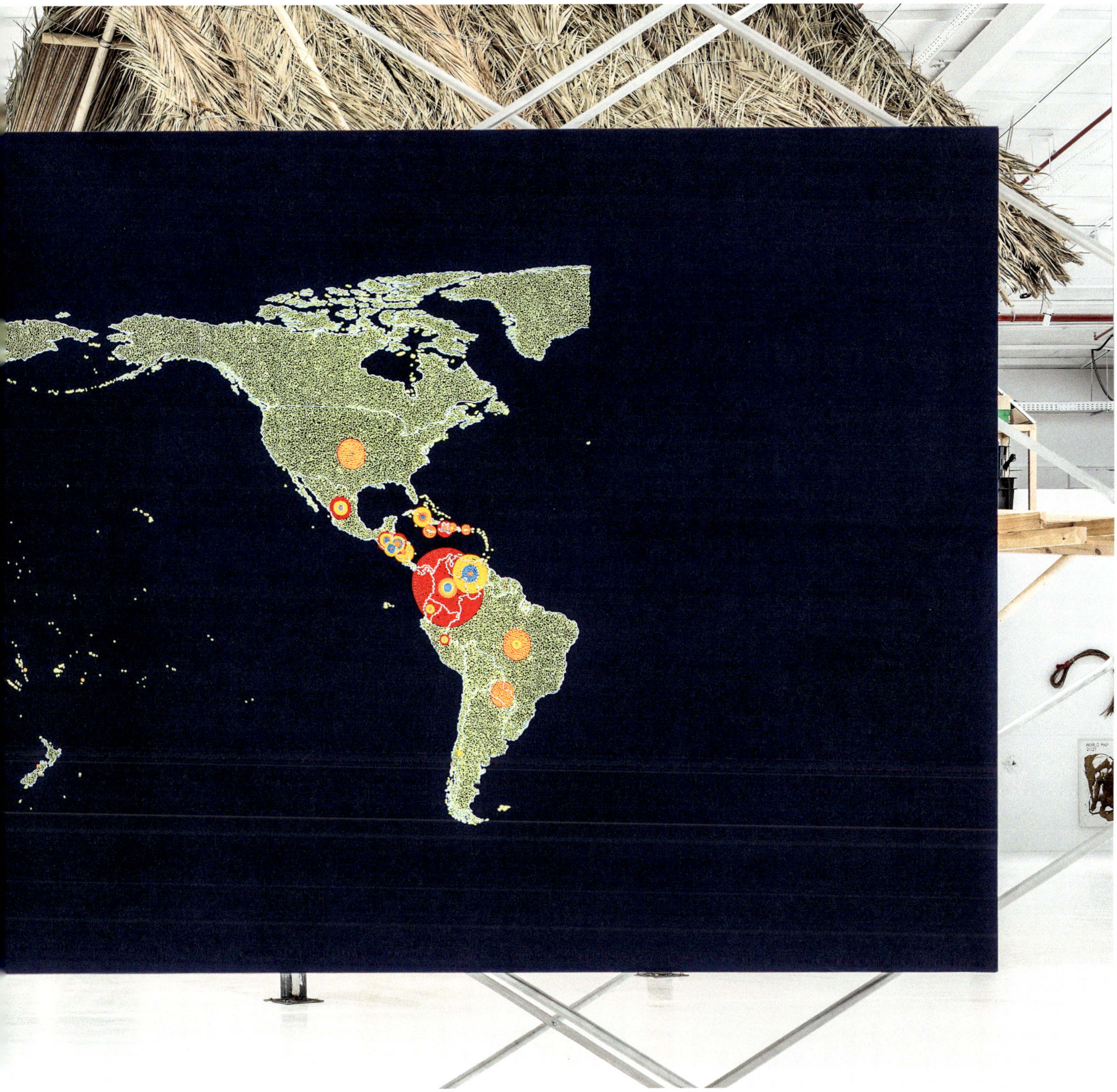

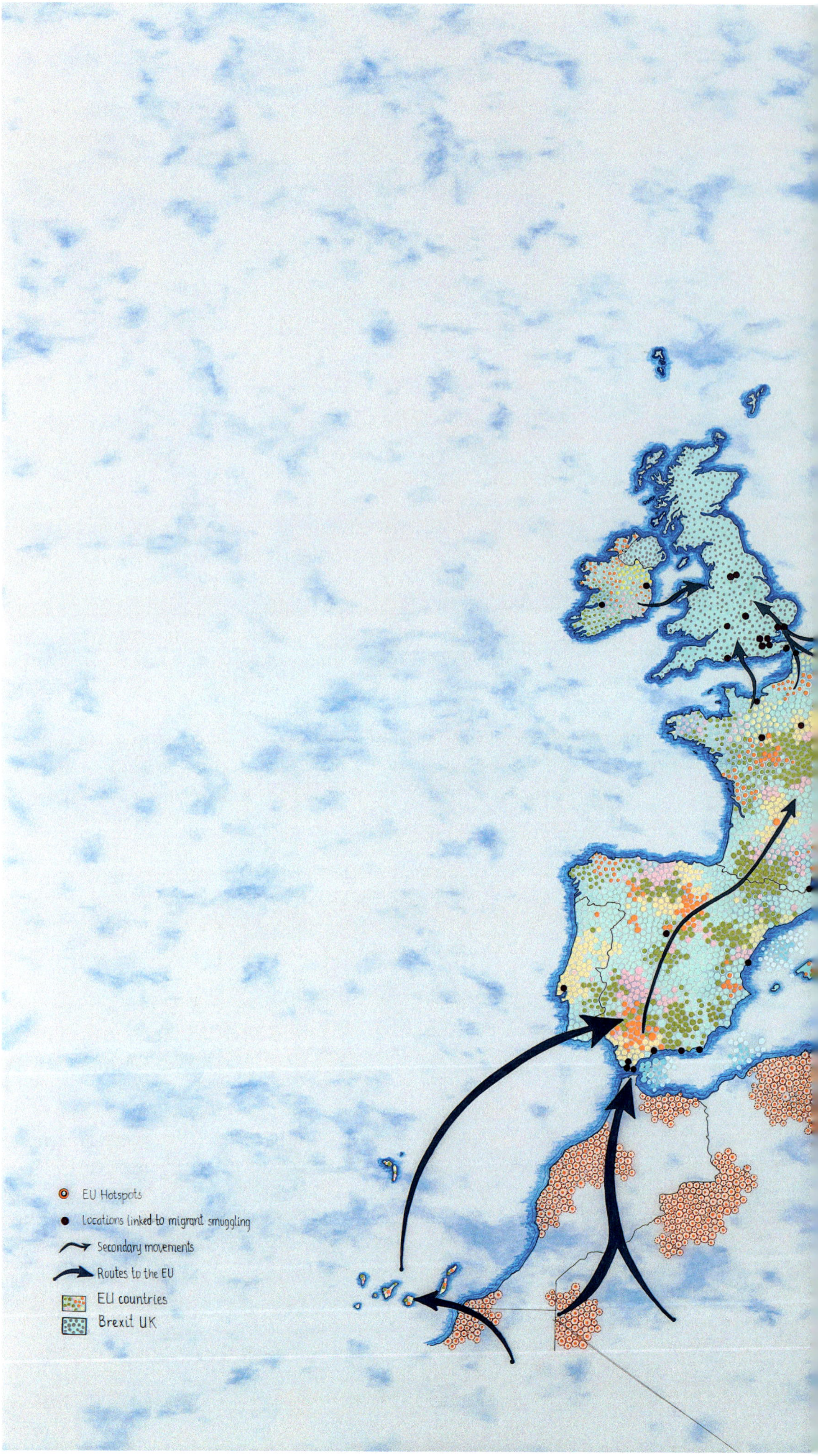

Europol, UK Parliament: tracking migrant smuggling routes to and within the EU, 2017
Acrylic, ink, and oil on vellum and paper
100 × 80 cm (39 ⅜ × 31 ½ in.)

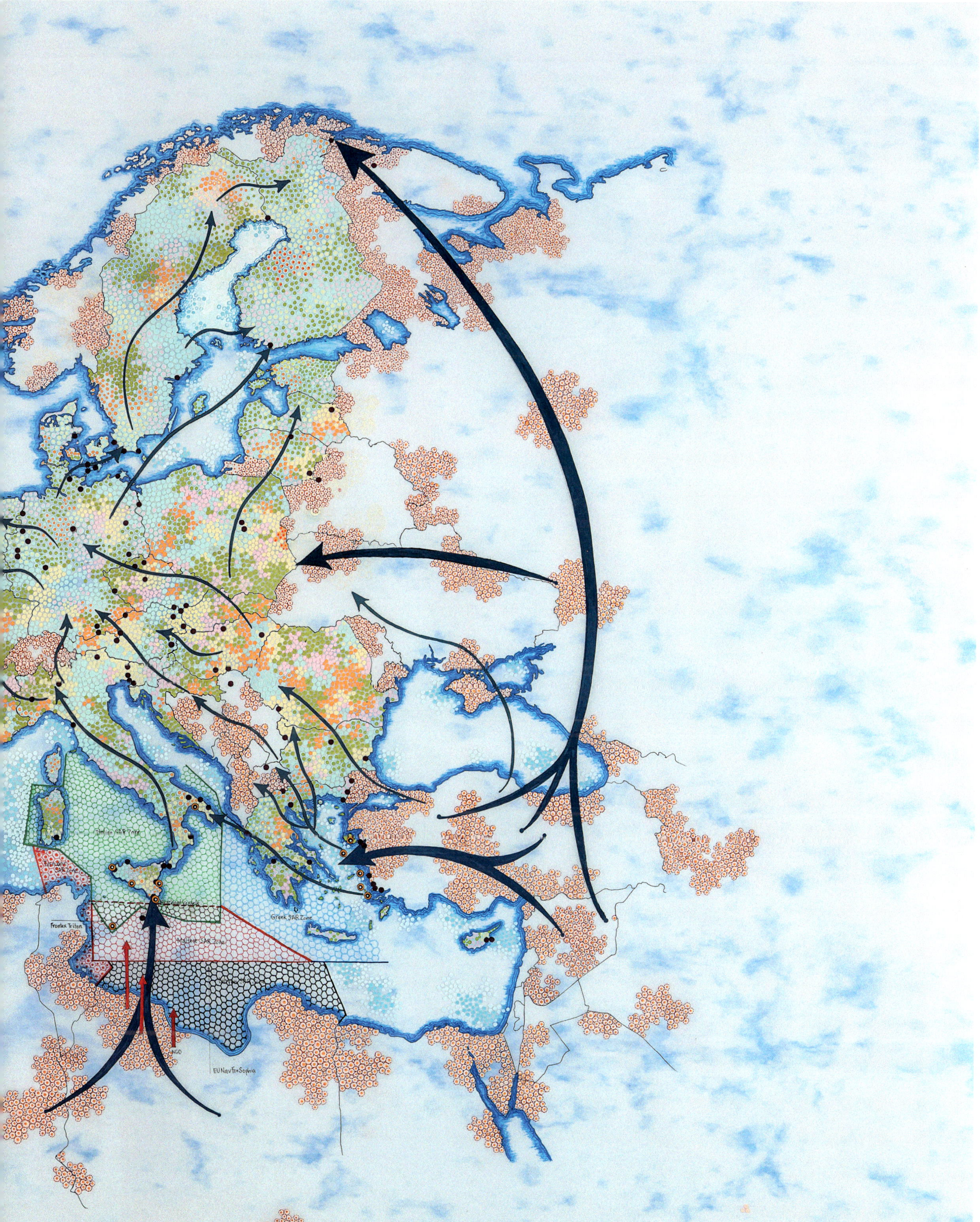

Italian SAR Zone
Tunisian SAR Zone
Merchant Vessels
Frontex Triton
Greek SAR Zone
Maltese SAR Zone
Libyan SAR Zone
NGO
EU NavForSophia

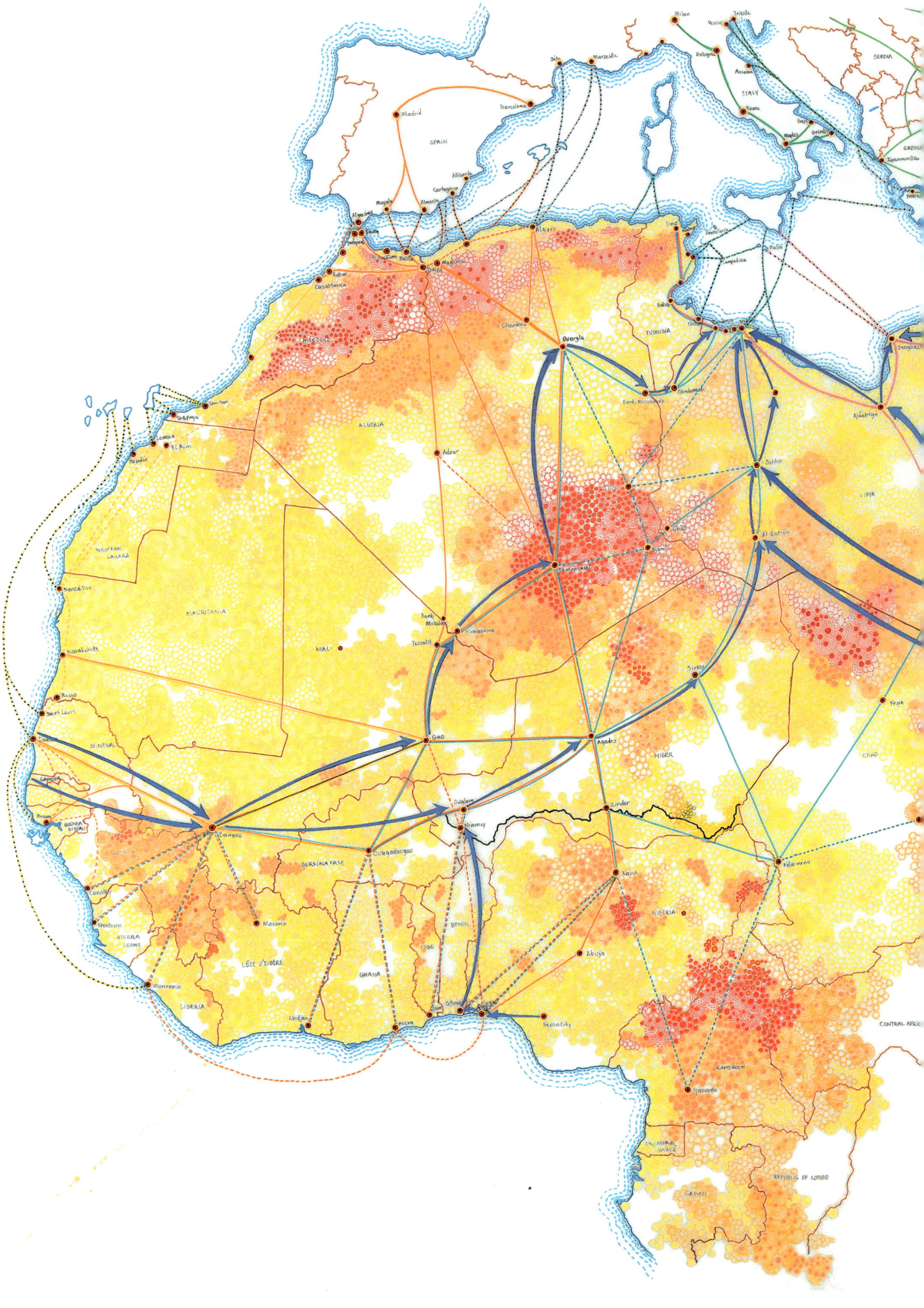
Milan
Trieste
Venice
Bologna
Ancona
ITALY
Rome
Naples
Bari
Brindisi
SERBIA
Madrid
SPAIN
Barcelona
Marseille
Alicante
Cartagena
Almeria
Malaga
Algeciras
Algiers
Oujda
Casablanca
MOROCCO
Ghardaia
Ouargla
TUNISIA
ALGERIA
Adrar
Tamanrasset
Djanet
Ghat
Sabha
Al Qatrun
LIBYA
Ajdabiya
WESTERN SAHARA
MAURITANIA
Nouadhibou
Nouakchott
Rosso
Saint Louis
MALI
Gao
Tessalit
SENEGAL
Bamako
Ouagadougou
BURKINA FASO
Niamey
Agadez
Dirkou
NIGER
Zinder
CHAD
Kano
NIGERIA
Abuja
Conakry
Freetown
SIERRA LEONE
Monrovia
LIBERIA
CÔTE D'IVOIRE
Abidjan
GHANA
Accra
TOGO
BENIN
Cotonou
Lagos
Benin City
CAMEROON
Yaounde
CENTRAL AFRICA
GABON
REPUBLIC OF CONGO

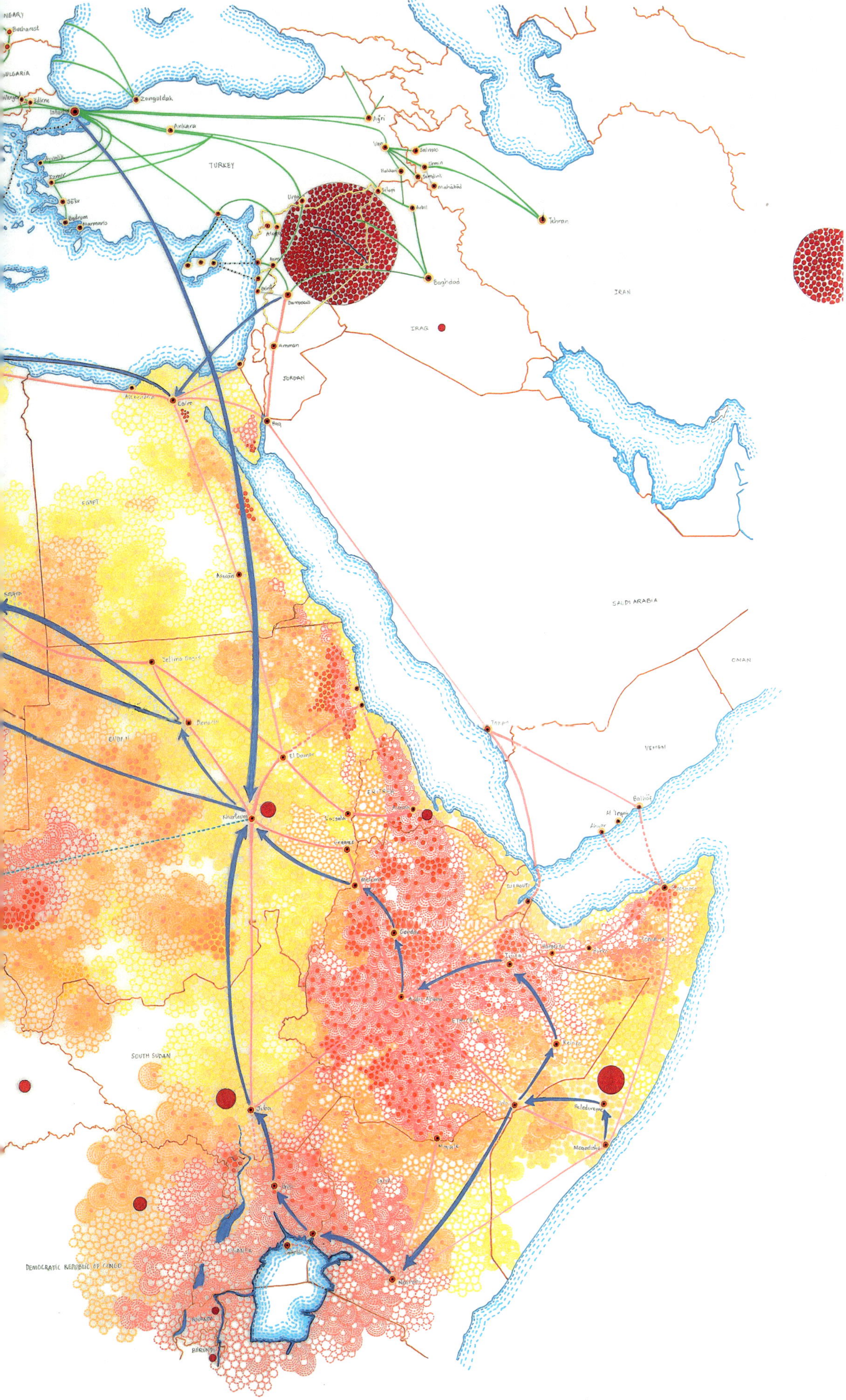

ICMPD, IOM Missing Migrants Project, Frontex, Reuters, NYT: migration routes through Africa to Europe, 2017
Acrylic, ink, and oil on drafting film
92 × 131 cm (36 ¼ × 51 ½ in.)

IOM Missing Migrants Project, EUROSTAT, FRONTEX, RAUL Analytics, ECHO: SAR zones, rescue operations by date, numbers of dead and missing in the Mediterranean, 2017
Ink and oil on vellum and paper
38 × 50 cm (15 × 19 5/8 in.)

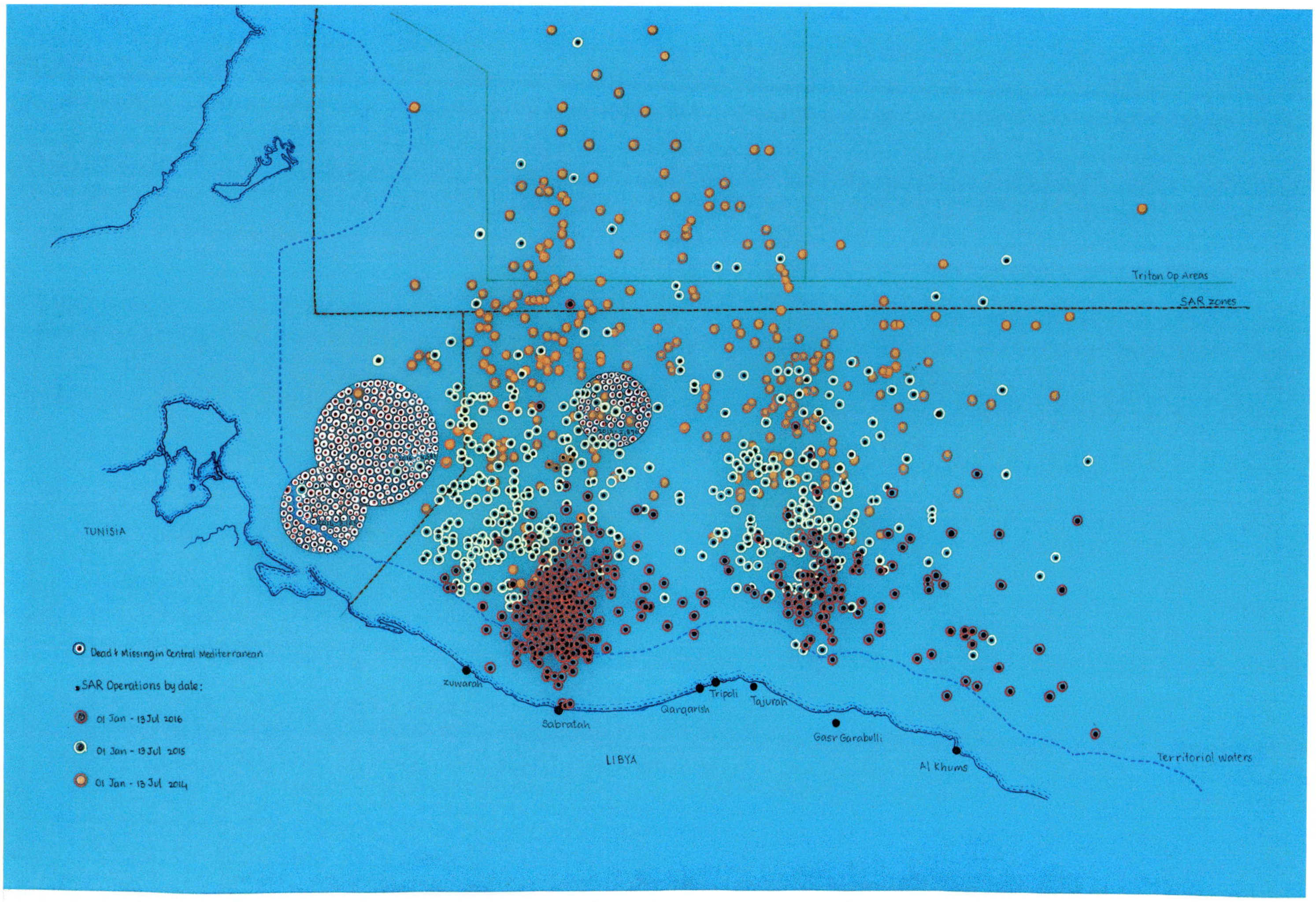
Triton Op Areas
SAR zones
TUNISIA
Dead & Missing in Central Mediterranean
SAR Operations by date:
01 Jan - 13 Jul 2016
01 Jan - 13 Jul 2015
01 Jan - 13 Jul 2014
Zuwarah
Sabratah
Qargarish
Tripoli
Tajurah
Gasr Garabulli
LIBYA
Al Khums
Territorial waters

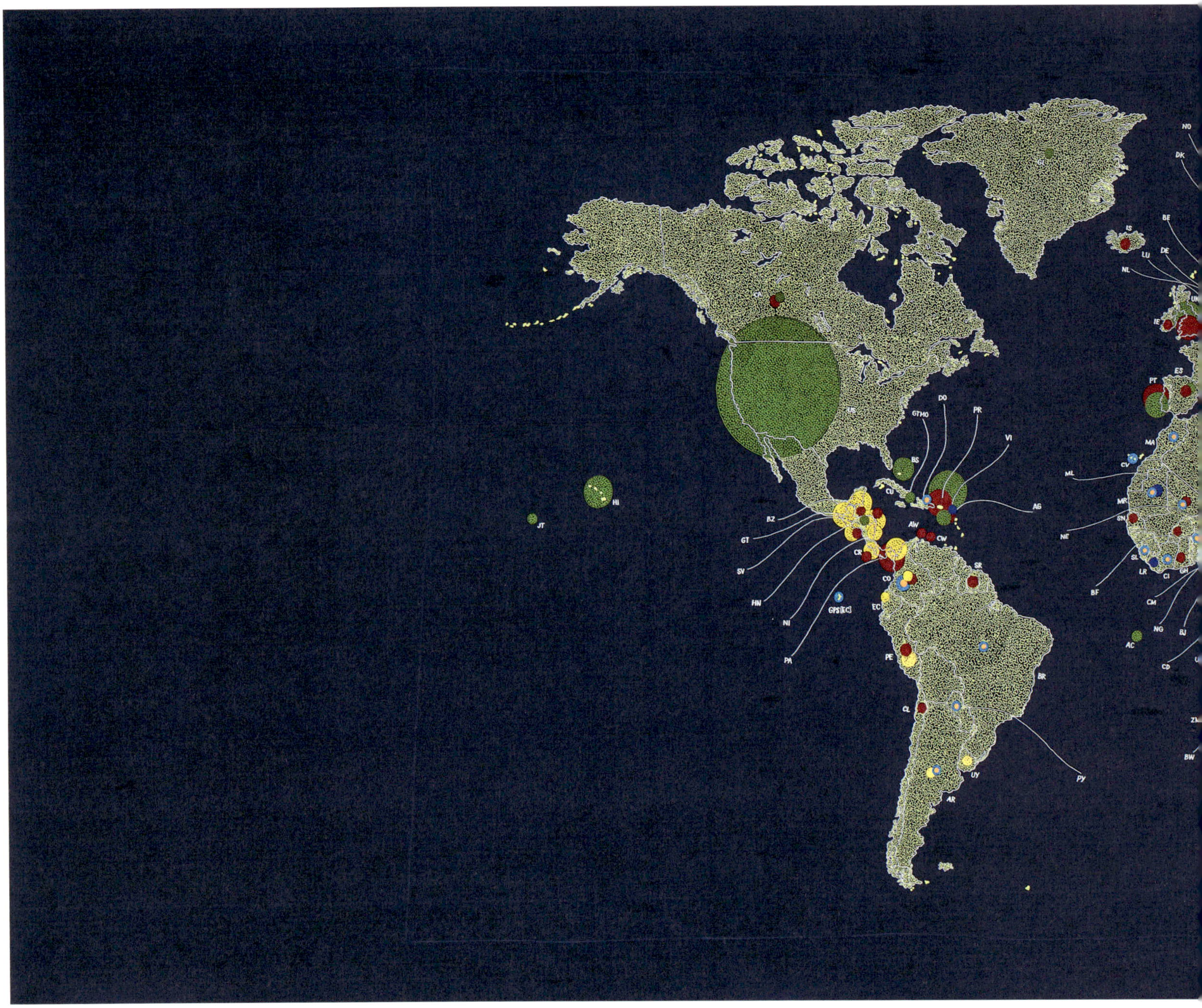

USM Global: tracing the US military global footprint, 2023
Embroidery on fabric
140 × 350 cm (55 ⅛ × 137 ¾ in.);
map key: 40 × 70 cm
(15 ¾ × 27 ¾ in.)

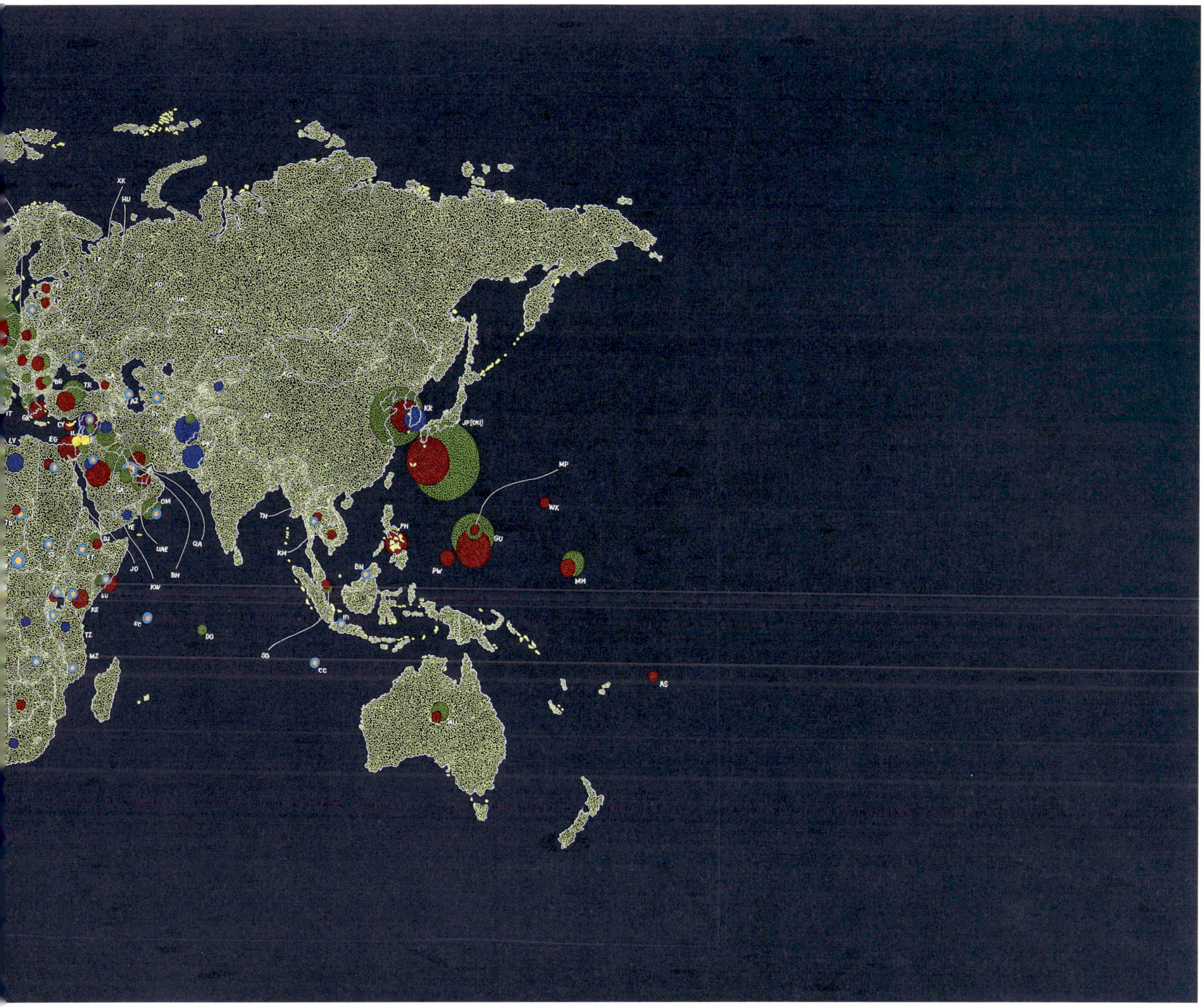
XK
HU
LT
SI
RO
UA
TM
GA
BG
TR
AZ
XG
IT
GR
CY
SY
IQ
AF
KR
JP [OKI]
LY
EG
IL
PK
SA
OM
MP
WK
TH
PH
YE
DJ
GU
QA
UAE
SS
ET
KH
PW
MH
JO
BH
BN
KW
SU
KE
SC
ID
DG
TZ
SG
MZ
CC
AS
AU

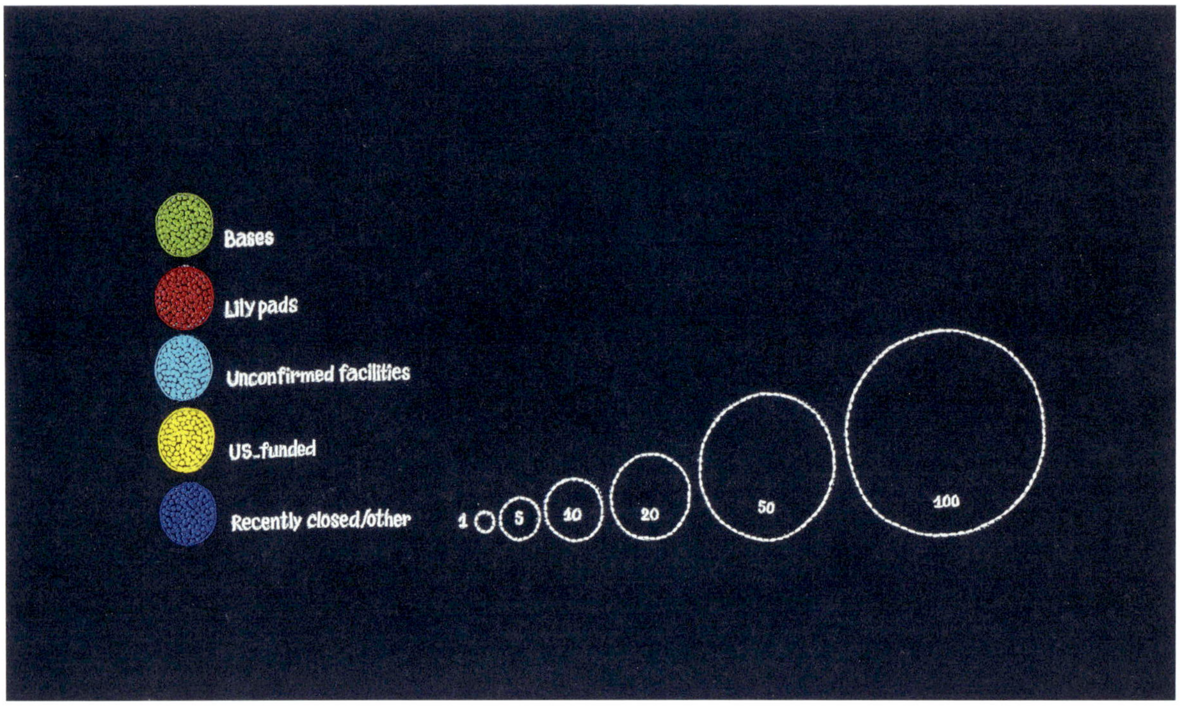

Bases
Lily pads
Unconfirmed facilities
US_funded
Recently closed/other
1
5
10
20
50
100

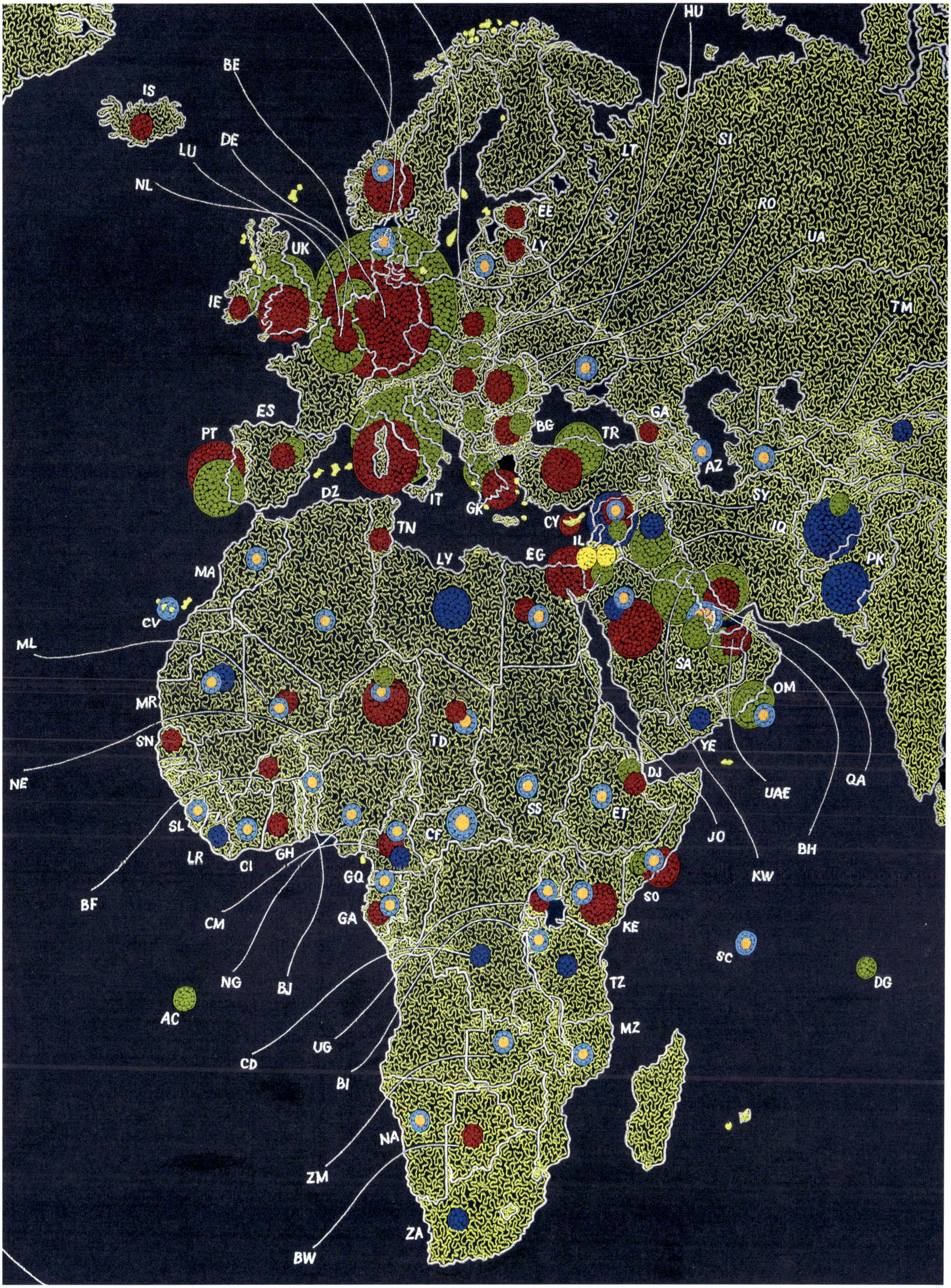

HU
BE
IS
SI
LT
LU
DE
NL
RO
EE
UA
LY
UK
IE
TM
ES
GA
PT
BG
TR
AZ
DZ
SY
IT
GK
CY
TN
IL
IQ
LY
EG
PK
MA
CV
SA
ML
OM
MR
TD
YE
SN
DJ
QA
UAE
NE
SS
ET
JO
SL
CF
BH
LR
CI
GH
KW
GQ
SO
BF
CM
GA
KE
SC
NG
BJ
TZ
DG
AC
MZ
CD
UG
BI
NA
ZM
ZA
BW

Africa in Focus: Refugees, IDPS, LIC Policy, Drone & Air Strikes, and Combat Engagement, 2021
Acrylic, ink, and oil on vellum and paper
113 x 68.7 cm (44 ½ x 27 1/16 in.)

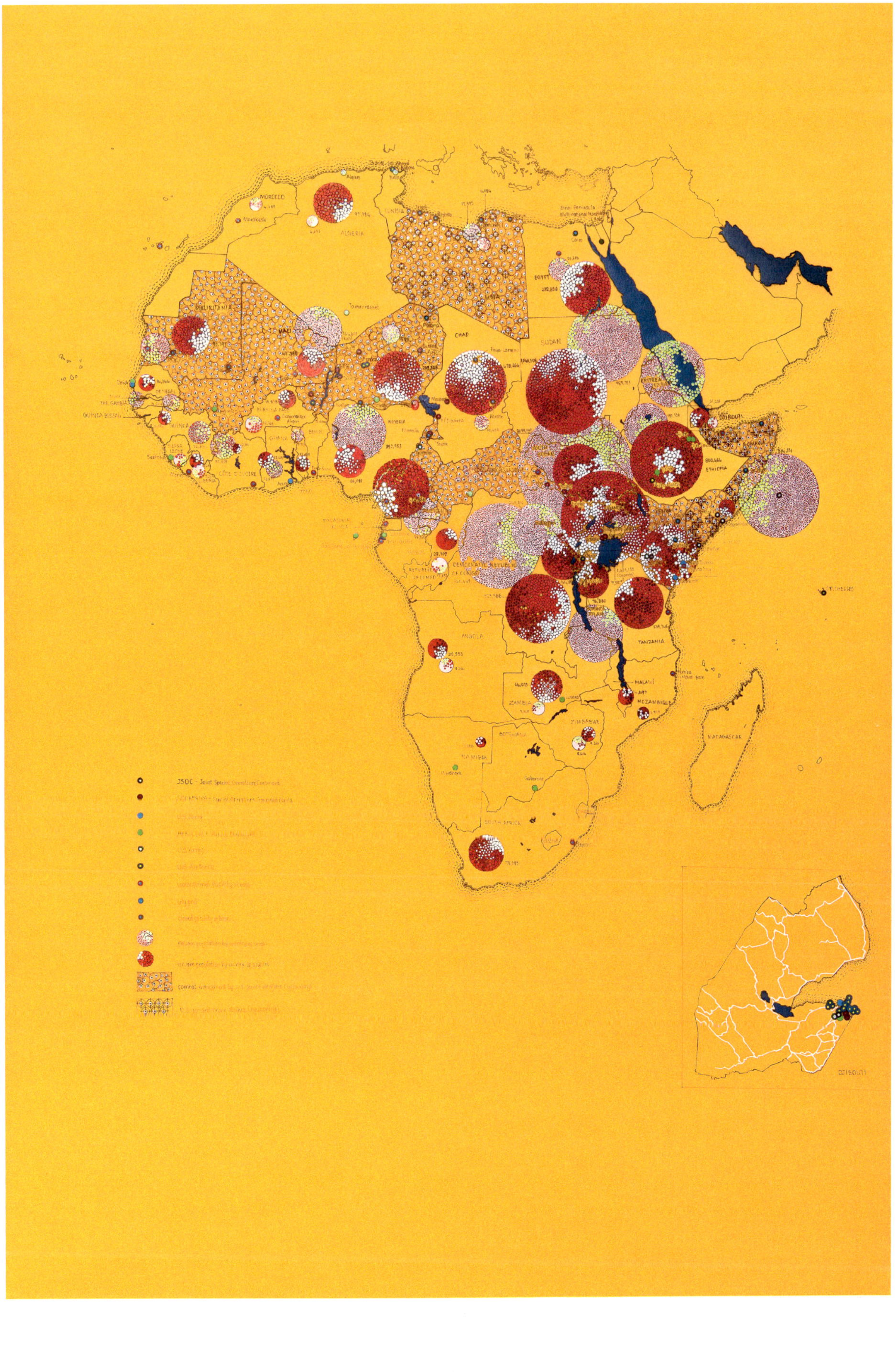
MOROCCO
ALGERIA
EGYPT
MAURITANIA
MALI
CHAD
SUDAN
ETHIOPIA
TANZANIA
ANGOLA
ZAMBIA
MALAWI
MOZAMBIQUE
MADAGASCAR
DJIBOUTI

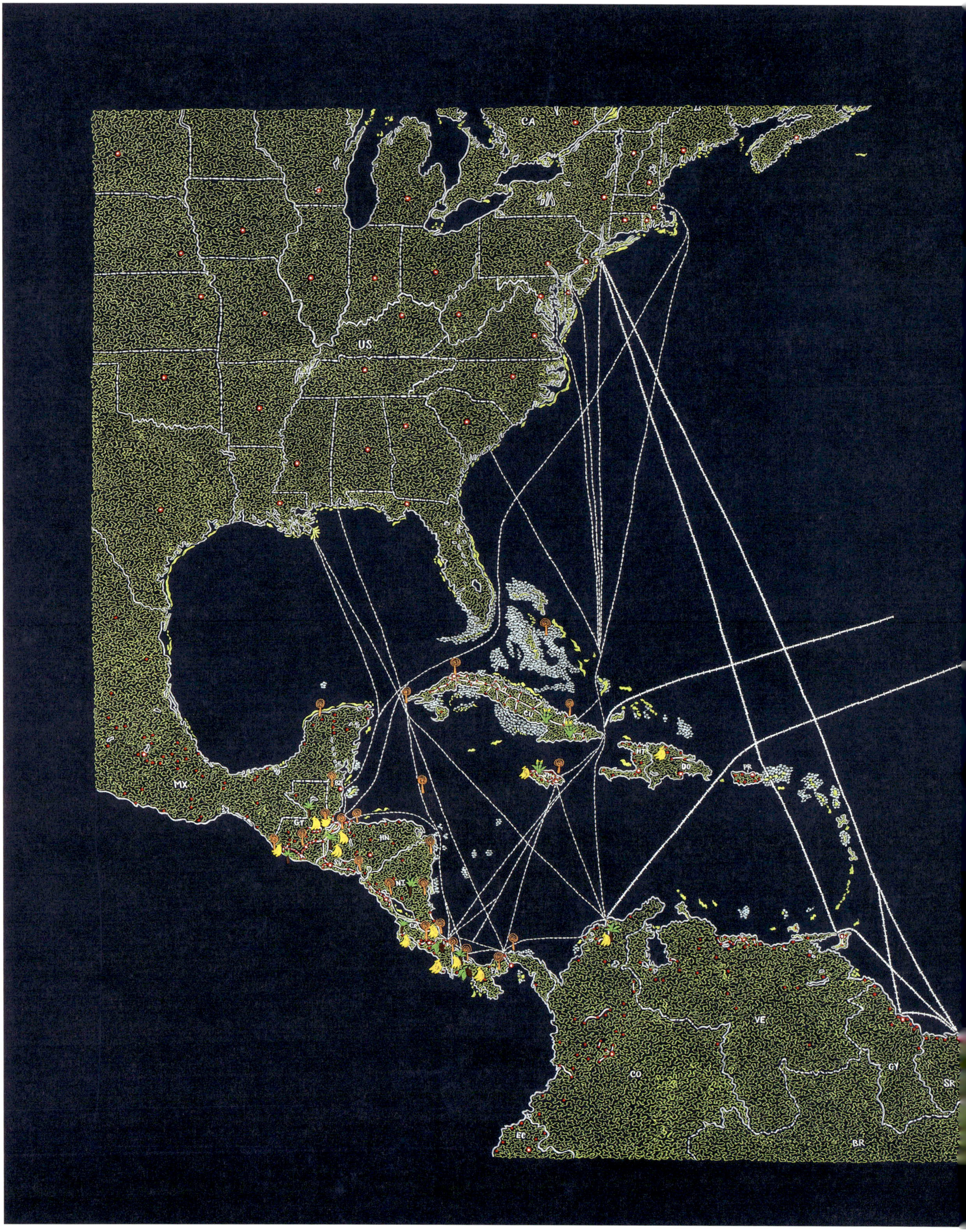
CA
US
MX
CU
VE
CO
GY
SR
EC
BR

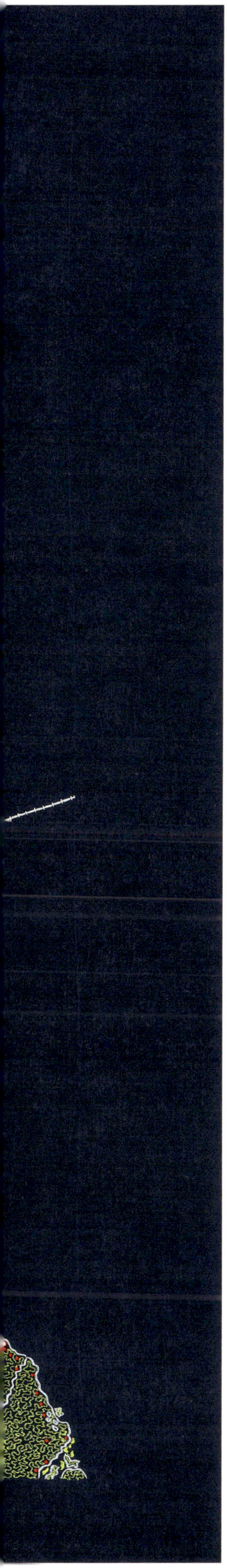

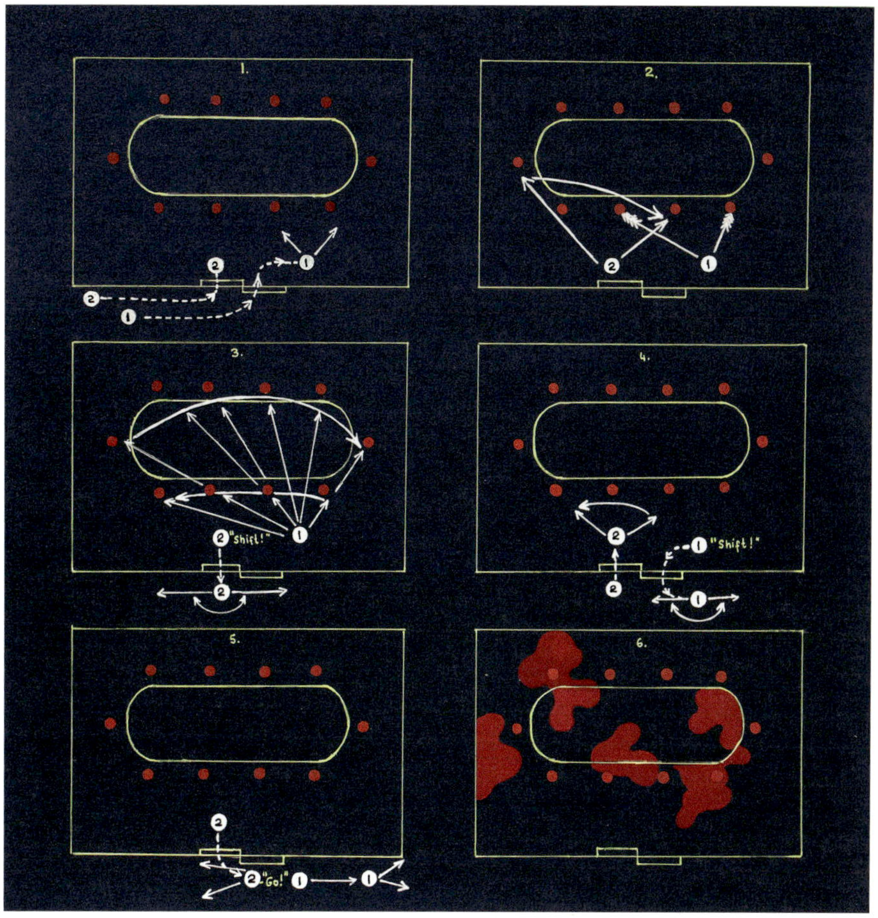

El Pulpo: UFCo's Great White Fleet routes and properties in Central America & the Caribbean, 2019
Embroidery on fabric
137 × 137 cm (54 × 54 in.)

CIA Study of Assassination sketch, 2019
Acrylic, ink, and oil on paper
30.5 × 30.5 cm (12 × 12 in.)

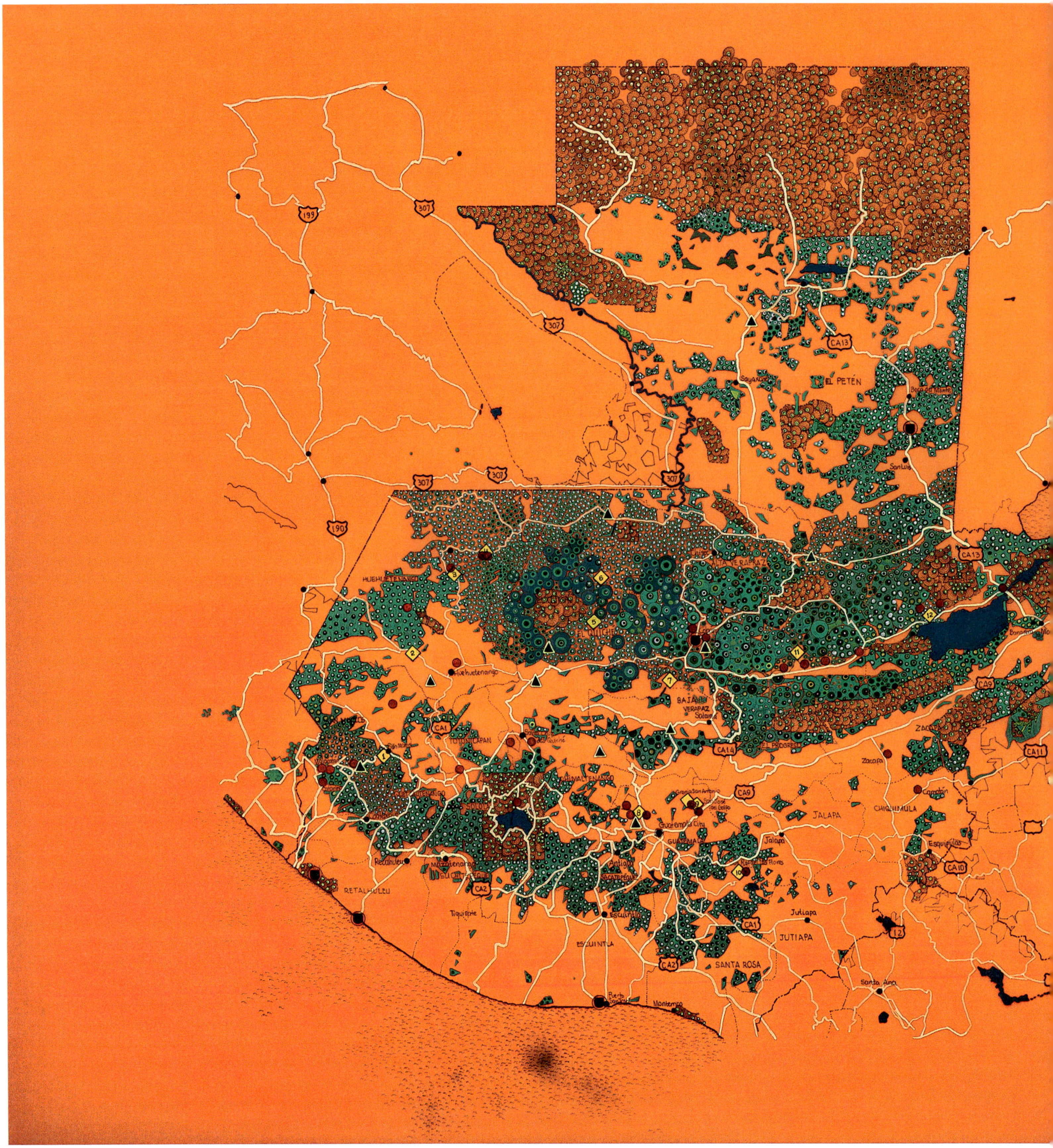
199
307
301
190
CA13
EL PETÉN
Sayaxché
San Luis
EL QUICHÉ
HUEHUETENANGO
Huehuetenango
TOTONICAPAN
CHIMALTENANGO
BAJA VERAPAZ
Salamá
CA1
CA14
CA9
CA2
CA10
CA11
Zacapa
JALAPA
Jalapa
CHIQUIMULA
Esquipulas
Guatemala City
Retalhuleu
RETALHULEU
Mazatenango
Tiquisate
ESCUINTLA
Escuintla
Monterrico
SANTA ROSA
JUTIAPA
Jutiapa
Santa Ana

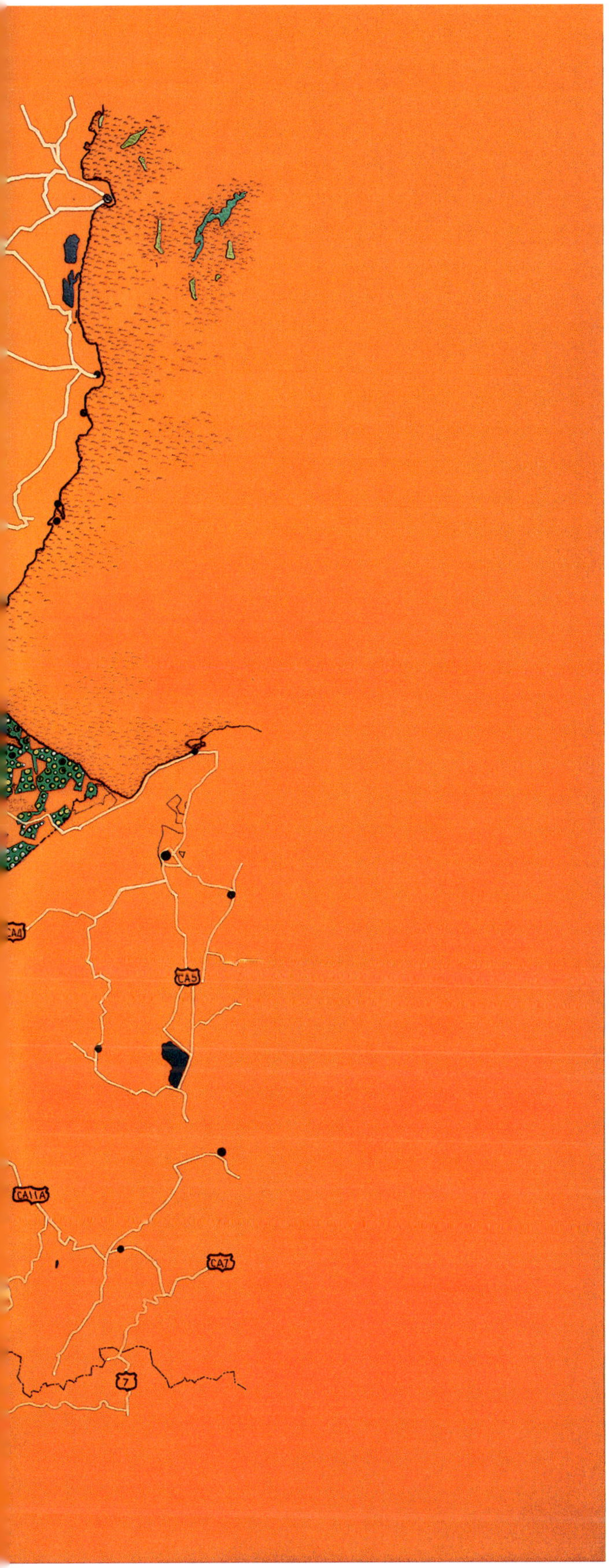

Guatemala Human Rights Commission: Selected cases of violence in relation to current mega projects, 2019
Acrylic, ink, and oil on vellum and paper
71 × 88.3 cm (28 × 34 ¾ in.)

from faraway lands to dust we return: Ewa Plantation Community Cemetery's Ledger Book, 2018
Acrylic, ink, and oil on vellum and paper
102 × 64 cm (40 ⅛ × 25 ¼ in.)

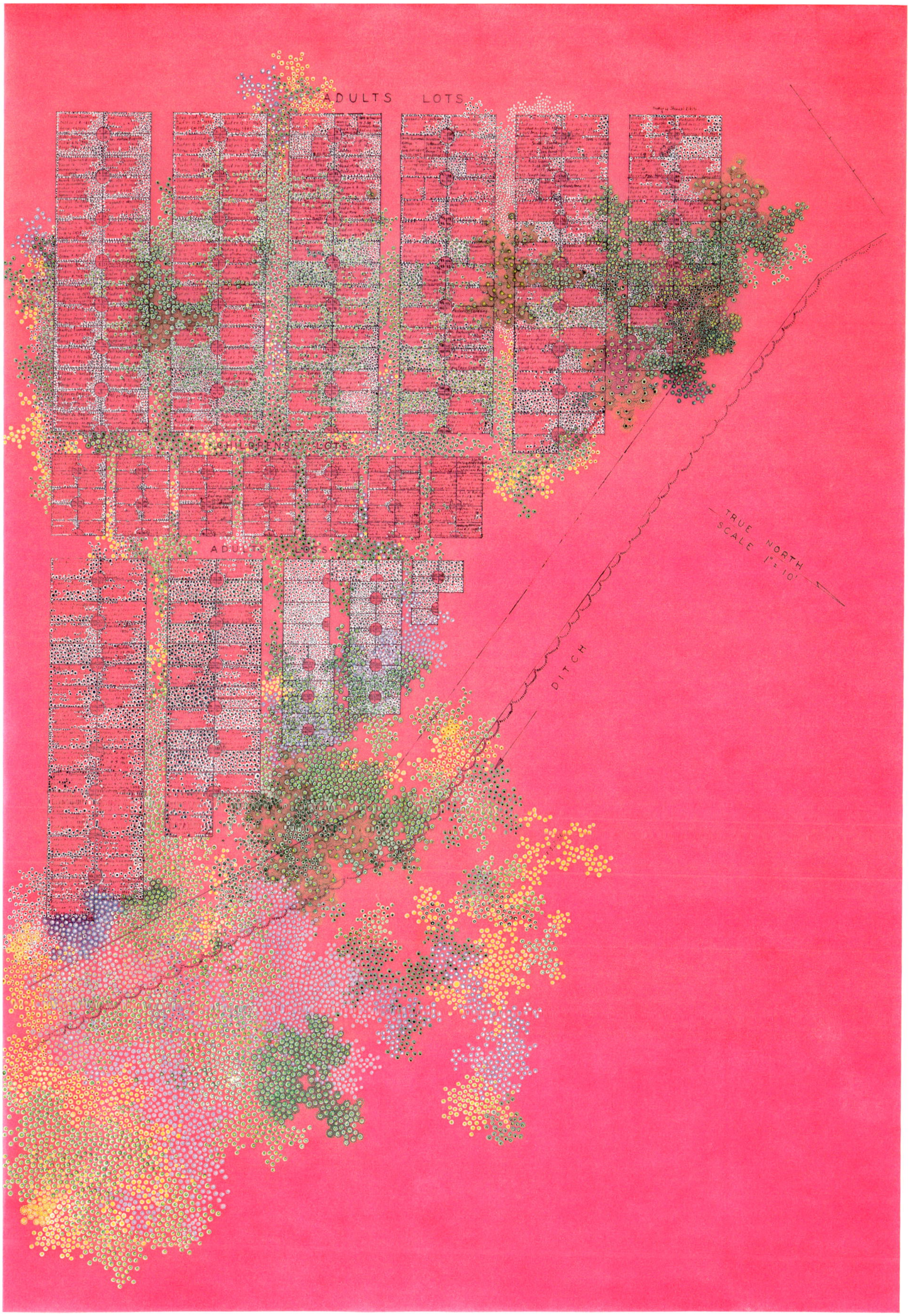
ADULTS LOTS
CHILDREN'S LOTS
ADULTS LOTS
TRUE NORTH
SCALE 1"=10'
DITCH

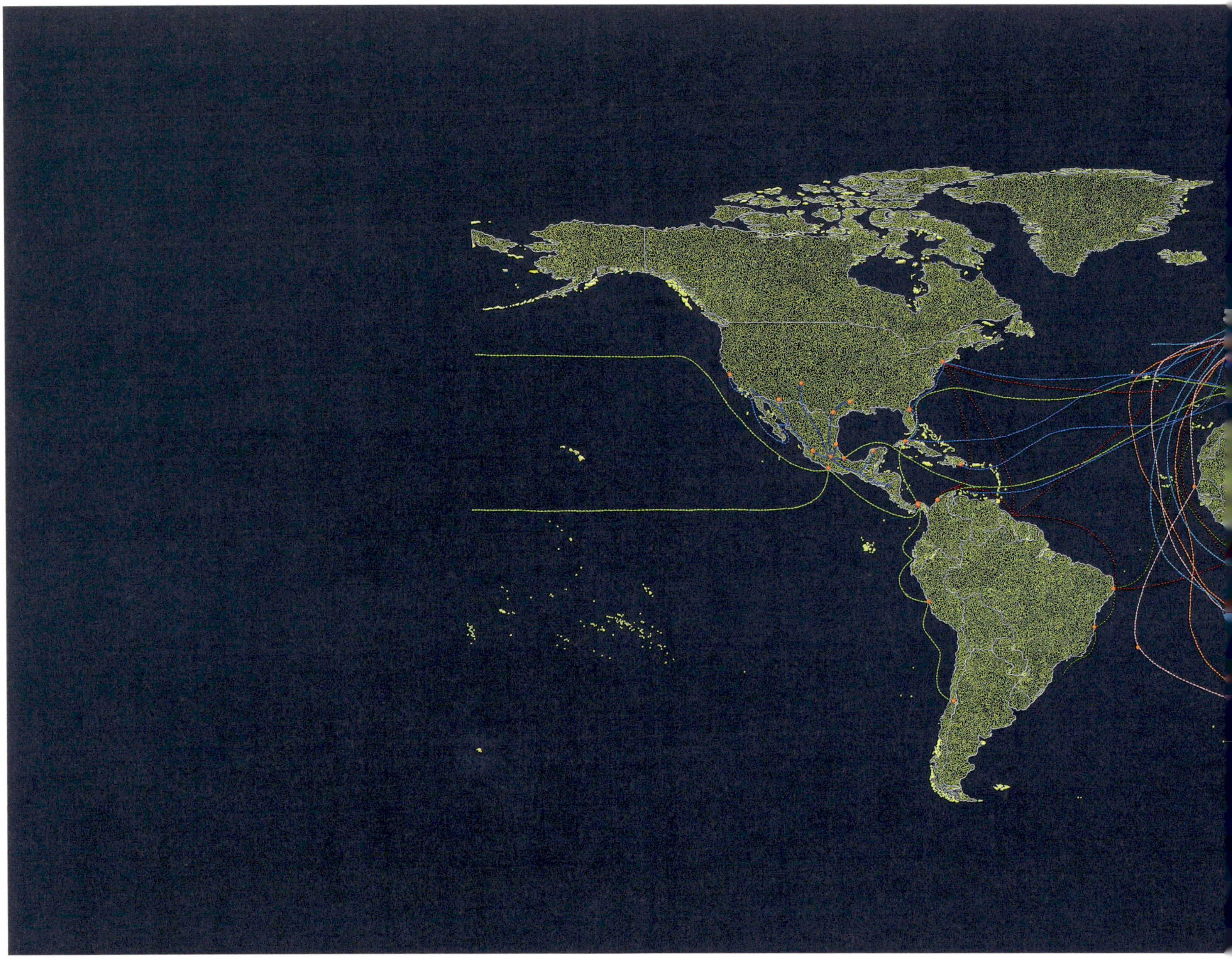

Global Spice Trade: routes from ancient times to the age of exploration/ exploitation, 2024–2025
Embroidery on fabric
140 × 380 cm (55 × 149 ½ in.); map key: 50 × 50 cm (19 ⅝ × 19 ⅝ in.)

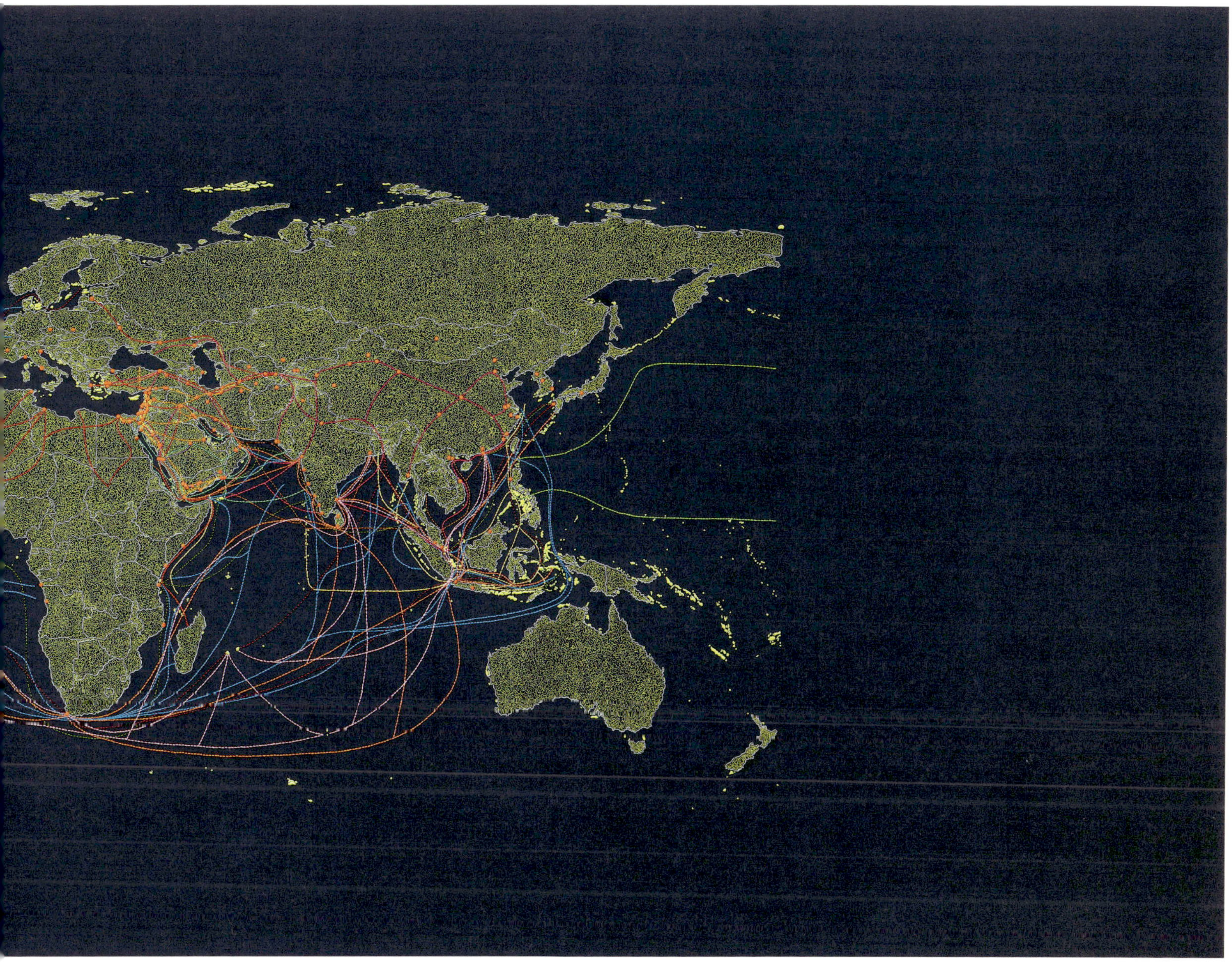

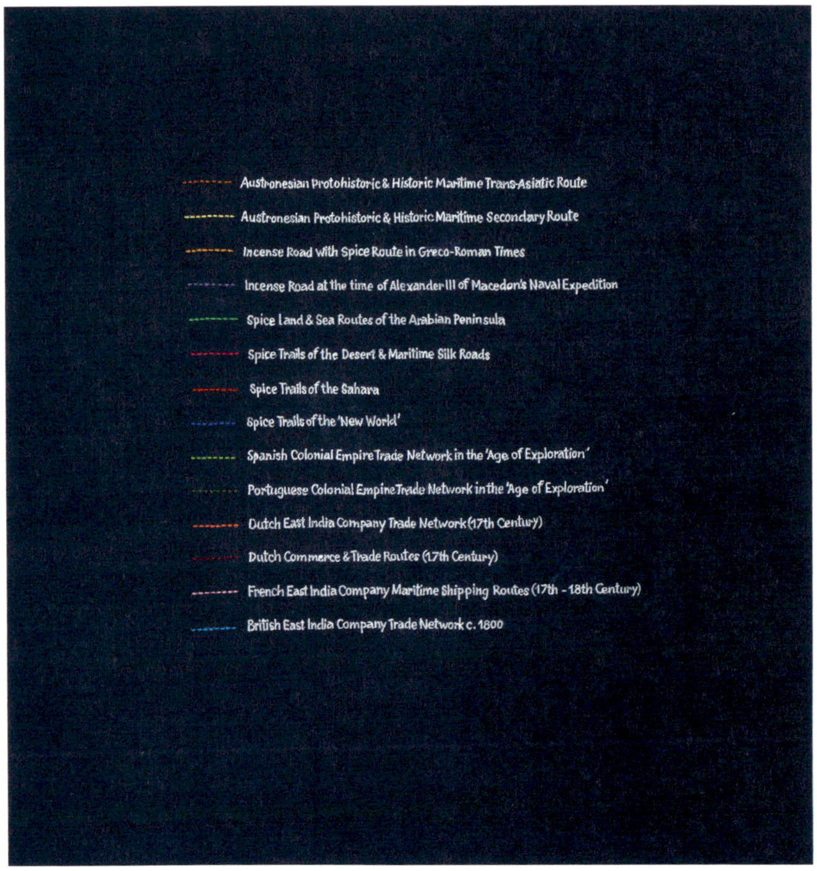
Austronesian Protohistoric & Historic Maritime Trans-Asiatic Route
Austronesian Protohistoric & Historic Maritime Secondary Route
Incense Road with Spice Route in Greco-Roman Times
Incense Road at the time of Alexander III of Macedon's Naval Expedition
Spice Land & Sea Routes of the Arabian Peninsula
Spice Trails of the Desert & Maritime Silk Roads
Spice Trails of the Sahara
Spice Trails of the 'New World'
Spanish Colonial Empire Trade Network in the 'Age of Exploration'
Portuguese Colonial Empine Trade Network in the 'Age of Exploration'
Dutch East India Company Trade Network (17th Century)
Dutch Commerce & Trade Routes (17th Century)
French East India Company Maritime Shipping Routes (17th - 18th Century)
British East India Company Trade Network c. 1800

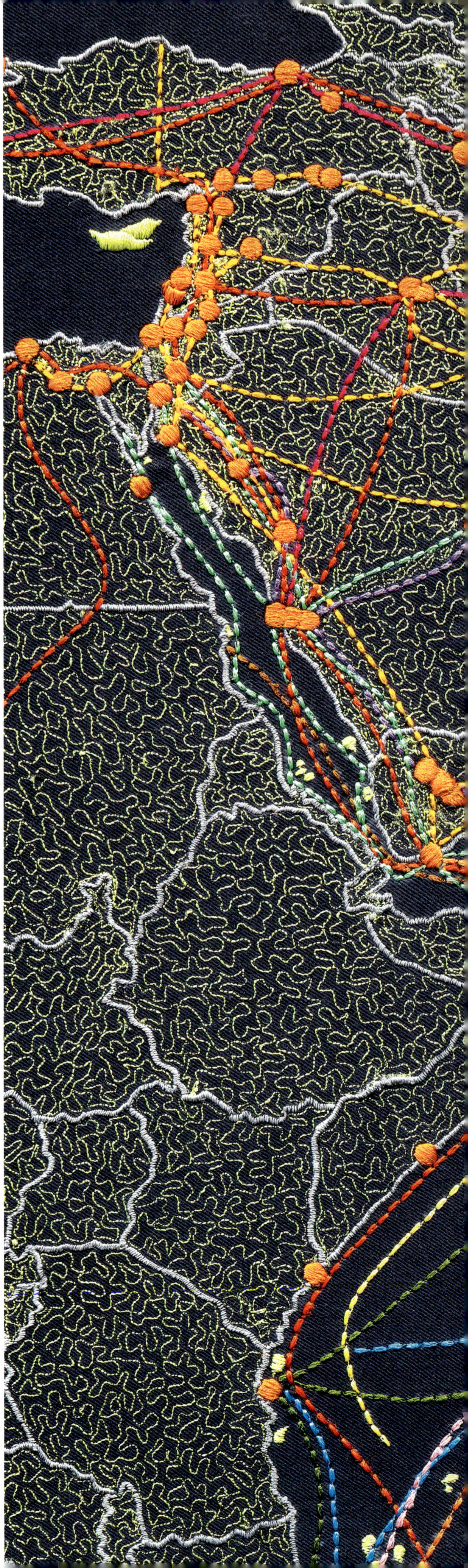

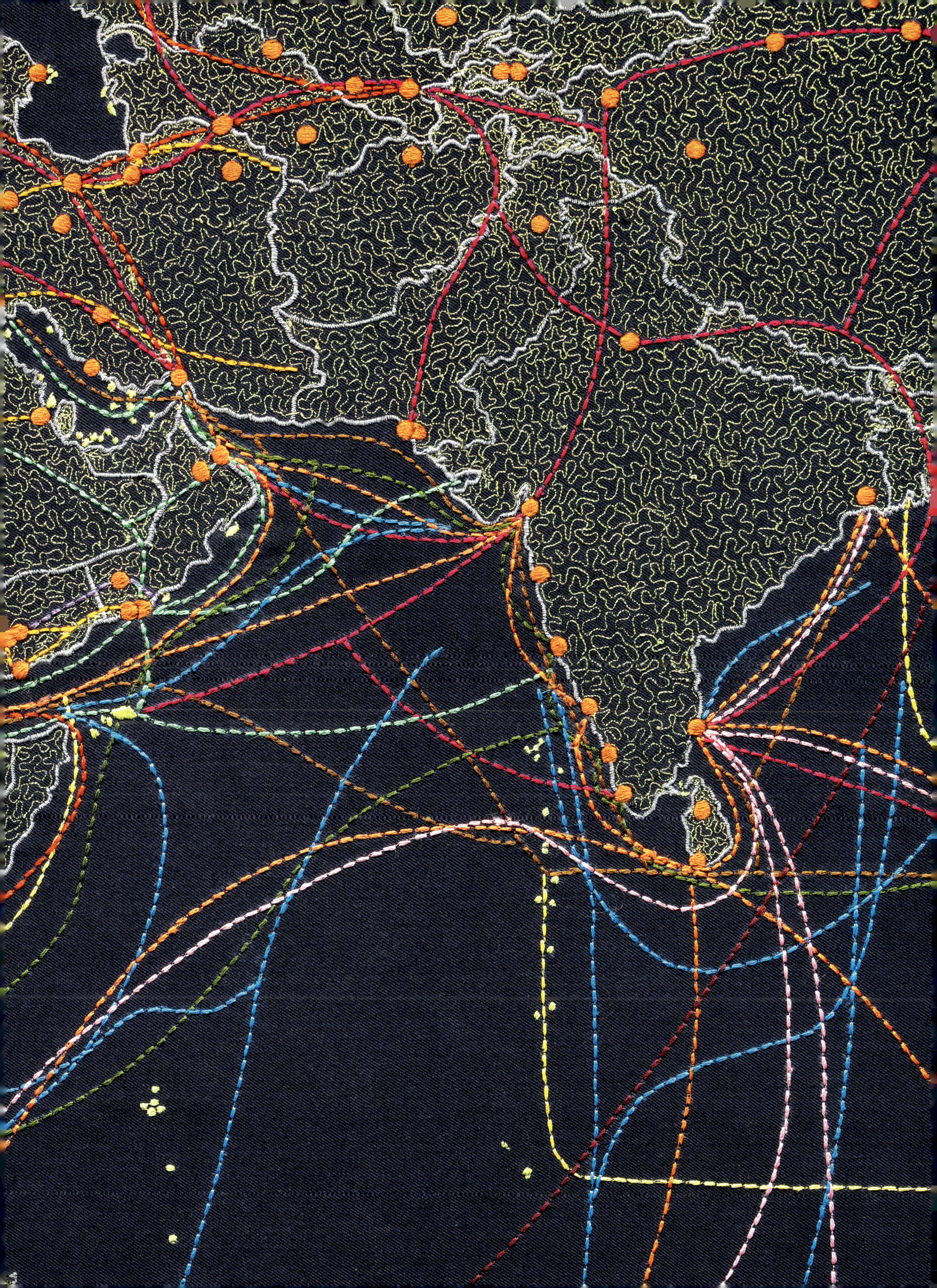

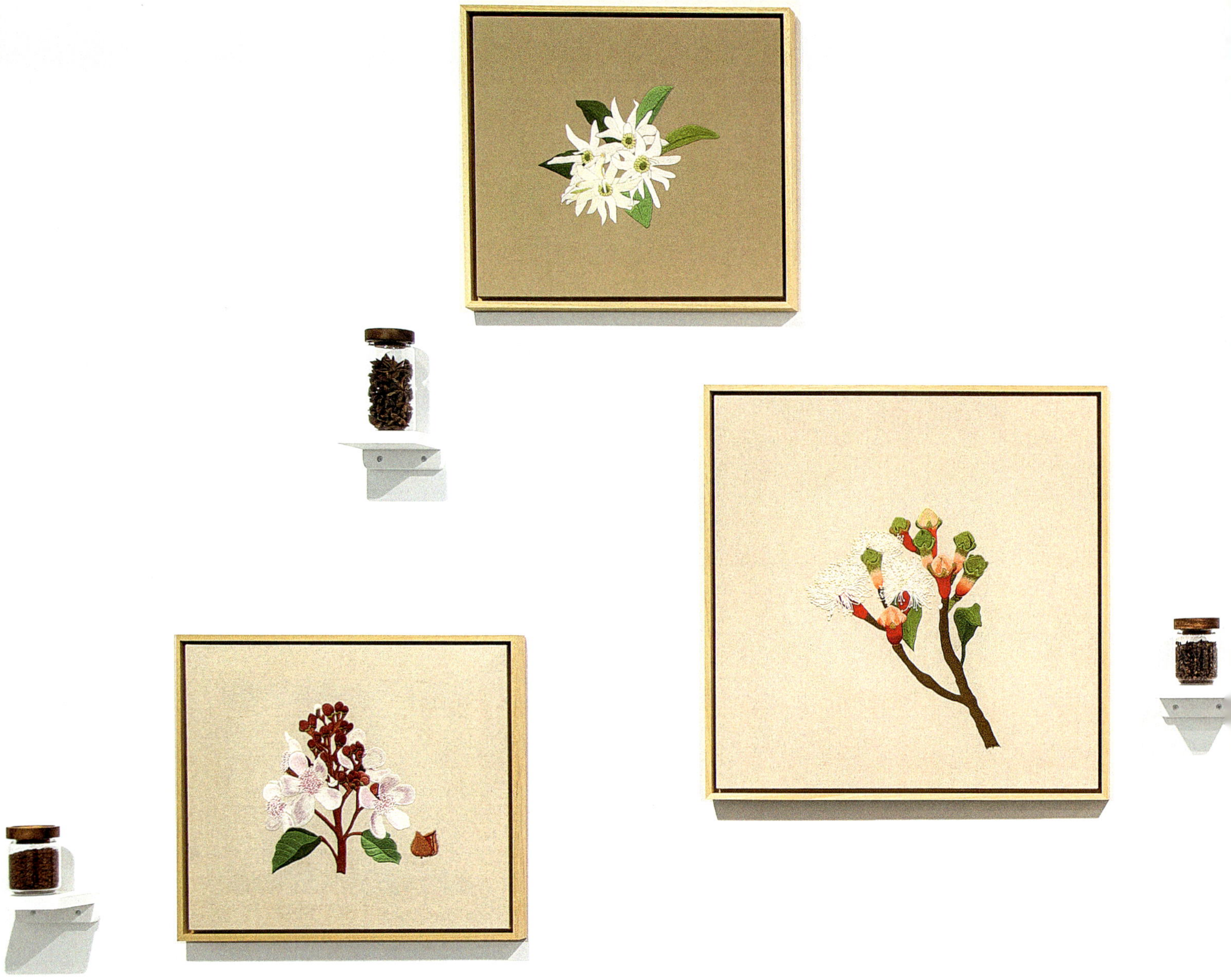

Studies of exotic botanical organisms and spices from the ends of the earth in quest of market dominance,
2024–2025
10 pieces of hand embroidery on linen, spices in glass jars
Dimensions variable

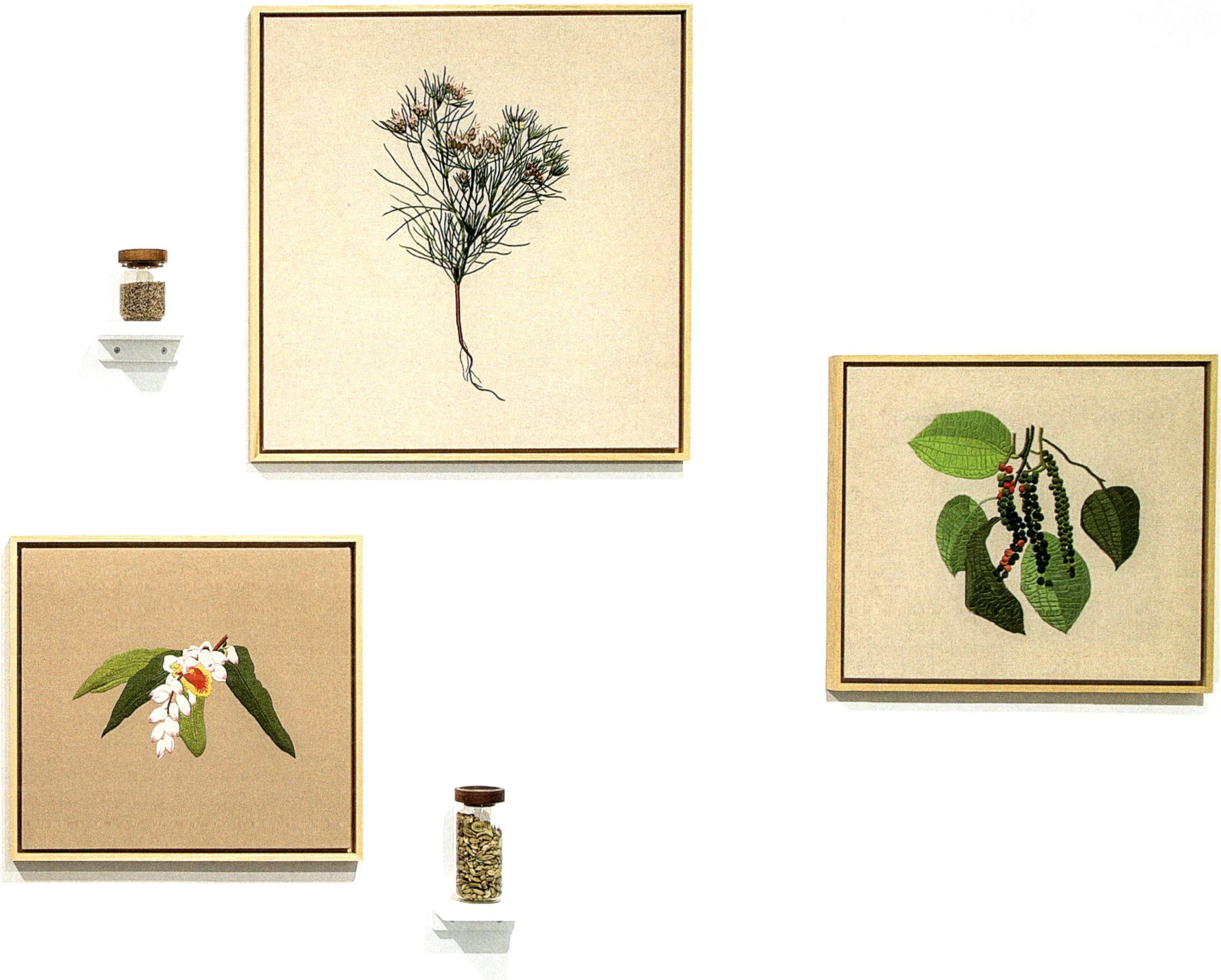

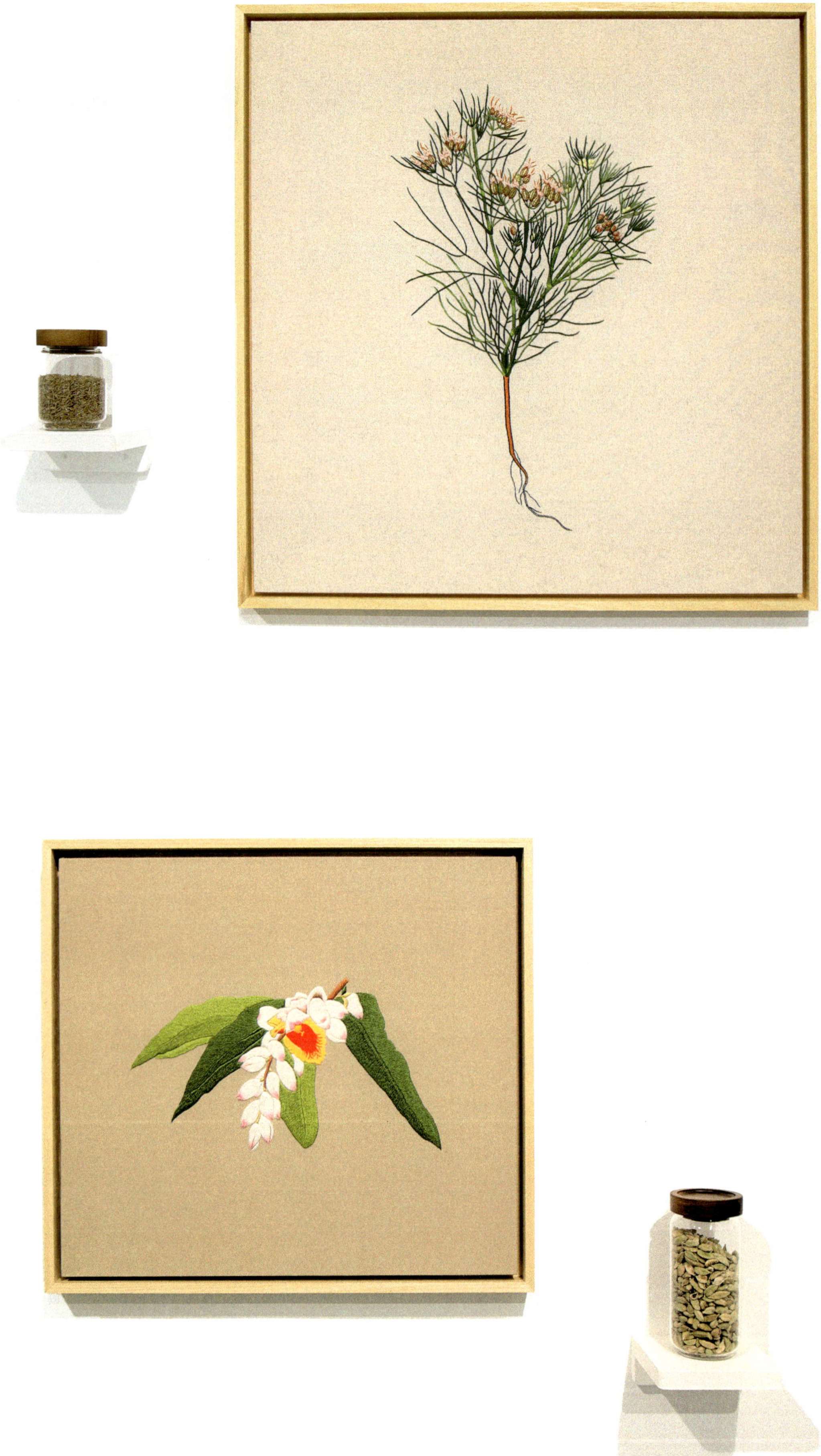

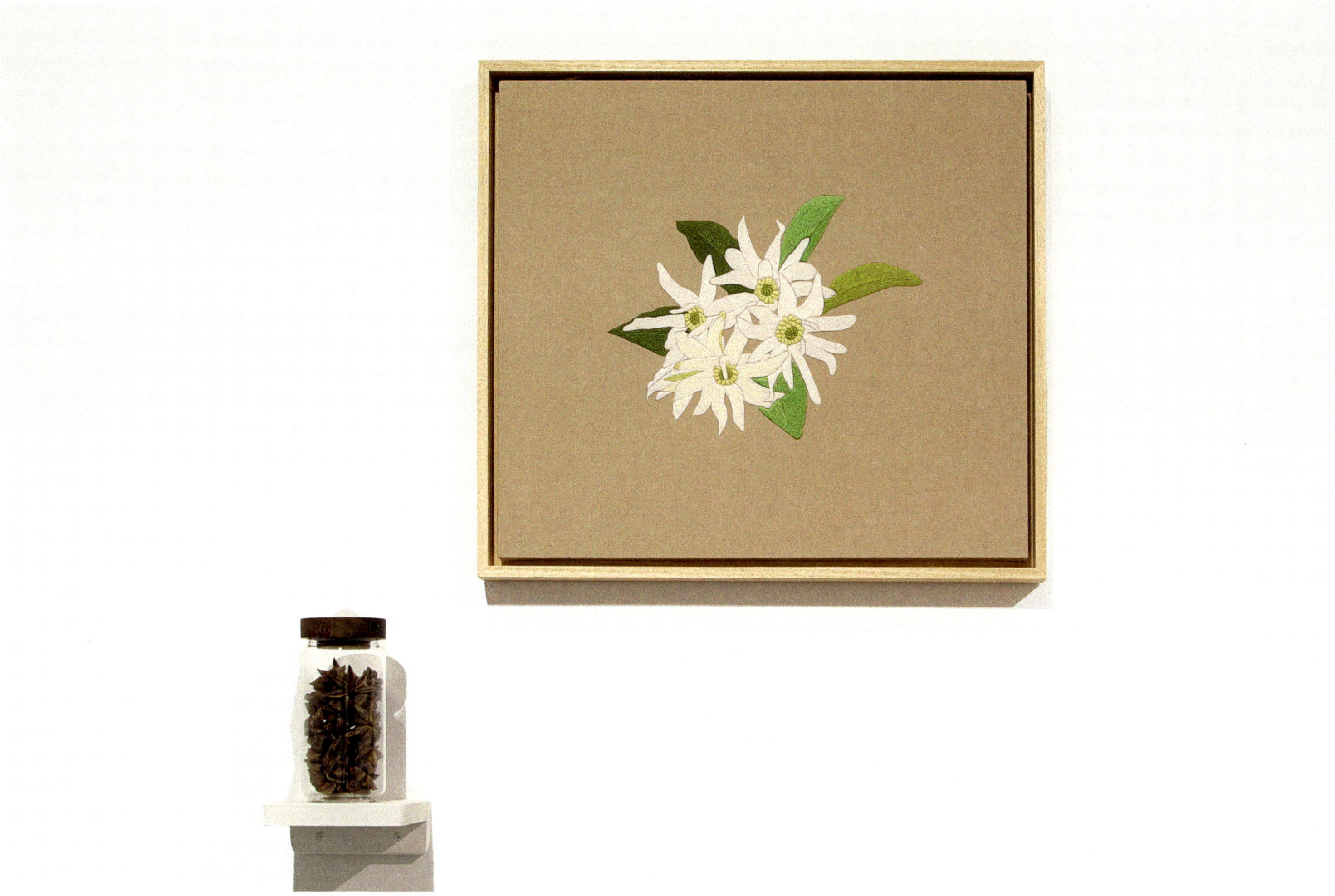

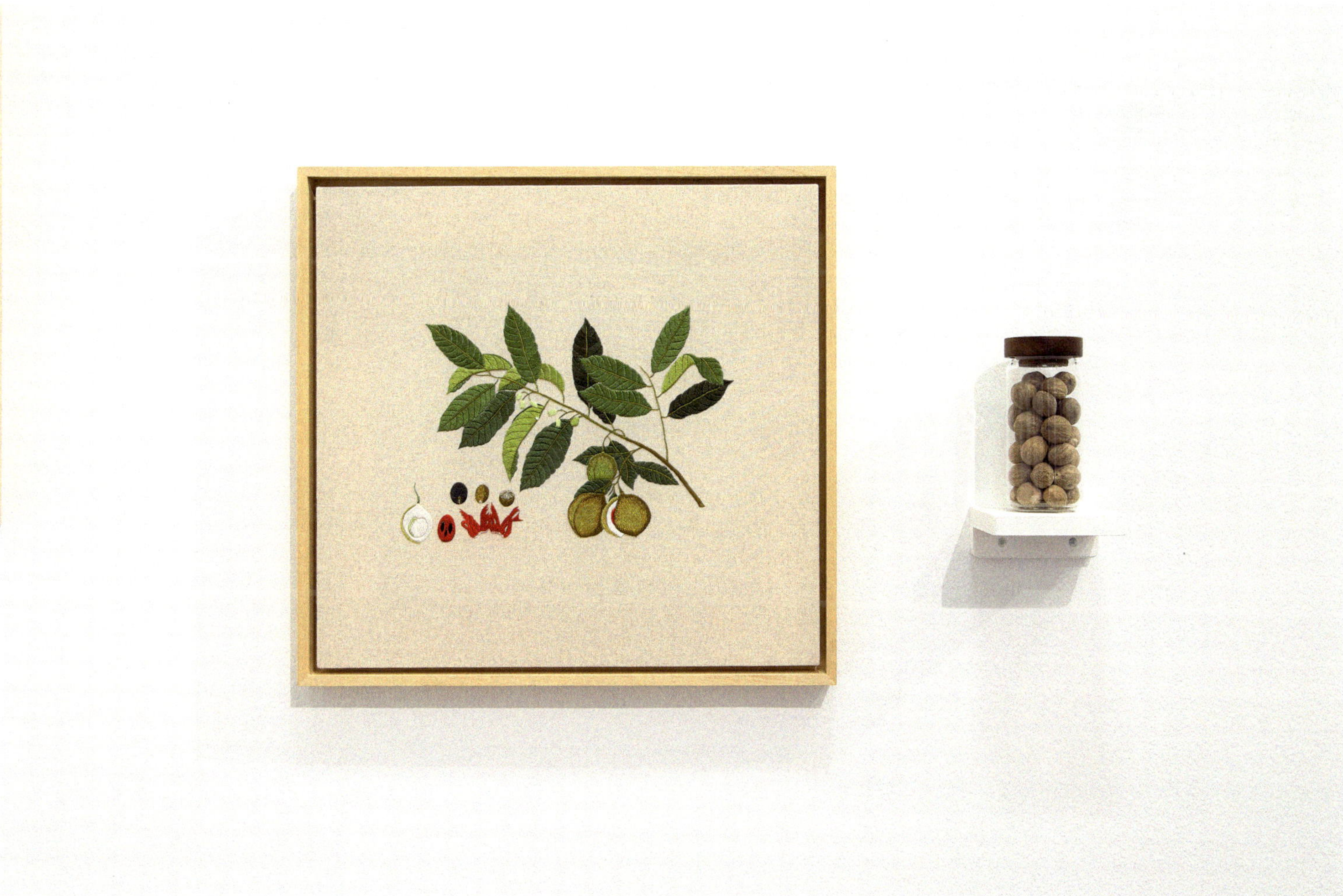

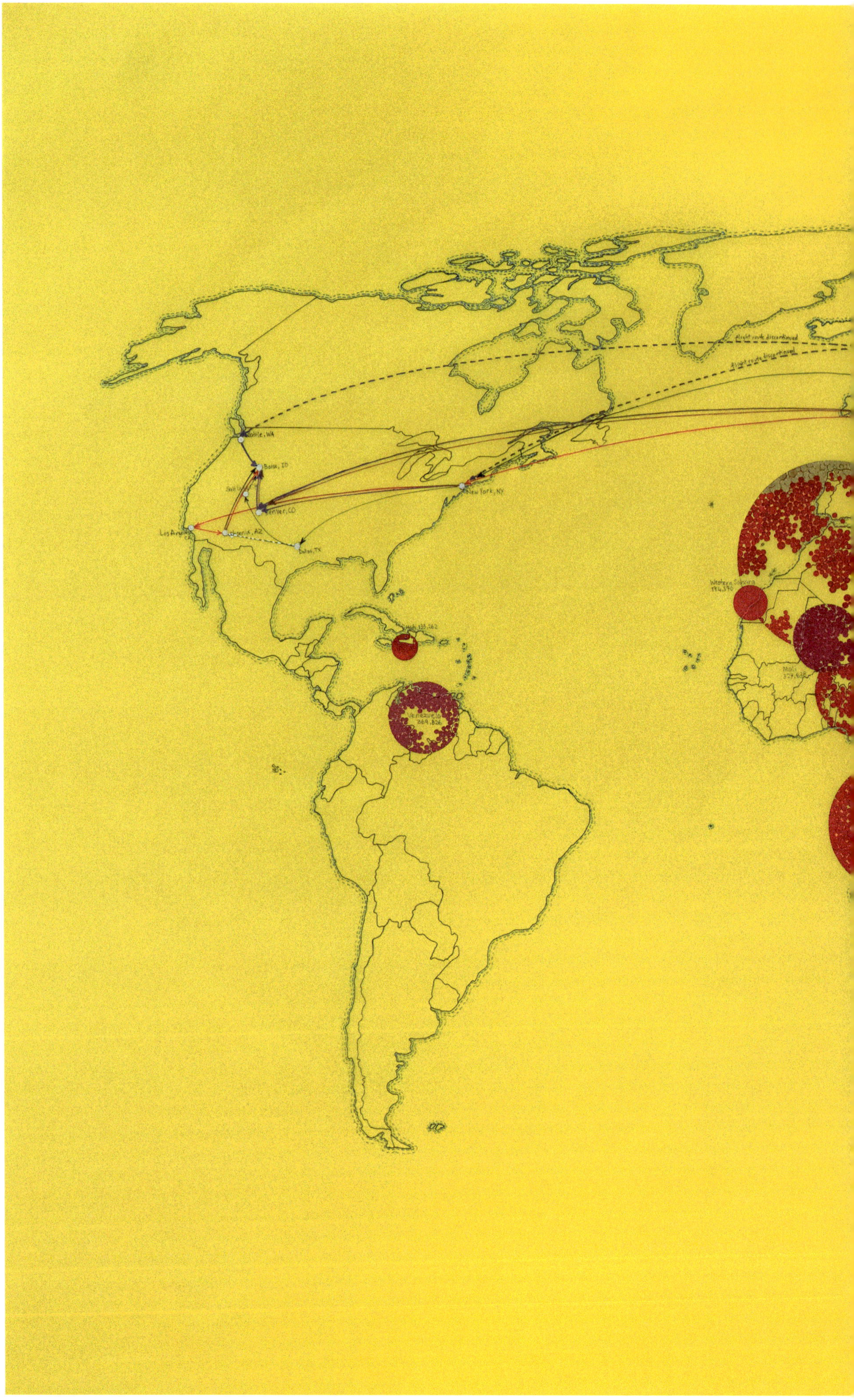

cracked heels and spices beyond my father's shoreline, 2025
Ink and oil on vellum and paper
77.5 × 100 cm (30 ½ × 39 ⅜ in.)

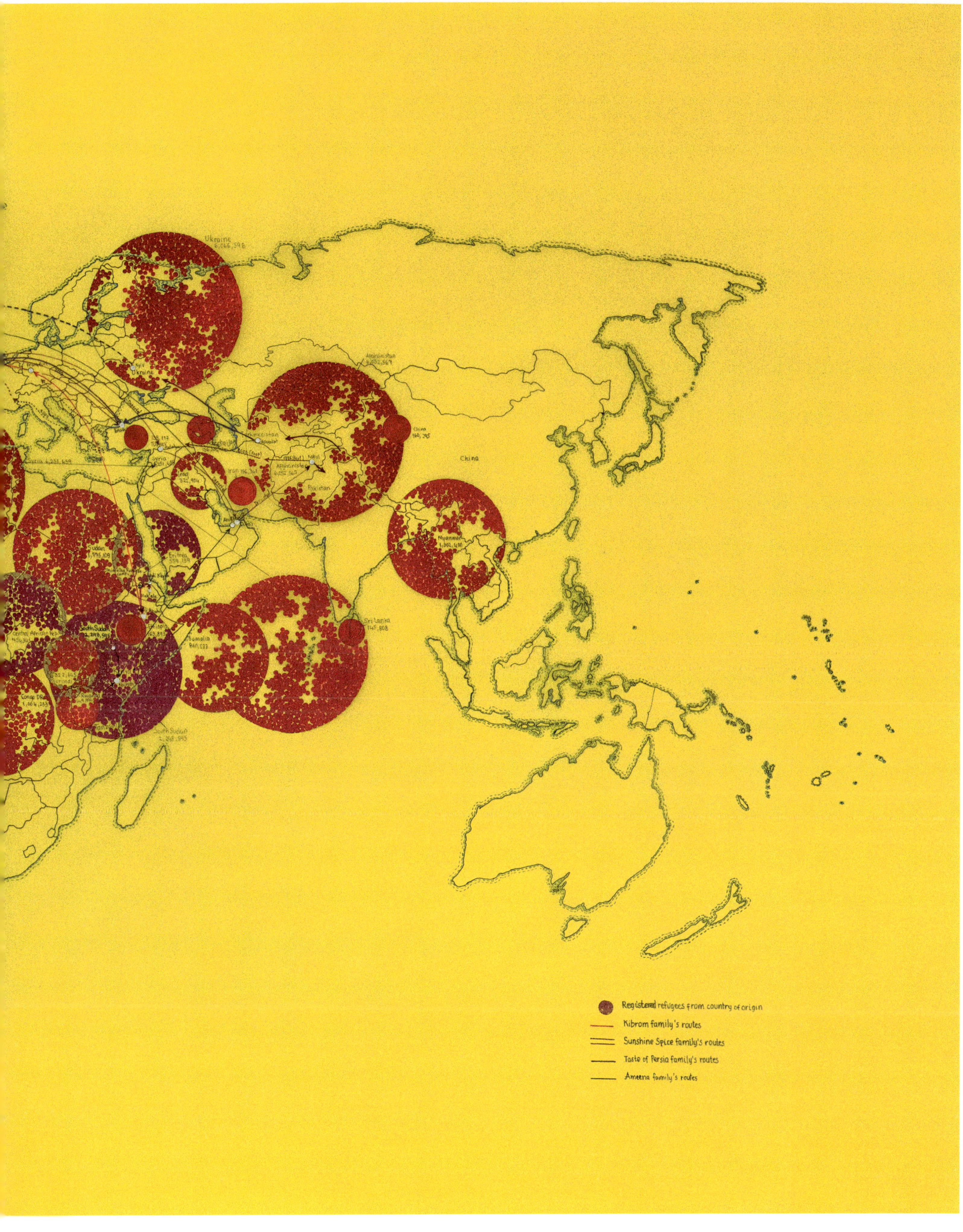

Ukraine
6,066,598
Afghanistan
6,052,567
China
160,295
China
Iran 156,341
Iraq
322,904
Kabul
Pakistan
Myanmar
1,302,400
Sri Lanka
145,808
Registered refugees from country of origin
Kibrom family's routes
Sunshine Spice family's routes
Taste of Persia family's routes
Ameena family's routes

Terra Rouge: CEW sites, rubber plantations, and abandoned airfields, 2022
Acrylic, ink, and oil on vellum and paper
113 × 70 cm (44 ½ × 27 ½ in.)

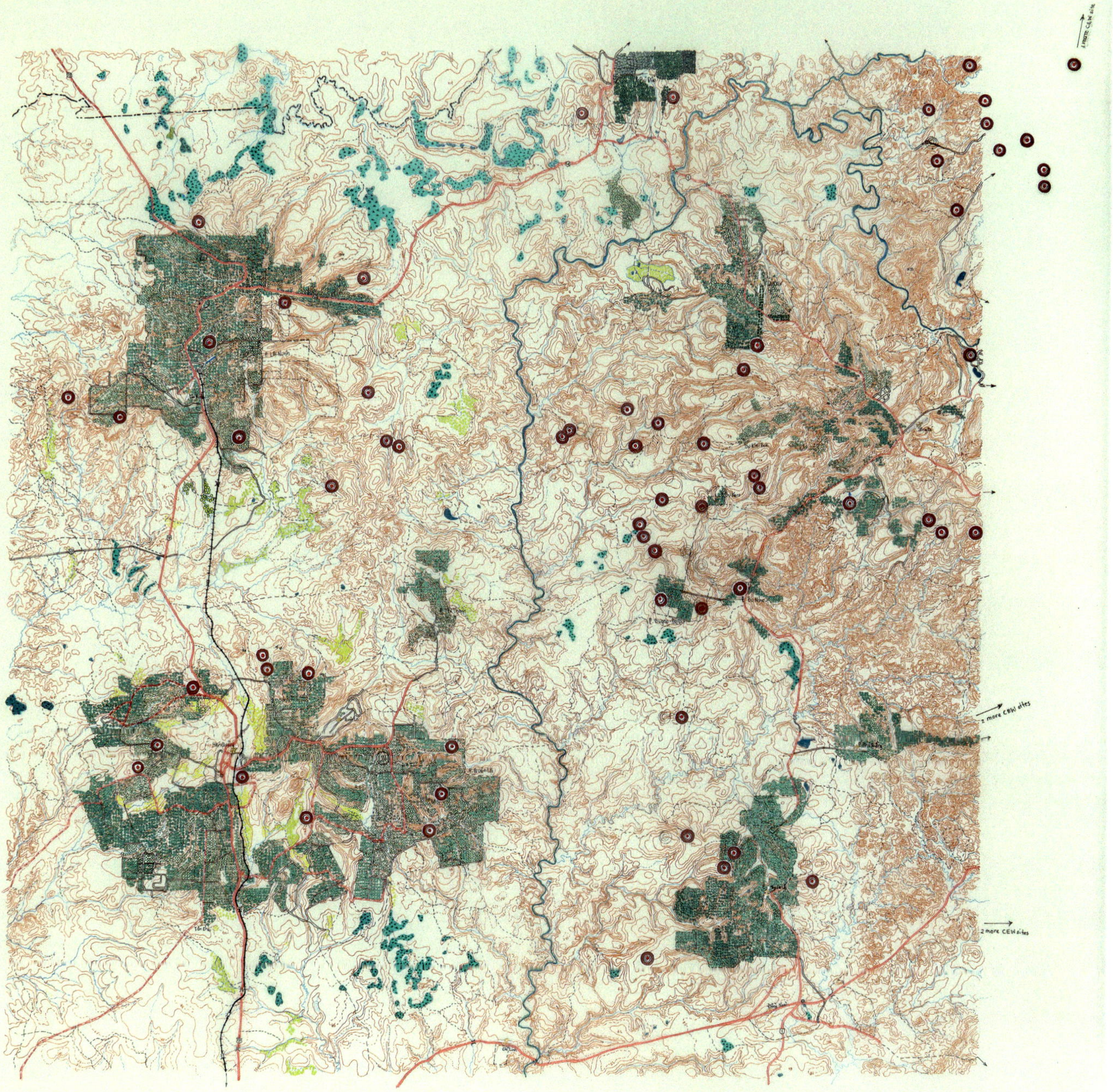
1 more CEW site
2 more CEW sites
2 more CEW sites

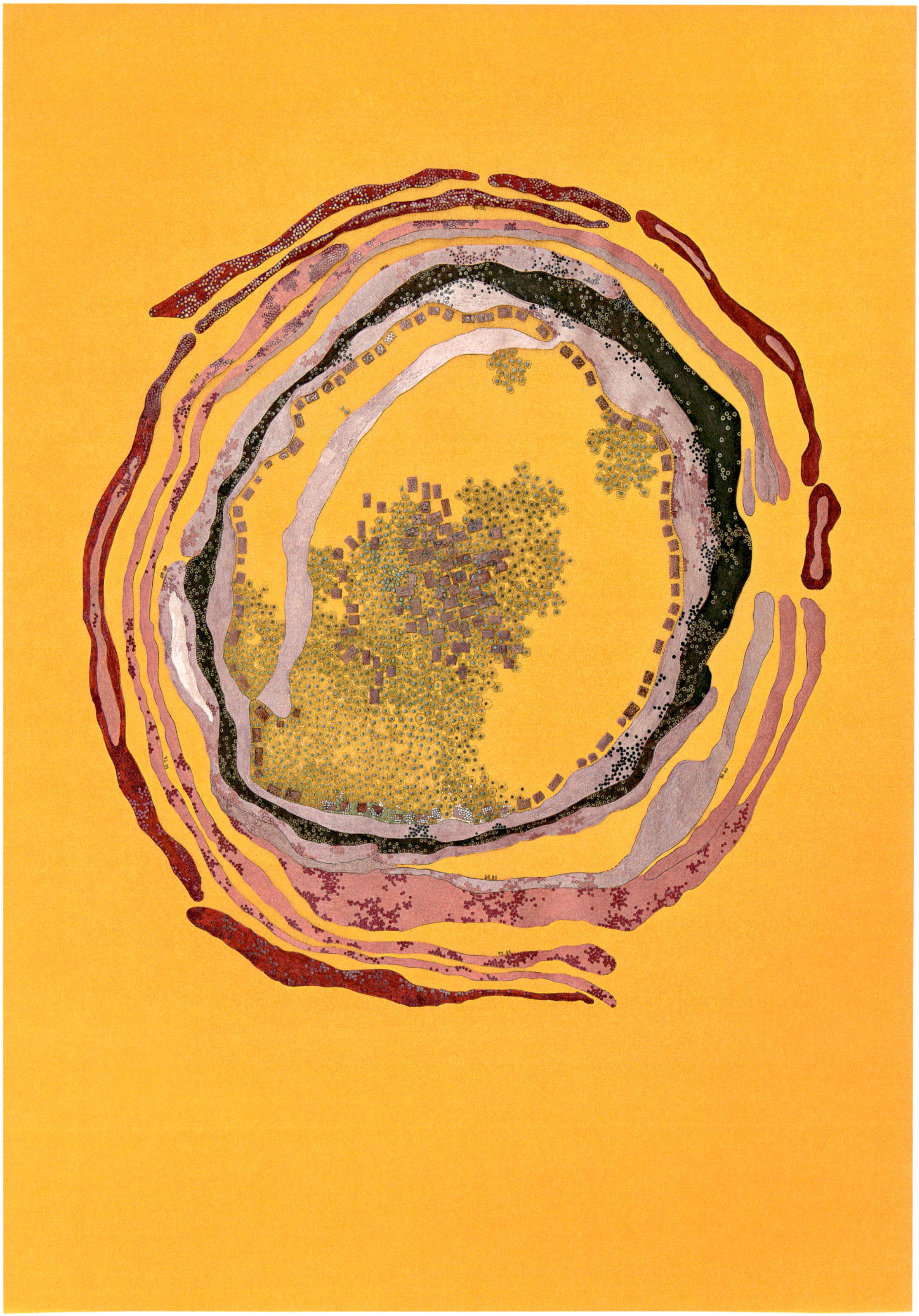

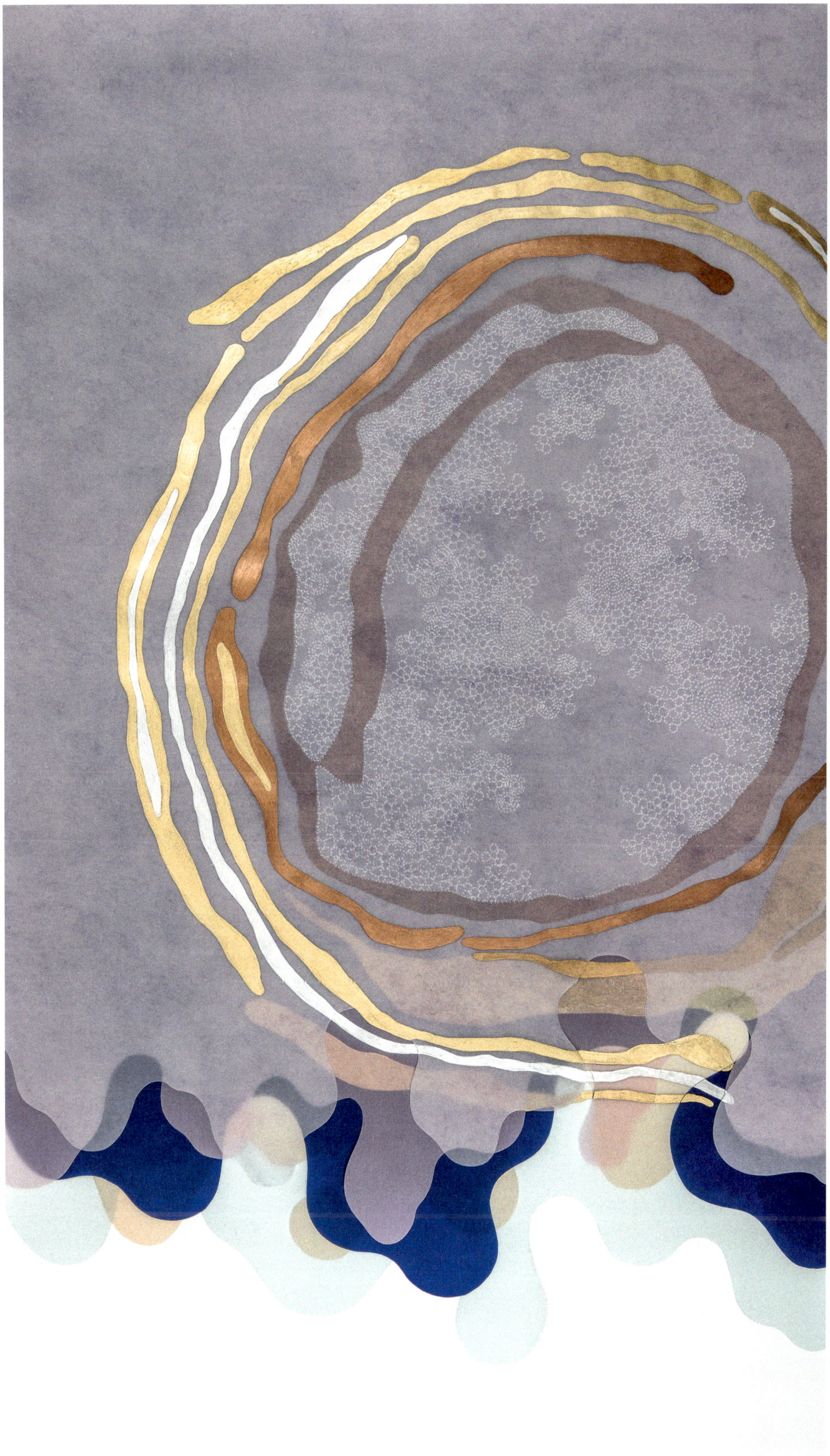

Terra Rouge CEW Study no. 1, 2022
Acrylic, ink, oil, and hand perforating on vellum and paper
113 × 70 cm (44 ½ × 27 ½ in.)

Terra Rouge CEW study no. 5, 2022
Ink, oil, and hand perforating on vellum and paper
94 × 54.9 cm (37 × 21 ⅝ in.)

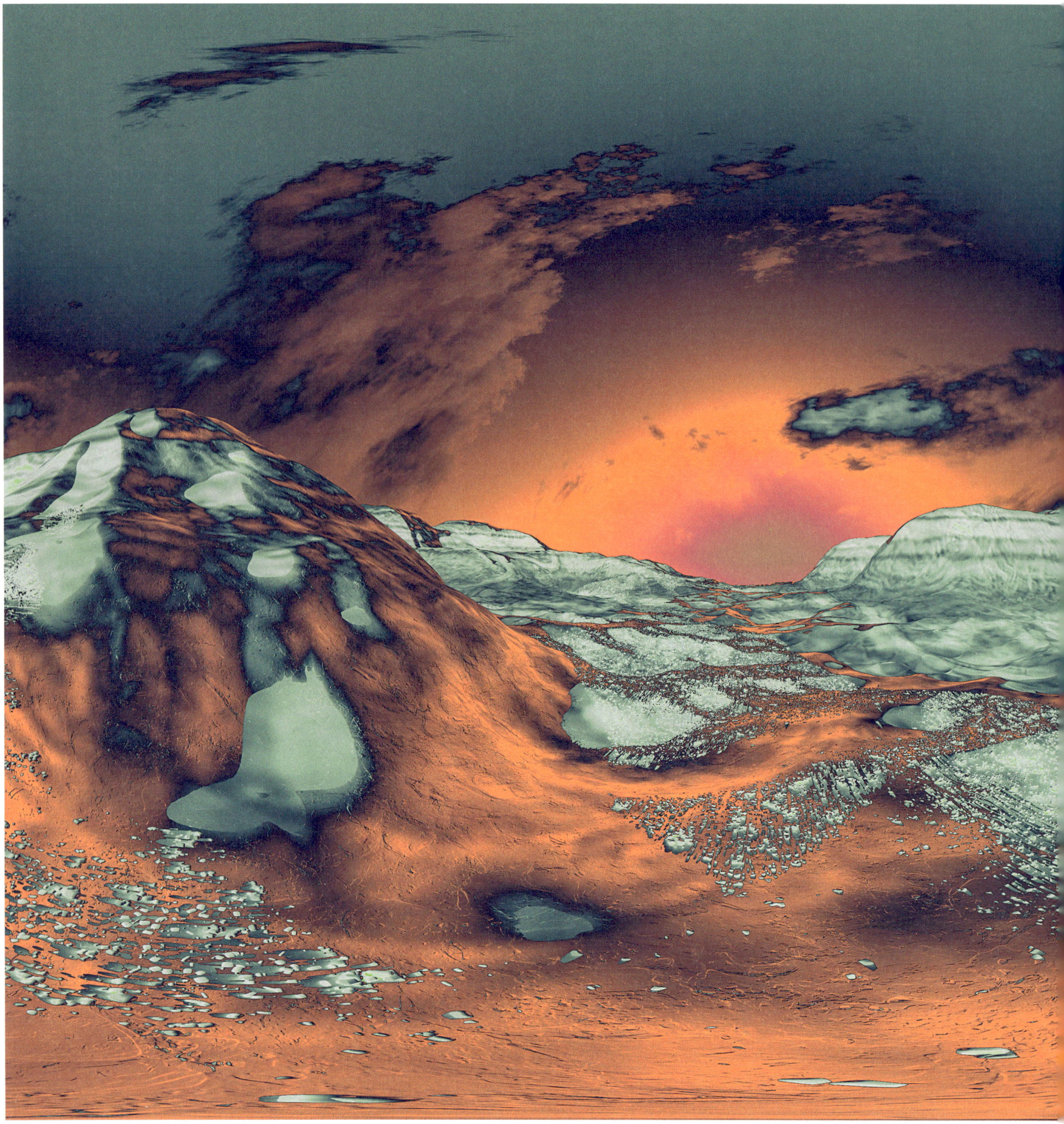

Spheres of Time, 2026
Immersive sound and
video installation
AlloSphere facility: 3-story metal
sphere, 26 video projectors,
and 54.1 audio channels

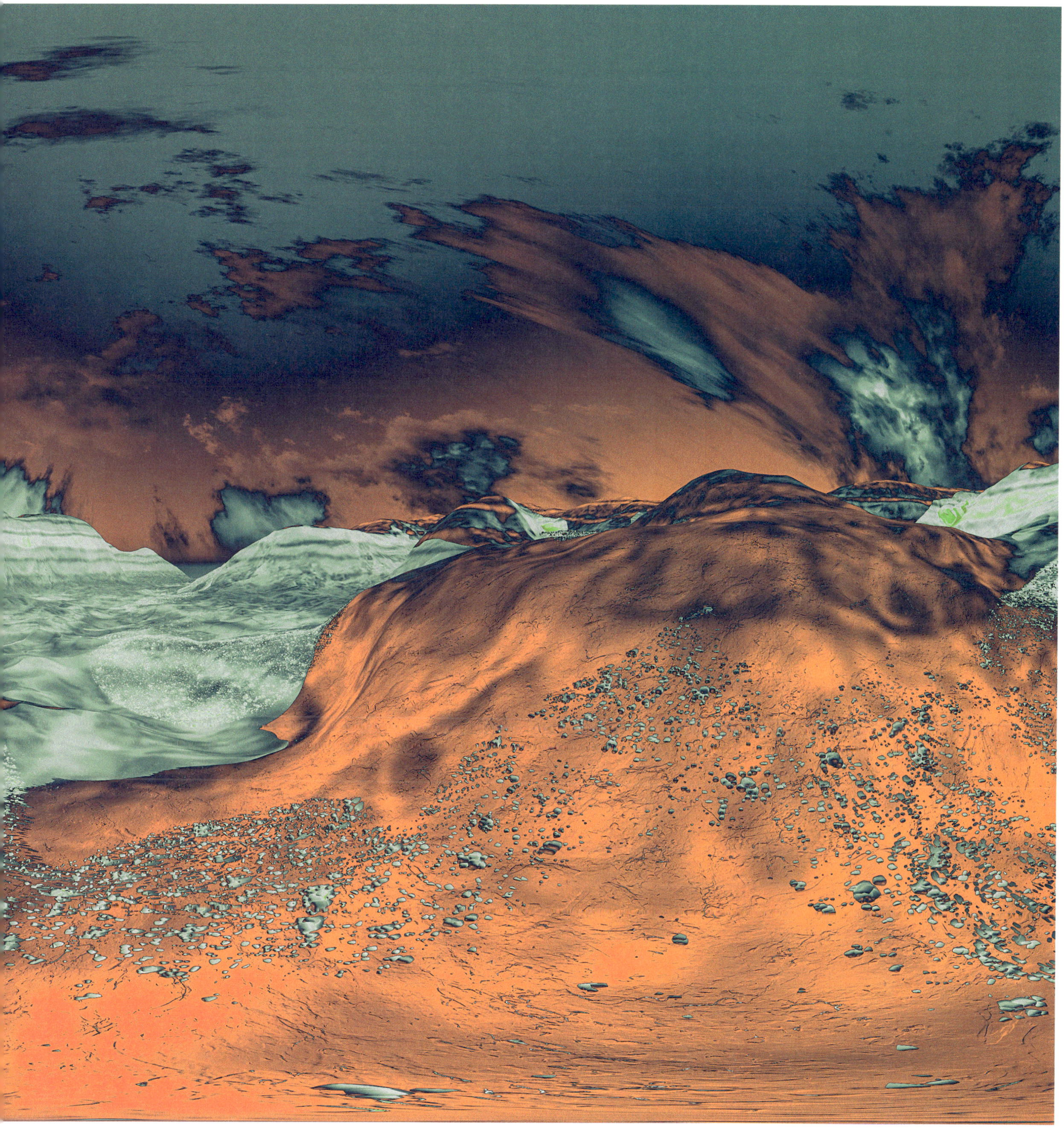

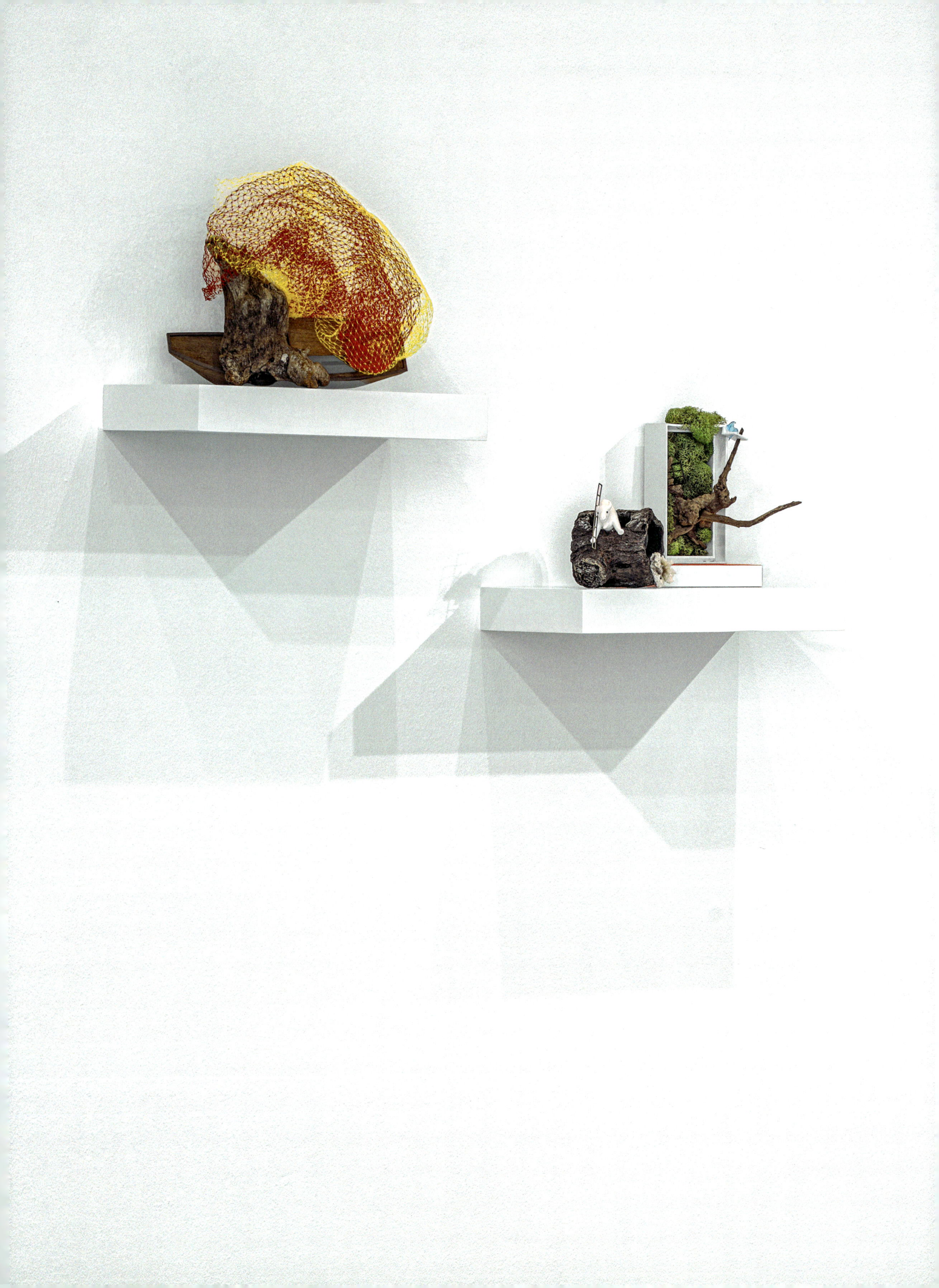

ESSAYS

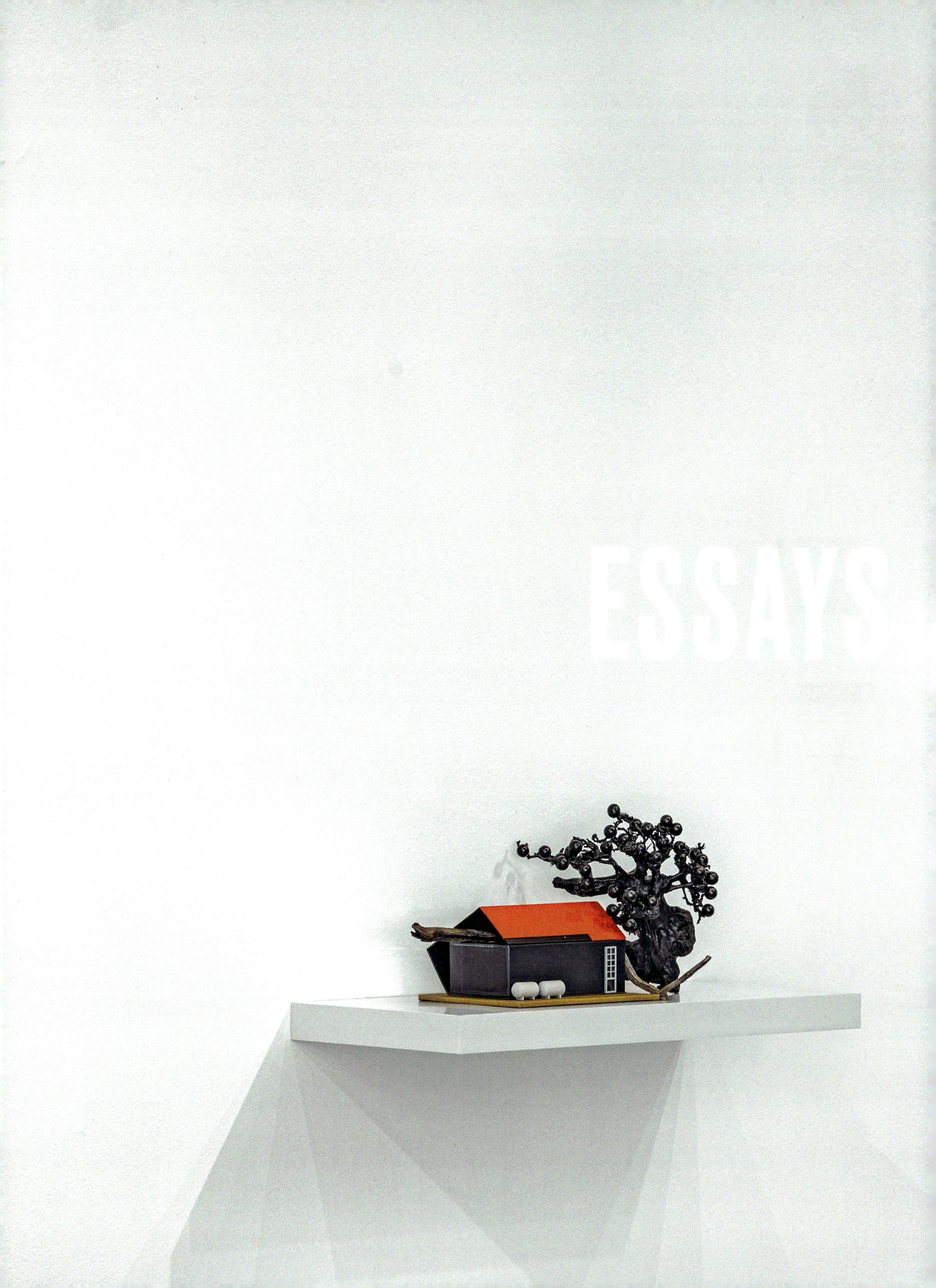

SHADOWS OF PLAY: TIFFANY CHUNG IN MILLENNIAL SÀI GÒN

Erik Harms

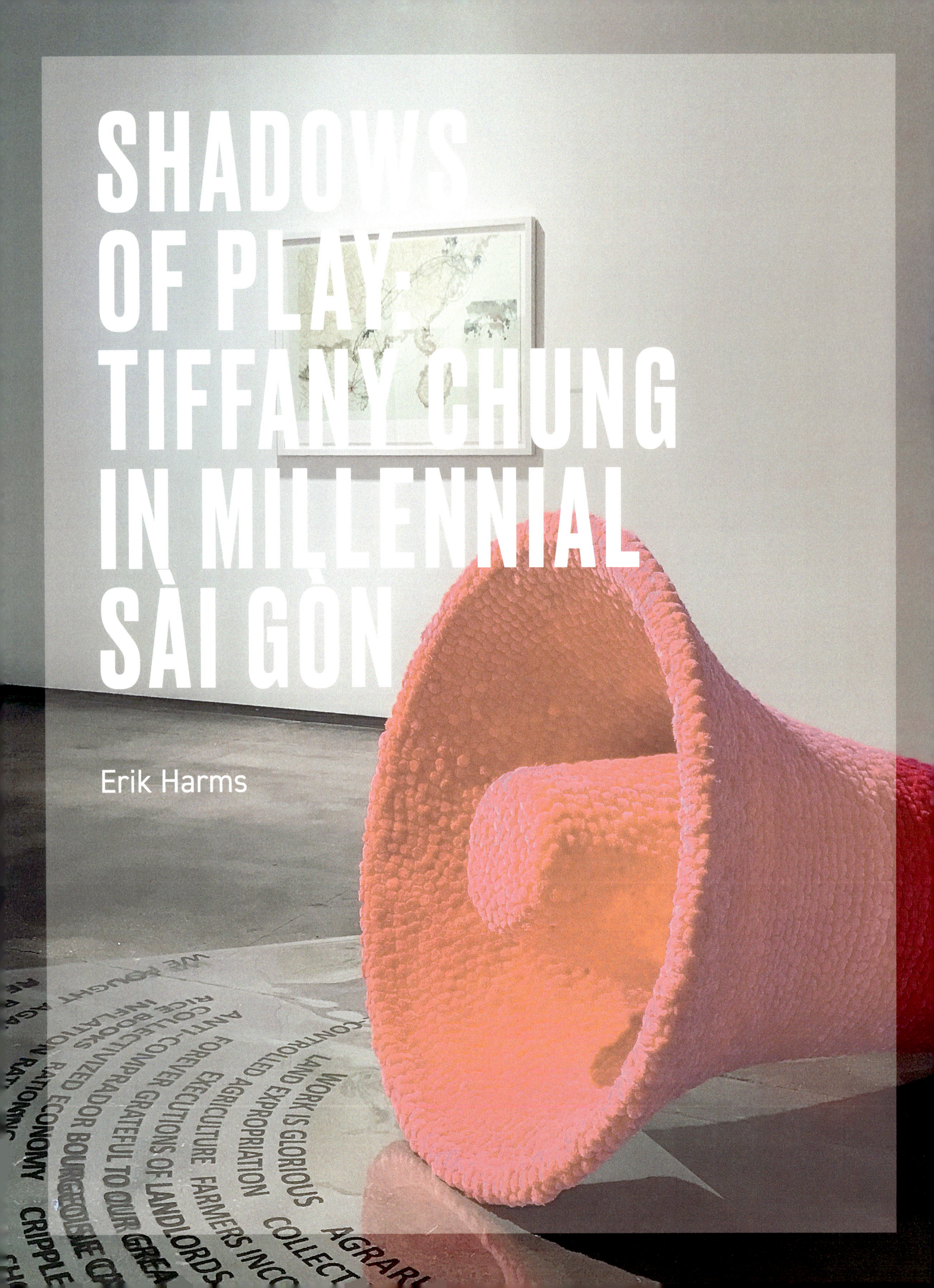

A fluffy megaphone. Stylized enoki mushrooms hybridized with berry trees. Ornate maps. Sherds of broken tiles and ceramics. These visually incongruous artworks were all produced during the decade or so after Tiffany Chung began living and working in Sài Gòn, starting in 2000. Twenty-five years after the end of the US/Việt Nam War, Sài Gòn was a far different place than it had been when Chung and her family fled the country as refugees during the immediate postwar period. After 1975, the city entered a period of extreme economic scarcity and political persecution so difficult that Vietnamese have now given it a name: the "subsidy era" (thời bao cấp, 1975–1986). It was a moment when official exuberance for high socialism was matched by everyday despondency about low living standards. During the subsidy era, the Communist Party leadership's zeal for building socialism was rivaled only by their desire to retaliate against people who had been associated with "the other side," a group that included Chung's family. Her father, a helicopter pilot during the war, had been captured as a prisoner of war in 1971, and was still imprisoned when the war ended. Back then, the city, which had been renamed Ho Chi Minh City by the new government, was a place from which to flee. By contrast, life in the millennial city, which most people had openly taken to calling Sài Gòn again, was supercharged. Chung's work was, too.

By the 2000s, overt political antagonisms had cooled somewhat, and Sài Gòn was enjoying a renaissance. Việt Nam was already in the second decade of political and economic reforms called *đổi mới* that the Party had officially introduced in 1986. Sài Gòn was increasingly flooded with new wealth, much of it coming from booming real estate enabled by market reforms that laws introduced throughout the 1990s had set in motion.[1] New art galleries—including Galerie Quynh, which opened in 2000, and Mai's Gallery, where Chung held one of her first solo exhibitions in 2003—were part of the urban transformation.

When Chung returned in 2000, the city's official population had reached over 5.25 million people. By 2010, the official population was 7,378,000, with some scholars estimating it was actually over 9.6 million, accounting for informal residents typically overlooked by the census.[2] The visual impact of all this growth was palpable. One of the first high-rises to be constructed in the postwar period, the thirty-three-story Saigon Trade Center, had opened in 1997 and others were going up across the city. Every new development seemed to infuse the visual landscape with striking symbolic juxtapositions. The Diamond Plaza, a high-end shopping mall that opened in 1999, is a case in point. A joint venture with South Korea, it was built at a prominent intersection next to April 30th Park, facing the boulevard where North Vietnamese tanks rolled in to capture Sài Gòn on that date in 1975. For the ruling Vietnamese Communist Party, April 30 commemorates the triumph of socialism over capitalism. By 2000, however, consumer capitalism was no longer banished, and it was possible to open a shopping mall in a symbolically central spot like this. Across the city, it was common to see temples of capitalism sitting cheek by jowl with memorials to socialist victory. Private corporations often held marketing seminars in Party-run hotels, and socialist propaganda posters competed for visual attention with advertising billboards. In this expanding consumer economy, the word *chơi* (play) was omnipresent and playfulness became something of an ethos, as many urban residents sought to prioritize enjoyment by partaking in new opportunities for pleasure, entertainment, and conspicuous consumption. The omnipresent emphasis on play sometimes made it seem as if the entire urban population was trying to compensate for the previous years of dearth they had endured.

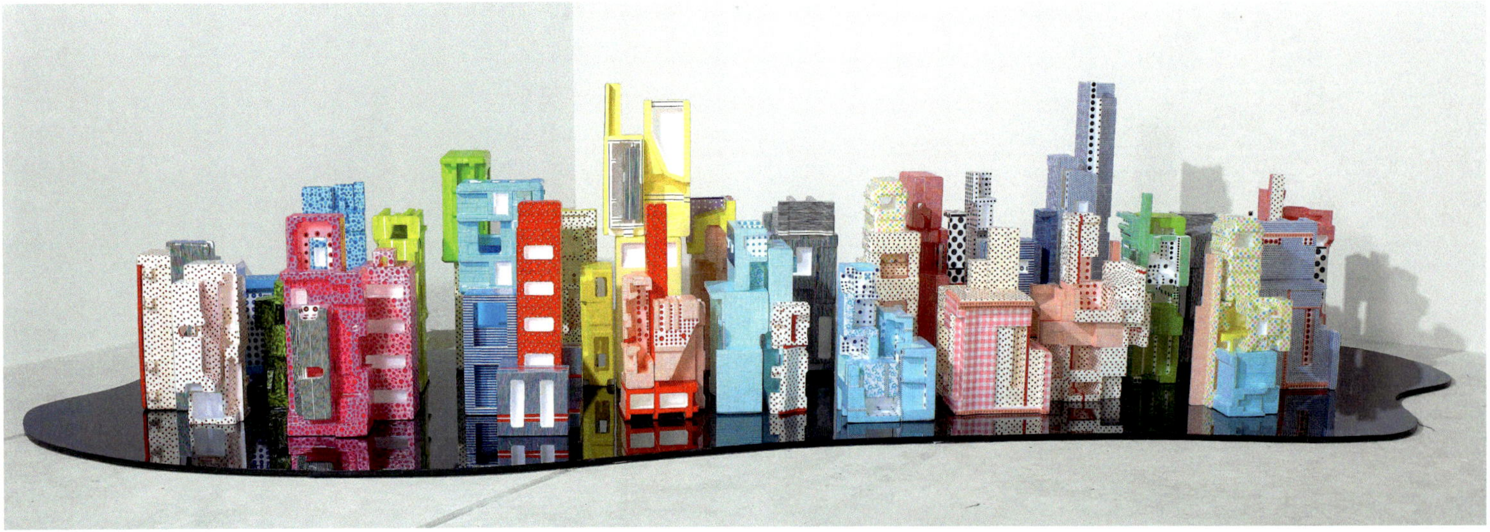

FIGURE 1 Tiffany Chung, *D-City: where sidewalk cafes meet the stars*, 2006/2010. Polystyrene, assorted tapes, thermoplastic adhesive, astro turf, painted plexiglass, and MDF, 200 × 600 cm (78 × 236 in.). Photograph by Brian Doan.

A visual semblance of this ethos is clearly on display, albeit tinged with a touch of irony, in a playful-looking installation called *D-City: where sidewalk cafes meet the stars* (2006/2010, fig. 1). Chung fashioned a mini cityscape out of Styrofoam salvaged from discarded electronic appliance boxes and decorated with multi-patterned assortments of tape and other forms of adhesive. The work calls attention to the vibrancy of growth, but its exaggerated whimsy also implicitly hints at how excessive this all is—the colorful fantasy of this urban dream is literally made from the waste of consumer capitalism. Sài Gòn's urban growth of that decade also produced new forms of socioeconomic inequality: luxury spaces were expanding to serve the new rich, but urban precarity was also widespread. The social inequalities were visible everywhere. At each crossing of a bridge over the city's canals, commuters on new motorbikes or passengers in air-conditioned taxis would see thousands of stilt houses hovering above malodorous waterways, black with pollution. Despite these inequities, the new urban landscape also showed glimmers of political and ideological permissiveness (at least toward consumerism) that stood out against a political backdrop that remained staunchly committed to defending socialist orthodoxies and the single-party state. This is what scholars began calling "market socialism," a hybrid form of socialism with neoliberal characteristics.[3] Full of visual contrasts, Sài Gòn was not only an artist's playground, but also a city in need of the critical vision that great art could offer.

Chung grappled with the tensions coursing through this playground of endless juxtapositions, where every urban corner was rich with symbolism. In her piece *Work Is Glorious, Long Live the Party* (2008/2019, fig. 2), a megaphone covered with fluffy magenta pom poms captures with brilliant directness the tug between consumerist enticement and the dogged resilience of Vietnamese socialist political ideologies. The artwork visually expresses what the social theorist Nguyễn-võ Thu-hương has called the "ironies of freedom," a condition in which formal political power at the time was deeply Leninist but modes of everyday self-expression and activity were more directly governed by markets and consumerism.[4] In Việt Nam's official political society, anyone authorized to hold a megaphone would be expected to amplify words of socialist mobilization. Urban neighborhoods still had cone-shaped speakers attached to telephone poles that would announce Party-approved news and other exhortations. In this way, Chung's megaphone evokes the Leninist state, with its penchant for announcing central plans loudly, while recognizing that city residents could still get arrested if they directly criticized the Party or "Ho Chi Minh Thought," no matter how playful the city seemed.[5] (This is still true today, fifty years after the end of the war.) At the same time, the scale, bright pink color, and textures of Chung's megaphone are inspired by plastic toys and Asian kitsch, highlighting the impact of Korean, Japanese, and Taiwanese cultural capital and money, and pointing to the strong social pressure people were under to become consumers and keep up with the latest trends.

For Sài Gòn residents at the time, government paperwork and neighborhood units were still regulated by bureaucratic socialism and a very formalized, ideologically correct type of language, even though business and entertainment opportunities (as well as school fees and health care) were increasingly dictated by the market economy. Chung's work offered visual responses to the contradictions of everyday life, encouraging viewers to grapple with the tensions coursing through the quickly growing city and the ironies of market freedom in a state that still insisted on calling itself socialist.

Play Tough Aim High (2008, fig. 3) not only looks ironically at socialism but also puts the idea of *play* under the spotlight. The photograph presents cute young men dressed up in the style of Japanese cosplay then popular in Sài Gòn while striking the kind of pose typically associated with socialist propaganda posters. Chung suggests that these saccharine expressions of outward-facing joyfulness barely conceal pernicious political ideologies.[6] She shows that play can only be understood by coming to terms with its shadow, ideology. The hyper-consumerist urban life that had emerged under conditions of neoliberal socialism were never fully liberating. Attending to the shadows of play might offer a way of understanding how urban exuberance is inseparable from certain aspects of state control.[7]

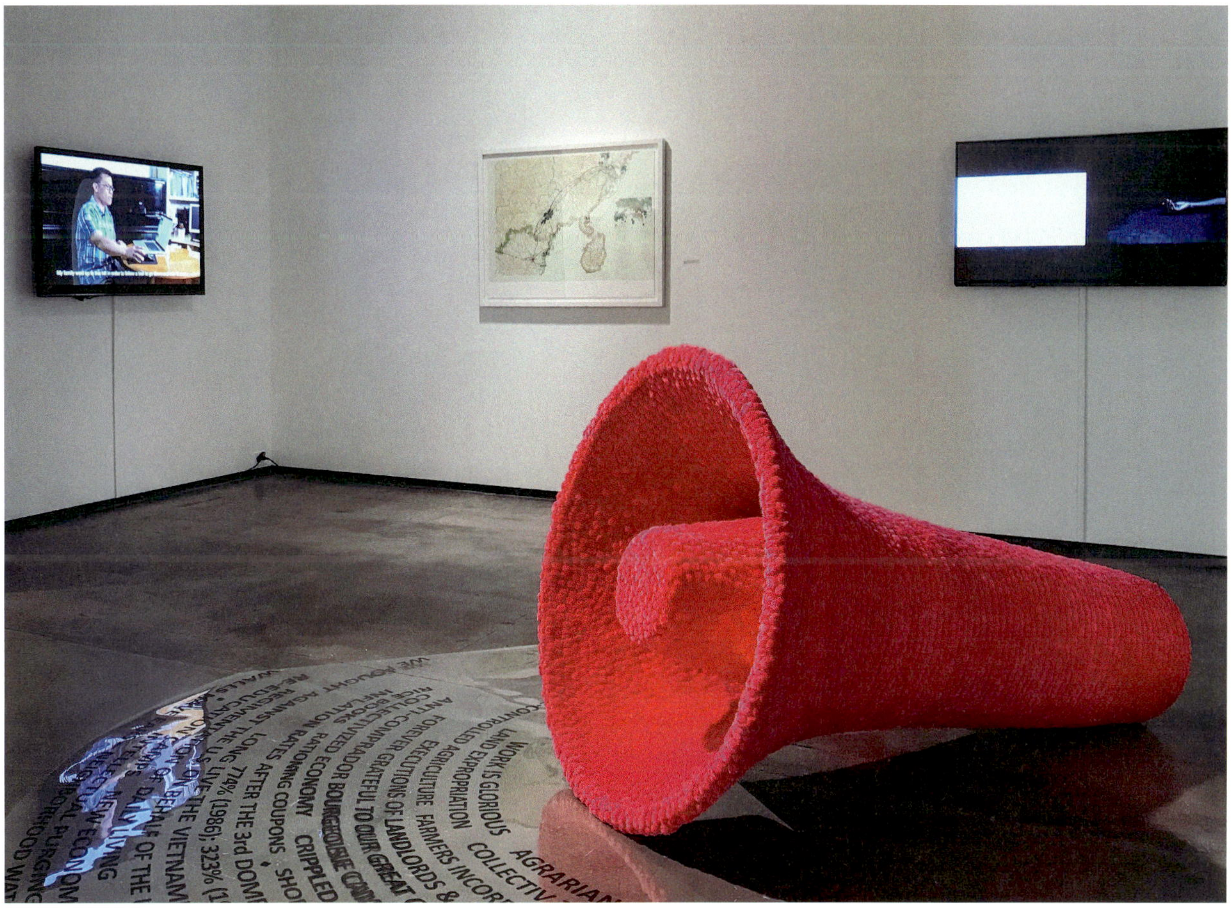

FIGURE 2 Tiffany Chung, *Work Is Glorious, Long Live the Party*, 2008/2019. Bamboo, wire, papier-mâché, pom poms, thermos adhesive and vinyl decals, sculpture: 101.6 cm × 172.7 cm (40 × 68 in.); decal text: 172.7 × 265.4 cm (68 × 104 ½ in.). Installation view, *Tiffany Chung: passage of time*, Tyler Rollins Gallery, 2019.

Such a reading of play would resonate with keen observers of Sài Gòn nightlife in the new millennium, wherein the Vietnamese word for play, *chơi*, implied a privileged existence available to the newly rich, who most often gained their wealth via nepotistic political connections. The player, *người ăn chơi*, was rarely innocent, and neither was play.[8] The fun colors in fashion, billboards, and consumer products that made the city seem increasingly vibrant could not conceal the continued controls on political expression in Việt Nam. In 2007, the year Chung joined Dinh Q. Lê and others to establish the nonprofit art space Sàn Art, scores of Vietnamese dissidents were arrested on exaggerated charges of "conducting anti-government propaganda" and twenty were sentenced to prison.[9] Against such a political backdrop, Chung's concept of play directly challenged viewers to question what might be concealed by the superficialities of the bubble tea palette that characterized commercialized urban life.

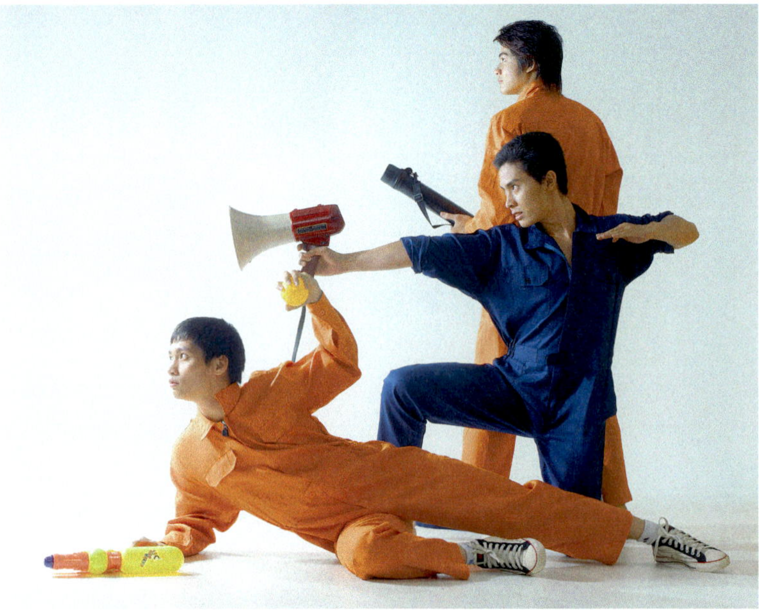

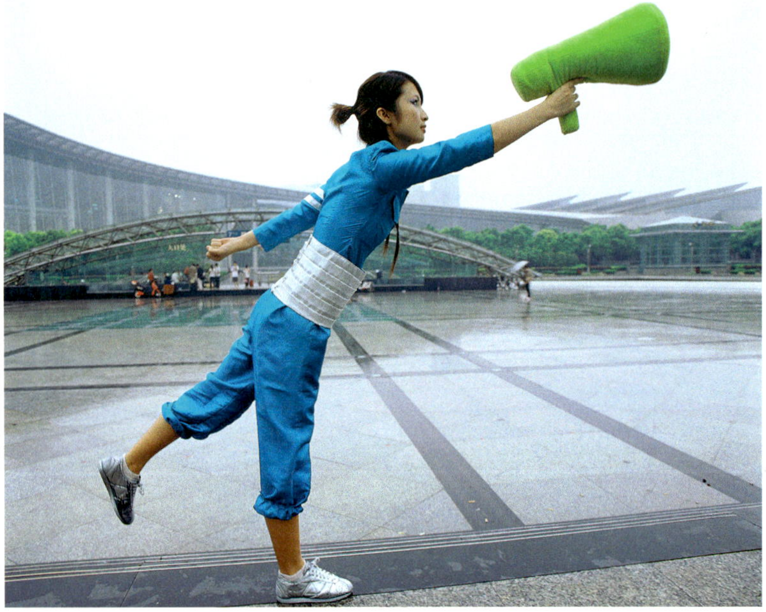

FIGURE 3 Tiffany Chung, *Play Tough Aim High*, 2008. C-Print, 99 × 149.8 cm (39 × 59 in.). Photograph by Truong Quoc Huy.

FIGURE 4 Tiffany Chung, *Blue Summer Girl from Enokiberry Tree in Wonderland, Episode 3*, 2008. C-Print, 120 × 150 cm (47 ⅕ × 58 1/10 in.).

Subsequent works, especially the *Enokiberry Tree* series, reflect on the hollowness of play in the face of political power, and draw critical attention to the excessive vacuity of lives lived in the colors of bubble tea and pom poms. To apprehend Chung's approach, it is necessary to recognize how a critique of state ideology is conveyed through the stylized propagandistic posture of the actors in the photographs, and in the process to see that the critique is leveled not only at socialism but at all forms of empty rhetoric. In *Blue Summer Girl from Enokiberry Tree in Wonderland, Episode 3* (2008, fig. 4), for example, a female cosplayer dressed in a blue space-age outfit wields a plush green megaphone while balancing in a socialist-inspired pose of forward advance, all against the background of a vacant, oversized plaza in Shanghai. The composition, part of a series of staged photographs, forces viewers to grapple with the vacuous, alienating urban spaces of commodified Asia—the kinds of urban non-places that are produced by rampant expansion and growth fueled by neoliberal developmentalism. The sculptural installation of *Enokiberry Tree in Wonderland* (2010, fig. 5), with its slender, red-tipped white mushrooms, towering above average adult human height, advances similar themes, albeit using different visual cues. Viewers need to know that the "enokiberry tree" itself is a fabulation. The conceit plays off the hybridized

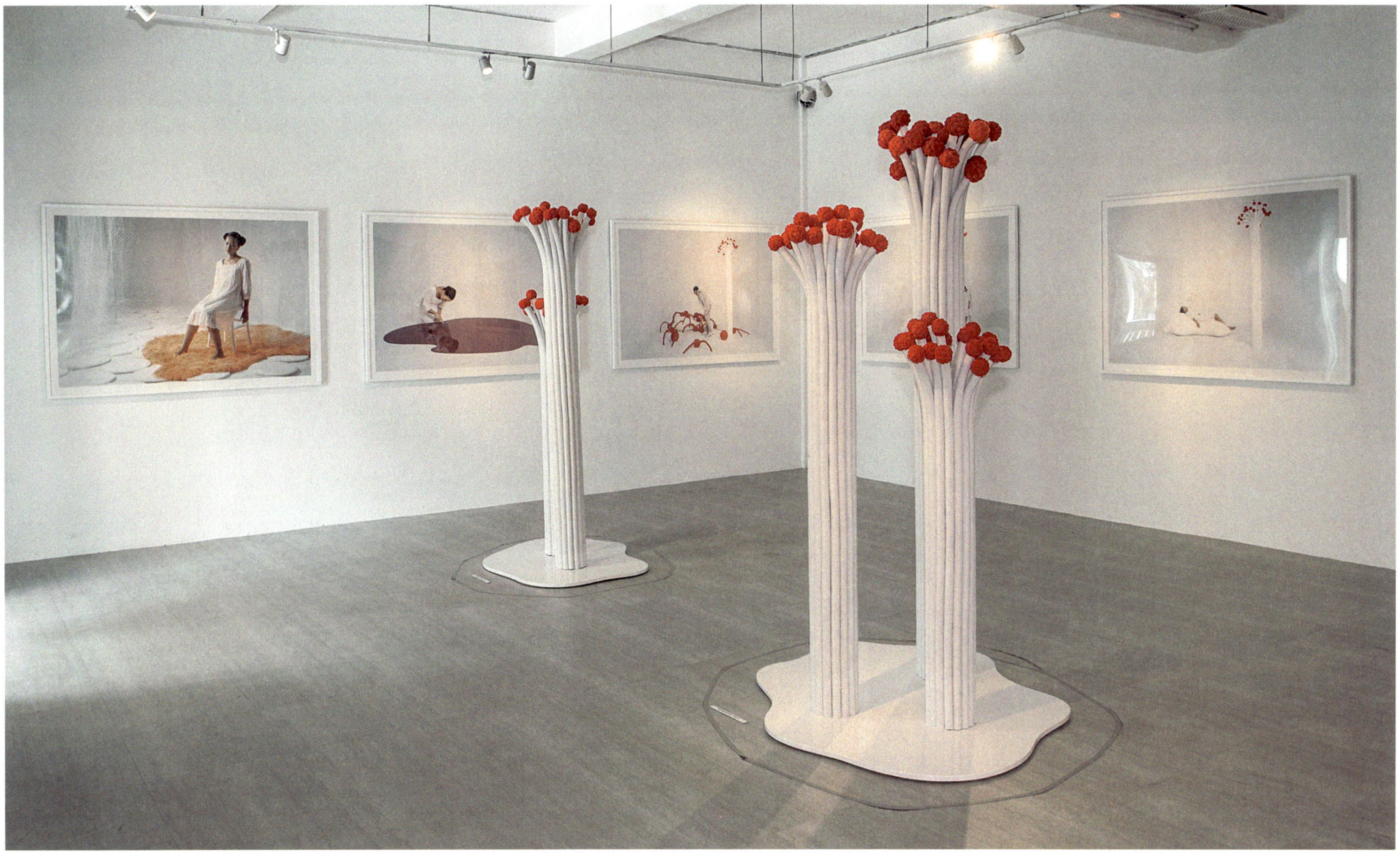

FIGURE 5 Tiffany Chung, *Enokiberry Tree in Wonderland*, 2010. Mixed media, dimensions variable. Installation view, *PANORAMA: Recent Art from Contemporary Asia*, Singapore Art Museum, Singapore, 2012. Collection of Singapore Art Museum. Image Courtesy of National Heritage Board.

form of thin enoki mushrooms—which can only be grown in a controlled lab environment—dipped in bright red so their caps look like berries, and growing as tall as trees. Enokis evoke spontaneous growth, and in the form Chung gives them, they call to mind the buildings popping up across Sài Gòn at the time, like mushrooms after a rain. Like apartment buildings, enoki mushrooms are thin, mostly white in color, and they sprout quickly, as if out of nowhere. Japanese in origin, enokis are available across Asia, pointing to the inter-Asian circulation of cultural capital that accompanied Sài Gòn's rapid growth, bringing with it both foreign direct investment and passion for Japanese-inspired cuteness that was changing the city. On the other hand, the enokiberry trees, despite their bright color scheme, populate a dark parable depicting what happens when societies let development grow out of control. In the photos that surround the sculptures, futuristic-looking actors, carrying plush megaphones and dressed in space-age costumes, wander among outcroppings of these imaginary trees, framed by the open voids of new kinds of Asian urbanism that were being built at the time in developments on the outskirts of the city, where newly widened multi-lane boulevards would cross modern new bridges into vast master-planned developments that combined high-end commodity housing and large-scale shopping malls with new government administrative districts and export-processing zones. If Việt Nam's economy could be described as a market economy with socialist characteristics, *Enokiberry Tree in Wonderland* seemed to express utopian urbanism with dystopian characteristics. These are the ironies of freedom.

Chung digs further into her excavations of unchecked urbanism in subsequent works, especially through her intense and sustained engagement with maps. The title of one of her first maps, *10.7747°N 106.6667°E* (2007, fig. 6) refers to

FIGURE 6 Tiffany Chung, *10.7747°N 106.6667°E*, 2007. Oil and alcohol-based markers on paper, 79.2 × 109 cm (31 ⅛ × 42 15/16 in.). Post Vidai Vietnamese Art Collection. Photograph by Nam Bui.

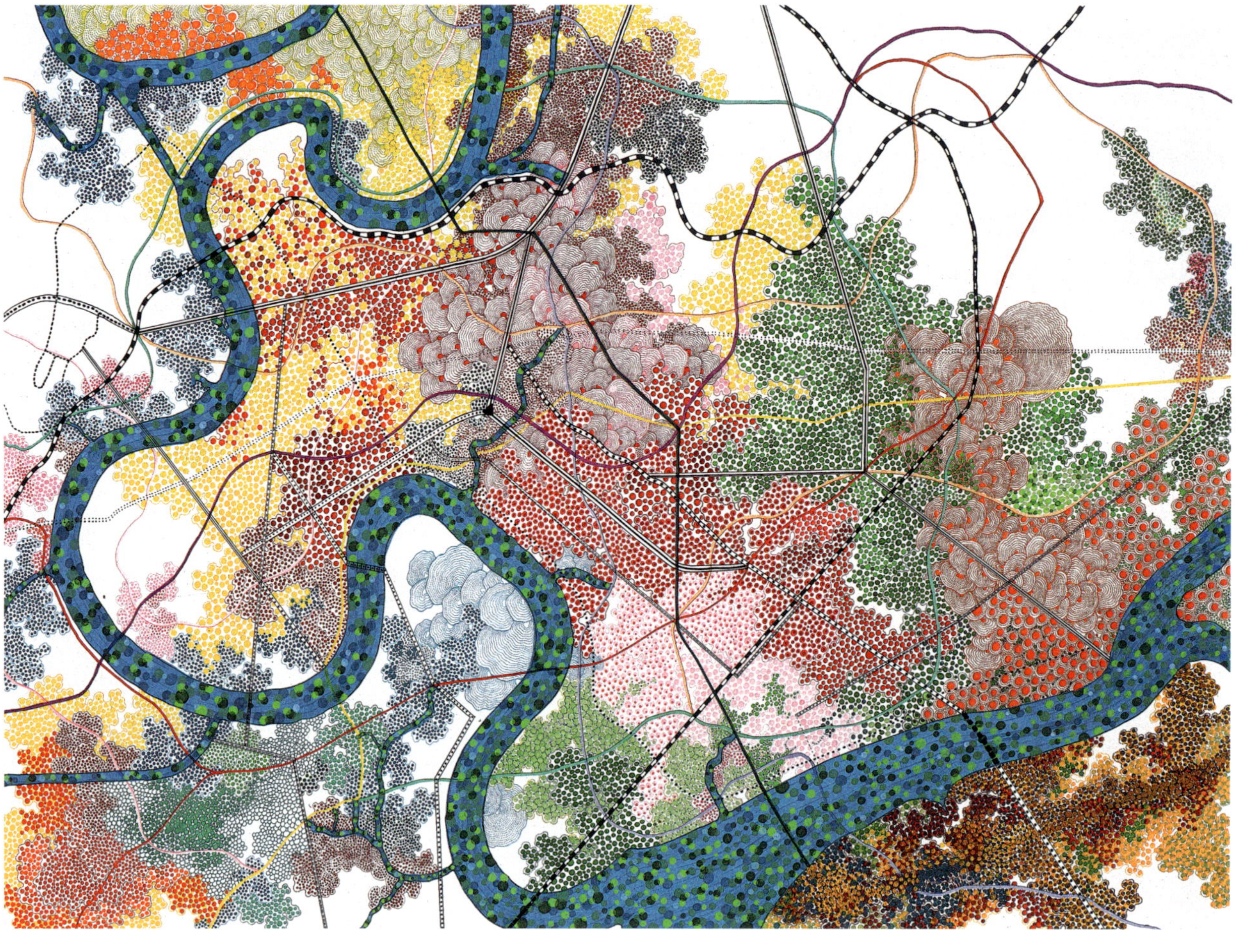

cartographic coordinates. Entering these coordinates into a web browser will take you to a digital map of Sài Gòn. Zooming in further brings you to a neighborhood surrounding Chí Hòa prison, a yellow, octagonal, French-built facility in operation since 1949, the waning years of colonialism. Interestingly, the coordinates do not take you to the exact place depicted on Chung's map. Her map is centered on a different part of the city, in what was once a rural area to the east of the meandering Sài Gòn River. The prominent oxbow in the bottom-left quadrant of the image encircles what in the 2000s was the site of a major urban development project called the Thủ Thiêm New Urban Zone.[10] I have previously described the devastation wrought upon the 14,600 working-class households that had been evicted so property developers could grab the land to build the project.[11] Across Sài Gòn, new urban projects delivered commodious housing to the Vietnamese middle class and made property moguls rich while displacing thousands of hard-working Vietnamese. Former farmers on the peri-urban fringes were swindled by dubious schemes that rezoned agricultural land only to transfer it at falsely deflated prices to real estate developers and land speculators with connections to corrupt government officials. The excitement of seeing all the city's new high-rises cannot be separated from alarming acts of destruction, land grabbing, and dispossession.

Chung's meticulous map overlays offer commentary on urban growth and words of pause about excess. Intricate hand-inked markings spill across *10.7747°N 106.6667°E* like some kind of organism growing across the landscape. Similar to the enokiberries, they look both artificial and organic at once. Viewed from the god's-eye perspective of the map, they also seem to be oozing, spreading. Perhaps they are the spores of enoki mushrooms? Personally, I see *hạt é*, sweet basil seeds that have been soaked in water, and the key ingredient in an old-school Vietnamese dessert that is both delicious and impossible not to stare at. When mixed with fruity flavors, *hạt é* seem oddly futuristic, like something a multinational bubble tea company might have engineered to achieve maximum cuteness and addictive mouthfeel. While *hạt é* are known to be healthy, eating too many of them can lead to an upset stomach, and while their color schemes make them seem playful at first, they can also spill out of control. With imagery like this, Chung's maps also call attention to the way urban growth both produces beautiful things and runs out of control. Growth creates the shadows of dispossession, another theme that runs through Chung's work.

If the maps offer a skeptical look at unbridled urban growth from a satellite view, her project *Archaeology for Future Remembrance* (see pp. 56–63) takes what might be called a ground up or "rubble's-eye view" of urban development. Chung has said publicly that much of her work is an act of "protest against this politically driven historical amnesia."[12] The amnesia she critiques is imposed by powerful forces that continue to propagate episodes of dispossession and displacement, imposed not only by government leaders, but also by overconfident urban planners and arrogant real estate titans who evade all attempts to hold them accountable. Such themes are sadly relevant throughout the world, but Chung focused her early work on the story of Việt Nam to draw attention to the inequitable ways in which the hubris of experts and leaders can lead to fields of rubble. When thinking of Việt Nam, most foreign observers associate rubble with the impact of war, but too many overlook the fact that dispossession has also been rampant after the war, often in the form of unbridled urban development and land grabbing. What happened to the people from Thủ Thiêm was, and still is, happening across the country.

One of Chung's works from 2013 takes us directly to the rubble of Thủ Thiêm. Named after a geolocation in Sài Gòn, *10°45'39"N 106°43'23"E* (see p. 54), the work itself consists of a large slab of what were once interior household tiles still attached to a rough layer of concrete. The coordinates referred to in the title denote the precise location in Thủ Thiêm where these tiles were excavated, directly within the rubble fields where an entire neighborhood had been demolished. The site also happened to be the location of a historic structure called the Đồn Cá Trê, the first guard tower erected to protect the river entrance into Sài Gòn during precolonial times. Excavating there allows Chung to stress the historical importance of the site in a thinly veiled rebuttal of assertions by developers that the area was a wasteland, with no significant historical vestiges worth preserving. This heavy slab is sometimes displayed alongside another work, *remnants of history* (2016, fig. 7), which consists of a museum-style vitrine within which Chung has laid out a collection of tile fragments and pieces of broken ceramic dinnerware. It is designed to look like the presentation of pot sherds commonly displayed in archaeology museums. The actual objects, like the slab of tiles, are real pieces of detritus Chung salvaged from the demolished neighborhood.

Chung's excavations were conducted during the tail end of a long period of eviction and displacement, at precisely the time when a landscape of habitation was being rendered into a blank slate for future urban development. Together they form an act of anticipatory memorialization, a kind of "activist archive," to borrow a useful phrase from Doreen Lee.[13] Chung's artistic archaeology inverts the standard directionality of time, curated by people who have come to understand that they are living in the middle of history and thus already know that it is their duty to collect artifacts for future remembrance. Curating these artifacts has allowed her to turn at least part of this space of mass dispossession into a memorial. In other iterations of this exhibit, Chung also displayed children's flip flops, metal window frames, and even excerpts from my own unpublished scholarly manuscript that documents the history of the place and the process of its destruction. In that essay, I questioned how it was possible for planners to have claimed that the place from which all these people were evicted was empty, even though those planners had copious knowledge of the place and its people—ranging from cadastral maps to land registries. Planners who know a given area is full of people and still mobilize expert knowledge to assert that it is empty engage in what I call "knowing into oblivion."[14] Through acts of remapping, Chung reclaims power from the state and demands that viewers pay attention to people who have been obscured by acts of cartographic erasure.

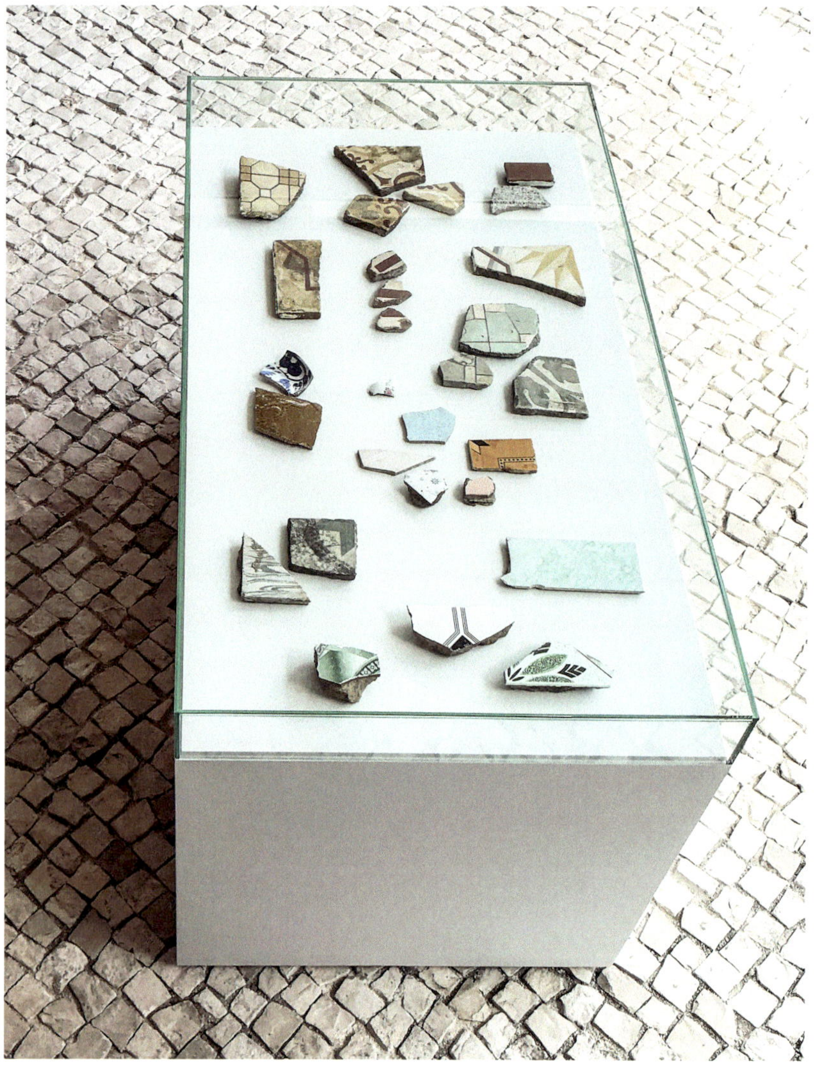

FIGURE 7 Tiffany Chung, *remnants of history: French colonial tile technology, pieces of home foundations, and traces of lived lives*, 2016. 28 retrieved pieces of cement/ceramic tiles and domestic objects, dimensions variable. Installation view, *Thu Thiem: archaeology for future remembrance*, Maumaus/Lumiar Cité, Lisbon, Portugal, 2019.

Thanks to Chung's work, viewers can move beyond scholarly theorizing; they can look through the fragments of that oblivion and remember it back into existence. In this way, her archaeology of a present crisis recalls the work of anthropologist Jason De León, who has used the tools of archaeology to preserve and memorialize artifacts left by those who have tried, and perished while trying, to make the perilous crossing of the US-Mexico border through the treacherous lands of the Sonoran Desert.[15] Chung's work, like De León's, takes a case of forced displacement and makes it into an object of memorialization and care, and in doing so posits a searing critique of the forces causing the displacement. In some showings, her collected artifacts are accompanied by a map, which Chung altered visually, but which she chose to name by simply adding the word "after" to the original title of a map produced by Americans during the war: *After 1972 USAID Thu Thiem Development Plan* (see p. 61). As with all the maps in her cartographic series, Chung applies her palimpsestic magic here, showing how this project of "development" is connected to a long history of displacement. De León and Chung are connected by a global history of migration and displacement, a theme about which Vietnamese people of Chung's generation and of her parents' know too much, intimately and personally. Viewers are drawn in by the playfulness of her art, bursting with color. But the more one stares at them, the more it becomes clear that even the most colorful things cast very dark shadows.

NOTES

1 Exchanging land had only become possible again in 1992 and planners were only allowed to use the term "market economy" in 1994.

2 The official population numbers are available in Government of Vietnam General Statistics Office, "Dân Số Và Lao Động [Population and Labor]" (Hanoi [Online]: Available Online: Trung tâm Tư liệu Thống kê–Tổng Cục Thống kê Việt Nam 2014). For the unofficial number, see Du Huynh, "The Misuse of Urban Planning in Ho Chi Minh City," *Habitat International* 48 (2015).

3 Christina Schwenkel and Ann Marie Leshkowich, "How Is Neoliberalism Good to Think Vietnam? How Is Vietnam Good to Think Neoliberalism?" *positions: asia critique* 20, no. 2 (2012).

4 Nguyễn-võ Thu-hương, *The Ironies of Freedom: Sex, Culture, and Neoliberal Governance in Vietnam* (University of Washington Press, 2008).

5 "Ho Chi Minh Thought" is not my term but an actual political ideology that combines Marxism-Leninism with ideas culled from the history of Ho Chi Minh's writing and speeches. Vietnamese political leaders regularly pen essays espousing their application of Ho Chi Minh Thought to various topics.

6 This approach might be called a "Frankfurt-school-style social critique," because it critiques superficiality in ways similar to the critiques popularized by Herbert Marcuse. See Herbert Marcuse, *One-Dimensional Man* (Beacon Press, 1964). For more on the Frankfurt School, see Martin Jay, *The Dialectical Imagination: A History of the Frankfurt School and the Institute of Social Research, 1923–1950* (University of California Press, 1996).

7 For a compelling discussion of how to think along with Freud, Derrida, and Jungian shadow work when conceptualizing Vietnamese and Vietnamese American artistic repertoires, which regularly grapple with history, and visual approaches to working through of trauma and memory, see Việt Lê, *Return Engagements: Contemporary Art's Traumas of Modernity and History in Sài Gòn and Phnom Penh* (Duke University Press, 2021), 66.

8 For extended discussions of the politics of play in Vietnam, see Tri Mac Phuong, "The Politics of Play: Digital Youth, New Media, and Social Movement in Contemporary Vietnam" (PhD diss., Yale University, 2021).

9 Sàn Art was started as a nonprofit artist-run art space in 2007 by Dinh Q Lê, Tuan Andrew Nguyen, Phu Nam Thuc Ha, and Tiffany Chung. The Vietnamese word "sàn" means "platform" and the space offered artists a platform for exhibition, education, meeting, and the exchange of artistic ideas. For more on Sàn Art, see Zoe Butt and Dinh Q. Lê, "Presentation About Sàn Art by Zoe Butt and Dinh Q Lê," *Asia Art Archive in America*, June 2010, https://www.aaa-a.org/programs/presentation-by-zoe-butt-and-dinh-q-le. On the arrests in 2007, see Human Rights Watch, "Vietnam: Events of 2007," *Human Rights Watch*, 2008, https://www.hrw.org/world-report/2008/country-chapters#:~:text=In%20July%20police%20and%20soldiers%20forcibly%20evicted,beating%20some%20of%20the%20villagers%20and%20bulldozing.

10 Thủ Thiêm is located in what was then known as District 2, directly across the Sài Gòn River from the city's central business district, known as District 1.

11 Erik Harms, *Luxury and Rubble: Civility and Dispossession in the New Saigon* (University of California Press, 2016).

12 Karishma Charai, "Tiffany Chung," *Brilliant Ideas*, Bloomberg Television, 10 November 2016, https://www.bloomberg.com/news/videos/2016-11-09/tiffany-chung-on-brilliant-ideas.

13 Doreen Lee, *Activist Archives: Youth Culture and the Political Past in Indonesia* (Duke University Press, 2016).

14 For an academic article exploring the ideas in that unpublished manuscript, see Erik Harms, "Knowing into Oblivion: Clearing Wastelands and Imagining Emptiness in Vietnamese New Urban Zones," *Singapore Journal of Tropical Geography* 35, no. 2 (2014).

15 Jason De León, *The Land of Open Graves: Living and Dying on the Migrant Trail* (University of California Press, 2015).

HISTORY AS METHOD: TIFFANY CHUNG AND THE TRAUMA OF DISPLACEMENT

Mark Philip Bradley

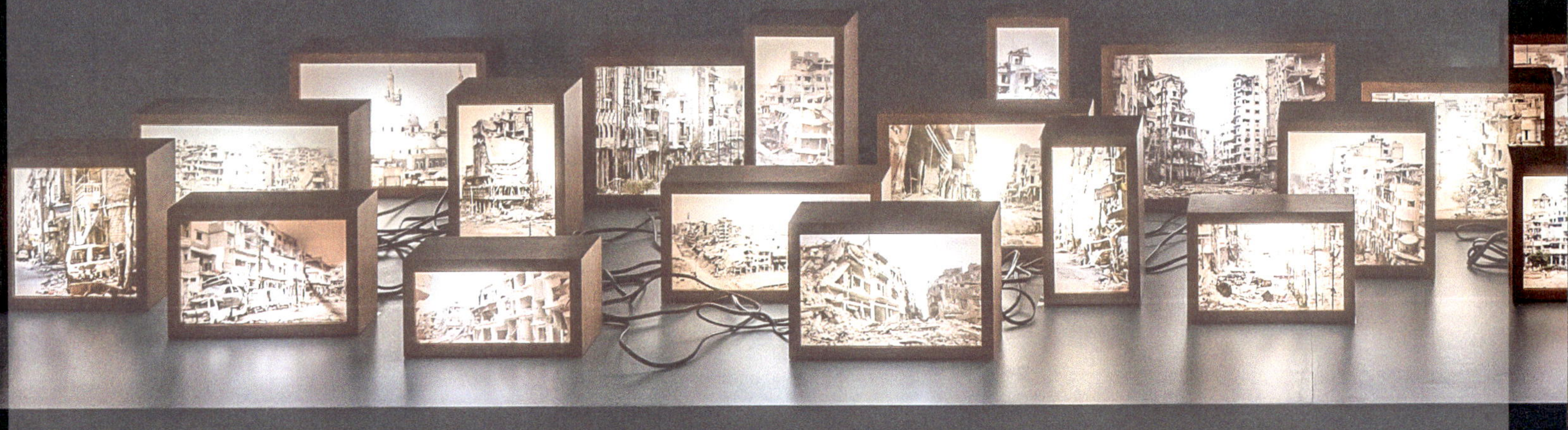

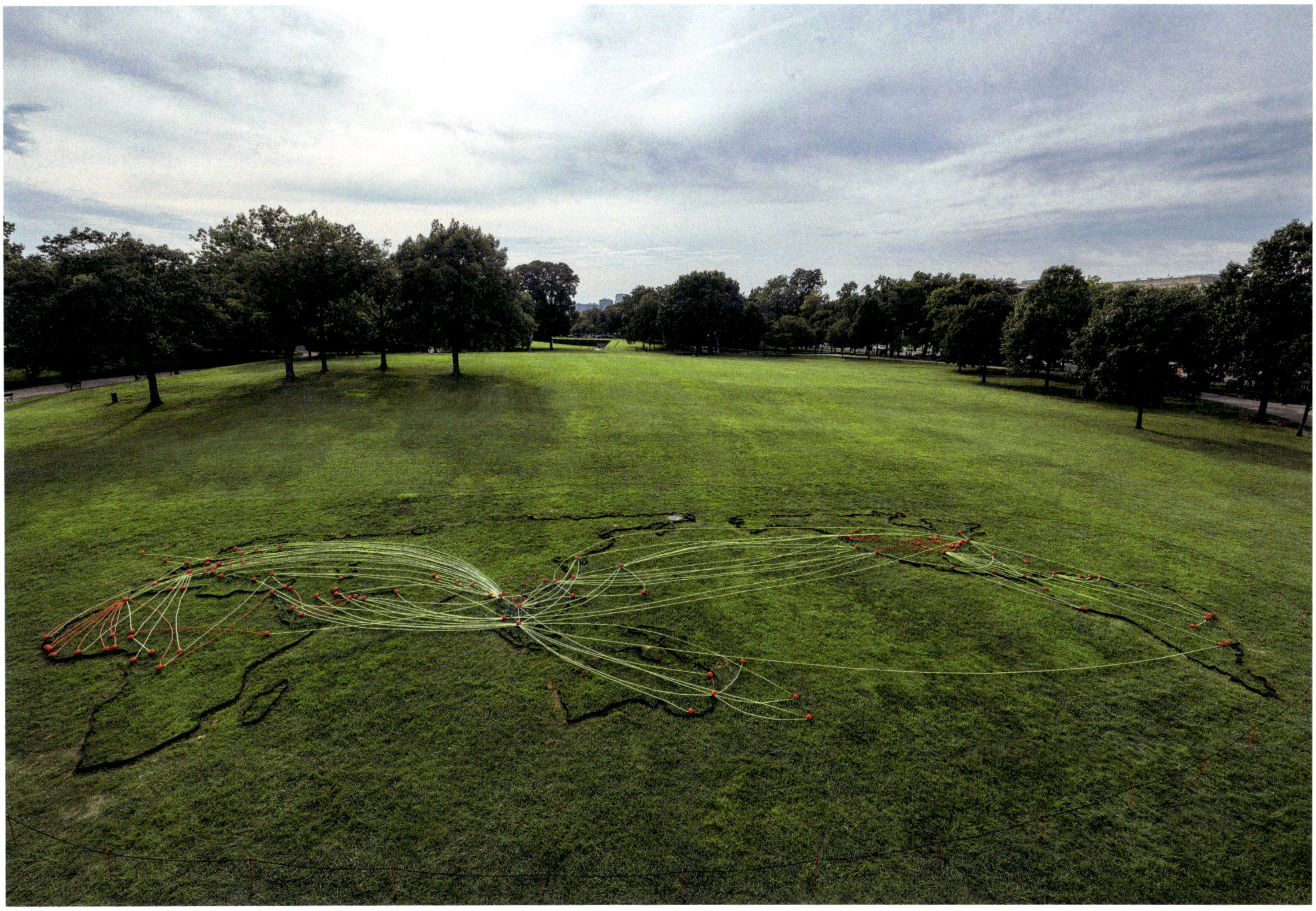

I met Tiffany Chung on the National Mall in Washington, DC, in August 2023. She was among six artists who had been commissioned by Monument Lab and the National Park Service to produce temporary installations aimed at envisioning alternative monuments and memorials for stories that remain untold on what is an almost sacred space of national memory in the United States. We met on-site to talk about her installation, *For the Living* (2023, fig. 1). Using the landscape of the Mall as her anchor, Chung explored the global routes of exile and displacement for 60,000 refugees from Việt Nam, Cambodia, and Laos in the aftermath of the American war in Southeast Asia. Positioned low to the ground adjacent to the Vietnam Veterans Memorial and, for Chung, in deliberate conversation with it, the massive artwork included color-coded ropes to trace out the sea, land, and air routes of Southeast Asian immigrants and refugees who crisscrossed the globe in the wake of the wars in Việt Nam. Indeed, the footprint on the ground of her installation was large enough that, from the window of my plane as I left DC, I could clearly see the outlines of the globe and the various linear rope tentacles conveying the architecture of displacement.

FIGURE 1 Tiffany Chung, *For the Living*, 2023. Mixed-media earthwork, approx. width 61 m (200 ft.). Installation view, *Beyond Granite: Pulling Together*, National Mall, Constitution Gardens West, near Vietnam Veterans Memorial, Washington DC, 2023. Photograph by Steve Weinik.

For the Living represented both a culmination and an intentional expansion of concerns around displacement and exile that have driven Chung's larger practice for more than a decade. At this writing in July 2025, the United Nations High Commissioner for Refugees reports that more than 123.2 million people are forcibly displaced around the world. Her work aims to make legible that almost unfathomable number and its larger meanings. We "need to unpack the root causes" of refugee migration, Chung told me on the Mall in Washington, and "talk about how the entanglements of imperial war and the environment are at the center of the humanitarian crises of our era."[1] Whether she is working on projects about the Việt Nam wars or colonial and postcolonial conflicts elsewhere in Asia, the Middle East, and Central America, empire and its aftermath frame her work. Chung's methods and practices fundamentally transform how we think about displacement and its resulting traumas by surfacing deeper histories and cartographies. Through these innovative new prisms, viewers can see connections to the past that might not have been visible to them otherwise.

Like *For the Living*, several of Chung's projects have been focused on making sense of the Việt Nam wars. The plural is important here. There were multiple wars for Việt Nam in the second half of the twentieth century. In the aftermath of World War II, Ho Chi Minh proclaimed Việt Nam an independent nation on September 2, 1945, throwing off more than eighty years of French colonial rule. But the French insisted on reclaiming its colony, fighting an ultimately failed nine-year imperial war. The French war soon became entangled in the emergent global Cold War. The United States financed as much as eighty percent of the French cost of the war in an attempt to beat back what American policymakers perceived as the dangers of the communist-led Ho Chi Minh government. When the temporary division of the country (part of the 1954 Geneva Agreement to bring an end to the French war) became permanent, Việt Nam was further enmeshed in global Cold War politics: Ho Chi Minh's Democratic Republic of Việt Nam, supported by the Soviet Union and Maoist China, ruled northern Việt Nam while the US-backed Republic of Việt Nam began to build a new state in the south. Tensions festered in this uneasy division. By the early 1960s, Việt Nam was increasingly on a wartime footing in what was both a civil war and, increasingly, a major battlefield in the Cold War. US ground troops arrived in 1965 to fight alongside the South Vietnamese army while Soviet and Chinese advisors supported the North and the southern communist insurgency.

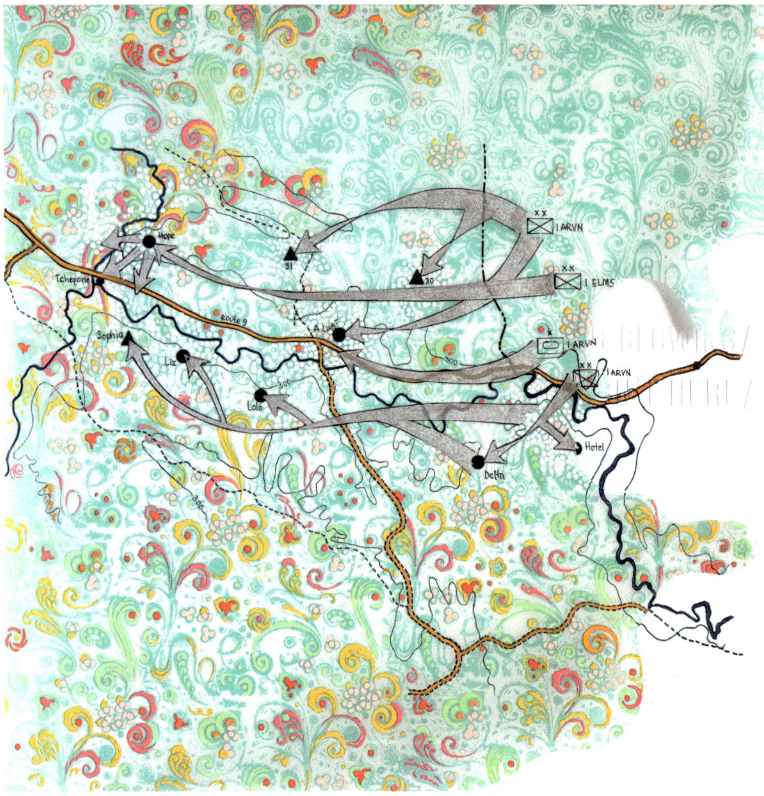

FIGURE 2 Tiffany Chung, *Operation Lam Sơn 719: ground attack and air assault plan*, 2016. Ink and oil on vellum and paper, 29.2 × 29.7 cm (11 ½ × 11 ⅝ in.).

The American war had a devastating effect across Việt Nam. Massive US bombing campaigns seriously disrupted both the urban and rural Vietnamese economies. Chemical warfare, including the use of Agent Orange, contaminated land and water. More than three million Vietnamese lost their lives in the American war, which came to an end in 1975. In the immediate postwar period, the socialist victors in the North sought to impose a collectivist economy on southern Việt Nam. It did not go well. In what is known as the "scarcity era" (thời bao cấp), lasting from the war's end in 1975 to 1986—the period of time in which Chung grew up—the Vietnamese economy stagnated. Putting food on the table was a challenge for many families, and indeed, some places in the countryside experienced spot famines. The forced resettlement of as many as one million southern Vietnamese to largely uninhabited and mountainous areas that the state dubbed "New Economic Zones" further impoverished many southern families. Political re-education campaigns, including re-education camps in which forced labor was common, put additional pressures on southern families whose members had served in the government or armed forces of the Republic of Việt Nam.[2]

Against this backdrop, upwards of three million Vietnamese fled the country, often by sea under precarious circumstances. Leaky boats, pirate raids, and stormy seas presented challenges, and some who left perished at sea. Those who survived initially came to refugee camps in Malaysia, Thailand, Indonesia, the Philippines, and Hong Kong. Chung and her family left Việt Nam for the United States through the US-sponsored Humanitarian Operations program, after several failed attempts to escape by boat. Most Vietnamese refugees permanently settled in the US, Australia, Canada, or France although the Vietnamese global diaspora, as Chung's work so vividly illustrates, stretched across Europe, Africa, the Middle East, Asia, and the Americas.[3]

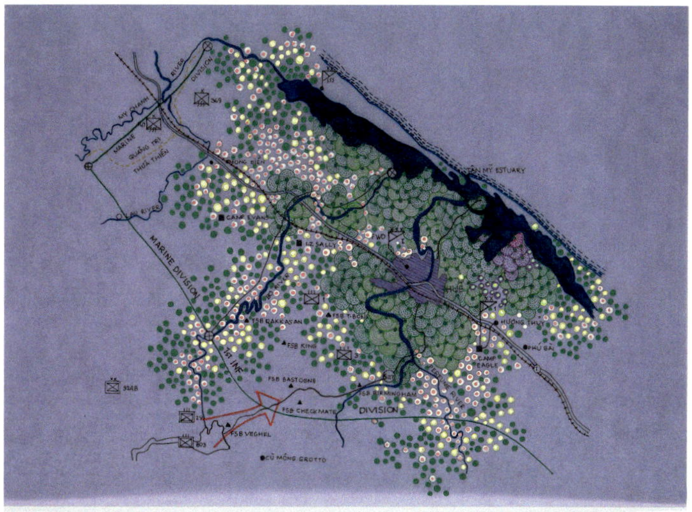

FIGURE 3 Tiffany Chung, *Easter Offensive: the defense of Hue, 5 May 1972*, 2015. Ink and oil on vellum and paper, 24 × 28 cm (9 ½ × 11 in.).

Chung visualizes critical aspects of these histories in several of her works. On one register, she explores the deeper sociopolitical and emotional meanings of the war's battlefields. The American war in Việt Nam operated at multiple levels. It was in part a village-level guerrilla war that pitted a southern communist insurgency against the South Vietnamese state and the firepower of the United States military. It was also an air war, with sustained US bombing campaigns over North Việt Nam. In time, Cambodia and Laos were drawn into the conflict; some of the most intensive US bombing took place in Cambodia, which endured heavier bombing than Japan during World War II. North Vietnamese troops entered Việt Nam in the early 1960s in ever larger numbers. Set piece battles that pitted northern soldiers against southern troops (and their American military supporters) became another important front in the war.

Chung has made a remarkable series of hand-drawn and embroidered works that recover the topographies of two of the most important late-stage battles of the American war in Việt Nam, the South Vietnamese Operation Lam Sơn 719 in 1971 (see fig. 2) and the North Vietnamese Easter Offensive of 1972 (see fig. 3). Operation Lam Sơn, in which Chung's father played a role as a helicopter pilot, was intended to thwart North Vietnamese military advances in the south but became a major defeat for the South Vietnamese with more than 9,000 of its troops killed or wounded. The North's successful Easter Offensive in 1972 had a devastating impact on the South with as many as 25,000 civilians killed and one million displaced persons crowding already growing southern refugee camps and urban centers.[4]

Chung is also concerned with representations of the war's aftermath. The United Nations High Commissioner's Orderly Departure Program (ODP) offered one foil for her work. The ODP was an international effort to facilitate resettlement of Vietnamese

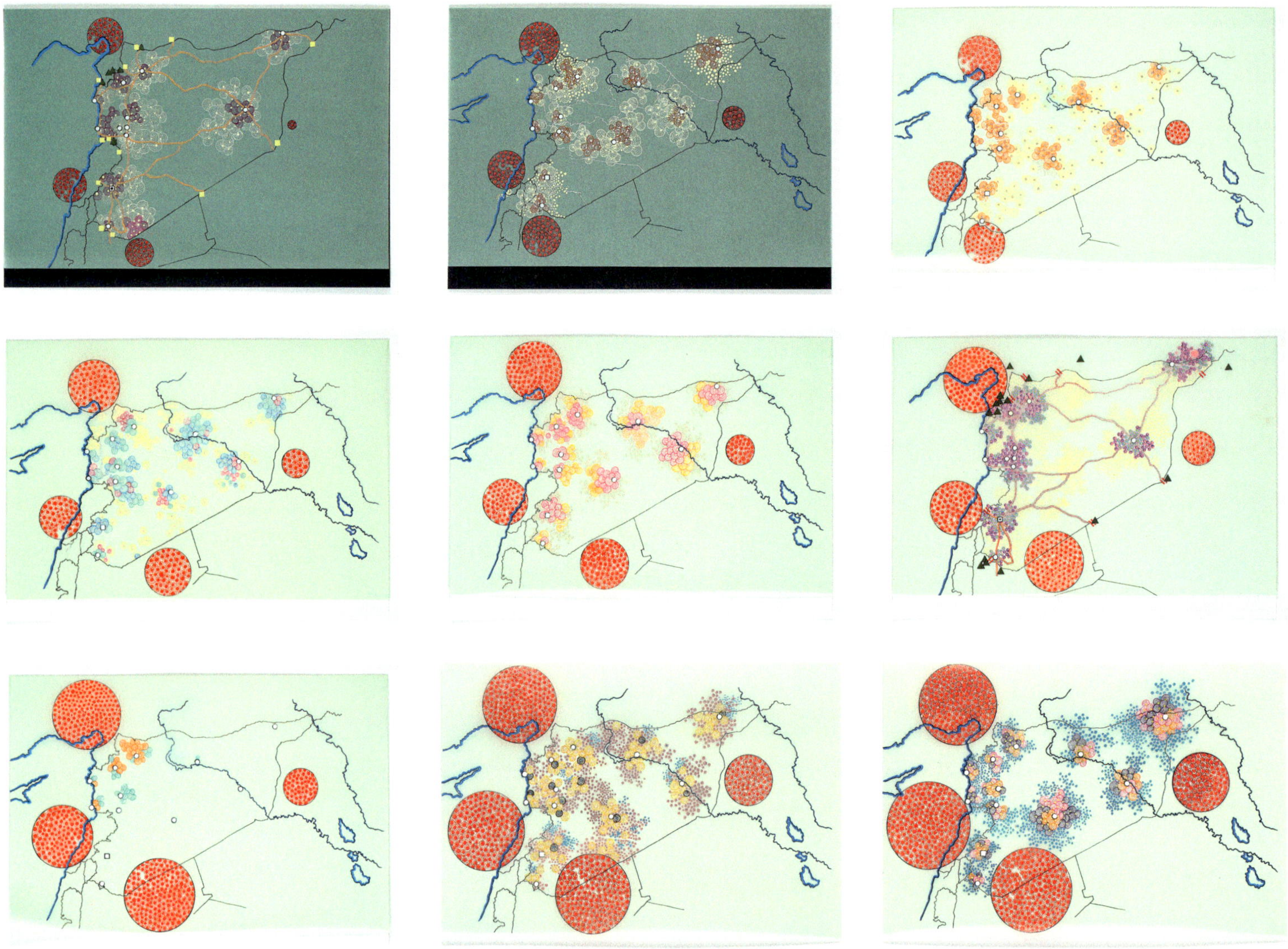

FIGURE 4 Tiffany Chung, *UNHCR Red Dot series: Tracking the Syrian Humanitarian Crisis, April–Dec 2012*, 2014–2015. Ink and oil on vellum and paper, each 21 × 30 cm (8 ¼ × 11 ¾ in.). Collection of British Museum. Photographs by Nam Bui.

who fled the country after 1975. Drawing on research she undertook in the United Nations archives, Chung captured aspects of postwar patterns of Vietnamese displacement and resettlement in her *For the Living* project on the Mall in Washington, DC, and in the *Vietnam Exodus Project* (fig. 4, see pp. 98–101). For this series she used embroidery on fabric to trace boat and flight routes from Việt Nam and the various refugee camps through the ODP.

Embroidery, beads, plastic gems, and stitched thread would become critical elements in her cartographic projects. Chung recalled in our conversations:

> I did a lot of puncturing using a grommet puncher on the canvas. I used my hands, and sometimes my fingers were bleeding. All the grommets, the fake rhinestones, the beads, made me feel textures of memories and their different layers, and the holes that I punctured through the canvas also had that quality of pain.

In elevating the tactile, these materials and methodologies allow her to recover in especially original ways the structures of feeling that make displacement palpable. The work Chung has made on the war and postwar period reflect not only her own lived experience, but also her enduring interest in the relationship between war and changes in land and the environment as catalysts for displacement and trauma.

In the early 2010s Chung also began tracking conflict and displacement in sites beyond Việt Nam. In detailed cartographic drawings she initially focused

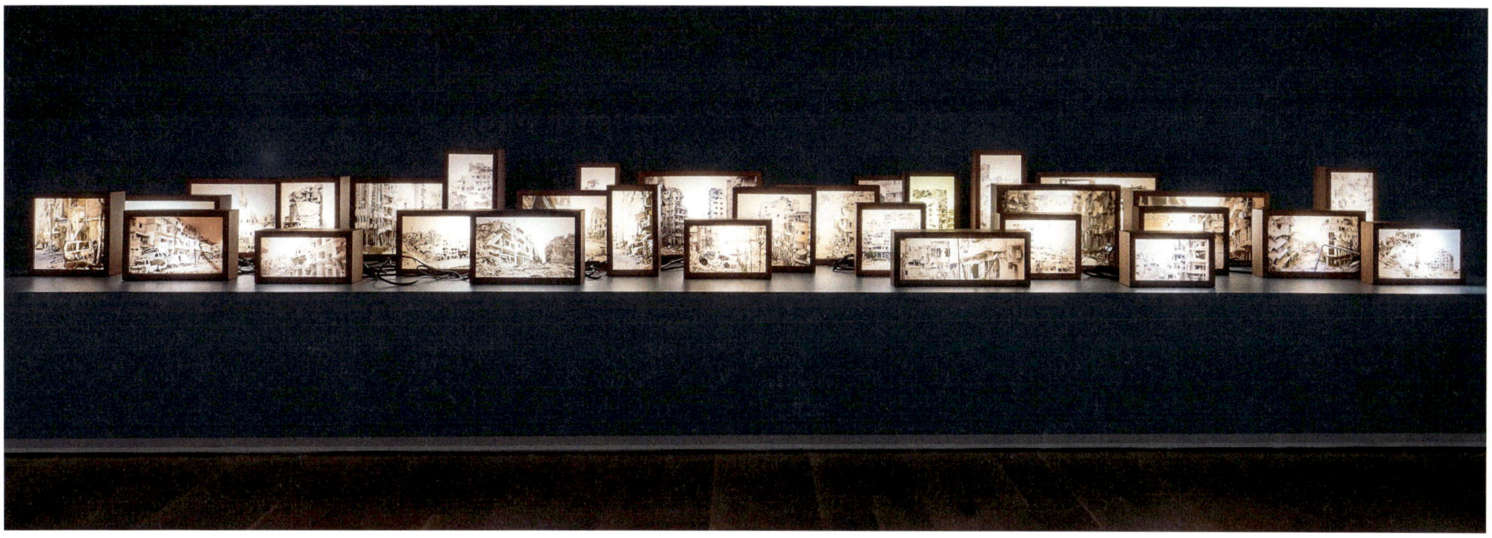

on the humanitarian crisis in Syria (see fig. 4) in the aftermath of a brutal civil war that forced more than fourteen million Syrians from their homes. Another work from this period, *finding one's shadow in ruins and rubble* (2014, fig. 5), presented arresting photographic documentation of the recent devastation in Syria's built environment through a set of thirty-one wooden light boxes. Over the span of her career, Chung has documented displacement in Tibet, Guatemala, North Africa, Lebanon, and Iraq. In addition, she has mapped the global footprint of the US military and economic interests in shaping geopolitics. Chung tracked British and French colonial mapping of the Middle East and the ongoing implications of imperial cartographic projects on the settlement of human populations in the region today (see p. 79). Her *USM Global* (2023, see pp. 134–135) plots US military bases around the world within the long histories of slavery and imperialism in an effort to trace the political, economic, and climatic forces over the *longue durée* that gave rise to American empire.

FIGURE 5 Tiffany Chung, *finding one's shadow in ruins and rubble*, 2014. 31 hand-crafted mahogany wooden boxes, Reuters-licensed photographs, glass, LED lights, dimensions variable. Installation view, *New Cartographies*, Asia Society Texas, 2018–2019. Photograph by Nash Baker.

As a historian, one of the affinities I share with Chung is a commitment to archival research and oral history. In her mapping of global Vietnamese refugee flows in *For the Living* and other related projects, she went to the archives of the UN High Commissioner for Refugees in Geneva to get the data to support her visualizations firsthand. Chung often found that these files were, in her words, "incomplete and fragmented." Sometimes they contained only a flight itinerary. Yet the files did allow her to see a truly global movement not only to the United States, Europe, and Australia, which Westerners more commonly think of as making up the Vietnamese diaspora, but to Africa, Latin America, and the Middle East as well. These unexpected patterns made her curious about the contingencies that propelled refugees to less familiar geographies. "To me it was mind blowing to learn about people who went to the Central African Republic," Chung told me. When she had the opportunity to meet one of the Vietnamese refugees who went to Côte d'Ivoire, in West Africa, she asked him why. He said he knew that several families had already successfully resettled there and he thought, "Why not? What do we have to lose?"

Chung is just as interested in people as in archives and has engaged in hundreds of informal conversations with former refugees from Việt Nam, Laos, and Cambodia. One project explores the lives of Vietnamese refugees in Hong Kong, many of whom remained in camps for extended periods of time. Her work on these forms of statelessness, a too often neglected sphere in Vietnamese refugee studies, usefully expands more conventional notions of displacement and trauma. She undertook sustained fieldwork in 2015 to 2018 with unhoused Vietnamese in Hong Kong who had been held in camps there in the 1990s. That research helped to shape a set of artworks for her *Vietnam Exodus Project*, including maps documenting individual journeys (see fig. 6, see also pp. 102–103), videos (see pp. 96–97), and the thirty-foot *water dreamscape scroll: the gangster named Jacky, the sleepers, and the exodus* (2017–18, see pp. 186–187), which Chung made in collaboration with a group of young painters in Ho Chi Minh City. They reveal the multiplicity of experiences from resettlement to statelessness that shaped lives in the Vietnamese diaspora.[5] These same archival and oral history methods have also informed her work on displacement in North Africa and the Middle East.

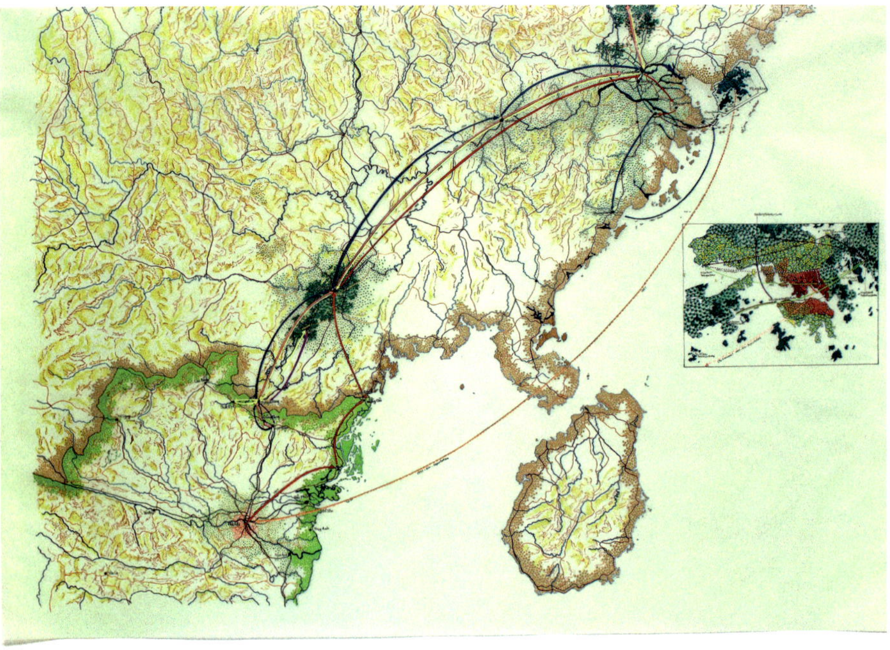

FIGURE 6 Tiffany Chung, *A Case Study of the UNHCR–Hong Kong Refugee Status Determination: escape journey of a stateless ethnic-Chinese Vietnamese between 1978–1997*, 2019. Ink and oil on vellum and paper, 79 × 100 cm (31 × 39 ½ in.).

Moving between data and visual representation has been critical to Chung's practice, and she continues to refine and develop it in her work on the traumas of climate-induced displacement and exile. In 2024, she created embroidered maps that reveal the operation of what policymakers and scholars have recently called the "Conflict, Climate, and Migration Nexus" in the Global South. Through two large-scale maps (see pp. 126–127 and 186), Chung juxtaposed global CO_2 emissions and worldwide production of oil, gas, and coal with documentation of recent refugees, asylum seekers, and internally displaced persons in the Global South to visually communicate the links between climate change and forcible displacement.

In my conversations with Chung, I was struck by the ways in which her own family history of displacement became productively intertwined with her broader historical research, and how in those interstices she offers a new methodology for understanding the histories of lived experience. "In 2009 and 2010, I still wasn't able to unpack the Việt Nam war," Chung told me. "But tracking the refugee and humanitarian crises in the Middle East and North Africa allowed me the kind of space I needed to reflect on my own history and to think about shared experiences." Her father had been a helicopter pilot in an elite squadron of the South Vietnamese Air Force. He was captured during the war and imprisoned in North Việt Nam for fourteen years. Chung had never really talked to him about his experiences of the war. With her research on Syria also came trips to former Vietnamese refugee camps in Singapore and Indonesia. A map collector, Chung had acquired a map of central Việt Nam on one of those trips and found its geographies to be puzzling. She called her father one day and told him about the map. As it turned out, the area was one that he had frequented as a pilot. "For the first time in my life," Chung said, "I was actually interviewing my dad, talking to him, listening to what he knew about the war, about his experience." In her 2015–19 work *Remapping History: an autopsy of a battle, an excavation of a man's past* (see pp. 80–81 and 195), which unfolds across forty feet of museum wall space, she used text, photographs, video, and maps to present a timeline and scrapbook-style narrative of her father's wartime experiences. In the supple ways through which it simultaneously and seamlessly blends the story of a single individual and his times, I feel this is one of her most compelling works. As a historian I know how hard it is to bring the past alive in ways that can surprise and engage an audience. Chung does that brilliantly in her work.

A guiding thread in Chung's practice has been her willingness to take risks and to work with partners in adjacent fields. Her recent collaborative project, *Rise Into the Atmosphere* (2024–25, see pp. 35 and 198), for the Dallas Museum of Art was inspired by centuries-old chants and hymns from the Syrian city of Aleppo. In this piece she joins those soundscapes with visualizations of landscapes from Syria, Morocco, Algeria, and Libya. Chung worked closely with a group of musicians and a collaborator specializing in media software to realize this immersive project. Coming into *Rise*, she said she didn't know much about composing music, but she learned as she went in order to tap into multiple ways of creating a "sonic landscape of shared memories that visitors might, or might not, have experienced or lived through."

Chung's most recent work-in-progress on spices (in which I am grateful to play a very modest collaborative role) also engages with the human sensorium. A planetary history that begins almost 3,500 years ago, it tracks the movement of spices and traditional recipes between and across the Middle East, Asia, Europe, and the Americas. In doing so Chung explores the circulations of plants, commodities, and food as they intersect and the realities of imperial conquest, trade, and labor.

Tiffany Chung's concerns with diaspora, traumatic memory, and displacement bring together her own lived experiences of the Việt Nam wars and a fierce commitment to documentation, archives, and oral history. In recovering what have too often been submerged stories of empire, war, political economies, and environmental change in the making of forced migration, her interdisciplinary methods open up entirely original and transformative conversations about the ways in which the past can illuminate and deepen our understanding of the present moment.

NOTES

1 All quotations are from my conversation with Tiffany Chung at the National Mall and in the offices of the American Historical Association in Washington, DC, on 25 August 2023 and subsequent Zoom conversations on 7 November 2024, 19 January 2025, and 9 July 2025.

2 For a short history of the Việt Nam wars that focuses on the multiplicity of Vietnamese experiences, see my *Vietnam at War* (Oxford University Press, 2009).

3 The best historical account of the making of the postwar Vietnamese diaspora is Jana K. Lipman, *In Camps: Vietnamese Refugees, Asylum Seekers, and Repatriates* (University of California Press, 2020).

4 The work of Vietnamese environmental historian David Biggs nicely complements some of the mapping dimensions in Chung's art. For his *Footprints of War: Militarized Landscapes in Vietnam* (University of Washington Press, 2018), Biggs joined archival research and oral interviews with Geographic Information Systems (GIS) data and satellite imagery to reconstruct critical dimensions of the experiences of war in central Việt Nam.

5 The story of one family's often surprising experiences of war and postwar displacement is the focus of Thi Bui's wonderful graphic novel *The Best We Could Do: An Illustrated Memoir* (Abrams Comic Art, 2017).

TIFFANY CHUNG'S FOOTPRINTS ACROSS DEEP TIME

Heidi Amin-Hong

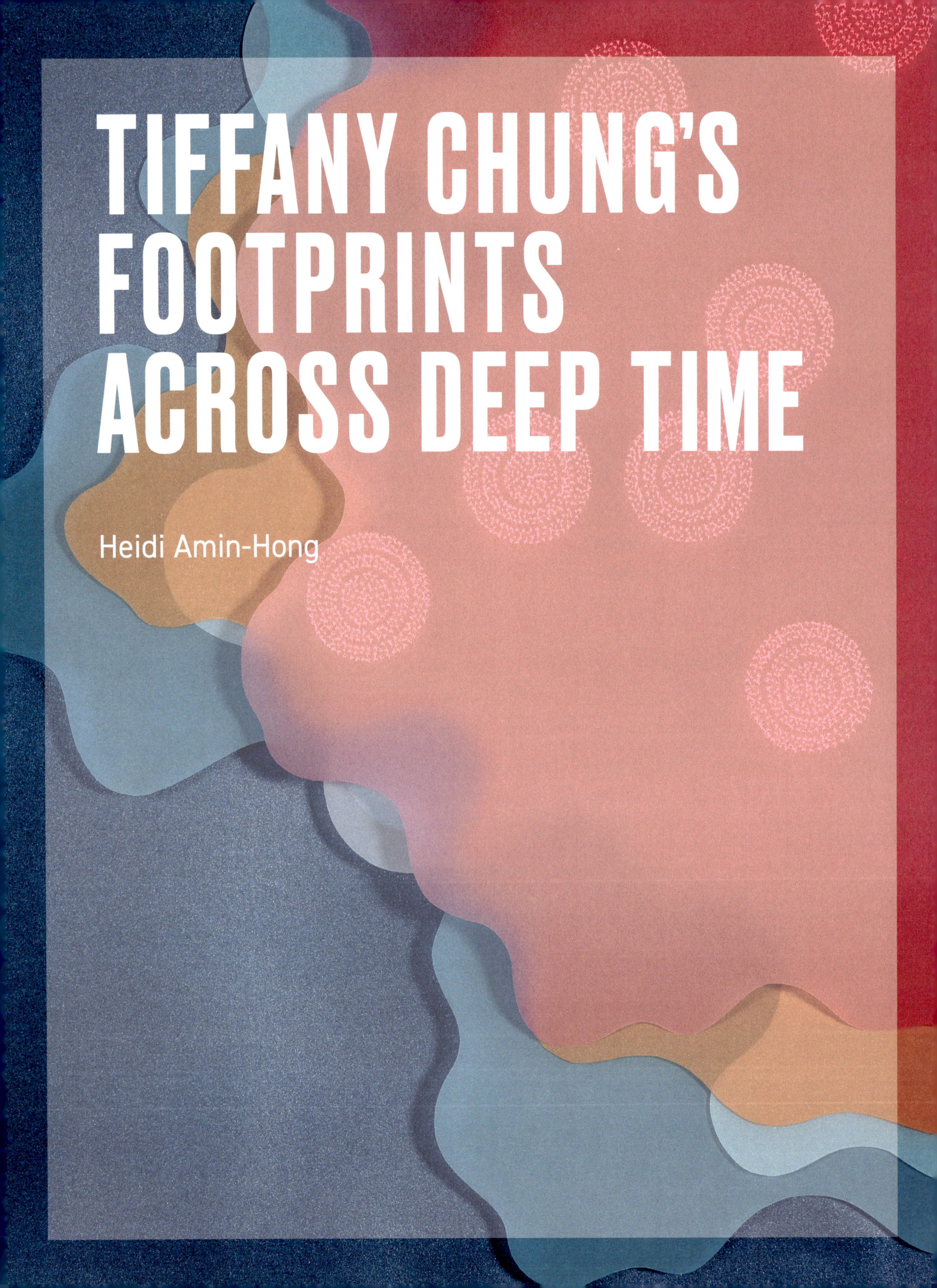

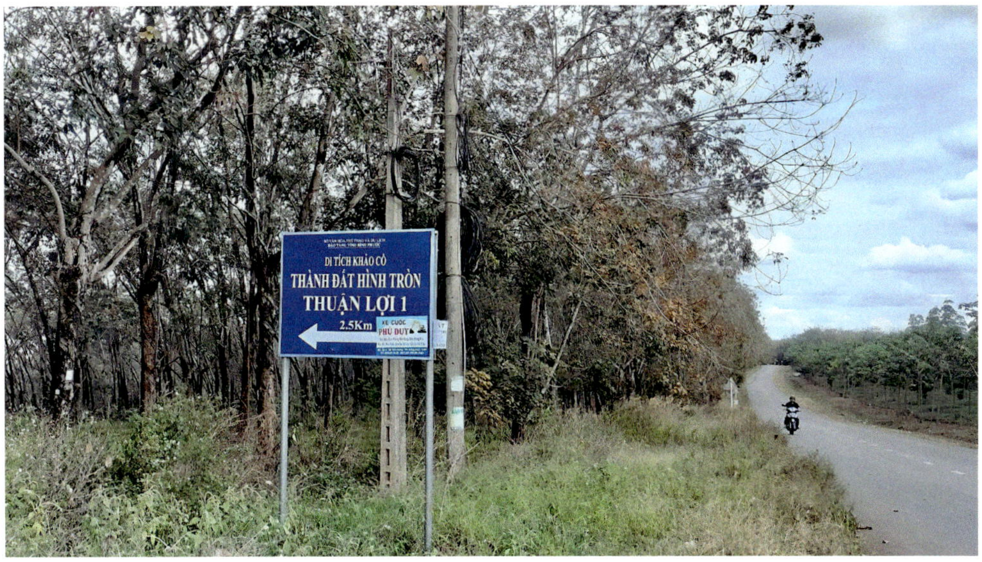

FIGURE 1 Sign to the archaeological site of circular earthwork "Thuận Lợi 2" in Bình Phước Province, Việt Nam. Photograph by Điểu Mơn.

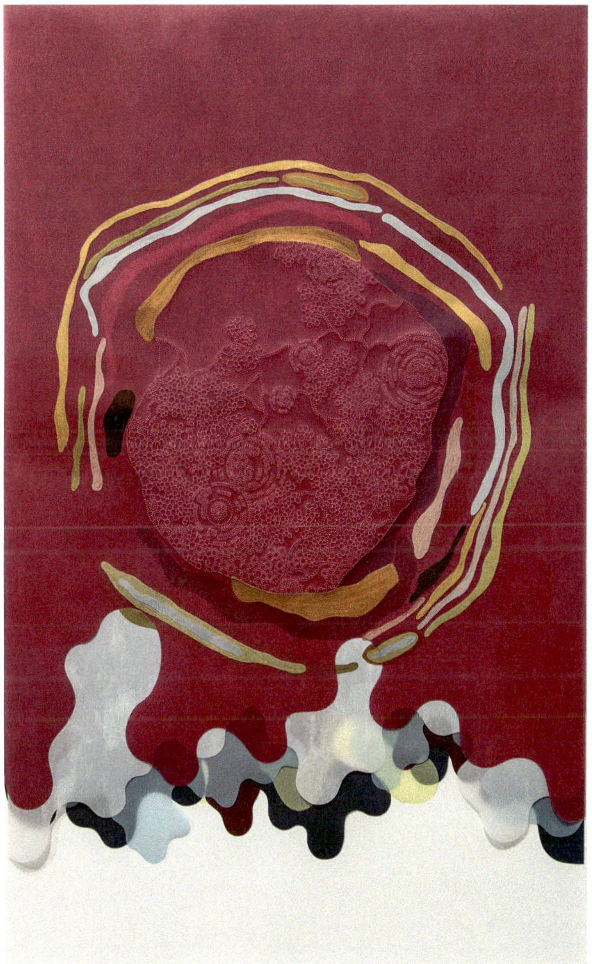

FIGURE 2 Tiffany Chung, *Terra Rouge CEW Study No. 17, Vietnam*, 2024. Ink, oil, and hand perforating on vellum and paper, 112 × 70.5 cm (44 ⅛ × 27 ¾ in.). Courtesy of the artist and Galería Max Estrella.

In 2014, Tiffany Chung traveled to southwest Việt Nam to track down and photograph abandoned airfields in Bình Phước (see fig. 1), a red soil plateau where Chung's father was often stationed as a helicopter pilot for the South Vietnamese Army prior to being captured as a prisoner of war (POW) in 1971.[1] Realizing that the same region was a site of the 1972 Easter Offensive and home to a network of rubber plantations established by French colonists in 1897, Chung set out to excavate a deep history of a landscape that is a palimpsest for many cycles of human settlement, colonialism, extraction, and migration. This investigation would become *Terra Rouge: circles, traces of time, rebellious solitude* (2022–ongoing, fig. 2, see also pp. 156–159), a series of artworks on paper and vellum that recreate Neolithic earthworks discovered through archeological excavations in the region that date back to 2300–300 BCE. These circular earthworks, composed of concentric rings, are traces of a prehistoric human settlement that was abandoned after 2,000 years, possibly due to economic conditions influencing the population's migration to the floodplains. Stone tools and pottery containing rice grains found in these sites suggest that their prehistoric inhabitants could have been farmers and horticulturalists who may have cultivated gardens within the concentric settlements.[2] Chung's interest in the earthworks and their inhabitants stems from their barely perceptible environmental footprint, presumably evidence of their sustainable practices and understanding of ecological relationships over a long period. Tracing and reconstructing these earthworks, she speculates: What if their residents never migrated into a new economic and political system? What rituals, practices, and ecological relationships would endure into our present from a society dwelling in what Chung calls "rebellious solitude?"[3]

The artworks in *Terra Rouge*, at a glance, are gestural and abstract, with curved lines rendered in gold and silver atop richly colored paper. With a closer look, this artwork is multidimensional and perhaps representational of specific landscapes. Sheets of translucent vellum and paper are cut along the bottom edge into rounded borders reminiscent of topographic features, evoking the curvature of mountains or rivers. The bottom layers of paper are subdued in color but not completely obscured, suggesting the liveliness of histories that have been temporarily muted. All the vellum layers are punctured with intricate patterns made by hand-perforations, with repeated circular motifs reminiscent of cells or microbes clustered next to labyrinth-like geometrical shapes. Chung characterizes this process of reconstruction as archeological, where the gestures of tracing and perforating resemble the careful labor of digging into the Earth's strata to reveal its buried histories.[4] The faint circular patterns also signal new life percolating on the surface, alluding to a possible alternative to our unsustainable forms of life.

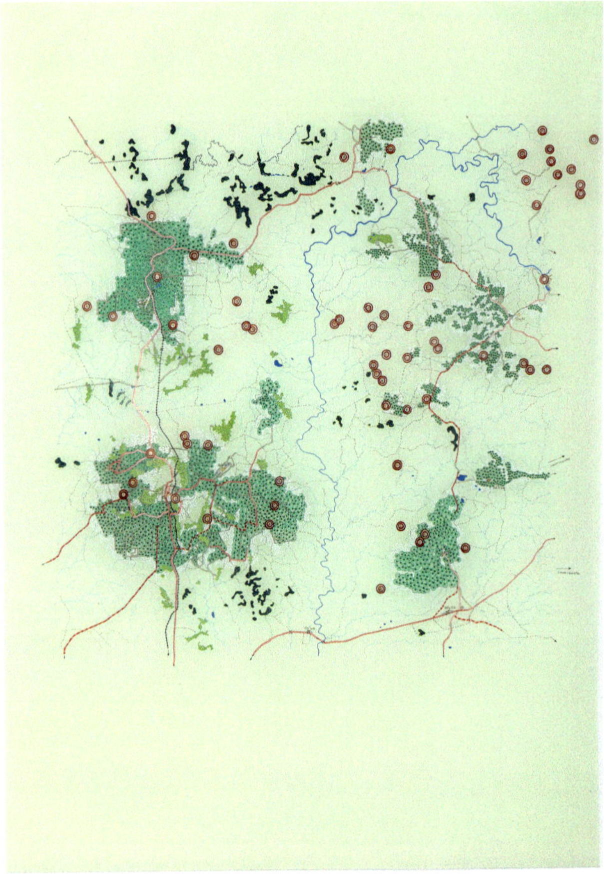

FIGURE 3 Tiffany Chung, *Entangled Landscape of Disremembering: CEW Sites, Rubber Plantations, Abandoned Airfields*, 2023. Acrylic, ink, and oil on vellum and paper, 113 × 70 cm (44 ½ × 17 ½ in.). Courtesy of the artist and Kiang Malingue Gallery, Hong Kong | New York. Photograph by Samson Wong.

Terra Rouge places the reconstructed circular earthwork images alongside a cartography of the archaeological sites, French colonial rubber plantations, and abandoned airfields from the US/Việt Nam War in this region (see fig. 3). In doing so, Chung extends our ability to sense human history as part of the vast stretch of geologic history, while bringing distant pasts and speculative futures to bear on contested landscapes in our present. In the environmental humanities, deep time describes an understanding of time spanning across geological eras and cosmic phenomena that far eclipse human lifespans. The limit of a human timescale is one of the foremost predicaments of the Anthropocene, a term coined by Paul J. Crutzen to describe the planetary impact of human activity hurling us into a new geologic era.[5] While human time is measured in hours and years, Earth's stratigraphic layers show that more-than-human life stretches far beyond human civilization and comprehension, into the past and future. Yet colonial and capitalist systems of extraction compress geologic time; fossil fuels formed from the remains of prehistoric life below the Earth's crust are mined and burned in an instant. Kathryn Yusoff thus describes geology as "a mode of accumulation, on one hand, and of dispossession, on the other, depending on which side of the geologic color line you end up on."[6] Writing about the parallel processes of anti-Black racism and extractive mining, Yusoff attests that the differentiation of human from inhuman matter enables violent geologic practices of extraction that sediment into material forms of racism. If modernity can only produce a singular truncated timeline of human progress for the few at the expense of others, Chung offers new blueprints to locate marginalized or deliberately obscured human histories on a geologic record. Such (re)orientations to natural history evoke what Adhy Kim describes as how "living (and dying) under capitalism may orient certain subjects toward speculative views of the human in natural history."[7] Situating human history as part of an expansive natural history, Chung shows us other modes of social and ecological relations that transcend national borders and developmentalist aims, or what Kim calls "a long natural history of capitalist destruction."[8]

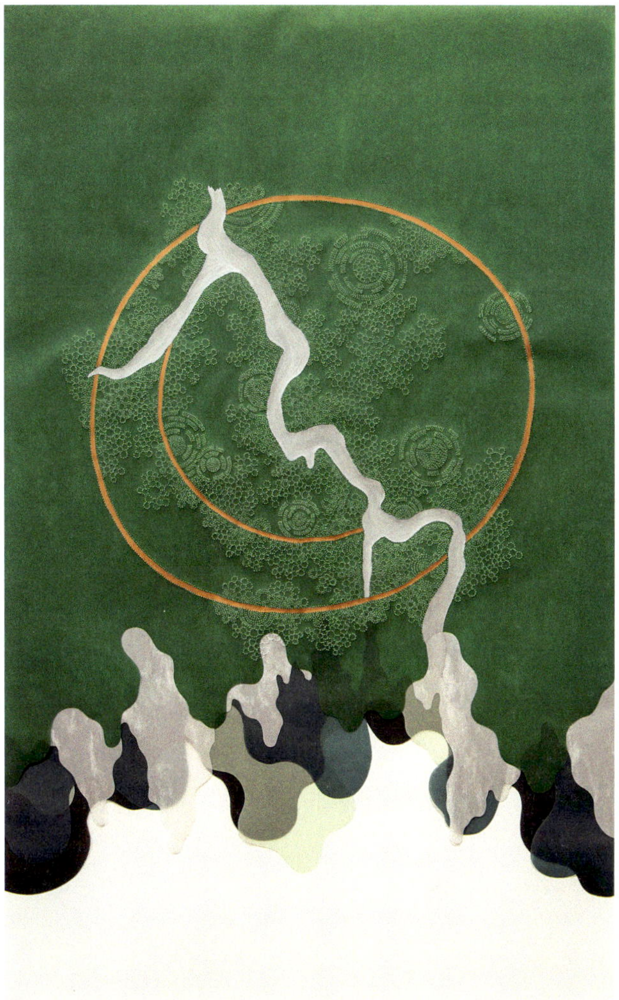

FIGURE 4 Tiffany Chung, *Ditched Enclosure La Pijotilla, Spain*, 2024. Ink, oil, and hand perforating on vellum and paper, 112 × 70.5 cm (44 ⅛ × 27 ¾ in.). Courtesy of the artist and Galería Max Estrella.

Histories of resource extraction to fuel imperial expansion have been recurring themes in Chung's art practice. As Imre Szeman and Dominic Boyer remind us, our dependence on fossil fuels has transformed all aspects of modern social and cultural life—from geopolitical conflicts over oil to our social relations and artistic practices.[9] Such extractive industries, from rubber plantations in the French colonial period to the petroleum-driven modern economy, convert nonhuman life and racialized labor into profitable resources to enrich the colonial center, rendering the land and its human and nonhuman populations disposable. Basaltic soil, prevalent throughout Southeast Asia and referenced in the *Terra Rouge* works, was formed from volcanic rock and considered ideal for growing rubber due to basalt's ability to deliver nutrients to plants.[10] The earthworks images evoke the materiality of the soil and its rich color to critique the extractivist logic of global capitalism and link us to a deep ecology that exceeds such unsustainable practices.

Drawing from both the personal and the planetary, Chung's artistic practice excavates global connections and shared histories that might be easily overlooked. This series of works focused on circular ditched enclosures pairs reconstructions of Neolithic earthworks found in Southeast Asia with similar earthworks found in the Iberian Peninsula (see fig. 4), another contested region with a violent imperial history. Economic and cultural exchanges with the Middle East and North Africa dating to the Neolithic and Chalcolithic periods shaped the Iberian Peninsula as a region with Muslim, Jewish, and Christian cultural influences. Under Catholic rule, Jews and Muslims were expelled from Spain and Portugal to North Africa and the Ottoman Empire. The Iberian earthworks were discovered to have been home to nomadic populations, who used the sites as meeting places and left their mark on the earthworks' architecture. Scholarly research revealed denser human activity in sites found on the Iberian Peninsula, including deeper pits filled with human remains and other materials, indicating that perhaps humans did not maintain harmonious and sustainable relationships with prehistoric environments after all.[11] Such early evidence of earthworks as transitory spaces presented antecedents to human migration across the Mediterranean region, suggesting that global movement and interrelationships have endured much longer than our static cartographies of nations and borders.

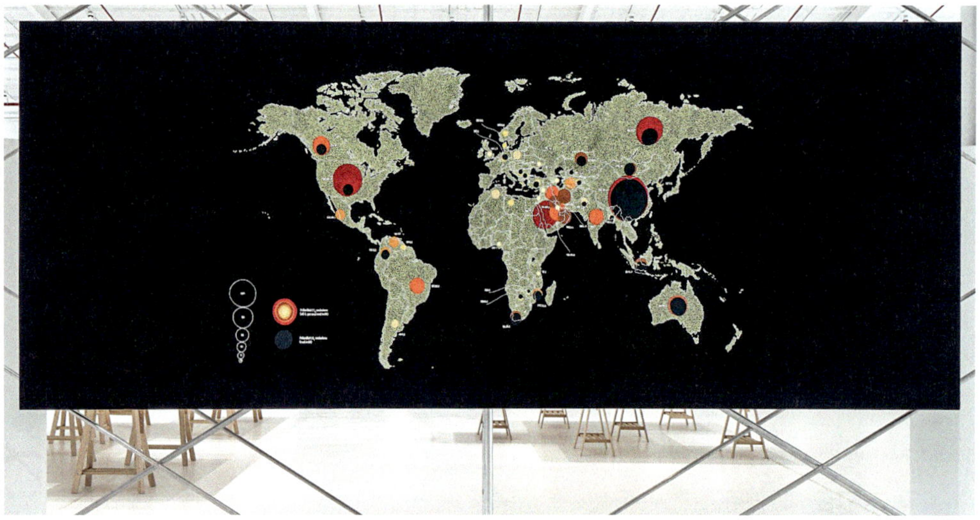

FIGURE 5 Tiffany Chung, *Energy Policy vol.166: potential CO_2 emissions until 2050 by key fossil fuel and coal extraction projects [each>1 Gt] worldwide*, 2023. Embroidery on fabric, 140 × 350 cm (55 ⅛ × 37 ¾ in.). Commissioned by the Diriyah Biennale Foundation for the Diriyah Contemporary Art Biennale 2024. Installation view, *After Rain*, Diriyah Contemporary Art Biennale, Saudi Arabia, 2024. Courtesy of the Diriyah Biennale Foundation. Photograph by Marco Cappelletti.

Chung's other cartographic works, often constructed from embroidery on canvas or layered vellum and paint, offer both expansive views of interconnected migration routes and intimate, microscopic patterns that represent individual displaced lives. Two large-scale maps from a series on the "Conflict, Climate, and Migration Nexus" visualize the impact of war and climate disasters on internal and cross-border migration.[12] Chung uses ArcGIS software to render data gathered from the United Nations Commission on Human Rights, World Bank, and Internal Displacement Monitoring Centre (IDMC) into digital infographics that are then transferred onto fabric through a labor-intensive prick and pounce embroidery process. *Mapping Global Displacement and Migration: nexus dynamics between conflict & violence and climate disaster [UNHCR, IDMC, EM-DAT: cross-border refugees, asylum-seekers, IDPs, and those affected in selected cases >2022<]* (2023, see pp. 126–127) presents circles symbolizing the global displacement of refugees, asylum seekers, and internally displaced persons, which Chung organizes according to their country of origin and the cause of migration. The brightly colored circles, overlayed directly upon each other, form hotspots concentrated in South and Southeast Asia, Central Africa, Eastern Europe, and Central America that clearly reveal links between war, migration, and human-induced climate change. Though the category of disaster-induced displacements does not account for resource extraction as a direct cause of so-called "natural" disasters, another map, *Energy Policy vol.166: potential CO_2 emissions until 2050 by key fossil fuel and coal extraction projects [each>1 Gt]*

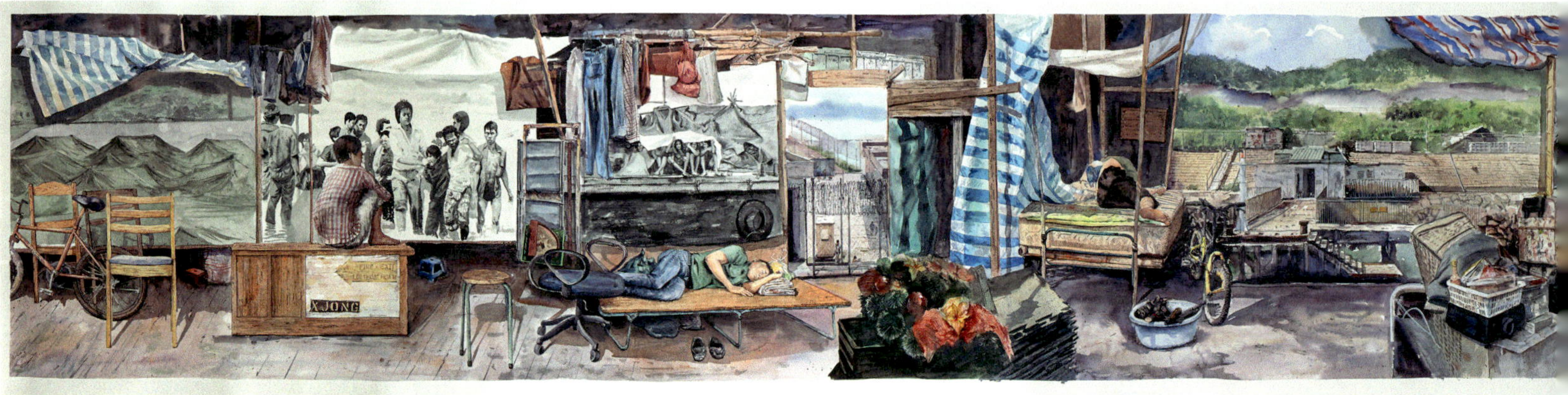

worldwide (2023, fig. 5) shows the potential CO_2 emissions of fossil fuel and coal extraction projects globally, highlighting countries with projected CO_2 emissions that exceed one gigaton. These circles, colored in shades of red and dark blue-green to indicate emissions from coal extraction, clearly picture the disproportionate impact of a handful of nations—the United States, China, Russia, and Saudi Arabia—as the center of consumption and fossil fuel extraction. These embroidered maps illuminate the power of these data visualizations while challenging the primacy of data. The faint lines on the map suggest the impermanence of geopolitical borders and the limitations of the cartographer's gaze, which only captures a limited view of the earth's surface from above and fails to account for the textures of networked lives across time and space.

Rooted in her personal history, the desire to understand the forced displacement of Vietnamese refugees in relation to other global displacements shapes many of Chung's works. The *Vietnam Exodus Project* assembles archival images and Chung's own photographs documenting the journey of stateless Vietnamese refugees in Hong Kong, taken on her visits to former refugee camps and detention centers. Chung commissioned and worked with a group of young artists from Sài Gòn to transform the photographs into paintings (see fig. 6), discussing with them a history of the exodus that has been erased from official state records during this process of making art. Her persistent exploration of the human and environmental costs of war led her to create *USM Global: tracing the US military global footprint* (2023, see pp. 134–135), a project that maps the US military's global footprint and archives Chung's extensive research in an interactive website. Drawing mainly from David Vine's 2021 list of US military bases abroad and cross-checking with records from the Department of Defense, Chung represents the global reach of US military activities, highlighting US military bases in sub-Saharan Africa and Okinawa. In this broader context, we may reevaluate the US/Việt Nam War as a global conflict with devastating environmental consequences that persist. Aerial bombings and herbicidal warfare, particularly the US military's spraying of chemical defoliants in Việt Nam, Cambodia, and Laos from 1962 through 1971, decimated Southeast Asian environments. Dioxin, a highly toxic byproduct of the infamous herbicide Agent Orange, continues to linger in human and nonhuman bodies today.[13] The shift to large-scale aerial bombing campaigns during the US/Việt Nam War also dramatically increased petroleum consumption. According to Department of Defense records, US, Vietnamese, and other US-allied military

FIGURE 6 Tiffany Chung, *water dreamscape scroll: the gangster named Jacky, the sleepers, and the exodus*, 2017–2018. Watercolor on paper, 113.5 × 924.5 cm (44 ⅝ × 364 in.). All watercolors are the result of the *Vietnam Exodus History Learning Project*, carried out in collaboration with Hồ Hưng, Huỳnh Quốc Bảo, Lê Nam Đy, Nguyễn Hoàng Long, Đặng Quang Tiến, Phạm Ái, Võ Châu Hoàng Vy, Nguyễn Văn Đủ, and Nguyễn Kim Tố Lan. Courtesy of the artist. Photograph by Nam Bui.

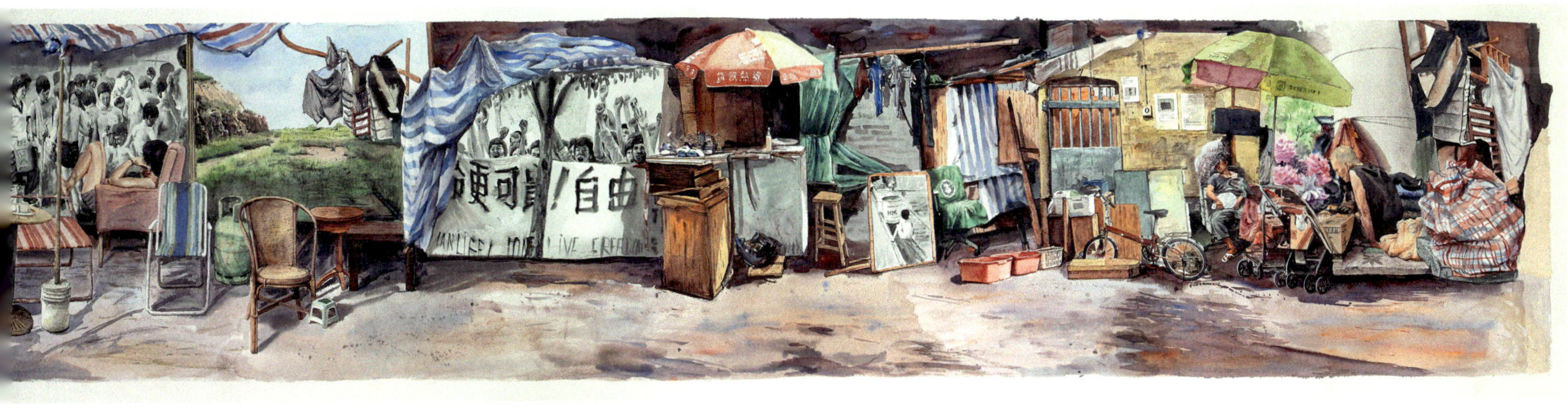

forces in Southeast Asia consumed 15.2 billion gallons of petroleum from the years 1966 to 1973.[14] This fuel was imported from refineries in the Pacific, the Caribbean, the Middle East, and Indonesia. The island of Okinawa, used as a launchpad for US airstrike operations in the Korean War and US/Việt Nam War, still hosts 70 percent of all US military facilities in Japan. In *Studying for USM Global*, Chung created an archive that bears witness to the nexus of military, economic development, and climate impacts, including toxic PFAS contamination from base activities and the environmental degradation of coral reefs due to commercial airport development in Okinawa.[15] This archive shows how entangled effects of US militarism, colonial occupation, and global tourism have disproportionately affected Indigenous Okinawans' ways of life.

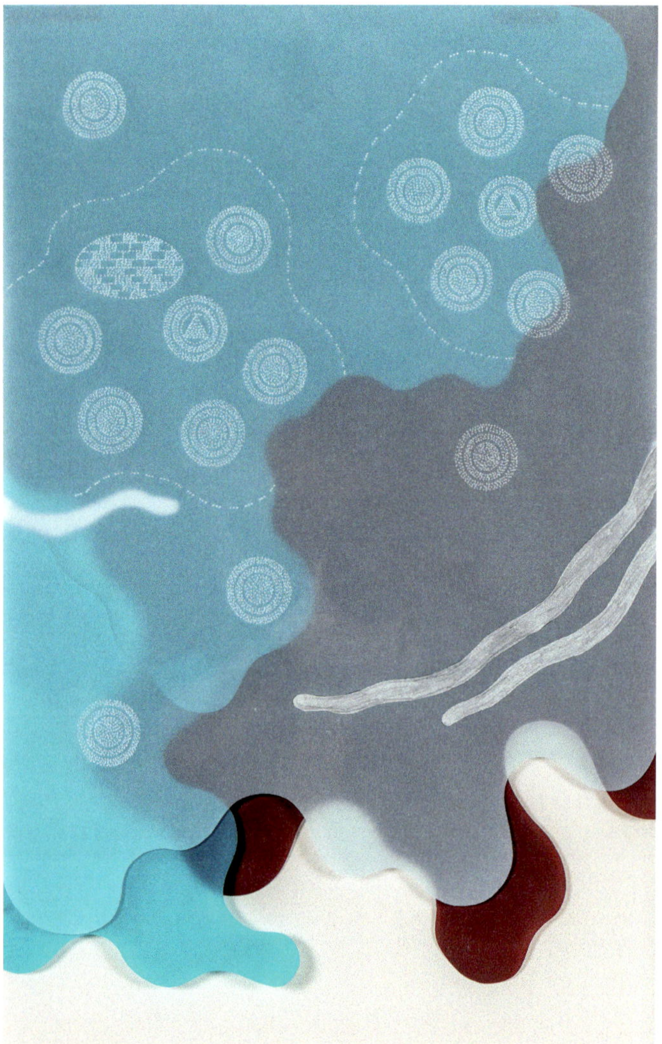

FIGURE 7 Tiffany Chung, *Dega-Latinis: CEW Hypothetical Inter-settlement Time Period 2*, 2022. Hand perforating on vellum and paper, 56.7 × 37 cm (22 ⅜ × 14 ½ in.). Courtesy of the artist and Kiang Malingue Gallery, Hong Kong | New York. Photograph by Samson Wong.

The exhibition's title, *indelible traces*, captures Chung's ability to sense the footprints that cannot be erased from the long memory of the Earth. As she redirects us to the staggering impact of war and colonialism, her artwork reminds us of the other possible worlds below ground that leave profound marks on the world we inhabit. In *Dega-Latinis: CEW Hypothetical Inter-settlement Time Period 2* (2022, fig. 7), Chung reinterprets drawings from Michael Dega and D. Kyle Latinis's research on prehistoric Cambodian earthworks to speculate on prehistoric trade and migration routes between settlements. Patterns resembling concentric circles are punctured into vellum, representing larger urban settlements and smaller sites across forest and floodplains that may have interacted, traded, or combined with one another.[16] Cultivating perspectives from below as an artist, archivist, and cartographer, Chung draws attention to our distinct but shared histories that overlap with others across deep time and space. *indelible traces* reveals that though entangled histories are often speculative and indeterminate, the geological traces that remain embedded in the earth are material reminders of our shared, migratory past. Chung visualizes a future that carries the imprint of our present actions; in doing so, her work inspires us to respond to the global environmental crises of our present by extending our imagination into the distant past and future to sense more sustainable ways of life.

NOTES

1 The 1972 Easter Offensive, known as Mùa Hè Đỏ Lửa in Việt Nam, was a military campaign led by the People's Army of Vietnam (PAVN) against the Army of the Republic of Vietnam (ARVN) and the United States military. In response, the US authorized large-scale aerial bombing campaigns in North Việt Nam via Operation Linebacker, which would determine ARVN's tactical victory.

2 Michael Dega and D. Kyle Latinis, "The Social and Ecological Trajectory of Prehistoric Cambodian Earthworks," *Asian Perspectives* 52, no. 2 (2013): 327–46.

3 Tiffany Chung, Artist Statement, "Circular Enclosures and Traces of Time" (2022).

4 Tiffany Chung, Artist Statement, "Circular Enclosures and Traces of Time" (2022).

5 Paul J. Crutzen, "Geology of Mankind," *Nature* 415 (2002): 23.

6 Kathryn Yusoff, *A Billion Black Anthropocenes or None* (University of Minnesota Press, 2018), 15.

7 Adhy Kim, "Han Kang's Speculative Natural Histories Beyond Human Rights," *Comparative Literature Studies* 58, no. 2 (2021): 431–54.

8 Kim, "Speculative Natural Histories," 437.

9 Imre Szeman and Dominic Boyer, "Introduction" in *Energy Humanities*, ed. Imre Szeman and Dominic Boyer (Johns Hopkins University Press, 2017).

10 Rubber production in Southeast Asia dates to the French colonial period in the late nineteenth century and continues to cause deforestation in the region today due to increasing demand. As of 2023, over 90 percent of the global production of rubber is in Southeast Asia. See Yunxia Wang, Peter M. Hollingsworth, Deli Zhai, et al. "High-resolution maps show that rubber causes substantial deforestation," *Nature* 623 (2023): 340–346 and Michitake Aso, *Rubber and the Making of Vietnam: An Ecological History, 1897–1975* (The University of North Carolina Press, 2018).

11 Felicitas Schmitt, Primitiva Bueno Ramírez, and Martin Bartelheim, "Just passing by? Investigating in the territory of the megalith builders of the Southern European plains. The case of Azután, Toledo," in *Megaliths–Societies–Landscapes: Early Monumentality and Social Differentiation in Neolithic Europe*, ed. Johannes Müller, Martin Hinz, and Maria Wunderlich (Dr. Rudolf Habelt, 2019), 601–19.

12 The titles for the maps reference what social scientists Kate Burrows and Patrick L. Kinney call the "conflict, climate, and migration nexus." See Kate Burrows and Patrick L. Kinney, "Exploring the Climate Change, Migration and Conflict Nexus," *International Journal of Environmental Research and Public Health* 13, no. 4 (2016): 443.

13 For more on Agent Orange's toxic legacies for both human and nonhuman populations, see Keva X. Bui, "Eugenic Ecologies of Herbicidal Warfare in the Vietnam War," *Journal of Asian American Studies* 26, no. 3 (2023): 315–37, and Natalia Duong, "Homing Toxicity: The Domestication of Herbicidal Warfare," *Catalyst: Feminism, Theory, Technoscience* 9, no. 1 (2023).

14 "Military Consumption of Petroleum in Southeast Asia," The Vietnam Center and Sam Johnson Vietnam Archive, Texas Tech University, accessed 29 June 2025, https://vva.vietnam.ttu.edu/images.php?img=/images/225/2250204004.pdf.

15 Tiffany Chung, "Studying for USM Global Archive," https://www.tiffanychung.net/studying-usmglobal-archive.

16 Specifically, Dega and Latinis hypothesize that based on the age of the sites, people from the hill and mountain settlements are likely to have moved toward the floodplains and lowlands at or after around 3000 BCE. See Dega and Latinis, "Prehistoric Cambodian Earthworks."

UNBOUNDED ATLAS: TIFFANY CHUNG'S VIEWS OF THE WORLD

Sarah Newman

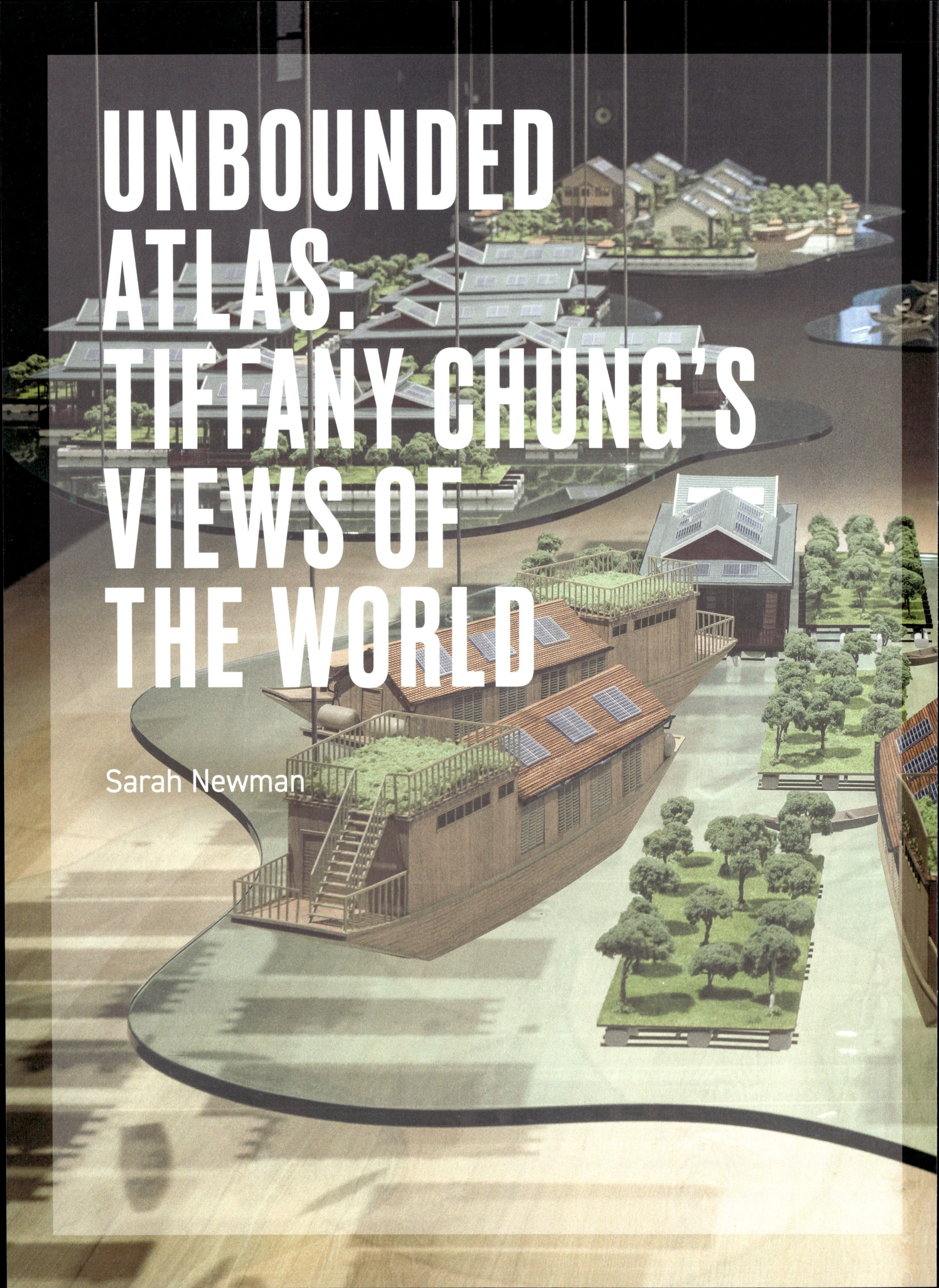

A man sets out to draw the world. As the years go by, he peoples a space with images of provinces, kingdoms, mountains, bays, ships, islands, fishes, rooms, instruments, stars, horses, and individuals. A short time before he dies, he discovers that the patient labyrinth of lines traces the lineaments of his own face.

—Jorge Luis Borges, 1960[1]

In *stored in a jar*, seventy miniature boats, forty-three tiny houseboats, and multiple diminutive farms hover above the ground. Nestled within green puffs of lollipop-like trees, the toylike structures are adorned with matchbox-sized windows, delicate staircases, and richly hued, orange-tiled roofs. Dramatically lit in a darkened space and suspended in the air above undulating watery shadows, they form a seemingly enchanted village, drifting together in a dreamlike haze (fig. 1, see also pp. 48–51).

The work's full title—*stored in a jar: monsoon, drowning fish, color of water, and the floating world* (2010–11)—reinforces the atmosphere of languid magic, hinting at both dangers and delights captured and presented for display. With its final words obliquely referencing *Ukiyo*, the Japanese Edo period's imagined floating universe of wit and leisure, it conjures the physical, sensual, and intellectual pleasures of modern life.

But Tiffany Chung's model village contains far more than its surface betrays, and her floating world is also a starkly literal one. Its title calls to mind modernity's amusements, yet at the same time tells of the anguishes of monsoons and drowning fish. In an answer of sorts to the watery threats she invokes, her houseboats and gardens propose a way to ride them out. Drawing from examples of traditional communities that thrived in natural floodplains throughout Asia,[2] Chung incorporates design principles developed over centuries of lived experience to create structures capable of floating above the rising tides of climate change and industrial development.

For Chung, these concerns resonate at a frequency that is at once historical, analytical, and urgently personal. As a child in Việt Nam in 1978, she endured the historic seasonal flooding of the Mekong Delta in a "New Economic Zone" where her family lived after having been forcibly relocated after the US/Việt Nam War. Her model scene is in part a distanced reflection on these events, thirty-two years later; *stored in a jar* presents a jewel-like capsule vision of society's wonders and ills. It also offers a distillation of her artistic practice, which traverses media and disciplines to examine the entanglements of nature, politics, and human experience.

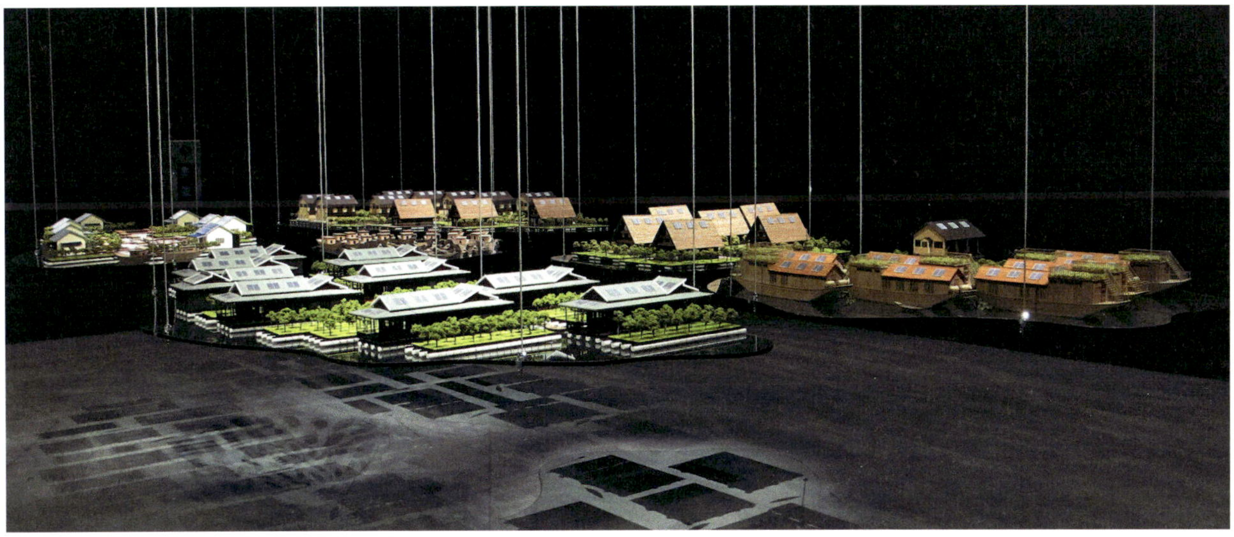

FIGURE 1 Tiffany Chung, *The River Project, stored in a jar: monsoon, drowning fish, color of water, and the floating world*, 2010–2011. Mixed media 1:50 scale model of a floating town, dimensions variable. Post Vidai Vietnamese Art Collection. Installation view, *Open House*, Singapore Biennale, National Museum of Singapore, Singapore, 2011.

Over the past two decades, Chung has explored the devastating effects of major world events, including the American Dust Bowl of the 1930s, the earthquakes in Kobe, Japan, and San Francisco (see fig. 2), the Syrian Refugee crisis, the civil war in Guatemala, and the war in Việt Nam. She probes how political breakdowns affect what people feed their families, how commercial interests intersect with policy, how climate shapes geography, how war shapes the trajectory of cultures around the globe, and how all these elements and more overlap. Beginning with surface information, her art works its way into deeper layers of complexity. She shows how the archives and atlases we rely on to make sense of the world can be understood as contested spaces of memory and erasure. And she shows the pathos—and the absurdity—of trying to represent forces too large to understand within a map, a document, or a deceptively simple tiny floating village.

Chung's broad research-based practice is nearly impossible to classify, as she draws freely from the fields of history, anthropology, investigative journalism, geography, and archaeology. To chart the delicately embroidered paths in her *Global Spice Trade: routes from ancient times to the age of exploration/exploitation* (2024–25, see pp. 146–147), for instance, she studied colonial maritime logs and correspondence and historic nautical charts, collected botanical samples of cinnamon and cloves, among other spices, mined histories of the Silk Road and earlier incense routes, and conducted oral histories with refugees resettled in the United States from countries along these routes.

In many ways, Chung's meticulous methodology grows out of and shares the "archival impulse" of artists who, in the words of art historian and theorist Hal Foster, "seek to make historical information, often lost or displaced, physically present," often with the goal of directing the audience to a larger social or political insight.[3] Art historian Claire Bishop has expanded on Foster's insights, examining the growing prevalence of the artist-as-archivist over the last fifty years, and their reliance on models derived from the internet and other digital technologies.[4] The authors' writings offer a useful framework for understanding the larger context of Chung's research-based practice. However, while both Foster and Bishop note the dominant tendency of this work toward networked, aggregated information, as well as the presentation of unaltered texts and objects to privilege the viewer's synthesis over the artist's voice, Chung pursues a different strategy. Her maps, installations, and floating village are the products of deep research, but they foreground aesthetic complexity and human experience as much as they do visibility and (il)legibility. Through exquisite hand-drawn cartographies, vibrating color, and obsessive detail, she complicates the easy consumption of the material she presents, inviting the

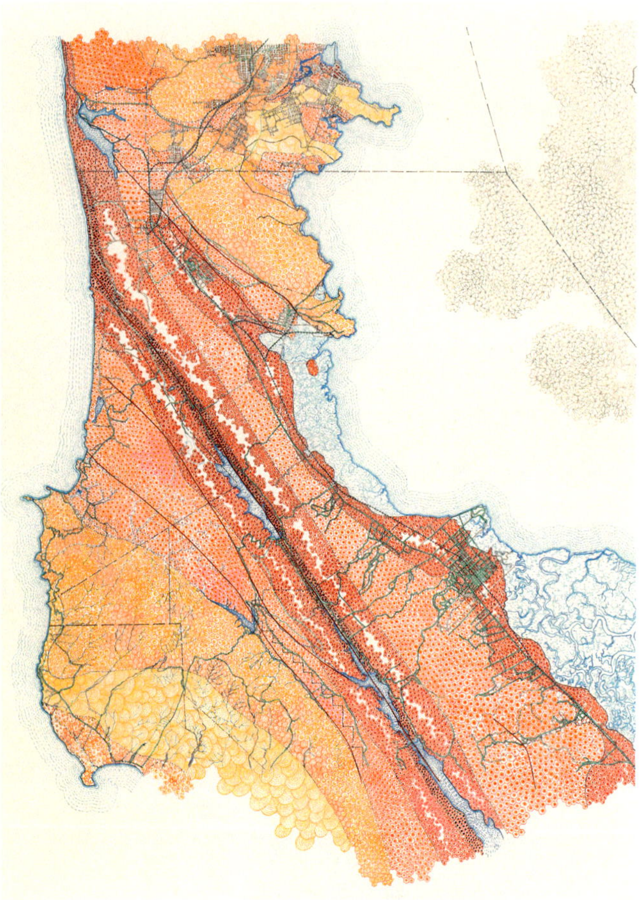

FIGURE 2 Tiffany Chung, *San Francisco, 1895 USGS map: distribution of apparent intensity based on Rossi-Forel scale, the known faults, and the routes examined*, 2012. Micro Pigment ink and gel ink on paper, 96 × 62.6 cm (37 13/16 × 24 5/8 in.). San Francisco Museum of Modern Art, Accessions Committee Fund Purchase.

viewer into the complex ways in which her many references and forms relate to her source material. In Bishop's terms, Chung is not offering an amateur anthropology or a documentary record, but rather a critical reimagining of how histories can be assembled, mourned, and resisted.

At the heart of Chung's research are individual people and their lived experiences. Throughout her work, including her projects on Syria, Việt Nam, and the spice trade, she has pursued what she refers to as "fieldwork," or close collaboration with displaced people and refugees, "connecting with people, listening to their stories, and trying to be a part of their community."[5] This firsthand research informs her art in ways that are both immediate and indirect, allowing her to understand the context and personal stakes as well as specific data points. During research in Hong Kong between 2015 and 2017 for the *Vietnam Exodus Project*, Chung engaged with a community of Vietnamese refugees and involved them in participatory fieldwork, tracking the sites of former detention centers, listening to individual refugees about their personal experiences of forced migration, and organizing three public discussions on asylum policy and the refugee experience. The video *km 0–Son's story* (2017, fig. 3 and 4) documents the story of Son, an ethnic Chinese-Vietnamese man who was forced to leave the county during the 1987 Sino-Vietnamese border war.

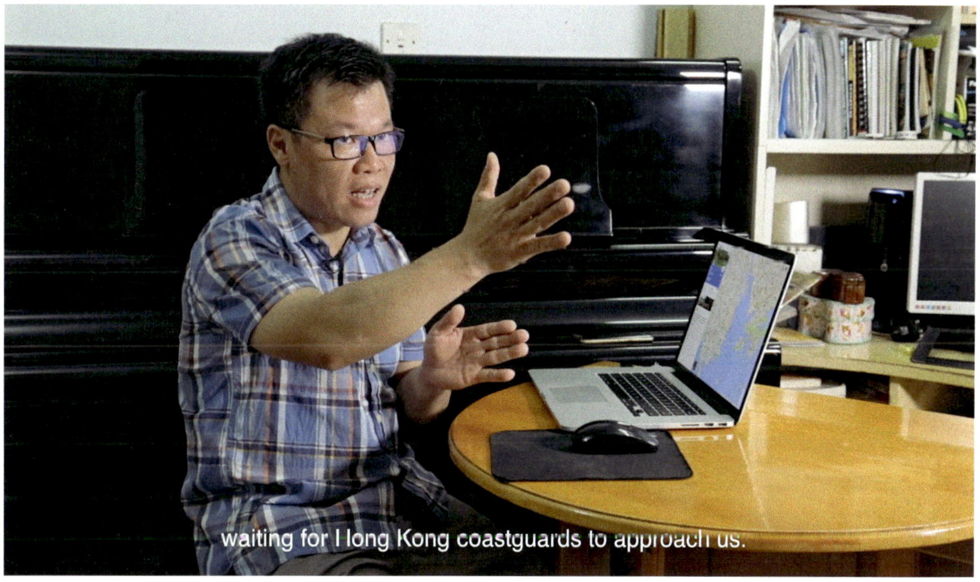

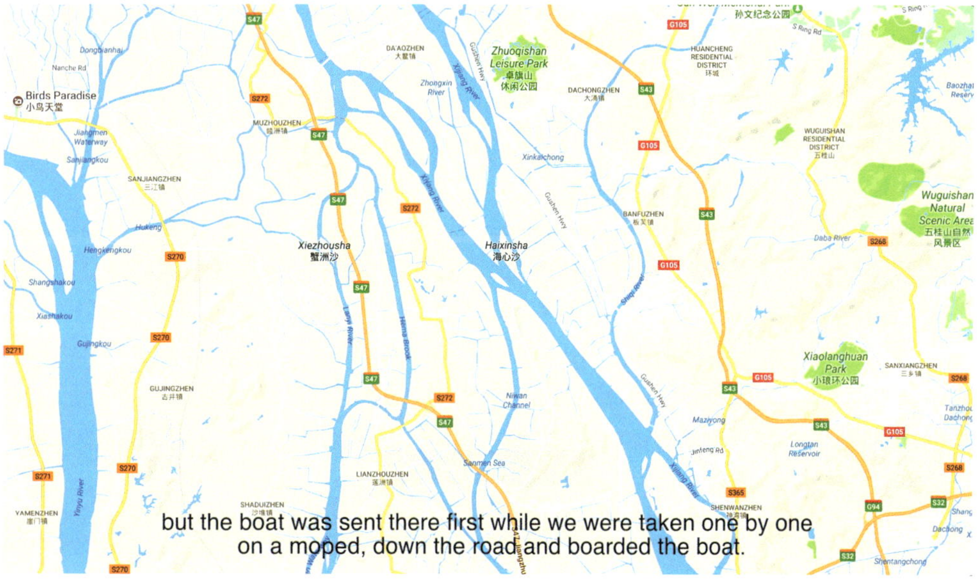

FIGURES 3 AND 4
Tiffany Chung, *km 0–Son's story*, 2017.
HD video, audio, color, 33:19 mins. Video still.

Son narrates his family's travels from their hometown of Bình Gia, Lạng Sơn in Northern Việt Nam to Pingxiang in Guangxi province, China, and then to Nanning and back to Pingxiang, where they hoped to reenter Việt Nam. By that point, the Friendship Gate separating the two countries was closed, leaving Son's family at what many refugees called km 0, between Việt Nam and China. The video continues to map his multiple harrowing escapes from Việt Nam and China to Hong Kong, his deportation back to Việt Nam, and his final escape journey to Hong Kong that ended with his refugee and stateless status.

For an iteration of her ancient spice trade project at the Sun Valley Museum of Art in Idaho, Chung describes her discussions with migrants to the region:

> I visited four restaurants owned by resettled refugees in Boise and talked to them about the spices used in their recipes. They're from countries along the Silk Road, including Afghanistan, Ethiopia/Eritrea, and Somalia/Tanzania/Kenya. Through meals and conversations around spices and foods, they shared with me their zig-zagged journeys to refugee camps where their children were born and raised, [as well as] their final journeys to the US, which were as complex as the previous ones.[6]

Crucially, Chung's process is not only grounded in broad human experience—it is also personal, informed by her experiences during the Việt Nam War and its aftermath.[7]

Chung has been justly cautious about the way that her biography has sometimes been used to provide a "key" to her work, knowing that her life cannot stand in for the vast array of circumstances she addresses, and remaining conscious of the impulse to personalize structural forces. But her "complex relationship to war and power," as she describes it, nurtured a curiosity about the human consequences of global events and an acute sensitivity to how those stories get told, codified, and distorted.

Her firsthand view of the Việt Nam War, and her understanding of how it has been narrated—whose stories had and had not been told—has offered a bracing example of that lesson. As the historian and writer Viet Thanh Nguyen has argued, the history of the period has been written by its two opposing "sides."[8] The official record in today's Socialist Republic of Việt Nam chronicles the profound devastation inflicted by and eventual triumph against US aggression; the United States, for its own part, has struggled to fully acknowledge the magnitude of Việt Nam's loss. Nguyen notes that this divided narrative has largely left out a central third perspective—that of the South Vietnamese, who had fought for the preservation of their way of life and their country, and on whose behalf the Americans entered the War. Chung, whose South Vietnamese father served alongside US forces, and whose family immigrated to this country after North Việt Nam's victory, is powerfully attuned to this absence, and the way that official history and personal memory can be strikingly at odds.

Chung's work excavates what lies beneath the surface of the world we think we know. The writing of history, for her, is underlaid by what is unsaid and unrepresented. She speaks about this hidden well of stories in terms of the Japanese concept of *ma*—roughly, negative space—which suggests that areas of emptiness are as meaningful as those that are full.[9] But her ideas also evoke dark matter: the presence of an unseen yet equally weighted universe that is inextricable from the one we see, and that we can occasionally glimpse using the right tools. In her attention to personal stories and unwritten accounts as much as to official records and documents, Chung does not claim to build a comprehensive understanding of her chosen subjects, but she does offer a different, perhaps more complete one. Similarly, she makes extensive use of archives with the awareness that records only reflect certain perspectives. She employs them as a fundamental tool of historians, cross-referencing and applying a critical eye to what she finds inside, combing through documents and primary materials and speaking directly to people in order to piece together a picture, however fragmentary. History, she acknowledges, is always viewed from a particular place, and always told by someone.

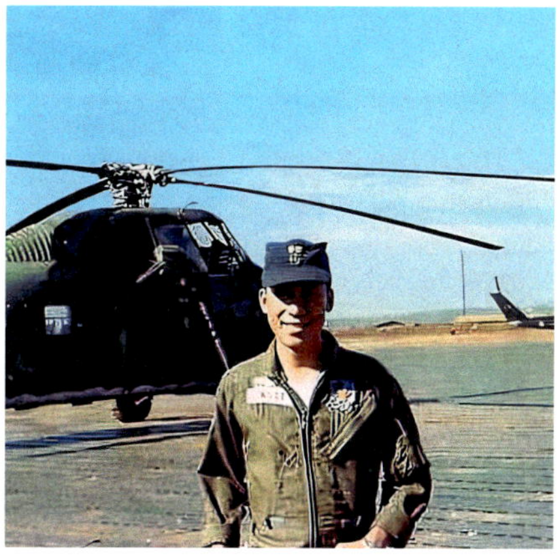

FIGURE 5 Image of Tiffany Chung's father in uniform from *Remapping History: an autopsy of battle, an excavation of a man's past,* 2015. Mixed media, approx. length 12.2 m (40 ft.). Installation view, *Tiffany Chung: Vietnam, Past Is Prologue*, Smithsonian American Art Museum, Washington, DC, 2019.

Throughout her career, Chung has constructed an ever-growing portrait of the world, at various points of crisis and change. To create it, she has mustered all the tools at her disposal, from as many angles and points of view as she can occupy. The different media and materials with which she has approached her subjects include, but are not limited to, dance, map-making, performance, drawing, painting, sculpture, watercolor, video, interviews, embroidery, photography, and archival installation. Everything is marshaled, and it is not enough.

Perhaps the most salient example of her maximalist methodology is ultimately one of her most vexing. *Remapping History: an autopsy of a battle, an excavation of a man's past* (2015, see pp. 80–81) documents Chung's attempts to understand her father's life as an elite helicopter pilot and prisoner of war by retracing his steps forty-five years later (see fig. 5).[10] In a work that is part timeline and part personal scrapbook, she assembled snapshots, archival photographs, videos, found images and audio recordings, handmade maps, drawings, and her own written text, meticulously diagramming the discoveries she made over two separate trips to Việt Nam. On its surface, Chung's non-hierarchical presentation of her research has much in common with the data visualization projects of the conceptual artist Hans Haacke, or the aggregation style of more recent information-based art discussed by Bishop. Yet in contrast to those works, *Remapping History* is deeply personal. Its double narrative tells the story of a young man at war and his daughter's failed attempts to connect with her father's past; Chung's own records, mixed in with found images, are colorful hand-drawn maps and her own journal entries. The viewer is invited to share the artist's private ruminations and struggles.

Chung details the ways in which her father's life intersects with and departs from larger historical narratives in equal measure. Anchored by major battles and well-known events, such as US President Richard Nixon's visit to China in 1972, the timeline most powerfully explores Chung's own efforts to recreate her father's story. Her present-day, prosaic journey is continually contrasted with his heroic one. One of her journal entries, transcribed on the wall, reads:

> *March 10, 2015*
> *45 years later*
> *Abandoned Quan Loi airfield is covered in red dirt and rubber trees.*
> *Pretending to taxi on the very airstrip of my father's youth,*
> *I could hardly see the asphalt.*
> *It's just another red dirt road.*
> *It took him 10 minutes to fly his helicopter between Quan Loi*
> *and Loc Ninh airfields.*
> *It took me 45 minutes in a Toyota 4Runner.*[11]

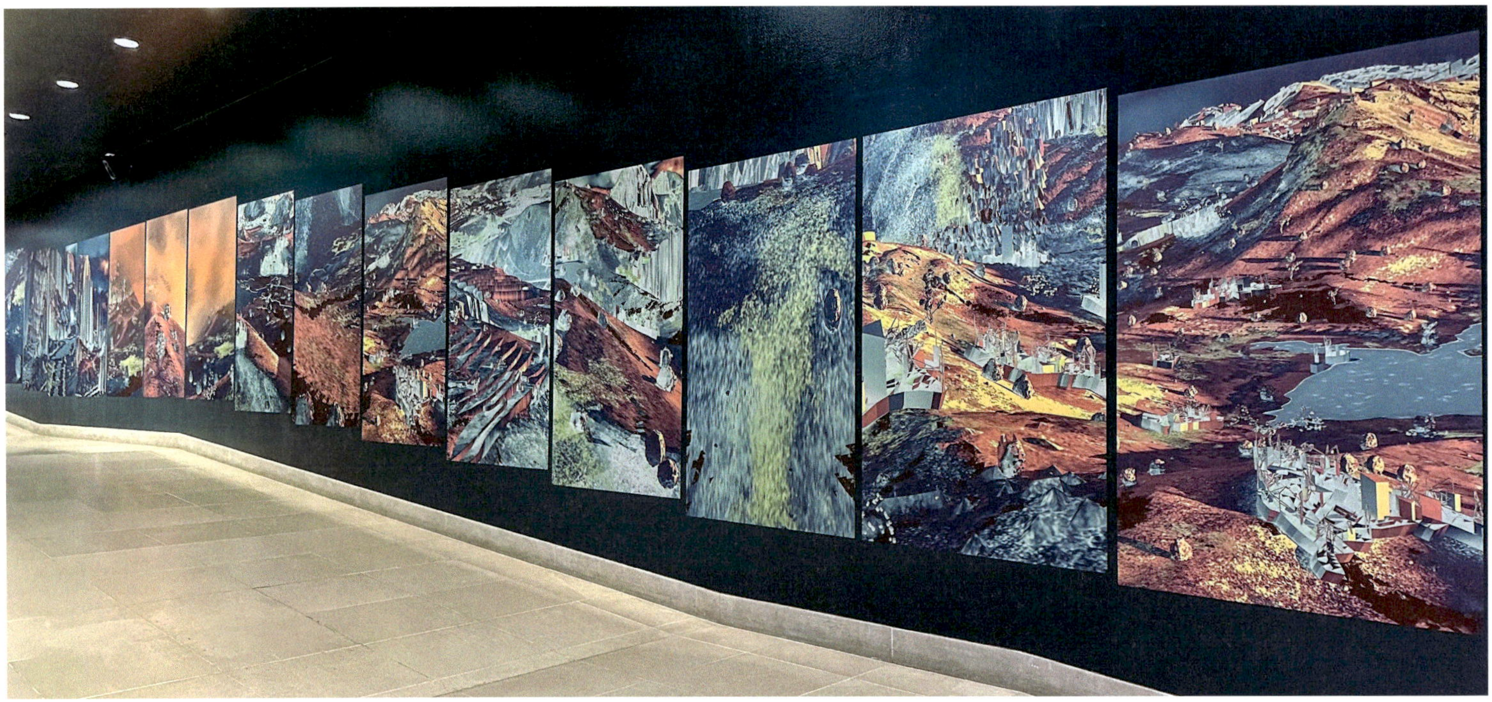

FIGURE 7 Tiffany Chung, *Poetic Landscapes Remembered*, 2023. Printed vinyl decals distilled from video animation, approx. length 45 m (150 ft.). Installation view, *Tiffany Chung: Rise Into the Atmosphere*, Dallas Museum of Art, Texas, 2023–2025.

Chung made her drawings on translucent jewel-toned vellum, perforating each sheet with intricate patterns and overlaying it with colorful and expressive drips and lines of paint. Viewed as a series, and in conjunction with the interpretive key she created as a complementary yet distinct work of art, the maps chart the ways in which the ancient earthworks created the physical template for the various regimes of power that followed.[16] Yet the clusters of scaled dots and sinuous lines do not immediately offer up their historical bounty. Without reference to their interpretive anchor, the drawings' organicism and formal echoes threaten to overtake their informational specificity. Tiny dots bloom across the ground like clouds of fungus, and the painted rings appear to breathe rhythmically from one sheet of vellum to another. In Chung's hands, maps forego their traditional role as legible instruments of accessibility and instead communicate in the ways that she understands history to speak: through gulfs of space and veils of time, without clarity and without completeness, blossoming largely within the mind of the individual.

In *Rise Into the Atmosphere* (2023, fig. 7), Chung expands this experiential ethic in both process and form, incorporating even more voices and employing the affective media of time and space. Commissioned for the Dallas Museum of Art, Chung created a music composition in collaboration with composer Isaac Hernández and twenty-six participants from around the world, some of whom had themselves undergone displacement and used sounds and poetry to represent their individual experiences. Chung then worked with media artist Mario Norton to translate the score into visual form using animation software, creating an abstracted landscape of rising teal blue cliffs and falling sepia-toned valleys. The original pool of information becomes a poetic, musical, multisensory encounter that asks us to understand not only what happened, but how we feel in response.

As with the *Terra Rouge* series, *Rise Into the Atmosphere* brings viewers into a space at once disorienting and clarifying, where it is possible to glimpse how geology, social life, and individual agency might coexist or even amplify each other. Embodying the questions that animate her work as a whole, these projects ask how it is possible—when faced with a flood of information and armed with imperfect tools to interpret it—to separate history from experience. How can we disentangle the world from how we see it? Chung—elusively, contrarily, compellingly—argues different sides at once: constructing a more complete narrative through meticulous research, she reveals its subjectivity. By always adding more and always falling short, by holding the smallest experiences together with the largest events, and by drawing on her own embodied knowledge, Chung creates a new kind of space.

NOTES

1 Jorge Luis Borges, *The Maker (Prose Pieces 1934–1960)*, trans. Norman Thomas di Giovanni, https://libraryofbabel.info/borges/themaker.pdf, 61.

2 These include communities in Tonlé Sap Lake in Cambodia, Hạ Long Bay in Việt Nam, Song Kalia River in Thailand, Srinagar in India, and Gifu and Yamaguchi in Japan.

3 Hal Foster, "An Archival Impulse," *October* 110 (Autumn 2004): 4.

4 See Claire Bishop, "Information Overload," *Artforum*, April 2023, https://www.artforum.com/features/claire-bishop-on-the-superabundance-of-research-based-art-252571/. Bishop notes antecedents including "photodocumentary captioning in the tradition of Lewis Hine; the film essay as defined by Hans Richter and practiced by auteurs ranging from Chris Marker to Harun Farocki; and the interdisciplinary Conceptualism of artists like Mary Kelly, Susan Hiller, and Hans Haacke…."

5 Joella Kiu, "'We can let people narrate their memories as they remember them': In Conversation with Tiffany Chung," Singapore Art Museum, https://www.singaporeartmuseum.sg/About/Our-Collection/Stories/In-Conversation-with-Tiffany-Chung.

6 Tiffany Chung, correspondence with the author, 24 May 2025. The work was included in the exhibition *Uncharted: Artists as Wayfinders*, Sun Valley Museum of Art, 2025.

7 During this period, Chung withstood losses to her home and family in ways that were at once distressingly common and profoundly individual. See Tiffany Chung, "While the World Stands Still: Remembering the Swelling River," *After Hope* (Summer 2021), https://www.afterhope.com/while-the-world-stands-still.

8 Viet Thanh Nguyen, "Industries of Memory: The Viet Nam War in Art," in *American Studies as Transnational Practice: Turning toward the Transpacific*, ed. Yuan Shu and Donald E. Pease (Dartmouth College Press, 2015), 331–32. I cited Nguyen in a similar context in an essay for Chung's 2019 exhibition at the Smithsonian American Art Museum. See Sarah Newman, *Tiffany Chung: Vietnam, Past Is Prologue* (Smithsonian American Art Museum, 2019), 8.

9 Tiffany Chung, telephone interview with the author, 23 March 2024. See also, Tiffany Chung, "Artist Statement," *Tiffany Chung: Scratching the Walls of Memory* (Tyler Rollins Fine Art, 2010), 6.

10 My discussion of this work, as well as *reconstructing an exodus history: boat trajectories from Vietnam and flight routes from camps and of ODP cases* (2020), is indebted to my earlier work and accompanying essay for Chung's exhibition at the Smithsonian American Art Museum, *Tiffany Chung: Vietnam, Past Is Prologue*. See Newman, *Past Is Prologue*.

11 Excerpt from Chung's *Remapping History: an autopsy of a battle* text.

12 Chung, *Remapping History*.

13 At the Smithsonian American Art Museum, it stretched across three walls.

14 Tiffany Chung's *For the Living* (2023) was in the exhibition *Beyond Granite: Pulling Together* at the National Mall, Washington, DC, 2023. The exhibition was curated by Paul Farber and Salamishah Tillet for Monument Lab. The Beyond Granite initiative was presented by the Trust for the National Mall in partnership with the National Capital Planning Commission and the National Park Service, https://www.beyondgranite.org/exhibition.

15 "Beyond Granite: Pulling Together | Artist Preview: Tiffany Chung," posted by Trust for the National Mall, video, 1:45, https://www.youtube.com/watch?v=c6FWgmVa0fI.

16 Diana Seo Hyung Lee, "Mapping the Past: Tiffany Chung at Davidson Gallery," *Art in America*, 16 November 2022, https://www.artnews.com/art-in-america/aia-reviews/tiffany-chung-terra-rouge-at-davidson-gallery-1234646035/.

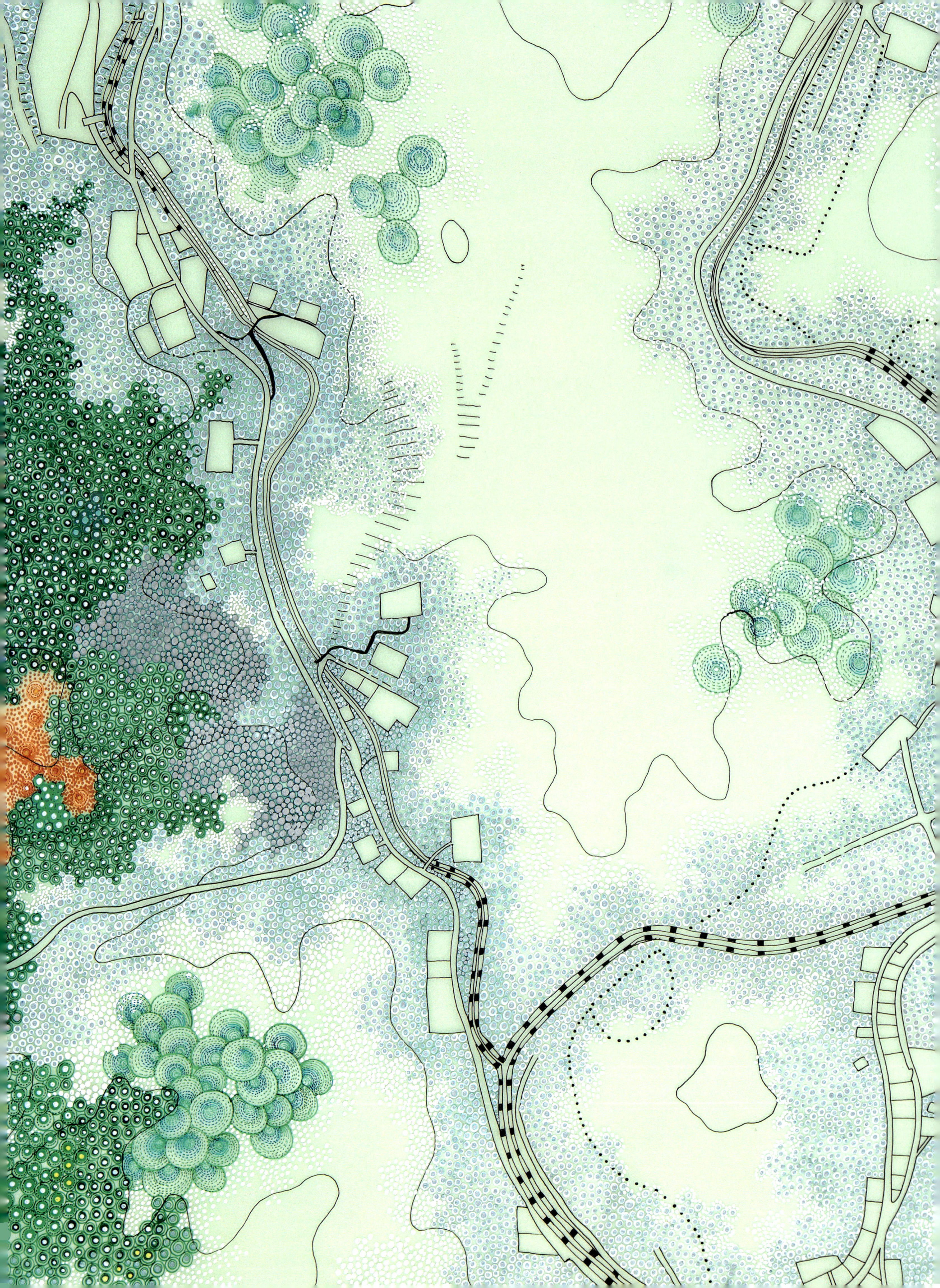

CHECKLIST

All artworks are listed in the order they appear in this catalog.

HCMC extreme flood prediction 2050–ADB & ICEM reports
2013
Ink and oil on vellum and paper
110 × 70 cm (43 ¼ × 27 ½ in.)
Jack and Jennifer Howell

Flora and Fauna Outgrowing the Future
2010
Ink and oil on vellum and paper
110 × 70 cm (43 ¼ × 27 ½ in.)
Collection of the Herbert F. Johnson Museum of Art, Cornell University
Acquired through the George and Mary Rockwell Fund
*Art, Design & Architecture Museum only

One Giant Great Flood 2050
2010
Ink and oil on vellum and paper
110 × 70 cm (43 ¼ × 27 ½ in.)
San Francisco Museum of Modern Art, Accessions Committee Fund purchase
*Blaffer Art Museum only

stored in a jar: monsoon, drowning fish, color of water, and the floating world
2010–2011
Mixed media
Dimension of installation:
approx. 6 × 3.6 m (20 × 12 ft.)
Post Vidal Collection

10.9677°N 106.4667°E
2007
Ink, oil, and collage on paper
79 × 109 cm (31 ⅛ × 43 in.)
Private Collection

10°45'39"N 106°43'23"E
2013
Excavated concrete slab with ceramic tiles
128 × 64 × 30 cm (50 ⅜ × 25 ⅛ × 11 ¾ in.)
Courtesy of the artist

landscapes and traces of a people yet to come
2013
3-channel video, HD, color, sound
6:26 minutes
Courtesy of the artist

knowing into oblivion
2013
Digital C-type printing on 26 glass plates
16 × 23.4 cm (6 ¼ × 9 ¼ in.) each
Courtesy of the artist

Saigon en 1795–On aperçoit le tracé de la Citadelle de Gia-Long et des Forts du Nord et du Sud
2016
Ink and oil on vellum and paper
35 × 23 cm (13 ¾ × 9 in.)
Private Collection

After 1972 USAID Thu Thiem Development Plan
2013
Ink and oil on vellum and paper
110 × 70 cm (43 ¼ × 27 ½ in.)
Courtesy of the artist

landscapes of a people yet to come–HCMC ICA plans for New Thu Thiem Urban Area
2013
Ink, oil, pencil, and image transfer on vellum and paper
79 × 100 cm (31 ⅛ × 39 ⅜ in.)
Courtesy of the artist

snow covered paths, winter evergreens and defunct coal mines in Yamaguchi
2012–2013
Ink and oil on vellum and paper
110 × 70 cm (43 ¼ × 27 ½ in.)
Courtesy of Keith Buck

1946 survey #37–semi-blank space: Hitachi Factory
2016
Acrylic, ink, and oil on vellum and paper
65 × 64.7 cm (25 ⅝ × 25 ½ in.)
Courtesy of the artist and RYAN LEE Gallery, New York

1946 survey: Hitachi Urban Damage Plan
2016
Acrylic, ink, and oil on vellum and paper
75 × 62.5 cm (29 ½ × 24 ⅝ in.)
Courtesy of the artist and RYAN LEE Gallery, New York

1946 survey #28–blank space: Hitachi Factory, seaside
2016
Acrylic, ink, and oil on vellum and paper
70 × 47.5 cm (27 ½ × 18 ¾ in.)
Private Collection, Minnesota

Scratching the Walls of Memory
2010
Mixed media (children's desk set; 38 handmade children's chalkboards with recycled wood, engraving, and chalk; 24 hand-stitched satchels made from used army tents and embroidery)
Dimensions variable
Courtesy of the artist

Frontier of Tibet as claimed by Tibetans in 1914/Frontier of Tibet as claimed by Nationalist Chinese in 1914
2010
Ink and oil on vellum and paper
100 × 62.8 cm (39 ⅜ × 24 ¾ in.)
Private Collection, New York

Frontier of Tibet as proposed at the Tripartie Simla Conference in 1914/ Territories under the control of the Dalai Lama's Government (1918–1950)
2010
Ink and oil on vellum and paper
100 × 62.8 cm (39 ⅜ × 24 ¾ in.)
Private Collection, New York

Berlin Wall
2010
Embroidery, metal grommets, and buttons on canvas
84 × 112.5 cm (33 ⅛ × 44 ¼ in.)
Private Collection

Kaesong Armistice Conference Site 1951
2010
Embroidery, beads, metal grommets, and buttons on canvas
112 × 86.5 cm (44 × 34 in.)
Orange County Museum of Art, Costa Mesa, California
Museum purchase with funds provided through the prior gift of the Estate of Carl S. Dentzel

Iraqi State Railways after Anglo-Iraqi Treaty 1930 & Current Pipelines
2010
Ink and oil on vellum and paper
100 × 63 cm (39 ⅜ × 24 ½ in.)
Private Collection, New York

Remapping History: an autopsy of a battle, an excavation of a man's past
2015
Mixed media
Dimensions of installation:
length 12.2 m (40 ft.), height variable
Courtesy of the artist

Crossing the DMZ–1972 Easter Offensive
2022
Ink and oil on vellum and paper
38 × 25.5 cm (15 × 10 in.)
Courtesy of the artist

Easter Offensive 1972,
Defense of An Lộc
2015
Ink and oil on vellum and paper
24 × 28 cm (9 ½ × 11 in.)
Collection of Alan Lau

Easter Offensive 1972, NVA base areas
on the Cambodian-RVN border
2015
Ink and oil on vellum and paper
29.8 × 21 cm (11 ¾ × 8 ¼ in.)
Collection of Alan Lau

Easter Offensive 1972,
Battle for Kontum MR III
2022
Ink and oil on vellum and paper
34.3 × 30.5 cm (13 ½ × 12 in.)
Courtesy of the artist

Easter Offensive 1972,
NVA bases, regimental dispositions
and attacks, MR-IV
2015
Ink and oil on vellum and paper
42 × 29.7 cm (16 ½ × 11 ¾ in.)
Collection of Alan Lau

Operation Lam Sơn 719,
30 Jan–6 April 1971
2018
Acrylic, ink, and oil on vellum, and paper
31.1 × 34.3 cm (12 ¼ × 13 ½ in.)
Courtesy of the artist

Operation Lam Sơn 719,
Feb 1971–ARVN movements
2018
Ink and oil on vellum and paper
34.3 × 30.8 cm (13 ½ × 12 ⅛ in.)
Courtesy of the artist

Operation Lam Sơn 719, Feb 1971–
Operation Dewey Canyon II & the attack
toward Khe Sanh
2018
Acrylic, ink, and oil on vellum and paper
34.3 × 30.8 cm (13 ½ × 12 ⅛ in.)
Courtesy of the artist

Operation Lam Sơn 719,
Feb 1971–NVA attack of FSB 31
2018
Acrylic, ink, and oil on vellum and paper
25.4 × 29.8 cm (10 × 11 ¾ in.)
Courtesy of the artist

Operation Lam Sơn 719–military
dispositions & attacks 1971
2018
Acrylic, ink, and oil on vellum and paper
29.8 × 32.4 cm (11 ¾ × 12 ¾ in.)
Courtesy of the artist

Operation Lam Sơn 719–the border
area, MR I-II
2018
Embroidery on canvas
45.7 × 30.5 cm (18 × 12 in.)
Courtesy of the artist

Recipes of Necessity
2013
Single-channel video, HD, color, sound
33 minutes
Courtesy of the artist, Kiang Malingue Gallery,
Hong Kong | New York, and
RYAN LEE Gallery, New York

Collective Remembrance of the War:
voices from the exiles
2018–2019
HD, color, sound [21 video interviews]
Durations variable
Courtesy of the artist

reconstructing an exodus history: boat
trajectories from Vietnam and flight routes
from refugee camps and of ODP cases
2020
Embroidery on fabric
140 × 350 cm (55 × 137 ¾ in.)
Smithsonian American Art Museum,
Museum purchase through
the Luisita L. and Franz H. Denghausen
Endowment and through the American
Women's History Initiative
*Art, Design & Architecture Museum only

reconstructing an exodus history:
boat trajectories in Asia
2017
Acrylic, ink and oil on drafting film
92 x 119 cm (36 ¼ × 46 ⅞ in.)
Courtesy of the artist and
RYAN LEE Gallery, New York
* Weisman Art Museum and
Blaffer Art Museum

from the sea and back to the sea–
the ten-year journey of a stateless,
unaccompanied minor
2016
Embroidery on canvas;
etching on stainless steel plaque mounted
on plexiglass
80 × 100 cm (31 ½ × 39 ⅜ in.);
20 × 34 cm (7 ⅞ × 13 ⅜ in.)
The Living Collection

Destination Pulau Bidong,
Dec 1985–June 1986
1999/2019
Acrylic, glitter, fabric, and thread on
19 cotton handkerchiefs
39.4 × 39.4 cm (15 ½ × 15 ½ in.) each
Courtesy of the artist

Destination Songkhla:
pirate attacks in the Gulf of Thailand,
Oct–Dec 1985
1999/2019
Acrylic, glitter, and fabric on
19 cotton handkerchiefs
39.4 × 39.4 cm (15 ½ × 15 ½ in.) each
Courtesy of the artist

selected cases of pirate attacks
in the Gulf of Thailand, Oct 1985–June 1986
2019
Ink and oil on vellum and paper
96.5 × 63 cm (38 × 24 ¾ in.)
Courtesy of the artist, and
RYAN LEE Gallery, New York

If Water Has Memories
2022
3-channel video, HD, color, 5.1 sound
6 minutes
Courtesy of the artist and Kiang Malingue
Gallery, Hong Kong | New York

life, which you look for, you will never
find–the ancient Near East
2015
Embroidery, beads, and plastic gems
on canvas
85 × 115 cm (33 ½ × 45 ¼ in.)
Courtesy of the artist

UNHCR/HIU/IDMC: Syria Crisis
Displacement–686,851 refugees, camps
and conflict areas, January 2013
2015
Ink and oil on vellum and paper
36 × 29.8 cm (14 ⅜ × 11 ⅞ in.)
The Living Collection

UNHCR Regional Data Analysis Group:
857,712 Syrian Refugees, February 2013
2015
Ink and oil on vellum and paper
27 × 28 cm (10 ¼ × 11 ¼ in.)
The Living Collection

UNHCR/Guardians/Your Middle East:
over 1 million Syrian refugees,
camps and border crossings, March 2013
2015
Ink and oil on vellum and paper
42 × 29.8 cm (16 ½ × 11 ⅞ in.)
The Living Collection

HIU: 1,245,570 Syrian Refugees, 3.6 million IDPs, April 2013
2015
Ink and oil on vellum and paper
21 × 28 cm (8 3/8 × 11 1/4 in.)
The Living Collection

UNHCR/VOA/HIU: 1.5 million have fled Syria, May 2013
2015
Ink and oil on vellum and paper
30 × 29.8 cm (11 7/8 × 11 in.)
The Living Collection

UNHCR/HIU: Syria Regional Crisis 1,658,177 camp and non-camp refugees, June 2013
2015
Ink, oil, and embossing on paper
42 × 29.8 cm (16 1/2 × 11 3/4 in.)
The Living Collection

Focus on Syria: The humanitarian crisis, July 2013
2015
Ink and oil on vellum and paper
21 × 30 cm (8 3/8 × 11 7/8 in.)
The Living Collection

UNHCR/REUTERS: Syrian Refugee Crisis–1.9 million refugees in the region, August 2013
2015
Ink and oil on vellum and paper
24 × 30 cm (9 1/2 × 11 7/8 in.)
The Living Collection

UNHCR/WSJ: 4.25 million IDPs, 2 million Syrian Refugees–September 2013
2015
Ink and oil on vellum and paper
21 × 30 cm (8 3/8 × 11 7/8 in.)
The Living Collection

UNHCR/HIU/MERCY CORPS/ OREGONIAN: Syrian Displacement–camps, refugees and IDPs, October 2013
2015
Ink and oil on vellum and paper
21 × 29.8 cm (8 3/8 × 11 7/8 in.)
The Living Collection

Syria Tracker: 92,120 Documented Killings in Syria, 18 March 2011–31 December 2013
2015
Ink and oil on vellum and paper
21 × 30 cm (8 3/8 × 11 7/8 in.)
The Living Collection

ISW: areas of control; UNHCR: numbers and locations of Syrian refugees and IDPs as of April 2019
2019
Acrylic, ink, and oil on vellum and paper
76 × 93 cm (30 × 37 in.)
Purchase with funds from the Morton R. Hirschberg Bequest and Vicar's Landing.
On loan from the Cummer Museum of Art & Gardens, Jacksonville, Florida

Dignity Revolution
2014–2020
Oil and hand perforating on vellum and paper
76 × 52.5 cm (30 × 20 5/8 in.)
Courtesy of the artist

Mapping Global Displacement and Migration: nexus dynamics between conflict & violence and climate disaster [UNHCR, IDMC, EM-DAT: cross-border refugees, asylum-seekers, IDPs, and those affected in selected cases >2022<]
2023
Embroidery on fabric
140 × 350 cm (55 × 137 3/4 in.)
Courtesy of the artist

Europol, UK Parliament: tracking migrant smuggling routes to and within the EU
2017
Acrylic, ink, and oil on vellum and paper
100 × 80 cm (39 3/8 × 31 1/2 in.)
Ford Foundation

ICMPD, IOM Missing Migrants Project, Frontex, Reuters, NYT: migration routes through Africa to Europe
2017
Acrylic, ink, and oil on drafting film
92 × 131 cm (36 1/4 × 51 1/2 in.)
Courtesy of the artist

IOM Missing Migrants Project, EUROSTAT, FRONTEX, RAUL Analytics, ECHO: SAR zones, rescue operations by date, numbers of dead and missing in the Mediterranean
2017
Ink and oil on vellum and paper
38 × 50 cm (15 × 19 5/8 in.)
Collection of Eddie and Chinhui Allen

USM Global: tracing the US military global footprint
2023
Embroidery on fabric
140 × 350 cm (55 1/8 × 137 3/4 in.);
map key: 40 × 70 cm (15 3/4 × 27 3/4 in.)
Courtesy of the artist and Kiang Malingue Gallery, Hong Kong | New York

Africa in Focus: Refugees, IDPS, LIC Policy, Drone & Air Strikes, and Combat Engagement
2021
Acrylic, ink, and oil on vellum and paper
113 × 68.7 cm (44 1/2 × 27 1/16 in.)
Pennsylvania Academy of the Fine Arts, Philadelphia
Museum Commission and Purchase, 2023.16
*Art, Design & Architecture Museum only

El Pulpo: UFCo's Great White Fleet routes and properties in Central America & the Caribbean
2019
Embroidery on fabric
137 × 137 cm (54 × 54 in.)
Courtesy of the artist and Kiang Malingue Gallery, Hong Kong | New York and Galería Max Estrella, Madrid

CIA Study of Assassination sketch
2019
Acrylic, ink, and oil on paper
30.5 × 30.5 cm (12 × 12 in.)
Private Collection, Hong Kong

Guatemala Human Rights Commission: Selected cases of violence in relation to current mega projects
2019
Acrylic, ink, and oil on vellum and paper
71 × 88.3 cm (28 × 34 3/4 in.)
Courtesy of the artist

from faraway lands to dust we return: Ewa Plantation Community Cemetery's Ledger Book
2018
Acrylic, ink, and oil on vellum and paper
102 × 64 cm (40 1/8 × 25 1/4 in.)
Courtesy of the artist and Kiang Malingue Gallery, Hong Kong | New York

Global Spice Trade: routes from ancient times to the age of exploration/exploitation
2024–2025
Embroidery on fabric
140 × 380 cm (55 × 149 1/2 in.);
map key: 50 × 50 cm (19 5/8 × 19 5/8 in.)
Courtesy of the artist, Kiang Malingue Gallery, Hong Kong | New York, Galería Max Estrella, Madrid, and RYAN LEE Gallery, New York

Studies of exotic botanical organisms and spices from the ends of the earth in quest of market dominance
2024–2025
10 pieces of hand embroidery on linen, spices in glass jars
Dimensions variable
Courtesy of the artist, Galería Max Estrella, Madrid, and RYAN LEE Gallery, New York

cracked heels and spices beyond my father's shoreline
2025
Ink and oil on vellum and paper
77.5 × 100 cm (30 ½ × 39 ⅜ in.)
Courtesy of the artist

Terra Rouge: CEW sites, rubber plantations, and abandoned airfields
2022
Acrylic, ink, and oil on vellum and paper
113 × 70 cm (44 ½ × 27 ½ in.)
Courtesy of the artist

Terra Rouge CEW Study no. 1
2022
Acrylic, ink, oil, and hand perforating on vellum and paper
113.03 × 69.85 cm (44 ½ × 27 ½ in.)
Perry Guariglia and Haewon Jo

Terra Rouge CEW study no. 5
2022
Ink, oil, and hand perforating on vellum and paper
94 × 54.9 cm (37 × 21 ⅝ in.)
William and Rosemary Hankowsky

Spheres of Time
2026
Immersive sound and video installation
AlloSphere facility: 3-story metal sphere, 26 video projectors, and 54.1 audio channels
Commissioned by the Art, Design & Architecture Museum in collaboration with the AlloSphere Research Facility, Isaac Hernández Campos, Adam Kaleta, and Mario Norton
*Art, Design & Architecture Museum only

Checklist accurate at time of printing

CONTRIBUTOR BIOGRAPHIES

TIFFANY CHUNG (b. 1969, Đà Nẵng, Việt Nam; lives in Houston, Texas) is an interdisciplinary artist globally noted for her research-driven practice exploring the intersections of history, culture, and geography on local and global scales. Working across media such as cartography, embroidery, painting, photography, sculpture, video, text, and music, her projects trace shifts in cultural, geopolitical, and natural landscapes driven by the upheavals of war, displacement, disaster, and global trade. Chung earned a BFA in Photography at California State University, Long Beach (1998), and an MFA at the University of California, Santa Barbara (2000). She is currently an inaugural KAVAH Fermata Fellow at the University of Chicago. Previously, Chung was a Mellon Arts & Practitioner Fellow at the Yale Center for the Study of Race, Indigeneity, and Transnational Migration (RITM) (2021) and was named Jane Lombard Fellow for Art & Social Justice at the Vera List Center, New School (2018–20).

Chung has exhibited her artwork widely in the United States and abroad. Recent solo exhibitions include *Vietnam, Past Is Prologue* at the Smithsonian American Art Museum (2019) and *Rise Into the Atmosphere* at the Dallas Museum of Art (2023–25), as well as presentations at Lumiar Cité/Maumaus, Lisbon, Portugal (2019); Johann Jacobs Museum, Zürich, Switzerland (2018); Statens Museum for Kunst, Copenhagen, Denmark (2016); and Kenpoku Art at the Hitachi City Museum, Ibaraki, Japan (2016). Her work has been featured in major exhibitions and biennials throughout the world. Exhibitions include, most recently, *Breath(e): Toward Climate and Social Justice* (2024–25) at the Hammer Museum, Los Angeles, as part of PST Art; *Are You Ready? Surge to 2030: Enhancing Ambition in Asia-Pacific to Accelerate Disaster Risk Reduction*, United Nations Office for Disaster Risk Reduction (2024); *After Rain*, the Diriyah Contemporary Art Biennale (2024); *Beyond Granite: Pulling Together* at the National Mall in Washington, DC (2023). Biennials include the 56th Venice Biennale, Sharjah Biennial, Biennale of Sydney, Gwangju Biennale, Bienal de Cuenca (Ecuador), EVA International (Ireland), and Asia Pacific Triennial (Australia). Her work has also been presented at the Museum of Modern Art (New York), the British Museum (London), Schirn Kunsthalle (Frankfurt, Germany), the Nobel Peace Center (Oslo, Norway), Louisiana Museum of Modern Art (Humlebæk, Denmark), Centre de Cultura Contemporània de Barcelona, M+ museum (Hong Kong), 21st Century Museum of Contemporary Art Kanazawa (Japan), and the San Francisco Museum of Modern Art (San Francisco), among others. Chung has received the Asia Arts Game Changer Award (2020), the Asian Cultural Council Grant (2015), and Sharjah Biennial Artist Prize for Exceptional Contribution (2013).

HEIDI AMIN-HONG is assistant professor of English at the University of California, Santa Barbara. Her research and teaching examine how Asian American and Pacific Islander literature and culture contend with the material effects of war, global capitalism, and forced migration on transpacific environments. She is working on a book that considers how Asian American writers and artists can contribute to healing damaged environments in the afterlives of the Cold War. Her writing has been published in *Journal of Asian American Studies*, *ISLE: Interdisciplinary Studies in Literature and Environment*, *Atlantic Studies: Global Currents*, and *Verge: Studies in Global Asias*.

MARK PHILIP BRADLEY is the Bernadotte E. Schmidt Distinguished Service Professor of History and the College at the University of Chicago and the editor of the *American Historical Review*. Bradley is the author of *The World Reimagined: Americans and Human Rights in the Twentieth Century* (2016), *Vietnam at War* (2009), and *Imagining Vietnam and America: The Making of Postcolonial Vietnam* (2000), which won the Harry J. Benda Prize from the Association for Asian Studies, and has co-edited multiple publications. Bradley also served as the general editor for the four-volume *Cambridge History of America and the World* (2022). His current project, a cultural and visual history of the Global South, is supported by a fellowship from the Guggenheim Foundation. In 2024–25 he was the George E. Bogaars Professor of History at National University Singapore.

ORIANNA CACCHIONE is deputy director and curator of exhibitions at the University of Richmond Museums and was previously assistant director at the Art, Design & Architecture Museum at University of California, Santa Barbara. Committed to expanding the canon of contemporary art to respond to the circulations of art and ideas, her recent exhibitions include solo presentations of Haegue Yang, Samson Young, Tang Chang, and Zhang Peili, as well as the thematic exhibitions *Monochrome Multitudes* and *The Allure of Matter: Material Art from China*. A specialist in contemporary Asian art, Cacchione holds a PhD in Art History, Theory and Criticism from the University of California, San Diego.

ERIK HARMS is professor of Anthropology and chair of the Council on Southeast Asia Studies at Yale University. An urban anthropologist, he has been studying Vietnamese urban life and social change for more than two decades. He is the author of *Luxury and Rubble: Civility and Dispossession in the New Saigon* (2016) and *Saigon's Edge: On the Margins of Ho Chi Minh City* (2011). He has been following Tiffany Chung's work since the early 2000s.

SARAH NEWMAN is the James Dicke Curator of Contemporary Art and deputy head curator at the Smithsonian American Art Museum. At SAAM, she recently led a major reinstallation of the museum's contemporary permanent collection, *American Voices and Visions*, and has organized the exhibitions *Tiffany Chung: Vietnam, Past Is Prologue*, *Do Ho Suh: Almost Home*, and *Kara Walker: Harper's Pictorial History of the Civil War (Annotated)*. Prior to working at the Smithsonian, she held positions at the National Gallery of Art and the Corcoran Gallery of Art in Washington, DC.

IMAGE CREDITS

Details: p. 4 Tiffany Chung, *HCMC extreme flood prediction 2050–ADB & ICEM reports*, 2013. Photograph by Nam Bui; p. 6 Tiffany Chung, *El Pulpo: UFCo's Great White Fleet routes and properties*, 2019. Courtesy of the artist and Kiang Malingue Gallery, Hong Kong | New York. Photograph by Samson Wong; p. 12 Tiffany Chung, *13 Oct 2013 NYT/UNHCR: Syria 4,250,000; Jordan 543,000; Turkey 504,000; Lebanon 790,000; Iraq 197,000; Egypt 126,000*, 2014; p. 30 Blue Mesa at the Petrified Forest National Park, Arizona, 2023; pp. 40–41 Tiffany Chung, *from faraway lands to dust we return: Ewa Plantation Community Cemetery's Ledger Book*, 2018. Courtesy of the artist and Kiang Malingue Gallery, Hong Kong | New York. Photograph by Samson Wong; pp. 162–163 Tiffany Chung, *the world through my mother's cabinets of curiosities*, 2025. Courtesy of the artist and Kiang Malingue Gallery, Hong Kong | New York. Photograph by Francisco Ramos; p. 164 Installation view, *Tiffany Chung: passage of time*, Tyler Rollins Gallery, 2019; p. 174 Tiffany Chung, *finding one's shadow in ruins and rubble*, 2014. Photograph by Nash Baker; p. 182 Tiffany Chung, *Dega-Latinis: CEW Hypothetical Inter-settlement Time Period 1*, 2022. Detail. Courtesy of the artist and Kiang Malingue Gallery, Hong Kong | New York. Photograph by Samson Wong; p. 190 Tiffany Chung, *stored in a jar: monsoon, drowning fish, color of water, and the floating world*, 2010–2011. Installation view, *Breath(e): Toward Climate and Social Justice*, Hammer Museum, Los Angeles, 2024–2025. Photograph by Jeff McLane; p. 200 Tiffany Chung, *snow covered paths, winter evergreens and defunct coal mines in Yamaguchi*, 2012–2013. Photograph by Nam Bui.

Artworks: pp. 43, 44, 45, 46, 47, 52–53, 54, 57–59, 60, 61, 62–63, 65, 66, 67, 68, 69, 83, 84, 87, 112, 113, 114, 115, 116, 117, 118, 119, 120, 121, 130–131, and 133 Photographs by Nam Bui; p. 44 Image courtesy of the Johnson Museum; p. 47 Photograph by Don Ross; pp. 48–49 and 50–51 Installation view, *Breath(e): Toward Climate and Social Justice*, Hammer Museum, Los Angeles, September 14, 2024–January 5, 2025. Photograph by Jeff McLane; pp. 54 and 56 Installation view, *Thu Thiem: an archeological project for future remembrance*, Maumaus/Lumiar Cité, Lisbon, Portugal, 2019; pp. 70–71 Installation view, *New Cartographies*, Asia Society Texas, 2018–2019. Photograph by Nash Baker; pp. 80–81 and 97 Installation view, *Tiffany Chung: Vietnam, Past Is Prologue*, Smithsonian American Art Museum, Washington, DC, 2019; pp. 98–99 Courtesy of the Smithsonian American Art Museum. Photograph by Lucia RM Martino; pp. 102–103 Images courtesy of The Living Collection; pp. 104–105, 106, 107, 122–123, 139, 142–143, 157, 158, and 159 Photographs by Nash Baker; p. 108 Installation view, *Lines—Aligning your consciousness with the flow*, 21st Century Museum of Contemporary Art, Kanazawa, Japan, 2024. Photograph by Tomoki Imai; pp. 126–127 Installation view, *After Rain*, *Diriyah Biennale of Contemporary Art*, 2024. Courtesy of the Diriyah Biennale Foundation, photo by Marco Cappelletti; pp. 128–130 Courtesy of Ford Foundation, Photograph by Nam Bui; pp. 134–135, 136, 137, 140, and 145 Courtesy of the artist and Kiang Malingue Gallery, Hong Kong | New York. Photograph by Samson Wong; pp. 146–147, 148, and 149 Courtesy of the artist and Kiang Malingue Gallery, Hong Kong | New York. Photograph by Andrea Rossetti; pp. 150–151 and 152–153 Courtesy of the artist and Galería Max Estrella; pp. 154–155 Photograph by Dev Khalsa for Sun Valley Museum of Art.